*Studies in Military and Strategic History*

General Editor: **William Philpott**, Professor of Diplomatic History, King's College London

*Published titles include*:

Martin Alexander and William Philpott (*editors*)
ANGLO-FRENCH DEFENCE RELATIONS BETWEEN THE WARS

Christopher M. Bell
THE ROYAL NAVY, SEAPOWER AND STRATEGY BETWEEN THE WARS

Peter Bell
CHAMBERLAIN, GERMANY AND JAPAN, 1933–34

Antony Best
BRITISH INTELLIGENCE AND THE JAPANESE CHALLENGE IN ASIA, 1914–41

Antoine Capet (*editor*)
BRITAIN, FRANCE AND THE ENTENTE CORDIALE SINCE 1904

Philippe Chassaigne and Michael Dockrill (*editors*)
ANGLO-FRENCH RELATIONS, 1898–1998
From Fashoda to Jospin

Michael Dockrill
BRITISH ESTABLISHMENT PERSPECTIVES ON FRANCE, 1936–40

Michael Dockrill and John Fisher
THE PARIS PEACE CONFERENCE, 1919
Peace without Victory?

John P. S. Gearson
HAROLD MACMILLAN AND THE BERLIN WALL CRISIS, 1958–62

John Gooch
ARMY, STATE AND SOCIETY IN ITALY, 1870–1915

Raffi Gregorian
THE BRITISH ARMY, THE GURKHAS AND COLD WAR STRATEGY IN THE FAR EAST, 1947–1954

Stephen Hartley
THE IRISH QUESTION AS A PROBLEM IN BRITISH FOREIGN POLICY, 1914–18

Ashley Jackson
WAR AND EMPIRE IN MAURITIUS AND THE INDIAN OCEAN

James Levy
THE ROYAL NAVY'S HOME FLEET IN WORLD WAR II

Stewart Lone
JAPAN'S FIRST MODERN WAR
Army and Society in the Conflict with China, 1894–95

Thomas R. Mockaitis
BRITISH COUNTERINSURGENCY, 1919–60

Bob Moore and Kent Fedorowich
THE BRITISH EMPIRE AND ITS ITALIAN PRISONERS OF WAR, 1940–47

T. R. Moreman
THE ARMY IN INDIA AND THE DEVELOPMENT OF FRONTIER WARFARE, 1849–1947

Kendrick Oliver
KENNEDY, MACMILLAN AND THE NUCLEAR TEST-BAN DEBATE, 1961–63

Paul Orders
BRITAIN, AUSTRALIA, NEW ZEALAND AND THE CHALLENGE OF THE UNITED STATES, 1934–46
A Study in International History

Elspeth Y. O'Riordan
BRITAIN AND THE RUHR CRISIS

G. D. Sheffield
LEADERSHIP IN THE TRENCHES
Officer–Man Relations, Morale and Discipline in the British Army in the Era of the First World War

Adrian Smith
MICK MANNOCK, FIGHTER PILOT
Myth, Life and Politics

Melvin Charles Smith
AWARDED FOR VALOUR
A History of the Victoria Cross and the Evolution of British Heroism

Martin Thomas
THE FRENCH NORTH AFRICAN CRISIS
Colonial Breakdown and Anglo-French Relations, 1945–62

Simon Trew
BRITAIN, MIHAILOVIC AND THE CHETNIKS, 1941–42

Steven Weiss
ALLIES IN CONFLICT
Anglo-American Strategic Negotiations, 1938–44

---

**Studies in Military and Strategic History**
**Series Standing Order ISBN 0–333–71046–0 Hardback   0–333–80349–3 Paperback**
(*outside North America only*)

You can receive future titles in this series as they are published by placing a standing order. Please contact your bookseller or, in case of difficulty, write to us at the address below with your name and address, the title of the series and the ISBN quoted above.

Customer Services Department, Macmillan Distribution Ltd, Houndmills, Basingstoke, Hampshire RG21 6XS, England

# AWARDED FOR VALOUR

## A History of the Victoria Cross and the Evolution of British Heroism

Melvin Charles Smith
*University of the Cumberlands*

© Melvin Charles Smith 2008

All rights reserved. No reproduction, copy or transmission of this publication may be made without written permission.

No paragraph of this publication may be reproduced, copied or transmitted save with written permission or in accordance with the provisions of the Copyright, Designs and Patents Act 1988, or under the terms of any licence permitting limited copying issued by the Copyright Licensing Agency, 90 Tottenham Court Road, London W1T 4LP.

Any person who does any unauthorised act in relation to this publication may be liable to criminal prosecution and civil claims for damages.

The author has asserted his right to be identified as the author of this work in accordance with the Copyright, Designs and Patents Act 1988.

First published 2008 by
PALGRAVE MACMILLAN
Houndmills, Basingstoke, Hampshire RG21 6XS and
175 Fifth Avenue, New York, N.Y. 10010
Companies and representatives throughout the world

PALGRAVE MACMILLAN is the global academic imprint of the Palgrave Macmillan division of St. Martin's Press, LLC and of Palgrave Macmillan Ltd. Macmillan® is a registered trademark in the United States, United Kingdom and other countries. Palgrave is a registered trademark in the European Union and other countries.

ISBN-13: 978–0–230–54705–6 hardback
ISBN-10: 0–230–54705–2 hardback

This book is printed on paper suitable for recycling and made from fully managed and sustained forest sources. Logging, pulping and manufacturing processes are expected to conform to the environmental regulations of the country of origin.

A catalogue record for this book is available from the British Library.

A catalog record for this book is available from the Library of Congress.

10  9  8  7  6  5  4  3  2  1
17 16 15 14 13 12 11 10 09 08

Printed and bound in Great Britain by
CPI Antony Rowe, Chippenham and Eastbourne

| LEEDS LIBRARY AND INFORMATION SERVICE ||
|---|---|
| LD39390306 ||
| HJ | 12/09/2008 |
| 355.13 | £20.00 |
| S035179 | |

# Contents

| | |
|---|---|
| List of Tables | vi |
| Acknowledgements | vii |
| Introduction: The Forgotten Hero | 1 |
| 1 'I've broken my arm, Dick, but never mind me now': The Hero in Victorian Popular Mythology | 5 |
| 2 The Institutionalization of Heroism in Britain | 26 |
| 3 Teething Problems, 1856–1867 | 43 |
| 4 Big Implications from Small Wars: The Imperial Vision of Heroism, 1860–1911 | 74 |
| 5 Fifty Years On: A Half-Century of Heroism | 94 |
| 6 1914: The Last Stand of the Thin Red Line | 110 |
| 7 The Middle Parts of Fortune: Heroism in Evolution, 1915–1916 | 132 |
| 8 'Courage isn't what it used to be': Heroism Emerges from the Great War, 1917–1918 | 152 |
| 9 The Hero Comes Home from the War: The Institutionalization of Modern Heroism | 165 |
| 10 Conclusion: The New Hero in Action, 1940–2006 | 185 |
| Appendix: The Victoria Cross Warrants | 207 |
| Notes | 230 |
| Bibliography | 263 |
| Index | 276 |

# List of Tables

| | | |
|---|---|---|
| 5.1 | Acts winning the Victoria Cross, nineteenth century: winners per decade | 96 |
| 5.2 | Enlisted versus officer in life-saving VCs, nineteenth century | 100 |
| 5.3 | The cost of courage: casualties among nineteenth-century VC winners per decade | 103 |
| 7.1 | Acts winning the Victoria Cross, 1915: winners by quarter | 138 |
| 7.2 | The cost of courage, 1915: casualties per quarter | 140 |
| 7.3 | Acts winning the Victoria Cross, 1916: Winners by quarter | 144 |
| 7.4 | Breakdown of Crosses won, 1915 and 1916 by quarter | 145 |
| 7.5 | The cost of courage, 1916: casualties per quarter | 145 |
| 8.1 | Acts winning the Victoria Cross, 1917: winners by quarter | 157 |
| 8.2 | The cost of courage, 1917: casualties per quarter | 161 |
| 8.3 | Acts winning the Victoria Cross, 1918: winners by quarter | 161 |
| 8.4 | The cost of courage, 1918: casualties per quarter | 163 |
| 10.1 | The cost of courage, the Second World War: casualties per year | 187 |
| 10.2 | Acts winning the Victoria Cross, the Second World War: winners per year | 189 |

# Acknowledgements

I would like to extend my firm thanks to all of the people who assisted in the research and writing of this work. First and foremost, my gratitude to my parents for the support both moral and financial over the years of my education and beyond. Many thanks are due to Major Tony Astle (retired) of the 22nd Regiment Museum and Archive in Chester, Lieutenant-Colonel Angus Fairie at Cameron Barracks in Inverness, and to the staff at the Argyll and Sutherland Highlanders Museum in Stirling and the staff at the Gordon Highlanders Museum in Aberdeen. To the Public Record Office desk workers at Kew, thank you for your patience and diligence. I would also like to thank Dr Margaret Sankey of Minnesota State University Moorhead for her assistance and critique. Lastly, my thanks to Dr Dan Szechi and his wife Jan Szechi, for direction, encouragement, bare threats, and venison curry.

# Introduction: The Forgotten Hero

Just under two years after the end of the First World War former Colour Sergeant Harry Hampton wrote to the private secretary of King George V, requesting an increase in the pension attached to the Victoria Cross, which at the time stood at £10 sterling per annum. Hampton, who had won his VC during the Boer War, alleged that the winners of gallantry awards from Canada and Australia enjoyed a variety of benefits that the British government failed to provide for its heroes. He closed with the observation that 'honour is all very well, but a little help is worth a lot of sympathy.'[1]

Hampton's dilemma is representative of a larger aspect of the concept of heroism, that of benign neglect. Of all the features of military history, heroism is the most elusive and difficult to quantify. It has thus been largely ignored by military historians; too often they focus on those who fail under pressure and neglect those who rise above it. This work explores one manifestation of the heroic ideal in the Western world, focusing on the evolution of the Victoria Cross from its foundation in 1856 to the current incarnation of the Cross, most recently awarded during operations in Iraq and Afghanistan. The study follows both the institutional history of the award and its popular history within and beyond the ranks of the armed forces.

Heroism, though wonderful for the headlines of the moment, has remained a phenomenon relatively untouched by modern military history. The hero makes an occasional appearance to add colour to an account of a battle scene. He is mentioned in passing, almost as an afterthought, in summing up the accomplishments of a campaign. Other than that he is startlingly absent, even from works dealing with the subject of military motivation or even courage itself. In *Soldiers: A History of Men in Battle* John Keegan and Richard Holmes noted the benefit of heroic action briefly in the second chapter, but limited their treatment to heroism as a factor in unit morale.[2] Nor did heroism figure in any important sense in Keegan's seminal work, *The Face of Battle*.[3] Neither Hew Strachan's *European Armies and the Conduct of War* nor Patrick Reagan's *Organizing Societies for War* address the question of the merits of heroism in any fashion.[4]

The works dealing specifically with the concept of courage do scarcely better when it comes to dealing with the hero. Lord Moran's landmark study of courage in combat dealt primarily with the factors that tear down the bravery of an individual rather than the exhibition of that courage in heroic acts.[5] Likewise were a series of lectures delivered at Fort Leavenworth during the First World War exploring the psychology of war.[6] The word 'heroism' was used only three times in the entire series, with far more attention paid to negative factors in troop morale and performance. Heroism has not been entirely ignored, however; Plinio Prioreschi devoted a substantial portion of a chapter in *Man and War* to a precise definition of heroism, and to differentiating between bravery and heroism on the battlefield.[7]

Even in the case of the Victoria Cross most of the specific works on the medal amount to little more than bullets of information, with each winner treated in a vacuum, entirely divorced from any circumstance beyond the rush of battle. The literary treatment of the Cross falls into four broad categories: reference works; works of jingoistic patriotism; studies limited to a specific region, war or service branch; and full-length Cross-winner biographies.

Works in the first of these categories amount to nothing more than encyclopaedias. There might be a few pages of introduction giving a thumbnail sketch of the origins of the Cross, but little more than anecdotal information.[8] The bulk of each is devoted to individual entries consisting of basic biographical information of the winners – date and place of birth, unit affiliation, place of death – and an account of the deed that won the award. Each is presented as a stand-alone article with a minimum of cross-reference in the case of multiple awards for the same action or family connections between Cross winners. The information presented can be quite useful for the compilation of statistics, but is entirely lacking in analysis.

This first category also has certain elements in common with the second. About the turn of the twentieth century several jingoistic, patriotic treatments of the VC came on the market.[9] This trend continued into the interwar years with the publication of the first volume of *The Victoria Cross, 1856–1920*, still widely accepted as the best early work on the Cross.[10] The thrust of this book and the genre are summed up in its introduction: 'Embracing the finest episodes in British Naval and Military History and the gallant exploits of the Royal Air Force – deeds which will forever live in the memory of man – it should prove a powerful incentive to uphold the honour of the Flag for generations to come.' Like the pure reference works, these patriotic works are compilations of individual records, strung together in either chronological or alphabetical order. Both of these categories fall far short of the mark of modern scholarship. In practical terms they are little more than anecdotal recollections supported by swathes of purple prose.

The third category of literature dealing with the Cross bears breaking down into three subcategories: regional or national histories of the VC, studies limited to a single war, and studies limited to a single service branch.

Regional studies run the gamut from the efforts of the local historian commissioned by the county council to the professional historian covering all the winners from an entire nation. Many of these works are private publications by hobby historians, and thus have limited usefulness for serious research.[11] Others represent a scholarly contribution to the study of the Victoria Cross, but due to their limited scope they offer only a partial snapshot of the process of the institution, and are primarily concerned with the individuals who won it, rather than what the Cross reveals about the development of the concept of heroism.[12]

The same problem arises with works limited to a specific conflict or service branch. Some of these histories are quite serviceable in their own realm, but by their very subject matter fail to come to grips with the evolution of heroic concepts.[13] Several studies published recently in this area incorporate more than the traditional recounting of the deed in question. John Laffin's *British VCs of World War 2* covers the Crosses won by British (but not Dominion) forces, and offers some analysis of heroism and the patterns of the award in addition to the standard tales of derring-do.[14] Mark Adkin's *The Last Eleven?* examines the Crosses won between the end of the Second World War and 1982, and places them in a larger context than a single battle.[15] An ambitious multi-volume project is currently cataloging the Victoria Crosses of the First World War, by detailing the exploits and giving short biographies of the winners.[16]

Biographies of the Victoria Cross winners are the most numerous type of work on the award, with over 40 published. They too exhibit a wide range of scholarship, from the insightful to the insipid.[17] While biographies sometimes offer wonderful information on the background of VC winners, the nature of the work focuses on the individual rather than the institutional mechanics that drove the VC's evolution.

Only one work approaches being a truly comprehensive, scholarly study of the VC: M. J. Crook's *The Evolution of the Victoria Cross: A Study in Administrative History*.[18] There are, however, some problems with Crook's work. While it is extensively annotated from primary sources, there are passages quoting memoranda and other correspondence that are not footnoted.[19] In many passages Crook relied on intuition and deduction rather than hard fact to reach his conclusions, and in some cases he reached the wrong conclusions. He also exhibits an almost Victorian sense of propriety in dealing with such ticklish issues as the questionable Cross granted to Lieutenant Henry Masham Havelock by his own father during the Indian Mutiny.[20]

The major drawback of Victoria Cross scholarship is the limited scope of the published body of knowledge. The subject lends itself greatly to 'puff without substance'; the deeds themselves are thrilling and entertaining, and far too often authors have stopped with the recounting of the act without setting it in context. In the instances where authors did go beyond the passion of the moment, moreover, their scope has been limited to a particular service branch, nationality, or era. This work fills the gap in the coverage of the Victoria Cross, analyzing what it has meant in the context of changing concepts of heroism and accomplishment on the battlefield. At first glance the organization of this book may seem unbalanced, with far too much time spent on the Victorian era and the First World War, and only a single chapter dealing with the Second World War and beyond. It also concentrates primarily on the Army. But the fact of the matter is that the basic ideas of what the Cross was were laid down during the nineteenth century and the new paradigm of what the Cross is was established during and immediately after the Great War. In both cases the criteria for what was and what was not VC-calibre heroism were established by Army representatives and test cases in the main, and the vast majority of Crosses have been won by land forces. As of this writing (2007) there have been 1356 VCs awarded. Of these, 521 were awarded before the First World War and 639 were awarded either during the First World War or in conjunction with immediate post-war operations, or in imperial police actions. Only 196 Crosses (14.5 per cent) were granted after the Great War, and no substantive changes have been made in the regulations governing the award since the major revision accomplished in 1920. Thus, to understand the nature of the Cross we must understand the circumstances of its creation and revision. The place to begin is an examination of the British concept of heroism as the Victoria Cross came into being.

# One

# 'I've broken my arm, Dick, but never mind me now': The Hero in Victorian Popular Mythology

> A British tar is a soaring soul,
> As free as a mountain bird,
> His energetic fist should be ready to resist
> A dictatorial word!

These lines from H.M.S. *Pinafore*, first performed in 1878, capture the exuberant essence of Victorian heroism: self-righteous, self-confident, and, thrusting a manly, square jaw forward, it offered a sound thrashing to any who might think otherwise. It was a curious combination of the romantic and the practical, all held in place with a stiff upper lip.

Victorian conceptions of heroism were complex and multi-faceted. Yet they profoundly shaped the values embodied in the Victoria Cross. The sources that might be used to explore this cultural backdrop to the institutionalization of courage that is the Victoria Cross are legion: poetry, literature, art, theater and music hall are just the most obvious. As a consequence a full analysis of popular conceptions of courage in the century preceding the First World War would be a dissertation in itself, and thus the phenomenon can only be registered, rather than fully explored here. This chapter will therefore deal with the subject only briefly, with a view to acquainting the reader with some of the assumptions underlying the genesis of the VC and its evolution. This is not an attempt to place a chronological matrix on the development of a popular heroic ideal, nor is it suggested that Queen Victoria and Prince Albert based their concept of the VC on popular books that had not been written at the time of the inception of the award. It is rather an exploration of the elements, both before and after the creation of the Victoria Cross, that went into the construction of an heroic ideal.

These elements are most clearly stated in the heroic poetry and literature of the Victorian era. These range from the upper crust of Alfred, Lord Tennyson and Thomas Babington Macaulay, both publishing at mid-century, through the middle ground of the late Victorian-era Rudyard Kipling and Henry Newbolt, to the vastly popular 'boys' Dumas,' George Alfred Henty, who published a prodigious number of juvenile novels between 1880 and 1902. Between them, their works reached the majority of the literate public and in the process shaped their conceptions of what heroism was.

In examining popular heroism, it is truly a case of the observer having an effect on the observed, a literary version of a self-fulfilling prophecy. As authors wrote of heroic deeds, their concepts of heroism were transferred to the readers, some of whom went on to perform heroic acts, which in turn provided inspiration for tales of derring-do even more daring in the doing. This cycle continued into the First World War, and was probably a factor in the number of underage volunteers in the first months of the war.[1]

Popular fiction underwent a transformation during mid-century; in the 1830s and 1840s most novels had a corporatist tone with main themes that revolved around the conflict between Tractarians and Evangelicals or the duty of the Church, and the characters merely served as spokespersons for a group view of morality. In the 1850s and 1860s individuality came to the fore, with greater emphasis on personal acts and consequences. Juvenile fiction changed as well. The stern, authoritarian morality stories of the past gave way to the 'ripping good yarn,' full of adventure in faraway places, with a stalwart hero taking center stage.[2]

These Victorian heroes did not spring from a vacuum, but rather from a melange of antecedents. The Classical World provided a crop of virtues to glean. The dim mists of Britain's origins furnished heroes both real and mythical. Anglo-Saxon resistance to the Norman Conquest also left a stamp on the Victorian heroic ideal.

Greek epic poetry abounded with examples of the archetypal Hellenic hero. He was self-sufficient yet self-centered; individualistic, yet required the constant recognition of the lesser mortals about him of his greatness; proud, yet petulant. He did not merely expect, but demanded honor for his heroism.[3] To do less would mark him as small minded and weak willed, and to be such was the greatest sin a Greek hero could commit.

It was the duty of the hero to be ever-mindful of his stature, and require those about him to do likewise. He did not necessarily court danger for the sake of proving his manhood, and was quite content to rest on his laurels. A challenge to his honor, however, would spur him into harm's way with reckless abandon.[4] It is worth noting that the key to action for the Greek hero was his own reputation more than the good of the *polis* or the needs of his comrades.[5] Achilles is a fine model for this archetype. Willing to sacrifice the better part of the Greek forces arrayed against the Trojans, he pouted until Agamemnon was forced to acknowledge the Hero's honor by declaring himself in the wrong and begging for his sword.[6] Likewise, Odysseus had no real need to hear the Sirens' song; it served no purpose other than inflating his ego and enhancing his reputation. This same courting of danger for reputation's sake is evident in Odysseus endangering an otherwise safe escape from the lair of the blinded Cyclops, Polyphemus, by shouting insults toward the shore as the ship pulled away. Despite his comrades' entreaties to silence, he insisted on haranguing the creature and shouting his own name, which gave the Cyclops a point at which to throw.[7]

The flawed heroes of the Greek epics reflected a very real image of the society that produced them, proud and independent city-states whose strongest virtues ultimately proved to be their downfall.[8] There is a certain amount of fatalism in the Greek view of the hero, it seems, recognizing hubris even in its brightest and best and merely acknowledging it as an unchangeable part of human nature. As such, the Greek ideal was acceptable to the Victorians, but with the admonition to pursue the virtues without developing the faults.[9]

The Roman hero was a man of action, action governed by sobriety, probity, and a sense of *gravitas*. His prime virtues were first and foremost an indifference to circumstances and a sense of civic duty in his actions. He was not governed by his passions or accidents of fortune, but rather by moral absolutes and proprieties that remained unaltered in any situation.[10] He was differentiated from his fellow man only by superior talents, not imbued with a congenital superiority of being. His greatness came not from the mere possession of talent, but from harnessing that talent to the service of the state.[11] This ideology dovetailed nicely into the ideology of the expanding Victorian Empire and prompted an identification with the same for poet Henry Newbolt:

> O strength divine of Roman days
> O spirit of the age of faith
> Go with our sons on all their ways
> When we long since are dust and wraith.[12]

Pius Aeneas – 'Dutiful Aeneas,' as his name might be translated – serves as the epic epitome for Cicero's ideal of heroic virtues. He is driven by his duty to his comrades, to his bloodline, and to the ideal of Troy to complete his task of founding a new city. War is a hateful but necessary thing to Aeneas; despite his prowess at arms, he would rather be honored for the fulfillment of his duty toward his gods, the state, and his family than to be remembered as the slayer of men.[13]

Tacitus's eulogy of his father-in-law Julius Agricola provides an example of the Imperial Roman hero:

> His first military service was in Britain under Suetonius Paulinus, a conscientious and cautious general, when he had been chosen to be the latter's aide; his performance satisfied his commander. Agricola did not behave with the license of young men who turn their military service into dissipation, nor did he, displaying no energy, take advantage of his rank as tribune and his inexperience to pursue his personal pleasure and obtain leaves of absence.[14]

Summed up in these few taciturn lines are the basic virtues of the Roman hero: duty, personal honor, and service to the state. No greater accolade could be ascribed by Tacitus than the phrase 'his performance satisfied his commander.'

On the opposite face of the classical coin were the native heroes of Britain resisting Roman expansion. None became more famous than the warrior queen of the Iceni, Boudicca.

In Boudicca we see a heroine who required several centuries passage to be rehabilitated into the pantheon of British folk-heroes. Some 500 years after her death the monk Gildas referred to her as a 'treacherous lioness [who] slaughtered the governors left to give fuller voice and strength to Roman rule.'[15] Writing in the dawn of the Middle Ages, it is understandable that he might wax nostalgic for the stability of imperial law. No positive mention was made of the warrior queen until she re-emerged as a minor nationalistic heroine during the reign of Elizabeth I, only to fall into ill-favor once again in the seventeenth century.[16] Milton's *History of Britain* dismissed her as the nadir of civilization, a madwoman who compared poorly with the male heroes who had previously resisted the Romans:

> Hitherto what we have heard of Cassibelan, Togadumnus, Venusius, and Carattacus hath bin full of magnanimitie, soberness, and martial skill: but the truth is that in this battel, and whole business, the *Britans* never more plainly manifested themselves to be right *Barbarians*; no rule, no foresight, no forecast, experience or estimation, either of themselves or of their Enemies; such confusion such impotence, as seem'd likest not to a Warr,

but to the wild hurrey of a distracted Woeman, with as mad a crew at her heeles.[17]

Not until the empire-building reign of her namesake ('Boudicca' can be translated as 'the victorious one,' or 'Victoria') did she become a popular heroine. Her image had been recast by the Victorian Romantics from that of a ruthless and bloodthirsty pagan queen into a personification of patriotism, justice, and propriety.[18] One thousand eight hundred and forty-two years after her brief and bloody career began Britain finally erected a statue to the warrior queen.[19] Although it is doubtful that many made the philosophical connection, the fanciful bronze of Boudicca in her war chariot was raised on the banks of the Thames at Westminster Bridge in 1902, in the wake of the unexpectedly long and embarrassingly costly Second Boer War. Ironically, like the Roman conquest of Britain, this conflict was also a ruthless and bloodthirsty affair, presented to the public as an exercise in patriotism, justice, and propriety.[20]

The Roman-Celtic era also gave rise to the Arthurian cycle of legends. The Victorians rediscovered these tales and they became quite popular with the aristocracy. Despite the military vocation of most of the male principals of these stories, the Victorians were delighted with them, though they focused primarily on the courtly love exhibited at Camelot.[21]

The Norman Conquest created a new crop of Anglo-Saxon heroes who injected a note of tenacity into the Victorian concept of heroism. As the Normans solidified their control of Anglo-Saxon England some savage guerrilla campaigns were waged against the invaders. Just as Celtic heroes had resisted the spread of Roman rule, now the Anglo-Saxons defied the Normans' expansion.

Most of the Anglo-Saxon rebels remained local figures. But one of their number, Hereward the Wake, was rediscovered and adopted by the Victorians as a national hero. He refused to recognize the new masters of England and waged a years-long revolt, striking from the fens and marshes where mounted men could not go. He was ultimately defeated, but injected a note of tenacity into the heroic paradigm. As was the case during the Civil War and the Glorious Revolution, there were a number of radical writers in Victorian England who railed against the 'Norman Yoke' of aristocracy. In Hereward they found a home-grown Noble Savage to prove that the (imagined) natural liberalism of Anglo-Saxon England had been ruthlessly suppressed by the viciously authoritarian Normans.[22]

These different conceptions of martial virtue came together in the Victorian concept of heroism, but were filtered through the lenses of romanticism and colored by a self-assured sense of national destiny. Elements of these earlier heroic ideals are found in the works of Victorian authors. So what were the tenets preached on the page?

First and foremost, war was seen as an honorable pursuit. This seems odd in a society that on the whole rejected militarism. Yet Tennyson, who himself was attacked in turn of the century reviews as a poet of 'innocuous sentimentality' and 'effeminate grace,'[23] listed among the blessings of a reflective Ulysses that he had 'drunk delight of battle with my peers,'[24] and is of course perhaps most famous for 'The Charge of the Light Brigade,' penned in 1855. Macaulay went even further, deeming a death in just battle the best way to die:

> Then out spake brave Horatius,
> The Captain of the Gate:
> 'To every man upon this Earth
> Death cometh soon or late.
> And how can man die better
> Than facing fearful odds,
> For the ashes of his fathers,
> And the temples of his Gods?'[25]

Lord Macaulay – who himself denigrated hero-worship as an indication of feeble-mindedness – could find nothing wrong with the person of brave Horatius, a man willing to sacrifice all, not for glory, but simply as his duty.[26]

Henry Newbolt epitomized the same sentiment in the famous lines of duty in the face of (implicitly) certain death, '*Vitai Lampada*':

> The sand of the desert is sodden red –
> Red with the wreck of a square that broke; –
> The Gatling's jammed and the colonel dead,
> And the regiment blind with dust and smoke.
> The river of death has brimmed his banks,
> And England's far, and Honour a name,
> But the voice of a schoolboy rallies the ranks,
> 'Play up! play up! and play the game!'[27]

Here we find both the dogged determination of Hereward the Wake and the Roman ideals of duty unto death.

Newbolt's contemporary, George Alfred Henty, not only deemed war an honorable pursuit, but one that should be eagerly sought. A declaration of war and the prospect of fighting were meat and drink to Henty's characters;

the knowledge that one might not get in on the action was a cause for remorse:

> 'A vessel has just come in from Plymouth with dispatches. Napoleon has escaped from Elba. He has landed in France, and has been received with enthusiasm. The troops have joined him, and he is already close to Paris, which he is expected to enter without opposition. The King of France has fled.'
>
> For a moment there was silence, then the major leaped to his feet.
>
> 'Three cheers, gentlemen;and all of those present joined in a hearty cheer.
>
> Then a sudden silence fell upon them. The first idea that had struck each man was that the news meant their again taking the field for another stirring campaign. Then the dismal thought occurred to them that the regiment was already under orders for America....[28]
>
> \* \* \*
>
> Three days later the expected order arrived.... Officers and men were alike delighted that the period of waiting had come to an end, and there was loud cheering in the barrack-yard as soon as the news came. At daybreak the next morning the rest of the baggage started under a guard, and three hours later the Mayo Fusiliers marched through the town with their band playing at their head, and amid the cheers of the populace.[29]

That this aspect of martial virtue was transferred to the real world (or perhaps was a reflection of the real world) is evidenced by the memoirs of Captain Arthur Kerr Slessor, who commanded a company of the Derbyshire Regiment in the Tirah Campaign of 1898:

> The sight of dingy figures clustered round standards on the top of a distant hill, conveyed no certainty of any immediate fighting, until the welcome sound of our guns booming from the Kotal stirred our pulses and quickened our footsteps like a band striking up at the end of a weary march, with the hope that now at last we were going to be engaged with this elusive enemy.[30]

Whether Captain Slessor accurately remembered the passions of the moment or if he was merely conforming to Victorian literary style is immaterial. What is important is that such a statement was expected of a proper Victorian officer. Likewise was the case of future Field Marshal Sir Evelyn Wood; denied a Victoria Cross in the Crimea, he resigned from the Royal Navy and took a commission with the 17th Lancers. En route to India in 1858 the regiment's transport made port at Cape Town 'where our spirits fell on hearing that Delhi had fallen, and the confident predictions that the Mutiny would be suppressed before the ship reached Bombay.'[31]

Henty's works in particular came to be closely identified with militarism, so much so that even the stories that did not deal with military scenarios were often published with militaristic cover art. *Facing Death*, published at the turn of the century, is the story of a working-class lad who saved the local coal mine from Luddite-style vandalism, then went on to rescue several trapped miners (and the mine owner) after an explosion in the pit. Although the hero at no point entered the military, nor did the military at any point enter the story, the cover depicts a cavalry trooper at full gallop, wielding a flashing saber.[32] *A Final Reckoning*, set in the Australian Outback, has a rather inexplicable Viking armed with broadaxe and sword on the cover.[33]

Henty had some definite ideas as to the proper conduct of the heroic individual. Once on the field, the hero should forget all except the goal assigned:

> His lips were parched with excitement and the acrid smell of gunpowder. Man after man had fallen beside him, but he was yet untouched. There was no thought of fear or danger now. His whole soul seemed absorbed in the one thought of getting into the battery.[34]

Tennyson gave a very good reason for this sort of behavior. Most quote only the second couplet of this often repeated verse as an example of the purity of the code of chivalry.[35] In so doing, an important motivational concept is missed:

> My good blade carves the casques of men,
> My tough lance thrusteth sure,
> My strength is as the strength of ten,
> Because my heart is pure.
> The shattering trumpet shrilleth high,
> The hard brands shiver on the steel,
> The splinter'd spear shafts crack and fly.
> The horse and rider reel:
> They reel, they roll in clanging lists;
> And when the tide of combat stands,
> Perfume and flowers fall in showers,
> That lightly rain from ladies hands.[36]

Martial virtue was the measure of manliness, and thus attractive to women. Although Galahad eschewed such carnal pleasures, the fact that they are noted – and more than once in the poem – indicate that military prowess and sexual reward were linked in the Victorian mind.

Even better than participating in combat was bringing back visible proof in the form of wounds. An honorable wound was not only proof that one had in fact seen the elephant; in light of the state of medical science in the nineteenth century, it marked one as a true survivor. Henty proved quite cavalier in the treatment of even the gravest of injuries, making permanent maiming seem positively desirable:

> 'How is Rawlinson going on?'
> 'Oh, I think he will do very well,' the surgeon said. 'Of course he's a little down in the mouth about himself. It's not a pleasant prospect for a man to have to go about on two wooden legs all his life. Still, it's been done in the service; and as the fight was a sharp one, and such an important capture was made, he will get his full pension, and I shall strongly recommend him for Chelsea Hospital if he likes to take it. But he tells me he was by trade a carpenter before he enlisted, and I expect he would rather go down and live among his own people. His wooden legs won't prevent him earning a living at his trade; and as he is rather a good-looking fellow I dare say he won't have much difficulty in getting a wife. Maimed heroes are irresistible to the female mind.'[37]

The preceding passage reveals another aspect of the hero's character: the loss of body parts was simply the cost of doing business. The Kipling stalwarts Mulvaney, Otheris, and Learoyd compared a variety of wounds in 'With the Main Guard.'[38] In Henty's world even the gravest wounds were treated as of little consequence:

> A few minutes later two surgeons entered the room and examined Ralph's arm. They agreed at once that it was necessary to amputate it three inches higher up....
> The operation was performed at once, and although he had to press his lips hard together to prevent himself from crying out, he did find it less painful than he had expected.

\* \* \*

> 'I saw the surgeon downstairs and he told me – ' and her lips quivered and her eyes filled with tears.

'That I had lost my left arm, mother. Well, that is nothing to fret about when thousands have been killed. One can do very well without a left arm; and I think, on the whole, that I have been wonderfully lucky.'[39]

What is more, injury should never interfere with completing the task at hand. In *Jack Archer* the hero and a companion, having lowered themselves down a cliff in the face of a storm to save shipwrecked comrades below, faced a minor annoyance:

'I've broken my arm, Dick,' Jack said; 'but never mind me now. How many are there alive?'

The hero and his companion went on to rescue 16 doomed souls before themselves returning to safety:

The Midshipmen were the last to leave the ship. Dick had in vain begged his companion to go up with one of the preceding batches, as the last pair would necessarily be deprived of the assistance from the lower rope, which had so materially aided the rest. Jack, however, refused to hear of it.[40]

Henty required his characters to be true to form to the very end:

'Fortescue, are you hit?'
'I am done for!' the young officer replied faintly; 'one of their bullets has gone through my body; but never mind me now.' As he spoke he tottered, and would have fallen had not the others supported him and gently laid him down on a heap of skins which served as an Afghan bed.[41]

It was important to the Victorian writers to die well, and self-sacrifice was the epitome of heroism. Henry Newbolt recounted heroism displayed during the American Civil War and compared it favorably with British heroes of the past:

> Into the narrowing channel, between the shore
> And the sunk torpedoes lying in treacherous rank;
> She turned but a yard too short; a muffled roar,
> A mountainous wave, and she rolled, righted, and sank.
>
> Over the manhole, up in the ironclad tower,
> Pilot and Captain met as they turned to fly;

> The hundredth part of a moment seemed an hour,
> For one could pass to be saved, and one must die.
>
> They stood like men in a dream: Craven spoke,
> Spoke as he lived and fought, with a Captain's pride,
> 'After you, Pilot:' the pilot woke,
> Down the ladder he went, and Craven died.
>
> *All men praise the deed and the manner, but we —*
> *We set it apart from the pride that stoops to the proud,*
> *That strength that is supple to serve the strong and the free,*
> *The grace of the empty hands and the promises loud:*
> *Sidney thirsting a humbler need to slake,*
> *Nelson waiting his turn for the surgeon's hand,*
> *Lucas crushed with chains for a comrade's sake*
> *Outram coveting right before command,*
>
> *These were paladins, these were Craven's peers,*
> *These with him shall be crowned in story and song,*
> *Crowned with the glitter of steel and the glimmer of tears,*
> *Princes of courtesy, merciful, proud and strong.*[42]

For these authors principle was more important than life itself. Henty echoed the same sentiment in *Beric the Briton*: ' "Tell Seutonius that we scorn his mercy," Beric said, "and we will die as we have lived, free men." '[43]

This attitude toward 'dying well' reached the highest levels of society. During the Crimean War, following the Battle of the Alma, Queen Victoria wrote to her daughter, the Princess Augusta: 'You will understand it when I assure you that I regret exceedingly not to be a man and to be able to fight in the war. My heart bleeds for the many fallen, but I consider that there is no finer death for a man than on the battlefield!'[44]

The heroic officer of literature always led from the front, where the fighting – and the glory – was thickest. Rudyard Kipling's Captain Crook O'Neil is an example of the officer who both shares the dangers and privations of his men on campaign, and inspires them with coolness and a clever phrase in even the most dire of situations:

> 'Knee to knee!' sings out Crook, wid a laugh whin the rush av our comin' into the gut shtopped, an' he was huggin' a hairy great Paythan, neither bein' able to do anything to the other, though both was wishful.
>
> 'Breast to breast!' he sez, as the Tyrone was pushin' us forward closer and closer.

'An' hand over back!' sez a Sargint that was behin'. I saw a sword lick out past Crook's ear, an' the Paythan was tuk in the apple av his throat like a pig at Dromeen fair.

'Thank ye, Brother Inner Guard,' sez Crook, cool as a cucumber widout salt. 'I wanted that room.' An' he wint forward by the thickness av a man's body, havin' turned the Paythan undher him. The man bit the heel off Crook's boot in his death-bite.[45]

Elsewhere in *Soldiers Three* and in 'The Ballad of Boh Da Thone,'[46] Crook O'Neil repeatedly won the undying loyalty of his men for his heroic leadership.

Henty attributed the same value to all cool and collected officers, though not in quite such a thick vernacular:

On the right, however, the Brunswickers were suffering heavily from the cannonade of the French, and were only prevented from breaking by the coolness of their chief. The Duke of Brunswick rode backward and forward in front of them, smoking his pipe and chatting cheerfully with his officers, seemingly unconscious of the storm of fire; and even the most nervous of his young troops felt ashamed to show any signs of faltering when their commander and chief set them such an example.[47]

Macaulay as well pointed out coolness and disregard for danger as one of the prime virtues of Lord Clive. Upon receiving a draft of rough men fresh from England in service with the British East India Company: 'Clive gradually accustomed them to danger, and, by exposing himself constantly in the most perilous of situations, shamed them into courage. He at length succeeded in forming a respectable force out of his unpromising materials.'[48]

The other ranks, on the other hand, were repeatedly enjoined to maintain discipline, follow orders, and do their duty, even under the most extreme of conditions. Kipling's advice was to maintain a stoic attitude:

> When first under fire and you're wishful to duck
> Don't look nor take heed at the man that is struck.
> Be thankful you're livin', and trust in your luck
>     And march to your front like a soldier . . .
>
> If your officer's dead and the sergeants look white,
> Remember it's ruin to run from a fight;
> So take open order, lie down, and sit tight,
>     and wait for supports like a soldier . . .

And in defeat, to remain defiant and deny the enemy his (or her) pleasure:

> When you're wounded and left on Afghanistan's plains,
> And the women come out to carve up your remains,
> Just roll to your rifle and blow out your brains
>     An' go to your God like a soldier.[49]

To do otherwise was to invite disaster and disdain; the survivors of the company that broke and ran in Kipling's 'That Day' lost the respect of their comrades and confidence of their officers, deemed fit only to tend the camels for the remainder of the campaign:

> There was thirty dead and wounded on the ground we
>     couldn't keep –
> No, there wasn't more than twenty when the front begun
>     to go –
> But, Christ! along the line o' flight they cut us up like sheep,
>     An' that was all we gained by doin' so.[50]

Henty agreed that discipline was the key to success:

> They were but halfway across the plain when a regiment of French cavalry were seen riding in pursuit. The regiments were at once formed into squares within fifty yards of each other, and Terence and Bull in the centre of one square, and Herrara and Macwitty in the other, exhorted the men to stand steady, assuring them there was nothing whatsoever to be feared from the cavalry if they did so. The French rode up towards the squares, but were met by heavy volleys, and after riding round them drew off, having suffered considerable loss, being greatly surprised at finding that instead of a mob of armed men, such as they had met at Avia, they were encountered by soldiers possessing the steadiness of trained troops.[51]

To Victorian authors the courage and heroism of the British soldier was intrinsic, and needed only sensible leadership to guide the natural impulses of the trooper, as Kipling's Private Mulvaney observed:

> Wid Bobs an' a few three-year-olds, I'd swape any army av the earth into a towel an' throw it away afterward. Faith, I'm not jokin'! 'Tis the bhoys – the raw bhoys – that don't know fwhat a bullet manes, an' wudn't care av they did – that dhu the work.[52]

Henty's view differed with that of Mulvaney, as he deemed a certain amount of seasoning necessary to produce an effective soldier:

> Just as brave, my lad, and when it comes to fighting the young soldier is very often every bit as good as the old one; but they can't stand the fatigue and hardship like old soldiers. A boy will start out on as long a walk as a man can take but he can't keep it up day after day. When it comes to long marches, to sleeping on the ground in the wet, bad food, and fever from the marshes, the young soldier breaks down, the hospital gets full of boys, and they die off like flies, while the older men pull through.[53]

For Henty, the natural bravery of youth required tempering; both Henty and Kipling, however, acknowledged the intrinsic heroism of British youth.

'Bobs' – Field Marshal Lord Roberts of Kandahar – was to Rudyard Kipling the living embodiment of the ideal. At the death of Lord Roberts, Kipling summed up his character as the archetype of Victorian heroism:

> Clean, simple, valiant, well-beloved,
> Flawless in faith and fame,
> Whom neither ease nor honours moved
> An hair's-breadth from his aim.[54]

Kipling's eulogy of the virtues of Lord Roberts compares nicely to that of Tacitus on Agricola.

Although Lord Roberts did operate within the system of patronage and connection that was the Victorian officer corps, Kipling cast him as a soldier to whom the accolades of heroism came justly and without self-promotion. By contrast, the poet denigrated what he saw as the political machinations of Sir Garnet Wolseley, thinking it unseemly that a soldier should seek to curry favor from civilians, that it was wrong for a military man to act in hope of reward. He articulated this position in 'The Taking of Lungtungpen,' where Mulvaney dismissed Sir Garnet as nothing more than a seeker of favor at Court, and in 'Bobs,' in which the true hero's virtues include the fact that he 'does – not – advertise.'[55] As with the sentiments expressed above by Captain Slessor and Evelyn Wood, the important point here is the concept projected, regardless of the actual actions of the individuals of whom the poet writes.

The theme of the modest hero was a constant in Henty's books, with the inevitable consequence that others would recognize the greatness of the great man:

'Well, Bob, so I hear you have been fighting and commanding ships and doing all sorts of things. I saw Captain Lockett in the town, and faith if you had been a dozen admirals rolled into one he couldn't have spoken more highly of you. It seems, Mrs. O'Halloran, that Bob has been the special angel who has looked after poor Jack on board the *Antelope*.'

'What ridiculous nonsense, doctor!' Bob exclaimed hotly.

'Not at all, Bob; it is too modest you are entirely.'[56]

It was important to Henty that the hero be mindful of his station until proven:

You will do, my lad. I can see you have got the roughness rubbed off you already, and will get along capitally with the regiment. I can't say that much for young Stapleton. He seems to be completely puffed up with the sense of his own importance, and to be an unlicked sort of cub altogether.[57]

The hero of *In Greek Waters*, Horace Beveridge, willingly placed himself under the discipline of the *Misericordia's* master, despite the fact that he was the owner's son, showing the proper humility of one yet unproven.

*In Greek Waters* served as a testament throughout to the natural justice of Albion. Set in the savage War of Greek Independence, it allowed Henty to assert the moral superiority of British heroism, and gave an opportunity to explain why the Philhellenes had been so disappointed by the barbarity of the Greeks they had come to free:

'Brutes!' Martyn exclaimed with great emphasis. 'How these fellows can be descendants of the old Greeks beats me altogether.'

'The old Greeks were pretty cruel,' Horace, who had just joined them, said. 'They used to slaughter their captives wholesale, and mercy wasn't among their virtues. Besides, my father says that except in Morea very few indeed are descendants of the Greeks; the rest are Bulgarian or Albanian, neither of whom the Greeks of old would have recognized as kinsmen.'[58]

How easily that explained it! The heroism of the ancient Greeks was not tarnished, because these chaps were actually barbarians in Greeks' clothing.

While in the eyes of the Victorians no native warrior could match the heroism and virtue of Newbolt's 'Island Race,' close association with a proper officer could impart the virtues of valour and fidelity, at least among the martial races:[59]

> Sons of the Island Race, wherever ye dwell,
> Who speak of your fathers' battle with lips that burn,
> The deed of an alien legion hear me tell,
> And think not shame for the hearts ye tamed to learn,
> When succor shall fail and the tide for a season turn
> To fight with a joyful courage, a passionate pride,
> To die at last as the Guides at Cabul died.

The Guides besieged, their officers slain, resisted the offer to save their lives by surrender. This was the effect of taming the native heart:

> Then the joy that spurs the warriors' heart
> To the last thundering gallop and sheer leap
> Came on the men of the Guides: they flung apart
> The doors not all their valour could no longer keep
> They dressed their slender line; they breathed deep,
> And with never a foot lagging or head bent,
> To the clash and clamour and dust of death they went.[60]

The perfidy of the East allowed Henty to make other points as to the proper conduct of a hero. As Gilbert and Sullivan pointed out in the lyric cited at the beginning of this chapter, a true man does not stand by and allow brutish behavior to go unchecked. The officers of the *Misericordia* dined with a regular British officer ashore, who related the following events:

> One old Albanian who told me he had done this [massacred an entire Muslim village], told me, sir, as if it were a thing to be proud of. I had the satisfaction of taking him by the scruff of the neck and the tail of his white petticoat and chucking him off the pier into the sea. When he scrambled out I offered him the satisfaction of a gentleman, seeing he was a chief who thought no small beer of himself. There was a good deal of difficulty in explaining to him how the thing was managed in a civilized country, and I never felt more satisfaction in my life than I did next morning when I put a bullet into the scoundrel's body.[61]

Such attitudes were not the province of gentlemen alone; shortly thereafter the owner of the *Misericordia* decided that rather than continuing as a Greek privateer, under which conditions he had engaged the crew, the ship would become a rescue vessel for any imperilled civilian, Greek or Turk. The men did not grumble at the prospect of losing the prize money they had expected from the voyage; instead:

> Three hearty cheers rang out from the sailors. They had all been ashore at Zante, and had heard enough from the soldiers they fraternized with there to fill them with disgust and indignation at the conduct of the Greeks, and this announcement that they would henceforth put a stop to such cruelty, even if they had to fight for it, filled them with satisfaction.[62]

The 'just cause' rang as a clarion call through all these works. For Tennyson, it was the one justification for a life otherwise wasted by foolishness and indecision:

> Let it flame or fade, and the war roll down like a wind,
> We have proved we have hearts in a cause, we are noble still,
> And myself have wakened, as it seems, to the better mind;
> It is better to fight for the good, than to rail at the ill;
> I have felt with my native land, I am one with my kind,
> I embrace the purpose of God and the doom assingn'd.[63]

Newbolt equated the extension of empire as the will of God, and invoked the blessings of Providence on the just cause:

> Remember, Lord, the years of faith,
> The spirits humbly brave,
> The strength that died defying death,
> The love that loved the slave:
>
> The race that strove to rule Thine earth
> With equal laws unbought:
> Who bore for Truth the pangs of birth,
> And brake the bonds of Thought.
>
> Thou wilt not turn Thy face away
> From those who work Thy will,
> But send Thy strength on hearts that pray
> For strength to serve Thee still.[64]

For Kipling, it was an intrinsic part of the White Man's Burden to take up the heroic racial cause:

> Take up the White Man's burden –
> Send forth the best ye breed –
> Go bind your sons to exile
> To serve the captive's need;
> To wait in heavy harness
> On fluttered folk and wild –
> Your new-caught sullen peoples,
> Half devil and half child.[65]

The evolving concept of the heroic ideal during the Victorian Era is demonstrated by a comparison of Macaulay and Henty. At mid-century the heroic paradigm was quite pragmatic. By the end of the century it had developed an artificial heroic morality that could not accept its heroes 'warts and all.'

The subject of one of Macaulay's most famous essays, Robert, Lord Clive, was not a terribly virtuous individual, and Macaulay presented him in his natural form, without any laundering of events.[66] In Macaulay's estimation, Clive's virtues outweighed his failings: 'But every person who takes a fair and enlightened view of his whole career must admit that our island, so fertile in heroes and statesmen, has scarcely ever produced a man more truly great in either arms or in council.'[67]

Henty, on the other hand, rewrote history to expunge the memory of a midshipman stripped of the Victoria Cross. Henty wove the true historical account of Captain William Peel into the tale of Jack Archer, placing the midshipman under his command in the Naval Brigade before Sevastopol. Much was made of the captain's leadership: 'Captain Peel... was just the man to get the greatest possible amount of work from them. Always in high spirits, taking his full share in all the work, and exposing himself recklessly in the heaviest fire, he was almost idolized by his men.'[68]

Jack was chosen to accompany the captain in the Battle of Inkerman, but was later commanded to lie down out of harm's way during the thick of the battle. Henty spent some considerable ink describing the exploits of various historical individuals during the Inkerman battle scenes, but on the conduct of Captain Peel he remained virtually mute.

Yet the real Peel was actually accompanied in his adventures by a midshipman, Edward St John Daniel, of HMS *Diamond*. Both Peel and Daniel, his young aide-de-camp received the Cross:

> Midshipman Daniel was one of the volunteers from HMS *Diamond*, who, under the command of the captain [Peel] brought in powder to the battery

from a waggon under very heavy fire, a shot having disabled the horses. On 5 November at the Battle of Inkermann he, as ADC to the captain, remained by his side throughout a long and dangerous day. On 18 June 1855 he was again with his captain in the first scaling party at the assault on the Redan binding up his superior officer's severely wounded arm and taking him back to a place of safety.[69]

Yet Henty passed up the opportunity to lionize two stalwarts for the price of one, and in fact never mentioned Daniel at any point during the story.

The problem was that Daniel had forfeited his Victoria Cross just four years after it was awarded.[70] Accused of taking homosexual liberties with subordinates, Daniel deserted rather than answer formal charges and his name was erased from the Register of the Victoria Cross at the War Office (the subject of forfeiture will be dealt with fully in Chapter 5). Such a figure could hardly be held up as a role model for the growing boys of England, so Henty simply made him an unperson. Instead, credit for being the loyal aide-de-camp was given to a Midshipman Wood of HMS *Queen* at the storming of the Redan.[71] As it would be impossible to report the actions of Captain Peel in any detail without mentioning the midshipman that accompanied him, Henty elsewhere remained purposely vague on Peel's conduct.[72]

The reality of war and heroism were thus not an exact fit with society's conception of the phenomenon. For the British public, the military consisted of the Officer Corps, a sort of modern incarnation of the paladin, riding forth to bring light to the darkness, and the Other Ranks, consisting of rogues with hearts of gold. War was a grand game to be played with good sportsmanship. The following passage comes from newspaper accounts of the storming of Dargai Ridge, 20 October, 1898:

> Stepping forward to the head of his regiment, Colonel Matthias addressed a few words to his men in loud, clear tones. The task before the troops was practically a forlorn hope. Four hours and more had been spent in similar attempts without success. Words to be a value in such an emergency must be well chosen. Colonel Matthias pitched his that afternoon in the right patriotic spirit. Having ordered the regiment to 'charge magazines, fixed bayonets,' Colonel Matthias said: – 'men of the Gordon Highlanders, listen to me. The General says this position must be taken at all hazards, and we will take it in front of the whole division; let every man follow his own officers and section leaders, and don't stop.'
>
> Loud huzzas greeted their colonel's words, and with eager faces the first company of the Highlanders formed up on the edge of the terrible

plateau, where the crowd of battered soldiers made way for their fresh and unblooded brothers.

'Are you ready,' again rang out the voice of Colonel Matthias, and a mad, wild cheer, bred of the courage which lies deep in the hearts of men, was the response. 'Come on,' shouted the Colonel.

Then the pipers skirled forth the regimental war song, 'and with the lilt of a big parade' the gay Gordons stepped forth. The gallant Colonel led his troops, offering the first mark to the enemy... The terrific roar of the guns, and the silence which followed, coupled with the stirring appeal of the Colonel and the roar of the slogan, had a wonderful effect. It was not ordinary enthusiasm, bred of natural courage. On, up the corpse-strewn steep, the Highlanders charged, whilst from the heights above, which commanded every soul of the advancing regiment, the enemy poured forth a blighting fire. The Gordons were seen dashing along the bullet-swept zone, and whilst men dropped in all directions the dust came up and hid the warriors momentarily from view.

On swept the undaunted band. Loud screeched the pipes, and the strains of 'Cock O' the North' and the 'Haughs O' Cromdale' – the charging tune of the Gordons – further infused the mad spirit of heroism into the storming party. Faster, more vivid, more tumultuous grew the music. The men saw their officers fall on all sides. The colonel at their head was shot; Lieutenant Lamont received his death wounds; and Major Forbes MacBean was shot in the abdomen, but even the whilst lying on the ground cheered on his men to the assault.

It was a maddened, infuriated scene. There was no halt in the advance. Wounded on the ground, shot in the legs, the pipers skirled on their compatriots to death and victory, and over the tumult of battle could still be heard the regimental war marches...

As Colonel Matthias, who had been outpaced in the final climb, came up, a tremendous cheer went up from all the Gordons, in which the men of other regiments and natives joined, while the native officers of the Sikhs and Gurkhas crowded round him to shake his hand.

Near the top of the hill the Colonel complained aloud about being blown, when Colour-Sergeant Mackie gave him a helping hand and exclaimed, 'Ye're gaun verra strong for an auld mon.'[73]

The Gordon charge up the heights of Dargai brought praise from the far corners of the empire, through official channels and from proud Scotsmen both in and out of uniform.[74]

Here in the storming of a native stronghold we see the epitome of the Victorian ideals of heroism, and indeed, four of those who made the mad rush up the heights of Dargai were recommended for the Victoria Cross.[75] Officers were expected to lead from the front, 'offering the first mark to the enemy,' while the other ranks were filled with a sort of disciplined berserker rage. When men were wounded they bore up under the pain with manly stoicism and carried on with their duty as long as they could stand (or in the case of Piper George Findlater, shot through both legs, got a Gurkha to prop him up on a rock so he could continue playing) and when they died, it was thanking God they had done their duty by Queen and Country. It was common knowledge that a Tommy Atkins or Jack Tar could easily whip thrice his weight in any foreign nationality you cared to name without mussing his mustache.[76]

The problem was that war was a horrible bloody business that left death and shattered survivors in its wake. Bullets did not leave neat holes in shoulders, and it was a rare man indeed who could press his lips together hard enough to prevent crying out during an amputation. Heroes were more often than not just too tired, too hungry, or too crazed with blood-lust to care anymore. Reconciling the myth and reality would prove to be a tedious task once the decision was made to institutionalize heroism. The Normans had their Tallifers, the Saxons their Herewards and the Celts their Warrior Queen; military virtues and the values of the hero had been common features of popular culture in the British Isles as long as there had been a population to cultivate these values. Why, then, did the British Government feel the need to institutionalize the hero in 1856?

# Two

# The Institutionalization of Heroism in Britain

A rather obvious question in dealing with the creation of a new thing is 'why?' In the case of the Victoria Cross the obvious answer is that it was created in recognition of the sacrifices made by the soldiers and sailors of the Crimean War. This is true insofar as the war served as a catalyst for change, but the change could not have occurred without some necessary preconditions. Hegel's *Zeitgeist* was in motion; changes had occurred in society, were reflected in politics, and were brought to a head through a combination of Romanticism, pragmatism, and personal ambition.

Since the fall of Rome, Europe had gone for centuries without any institutional means for the recognition of heroism. There were ways for kings and governments to signify their pleasure with the heroic individual, but no standard that endured over time or that was applied with any kind of continuity. With the exceptions of the Portuguese Military Order of the Tower and Sword, established in 1459, and the 1671 Danish Order of the Dannebrog,[1] there were no national standards of heroism until after the coming of the Enlightenment, with its core reliance on the rationality and perfectibility of the individual.

During the late eighteenth and early nineteenth centuries Europe rediscovered the value of military awards and decorations. The concept of the 'citizen soldier' and the *levée en masse* had changed the nature of warfare; an increasing number of soldiers were fighting for ideology rather than coin. Commanders and governments learned that the recognition of merit complemented the punishment of transgressions in motivating desired behavior in the ranks. Virtually the only provision proposed by the Royal Commission of 1837 on Army Reform (the Howick Commission) that was accepted by parliament was the creation of the Good Conduct Badge and merit pay bonuses for virtue in the ranks.[2] A soldier who had enlisted for the pay or because he had no other alternative required discipline. The soldier who enlisted in the name of duty or patriotism required recognition of his virtues.

By the end of the Napoleonic Wars virtually every other European nation had established some form of recognition for bravery. France had its Legion of Honor, created for officers by Napoleon in 1802. Prussia had established the famous 'Blue Max,' the Pour le Mérite, in 1810 and the equally famous Iron Cross in 1813. The Dutch instituted the Military Order of William upon their liberation from Napoleon's empire in 1815. One of the first things the Belgians did after winning their independence from the Kingdom of Holland was establish the Order of Leopold in 1832. Medals had become quite fashionable on the Continent.[3] This trend continued into mid-century, and even became somewhat egalitarian. In 1852 Napoleon III established the Médaille Militaire to recognize the heroism of the other ranks. When the Crimean War broke out the French Army regularly distributed these medals along with the Legion of Honor to deserving soldiers, a practice that soon excited comment in the British press.[4]

With the exception of the Médaille Militaire, these orders and awards were not egalitarian and usually came either in several grades that excluded the rank and file from the highest honors, or were open only to certain ranks. The Prussian Iron Cross, for example, came in four grades: The Blucher Cross (awarded only twice); The Grand Cross of the Iron Cross (awarded only 21 times since inception); The Iron Cross 1st Class; and the Iron Cross, 2nd Class (awarded so frequently as to become 'the most universally known award of bravery').[5] Likewise, the French Legion of Honor came in five classes, the lowest of which held the title of knight.[6]

The word 'order' generally meant that the award was open to the officer class alone. Many were not strictly military decorations; the Norwegian Order of Saint Olaf (1847), for example, could be awarded for either civilian or military service to the state. The Portuguese Military Order of Saint Ferdinand could be won both in combat for gallantry or in an office for outstanding staff work. The British Order of the Bath was similar in this respect, as it could be had for military gallantry, long and valuable service without a particular gallant act, or for civilian service to the Crown.[7] Britain lacked any national award purely for military service.

For the lower ranks of the British Army there were no national awards whatsoever; the various grades of the Order of the Bath were officer-only, and at that excluded lieutenants and captains. There were informal ways of recognizing the heroism of private soldiers and non-commissioned officers, the rare mention in dispatches or promotion being the most common. The former may have originated with Sir Charles Napier following the Battle of

Miani in 1843, but with one exception in 1846 it did not become common practice until the dispatches of Lord Raglan in 1855.[8] The latter of these two options presented a potential problem if the promotion made an officer of a common soldier. There was a very club-like atmosphere to the mid-Victorian officer corps. The officers were in the main drawn from the scions of the upper classes while the ranks were filled with refugees from the lowest levels of British society. A huge gap existed between officers and men, and little encouragement was given for the enlisted men to cross that gap.[9] The soldier who won a commission endured a miserable life in most cases, always an outsider, exiled from his origins by his new rank, ostracized from his new companions by his origins. It also had the undesired effect of promoting men who were not suited to command, in some cases turning a good senior NCO into a bad junior officer.[10]

Liberalism preached the doctrine of individual duty and individual reward for hard work.[11] Although Samuel Smiles did not publish *Self Help* until 1859, already in the 1840s the idea that the individual was personally responsible for his or her actions and that right conduct would be rewarded by society was a popular one. Indeed, it was his association with the members of a working-class mutual improvement society in 1845 that provided the core of *Self Help*.[12] This change in outlook was evident beyond the business office and seats in parliament. Recognition of the individual can be seen in the Nonconformist religious revivals of the early nineteenth century, with their special emphasis on personal salvation and personal responsibility for one's actions, as opposed to the more corporatist litany of the Anglican High Church. In government, in society, and in the pulpit, the early Victorian period was an era of growing importance for the concept of self.[13]

At the same time as the value placed on individuality increased, British identities were in transition. The American Revolution and the series of conflicts precipitated by the French Revolution fostered the growth of a 'British' identity that absorbed, but did not eliminate, the existing concepts of regional identity.[14] Increasing literacy rates played a part in the development of a British nationalism. More and more people had their basic letters as the century progressed. The circulation of the *Times* rose from about 5000 copies daily during the Napoleonic Wars to over 40,000 by the time of the Crimean conflict. In addition, the news carried by the mid-century newspaper was far more immediate due to the railroad and the telegraph.[15] While not every village was in the main stream, literacy provided a connection to events beyond the borough or parish boundary and gave access to vicarious pride in the accomplishments of distant fellow subjects.[16]

By mid-century the subjects of Queen Victoria were used to reading accounts of the latest British achievements and comfortable with the perception that they lived in the most advanced and stable country in the world. The Great Exhibition of 1851 reinforced this self-righteous self-perception, as a showcase of British technological and social superiority enclosed in crystal.[17] Britain saw itself as walking the via media between the political extremes of the Continent, neither a military despotism nor a state ruled by the passions of the mob.[18] It reaped the benefits of this middle path in terms of material prosperity and political stability.[19] It was ready to accept a national hero as another symbol of national greatness.

The general social climate of Britain was receptive to the idea of a national standard of heroism, but it took a special set of political circumstances to develop it. A combination of political uncertainty, royal anxiety, and public outrage came together to create the Victoria Cross. At the heart of these was the controversy concerning the Army's performance in the Crimean War. Among other issues, the controversy highlighted the ill-defined relationship between the Secretary of State for War and the Colonies and the Commander-in-Chief.

The Army's performance in the Crimea suddenly threw the deficiencies of its administration into high contrast, for the force dispatched to the Crimea brought something new with it as it made its landing on that peninsula: a professional war correspondent. The high command had never dealt with such a creature before and did not think to censor the dispatches William Howard Russell dashed off to *The Times* in London.[20] While some readers dismissed his stark reports from the front as defeatist or sensationalist, most reacted with first horror, and then outrage. As true privations set in during the winter of 1854–55 letters voicing the anger of readers appeared in the pages of *The Times*:

> the time has arrived when the abuses which are the bane of our military system must cease. The blood so wantonly wasted by mal-administration cries aloud, and calls for protection to the survivors. The means of reform are patent to every eye, excepting when viewed through the distorted medium of official spectacles, and yet, simple and honest as the question is, the remedy for the evil will never be applied, unless the public insists that the public work be wrought by the best men.[21]

The controversy came to center on two individuals, the Duke of Newcastle, Secretary of State for War and the Colonies in the Aberdeen Government, and the out-of-office Earl Grey. Grey, as Viscount Howick, had pushed for

Army reform when he served as Secretary at War in the 1830s and had served as Secretary of War between July 1846 and February 1852. Now he called once again for Army reform in the winter of 1854–55.[22] He was joined by an article in The Times demanding a 'real Minister of War.'[23] Grey also attacked any exertion of 'personal power' by the Crown over the Army as unconstitutional.[24] The Crown did not exert similar authority over any other governmental department; it was solely due to the unique construction of Army administration that the Crown had access to control through the person of the Commander-in-Chief. He sought the full subordination of that office to a 'responsible minister' under parliament's control.[25] This did not make him popular with the royal family.

The role of the crown in government was in transition at mid-century. The Glorious Revolution established a limited monarchy and the ensuing century-and-a-half saw a progressive erosion of Crown prerogative. Victoria had come to power determined to preserve as much of the influence and position of the Crown as possible, and military control in particular. Her refusal to submit what she considered her royal right to choose the ladies of her bedchamber to the will of Prime Minister Robert Peel during the 'Bed-Chamber Plot' indicates that from the outset Victoria was determined to defend what remained of the royal prerogative as a matter of principle, with little regard to the political cost.[26] This attitude did not mesh with reality; Victoria might claim that the government acted under her authority, but she could not rule by decree. All royal pronouncements, writs, and warrants had to be countersigned by one of the Secretaries of State, and those gentlemen were more responsible to parliament than the monarch.[27]

Victoria and Albert were determined to defend the position of the Commander-in-Chief as a bastion of royal prerogative.[28] The C-in-C operated out of Horse Guards and from those offices, within sight of Buckingham Palace on Birdcage Walk, he managed the Army. Through the Adjutant General's office he oversaw military discipline, punishment, and reward. The Quartermaster General's office undertook the distribution of supply from stores to the troops under his direction. The Military Secretary coordinated his communications with the various regimental depots and stations throughout the Empire. Most important, the C-in-C controlled Army patronage, determining who would get the plums of commission and assignment.[29]

The Commander-in-Chief's position thus held the potential for a great deal of power in the right (or wrong) hands. It was controversial because constitutionally there was no such thing as a C-in-C. The top commanders of the Army considered themselves direct servants of the Crown, not representatives of parliamentary policy and they answered to the monarch through the C-in-C. When there was no real divergence between Crown and parliament on an issue it did not matter, but when the two drew apart, as they did in the years of reform, it became a political hot topic. By mid-century the Commander-in-Chief represented one of the last vestiges of Crown prerogative, a direct link between the monarchy and the Army.[30] The Crown had lost control over the Navy during the eighteenth century, culminating with the 1831 reorganization of the Admiralty under Sir James Graham, in which administration of the Royal Navy was vested in an Admiralty Board over which the Crown had no formal control.[31] Victoria and Albert did not want to see the Army suffer the same fate.

On 7 April Grey again attacked the management of the Army, proposing the creation of a civilian board answering to the Commons to replace the existing structure.[32] Lord Panmure, who as the Honourable Fox Maule had been Secretary at War for the Russell Government, roundly supported Grey's proposal.[33] In 1850, during debates over officer pay rates he had circulated a confidential memorandum calling for revamping the Army's organization: 'Let the patronage of the Army be left to the C-in-C and its strategy to its officers, but let all other matters rest with a responsible minister of the crown.'[34] Now he had another opportunity to push for increased parliamentary oversight of the Army. While Grey's solution to the problem differed from Panmure's 1850 proposal, it did offer the potential to rectify the antiquated administrative problems of the Army. Prince Albert was horrified by the measure, as it would place the Army, like the Royal Navy, beyond formal Crown influence.[35]

Newcastle responded to the criticism by bluffly maintaining that the Army's administration was running like a well-oiled machine – a claim hardly sustainable in view of its performance – and by invoking the shade of Wellington to sanctify the existing system. Lord Hardinge, Commander-in-Chief since Wellington's resignation, vigorously supported Newcastle's assertions and warned that any diminution of the C-in-C's authority or changes in the system of military administration would seriously hamper the war effort.[36]

Lord John Russell, Aberdeen's Leader of the House of Commons, offered a different solution than Grey. He proposed separating the duties of War and Colonies into two positions and advocated giving the newly formed War Office to Lord Palmerston.[37] The new office of Secretary of State for War would amalgamate much of the existing administrative structure under its control.[38] Lord Aberdeen, the Prime Minister, accepted the proposal in principle but did not push for it; the cabinet was preoccupied with forming plans for offensive operations in the Black Sea. After one of his customary exhibitions of political pouting, Russell resumed his pressure for the change and was rewarded in June with formal severing of the two offices.[39] It was only a cosmetic victory, as the control that Newcastle had over the existing structure was not altered. The war effort still drew strong criticism and ultimately caused the fall of the Aberdeen government.

The government's situation deteriorated rapidly in January; Newcastle's proposal to form a permanent joint civil/military board similar to the Admiralty was rejected as too little, too late. John Arthur Roebuck, a pugnacious radical MP, announced his intention to call for a committee to inquire as to the condition of the Army before Sevastopol.[40]

Palmerston had the last word as Aberdeen's government died messily in the House of Commons, in a short speech that fully anticipated defeat in the Roebuck division. He defended coalition government, but more to support the one he expected to form than to defend the one in which he sat. A considerable number of Liberals did not take part in the vote, unwilling to condemn their colleagues, yet unable to support them. Aberdeen's coalition died with a whimper, losing the division 305 to 148 on 29 January 1855.[41]

Palmerston did not automatically receive an invitation to form a new ministry. Despite his partial rehabilitation, the Queen was still suspicious of him.[42] Victoria instead turned to Lord Derby on 31 January. The Tory leader claimed that despite a solid backing of 280 MPs he could not appease the public without 'other combinations' – that is to say, Peelites and Whigs. Chief on his list was Lord Palmerston, as according to Derby 'the whole country cried out for him.' Palmerston played his hand close to his chest in the turmoil of February, as he knew that Derby had virtually no chance of forming a government, but to refuse office would appear too self-serving. He therefore accepted Derby's invitation to join the new cabinet and then waited for Derby to fail.[43]

Upon Derby's failure the Queen turned to Russell. This act was simply a formality. It was well-known to everyone except Lord John that he had no hope of forming a government. In order to negate his potential opposition to a ministry that he did not head, it was necessary to demonstrate this fact to him. Once he had tried and failed to form a government, the torch was passed to Palmerston.[44]

Palmerston largely reconstituted the coalition Aberdeen had formed in 1852, with the exceptions of Newcastle, Russell, and Aberdeen himself. He chose Lord Panmure to take the War Office, an appointment that raised some protest. Palmerston's only stated concern was whether or not Panmure's gout would interfere with his ability to dispatch the duties of the office.[45]

Others were concerned with Panmure's intellectual capacity. Lord Clarendon wrote, 'Panmure is an honest good fellow but by no means of the calibre for such an office at such a moment and I am sure he *is* and will be thought inferior to Newcastle.'[46] Sir George Lewis described Panmure as one of the dullest men he ever knew.[47] The Duke of Argyll called him as 'a rough, strong-headed Scotsman,' but not 'a man to resort to in any great crisis of administration.'[48] Thus it was a challenge for both Panmure and Palmerston, who had ridden into office on the wave of popular discontent with the administration of the Army, to make the Army perform more efficiently. If they did not, the backwash of the wave would sweep them from office as surely as it had Aberdeen and Newcastle.[49]

They lost no time in presenting plans to revamp Army administration. On 10 February Panmure issued a set of proposals to the cabinet for the creation of two commissions of inquiry to be dispatched to the Crimea (an effort to blunt the still menacing Roebuck Commission) and for the absorption of the Secretary at War's powers into the Secretary for War's office.[50] This latter proposal was identical to one Russell had made in December that Palmerston had refused to support. Six days later Palmerston and Panmure expanded the new Government's plan to include the amalgamation of the civilian components of the Board of Ordnance under the direct control of the War Office.[51]

The reform of the Army's administration was by this point inevitable. Such reforms greatly concerned Victoria and Albert, as experience showed that any change in the system resulted in a loss of Crown authority. Although Albert had declined Wellington's suggestion that the Prince Consort become Commander-in-Chief in 1850, he fully agreed with the Duke's position on maintaining existing Crown prerogative.[52] Even before the matter drew to a head, during the discussions about the severing of War and Colonies, the Queen had cautioned Aberdeen to make sure the question of Army reform did not arise in parliament along with it. He assured her that the changes would be at ministerial level only and the structure of command would not be altered.[53] Like her husband, Victoria agreed with the Duke of Wellington's view of the relationship between the monarch and the military, that it was 'of the utmost importance to the stability of the Throne and the Constitution, that the command of the Army should remain in the hands of the sovereign, and not fall into those of the House of Commons.'[54] For Victoria, Crown, constitution, and command were woven inextricably into a single tapestry.[55]

The palace concomitantly maintained a vigil over reform proposals. On 20 January 1855 Secretary at War Sidney Herbert proposed a permanent

Civil/Military Army Board similar to the Admiralty. Victoria tried to barter her support for the measure in return for a clear description of the C-in-C's duty and a greater amount of autonomy for that office. It was clear that she was worried about the loss of Crown influence over the Army.[56] During the formation of the Palmerston ministry she objected to the proposed appointment of Frederick Peel as Under-Secretary of State for War on the grounds that his youth and inexperience 'may cause serious embarrassment and further exposure to successful attacks the already much-threatened maintenance of proper authority of the crown over the Army.'[57]

The formation of the new government did not allay her fears. Palmerston and Panmure had to appease the anger of the voting public and carry out a reform program. As Panmure observed concerning the appointment of the McNeill and Tulloch commission to inquire as to the state of the Army in the field, 'High personages are fearful least this opportunity be seized to get the administration of the Army placed, as the Admiralty, under the control of Parliament.'[58]

And while Victoria and Albert's worst fears did not materialize in the 1850s, enough changes were made to the administrative structure of the Army as to seriously limit the Crown's prerogative. During the further reorganization of the Army's administration the Crown lost one of the last remaining elements of royal control over the Army, when in July 1855 Panmure adopted a position that subordinated the office of the Commander-in-Chief to ministerial control. He pointed out that royal warrants and writs had to be countersigned by a principal secretary of state to be implemented, and that the C-in-C did not have this authority. He was therefore under the authority of the Secretary of State for War; if push came to shove, he could not act without the minister's approval.[59]

The Queen thus found herself in a distasteful position. To defend royal prerogative in the middle of the Crimean War controversy by opposing changes in the administration of the Army was to fly directly in the face of outraged popular sentiment. Any serious opposition to the changes in the offing would be wasted, and carry a political price far higher than the Crown was willing to pay. But Albert devised a way to numb the sting of the loss of yet another slice of the Crown's prerogative, replacing a concrete link to the military in the form of the Commander-in-Chief with an abstract link in the form of the Victoria Cross.[60]

The genesis of what became the Victoria Cross came from the Duke of Newcastle. At some point in 1854 he approached the Prince Consort and verbally suggested the need for either an expansion of the three classes of the Order of the Bath to include some of the lower ranks or the creation of a British 'Order of Merit' similar to the Médaille Militaire recently created by their allies. At the time Albert did not think such a measure advisable and the matter was tabled. However, in December of 1854, as the criticisms of the administration of the war climaxed, public calls in the press and in parliament for the recognition of British heroism appeared:

> while everyone is glowing with admiration of our noble Crimean Army, we seek in vain in the official dispatches with names of individuals in connection with specific deeds of daring, to become, as it were, household words among us. I venture, therefore, to suggest a partial remedy for the state of things – at any rate, until Lord Raglan shall add to his high reputation for courage by breaking through the red tape meshes of official routine, and giving the place of honour in his dispatches to those who have best deserved it without regard to rank or precedent.[61]

The writer went on to suggest that *The Times* establish an unofficial roll of honor to recognize the heroism that the government did not.

On 19 December 1854 Captain Thomas Scobell, RN (retired), proposed a motion in the House of Commons that the Queen institute an egalitarian award for valour. He pointed out that it would both aid recruitment and inspire those already in uniform 'to put forth their strength and exhibit their bravery.' After a brief discussion that included assurances from the government that medals had been struck and dispatched to the Crimea the captain agreed to withdraw his proposal: 'In withdrawing the motion, [he] trusted that the government would take the subject into consideration. To be of real utility, the "order of merit" ought to be given to all ranks, from the highest to the lowest. The motion was then withdrawn.'[62] It is unclear to what decorations the government spokesmen referred, as the Crimean Service Medal did not exist in December 1854. The Distinguished Conduct Medal had been created earlier in the year as an award for noncommissioned officers and men, but it was not open to all ranks.[63]

Scobell's comments precipitated new public calls for military recognition. In the press editors and letter-writers alike publicly wondered why the British soldier did not have similar rewards to those of his French ally to mark his merit. Some wanted campaign medals and clasps for all who participated in particular engagements:

> Why is there no clasp for Balaklava? If a medal has been justly earned by those who have taken part in the 'arduous and brilliant campaign in the Crimea,' why, of this gallant band, is a clasp alone undeserved by those

whose 'arduous' duty it was to stand in line against a charge of cavalry, or by those who cut their way, under three cross fires, through an opposing mass ten times their number, and, having slaughtered the enemy on all sides, returned in perfect order to their position?

Whatever may be the opinion of the Horse Guards, there is but one thought throughout the country, and that is this – that it will be a crying shame if such heroism is allowed to go unrewarded.[64]

Others pressed for recognition of individual acts of valour; that the French were more progressive in their recognition of individual heroism was unacceptable to some readers:

Sir, the attention of the public now being much directed to the proper mode of reporting those who distinguished themselves in the present war, it has occurred to me the very suitable mode would be by attaching to each of our great orders of Knighthood a new dignity by creating officers of the Orders of the Garter, Bath, Thistle, and Saint Patrick. A soldier who had eminently distinguished himself (as Captain Butler and Major Nasmyth at Silistria) might be created an officer of the order of the Garter, and those nearly as deserving might have given to them the decoration of any of the other orders.

This plan would, it appears to me, satisfy those who ask for the creation of an English 'Legion of Honour;' and such a decoration would be more highly prized than the medal given indiscriminately to all who 'are present' in a campaign, and would also afford a means of rewarding the devotion of our medical officers and of the commissariat.

In the case of our private soldiers being so decorated, there might also be conferred on them a pension for a limited number of years, with liberty to study, free of charge, at Sandhurst.[65]

The debate raised by Scobell's comments and by new letters to the editor of *The Times* in late December and early January prompted Newcastle to again approach Prince Albert on 20 January 1855:

Your Royal Highness mentioned several objections to the proposition of adding to the three classes of the Order of the Bath – and I hope I am not taking too great a liberty if I ask your Royal Highness' opinion upon the other suggestion – the institution of the new decoration to be confined to the Army and Navy but open to all ranks of either service.

> I confess it does not seem to be right or politic that such deeds of heroism as this war has produced should go unrewarded by any distinctive outward mark of honour because they were done by privates or by officers below the rank of major – and it is impossible to believe that Her Majesty's troops fighting side-by-side with those of France do not draw an invidious contrast between the rewards bestowed upon themselves and their allies
> 
> The value attached by soldiers to a little bit of ribbon is such as to render any danger insignificant and any privation light if it can be attained, and I believe that great indeed would be the stimulus and dearly prized the award of a Cross of Military Merit.
> 
> Of course great care would be requisite to prevent abuse – but I am sure your Royal Highness will not consider the danger of abuse a sufficient reason to reject this proposal if there appears sufficient good in it to justify its adoption.[66]

The Prince Consort sent a lengthy reply on 22 January, and still noted strong reservations to changing the existing structure for the recognition of heroism. He detailed the shortcomings of the Order of the Bath, remarking that the

> difficulty of distinguishing between the merits of different Officers in responsible situations and the unwillingness on the part of Commanders to incur the odium of making the distinction, have led them to mention nearly everybody in their Despatches and the government is thus left, either to do possible injustice, or to allow the reward to become a mere appendage of a certain Rank.[67]

He went on to discuss the limitations of medals for general campaigns and clasps for specific engagements:

> This mode is open to none of the former objections but is exposed to some of its own: – it leaves individual merit unnoticed & even here the necessity of distinguishing between actions becomes an embarrassment to the Govt. The troops which fought at Balaklava cry out at this moment at not sharing in the honours bestowed upon Inkerman, to which, it is true, the government can reply, that it marked an important success in the one instance, while the other was (to use the Duke of Wellington's expression) and '*untoward event*'. It has no reply however to the remonstrance of the troops: 'why are we to be punished for the mistakes of our

commanders? Have we not done all the troops could do under such difficult circumstances?'[68]

On the subject of the creation of a new award, Albert proposed strict regulations to insure against the abuses noted in connection with the Bath – granted too freely – and with the injustices inherent in issuing battle clasps – that deserving soldiers might be slighted:

> The only mode, I see, in which the difficulty could be overcome, seems to be something like the following:
> 1. That a small cross of merit for *personal deeds of valour* be established.
> 2. That it be open to all ranks.
> 3. That it be unlimited in number.
> 4. That an annuity (say, £5) be attached to each cross.
> 5. That it be *claimable* by an individual on establishing before a Jury of his Peers subject to confirmation at home, his right to the distinction.
> 6. That in cases of general actions it will be given in certain quantities to particular regiments, so many of the Officers, so many of the Sergeants, so many to the men (of the last say 1 per company) & that their distribution be left to a jury of the same rank as the persons to be rewarded.[69]

The peer-elective principle was intended to serve to both defuse the resentment soldiers might feel at not getting a decoration and to discourage commanding officers from recommending every man in the company or regiment in situations where an entire unit performed bravely. He closed with an admonition to avoid copying the French lead in creating the new medal:

> I would advise no reference to the Legion of Honour, the distribution of which is entirely arbitrary and guided by no principle, which is given indiscriminately to soldiers and civilians and has long been made a tool for corruption in the hands of the French Govt, the number of whose members extends to 40,000 & which has almost become a necessary appendage to the French Dress.[70]

Although Albert and Victoria at this point appear to have gotten behind the idea of a new gallantry award, going so far as authorizing approval of a public announcement of the intent to create a 'Cross of Military Merit,' political circumstances put the issue on the back burner for almost a year. The day after the Queen wrote to Newcastle granting permission for the announcement of intent, the Aberdeen Ministry fell.[71] Palmerston and Panmure had other fish to fry in setting up the new government and addressing the pressing issues of military administrative reform, while the press and parliament had new hobby horses to ride as the new government set to work. That the scope of those military reforms included the possible severing of the tie between the sovereign and the Commander-in-Chief and added a new dimension to Albert's conception of the new award. Newcastle's 'Cross of Military Merit' idea evolved into Albert's conception of the Victoria Cross, the design of which he sketched while traveling between Windsor and London by train.[72]

While the medal would not replace the direct and tangible control the Crown had held over the Army through the C-in-C, it could offer a direct, if abstract, link between the Crown and the officers and the rank-and-file of the Army. It carried with it the intrinsic understanding that this was a royal, not a government award – even the very name made that clear. It was the *Victoria* Cross, not a 'Parliamentary Order' or a 'Ministry Medal' or even a 'British Legion of Honor.' It was the personal recognition of valour by the Queen, and intentionally so. It maintained the fiction that the members of the armed services were soldiers of the Queen, not employees of parliament, even though in any meaningful sense they were now clearly the latter.

This conception fitted nicely into the Romantic perception Victoria had of herself and her relationship to the Army. She was proud of her father's military background and often made connection to it. Upon presenting new colours to the Royal Scots she remarked, 'I have been associated with your regiment since my earliest infancy, as my dear father was your Colonel. He was proud of his profession , and I was always taught to consider myself a soldier's child.'[73] She loved the military, often referring to the soldiers as 'her own,' or 'her children,' and cherished what she considered to be a personal bond between the sovereign and the lowest ranker.[74] After her first review of the 1st Regiment of the Life Guards and the Grenadier Guards as sovereign, 28 September 1837, she recounted: 'I saluted them by putting my hand to my cap like officers do, and was much admired for my manner of doing it . . . . The whole thing went off beautifully and I felt for the first time like a man, as if I could fight myself at the head of my troops.'[75]

The royal family had correspondingly perceived the war from afar and through a thick lens of romantic preconceptions. Victoria forthrightly stated she wished 'she were a man' so she could participate in the battles of the Crimean War alongside her soldiers. Even when news of the suicidal insanity at Balaklava reached Britain, she did not see incompetent communications or command stupidity but rather 'trembled with emotion, as well as pride, in reading the recital of the heroism of these devoted men.'[76] Queen Victoria experienced a vicarious romantic adventure through the war. To Victoria the Cross represented an opportunity to indulge her romanticism while strengthening the bond between herself and the military and, too, a way to recapture some of the influence she felt she had lost with the subordination of the position of the Commander-in-Chief to a civilian minister.

In November 1855 with a clear triumph on the books in the taking of Sevastopol in mid-September, the call for official recognition of British heroism resumed:

> In the *Moniteur* of 1st November we find eight columns devoted to the confirmations by the Imperial Government of the nominations to the Legion of Honour conferred by Marshal PELISSIER on the 11th of September... Merit is of no rank, and it is discriminated and rewarded in all... Now let us turn from the Army of our Allies to our own... In that memorable despatch in which general SIMPSON with his own hand so effectively demolished his own reputation as a commander, he stated that it was his intention to bring to the notice of the COMMANDER-IN-CHIEF those who had distinguished themselves in the assault on the Redan. From that day to this, as far as we have been able to learn, that promise has never been redeemed...[77]

The time appeared right to create the Victoria Cross, but to realize Albert's plan the royal couple needed the cooperation of the ministry, or at least that of a minister. The Crown had long ago lost the ability simply to decree the creation of a new order. In late November they began correspondence with Lord Panmure on the subject, hammering out the parameters of the award. On 28 December 1855 Albert and Victoria sent off the proposed draft of the royal warrant that would create the Cross to Lord Panmure at the War Office and anxiously awaited the outcome.[78]

In a sense their fears were misplaced, for the creation of the Victoria Cross gave Panmure an opportunity to mend fences with the royal family.[79] The Cross represented cheap balm to soothe the wounded pride of the Queen, and Panmure was happy to cooperate fully with the Crown's desires on a matter so apparently inconsequential. By mid-January 1856 the Crown and

War Office were in agreement as to the wording of the warrant and the design of the award.[80]

Chief among Victoria and Albert's desires was to make sure the Cross remained a purely royal award, that parliament could not take credit for its creation nor meddle in its administration. Panmure assured the Queen that the warrant 'Must declare throughout the Royal Will and Pleasure of the Queen – and bear the stamp of an act of Her Own prerogative. The sovereign is the fountain of all honours, and commands their institution as well as their revocation.'[81] This remained an active issue in the Queen's eyes; in 1857, writing on the subject of the first bestowals of the VC, she instructed Panmure:

> The Queen would wish the first notice of these awards to be in the Gazette & to have the explanations of the grounds upon which they are granted appended to each case as is done in the list submitted to her. To make such a report to Parliament by laying it on the table of the Houses, would look like an appeal to its discussion on a matter which clearly belongs solely & entirely to the discretion of the Crown.[82]

The Victoria Cross warrant was duly worded in such a way as to put as much of the selection process in military hands as possible, with final authority vested in the Queen as to who did and did not qualify.[83] Panmure's assurances were welcomed, but the suspicious Albert wanted to make doubly sure parliament could not interfere. Consequently the warrant was signed by the Queen and the Secretary for War on Saturday, 26 January 1856, while parliament was not in session. Even that was not enough to reassure Albert fully; on Monday he dashed off a note to Panmure demanding that he publish the warrant before parliament convened on Thursday, so as to present the House of Commons with a *fait accompli*.[84] The Warrant was thus published on Tuesday, 29 January 1856. By coincidence, this was the first anniversary of the fall of the Aberdeen Ministry.

The public had cried out for heroes; Victoria and Albert got the link to the soldier they wanted, and in the process created perhaps the most discriminating gallantry award in the world. From its inception it was determined to make the Cross an exclusive community and keep it free of political dilution. In Victoria's mind it was to be an award earned in the blazing moment of glory when one of her red-coated avatars performed a deed that, like the charge at Balaclava, made her 'tremble with emotion, as well as pride, in reading the recital of the heroism of these devoted men.' The official recognition of heroism had been formalized with the signing of the royal warrant. What remained was to make the Queen's pleasure a reality by creating an institutional framework to select the deserving men and bring them to Her Majesty's attention. The first few years would see a variety of problems addressed, questions answered, and policies set.

# THREE

# Teething Problems, 1856–1867

The Royal Warrant of 29 January 1856 created the award, but it was up to the War Office and Horse Guards to decide exactly how to implement the medal and select the individuals to be recommended to the Crown for the honor. As with any new bureaucratic creation, the Victoria Cross went through a developmental phase during the first years of its existence before departmental standards were established. Fifteen clauses were included in the original warrant governing everything from the color of the suspender ribbon (red for the army, blue for the Navy) to the circumstances by which a winner could be stripped of the honor. The operative clauses were quite vague, however, and offered no exact definition of what was to be considered heroic and worthy of reward.

The vagueness of these instructions insured the masters of the military would have ample opportunity to define the form of heroism they wished to institutionalize. The Crimea and the Indian Mutiny provided critical tests that established a distinct character for the Victoria Cross. By the time the last of the Mutiny claims had been processed, the parameters of heroism, both the officially demarcated and the institutionally understood, had permeated the fabric of the British military.

Clause V of the warrant, governing the conditions under which the award could be won, was typical of the nebulous character of the document. It made it clear that the award was indeed to be egalitarian, open equally to both officers and enlisted men, and that it was to be a combat award, but offered no standard by which to judge their actions:

> Fifthly – It is ordained that the Cross shall only be awarded to those officers or men who have served Us in the presence of the enemy, and shall have then performed some signal act of valour or devotion to their country.[1]

Exactly what constituted a 'signal act of valour or devotion' was the question that exercised Horse Guards and the War Office in the early days of the Cross.

There was also some initial confusion as to the intent of the Crown concerning eligibility. While the Fifth Clause stated that 'officers and men' were equally considered for the award, Lord Panmure apparently understood this to mean that the Cross was a supplement to the Order of the Bath, that although there was no official point of demarcation, the VC was intended to be a province of the enlisted ranks and the officers below the rank of colonel. He solicited the opinion of Viscount Henry Hardinge, the Army's top commander, on the matter:

> In order to more fully to give effect to her Majesty's gracious intentions, Lord Panmure proposes that the grant of the decoration, so far as the Army is concerned, only be made to all those officers in the lower grades of the Army, and non commissioned officers and soldiers who by the performance of deeds of gallantry since the commencement of the present war, may be enabled to substantiate their claim to it according to the conditions laid down in the enclosed instrument; and I request that you will move Lord Harding to favour Lord Panmure with his opinion on the subject.[2]

Before Hardinge could reply, Panmure either changed his mind or had it changed for him, as his secretary Godfrey Charles Mundy wrote Hardinge's military secretary, Major General Sir Charles Yorke:

> With reference to my letter of the 25th ultimo I am directed by Lord Panmure to request you will state to the Field Marshal Commanding in Chief that it is intended that the decoration of the Victoria Cross may be bestowed on officers of all ranks who have distinguished themselves by conspicuous bravery.[3]

This was the only time Hardinge was consulted as to the Victoria Cross, as he suffered an incapacitating stroke on 7 July 1856 and resigned two days later. As his successor, Victoria chose her cousin George, the Duke of Cambridge, to serve as the General-Commanding-in-Chief.[4] As a member of the royal family he would maintain the close connection between Crown and Army that the Queen so desired. He retained that office until 31 October 1895, and in the process left a deep imprint on the character of the Victoria Cross, for it was under his aegis that the War Office and Horse Guards established a selection process.[5]

Of more immediate importance, however, was the fact that the warrant did not specifically state that the VC could not be awarded for acts of valour predating the conflict in the Crimea. As a result, a number of aging heroes materialized out of the woodwork, petitioning the War Office for recognition of their deeds. Some were ludicrous: John W. Castin wrote the War Office on 15 March 1856 requesting a Victoria Cross apparently because he was a wonderful person; he did not specify any act of heroism, just that he was a deserving subject of her majesty. Others were more specific. C. J. Bourke laid claim to the medal for his part in the storming of Badajoz, although he did not specify if it was the first (1811) or second (1812) battle for possession of that city. A Lieutenant Colonel McDowell, C. B., felt himself deserving for services rendered 'during the American War' (we can only hope he meant 1812). The grandfather of all of these hoary heroes was a Frenchman, Monsieur le Baron Despiaux. His original letter of submission is no longer extant, but a draft of the reply to his claim informed him that the award was open only to British subjects, notwithstanding the 'services rendered by you in the years 1793 and 1794 to British Officers of distinction who had fallen into your power.' All such requests were quickly and firmly denied, as the War Office had no intention of dealing with a perpetual avalanche of self-seeking heroes long after the fact of their alleged heroism.[6] The reply to McDowell was typical, concise and leaving no room for argument:

> I am directed by Lord Panmure to acknowledge the receipt of your letter of the 22nd instant, forwarding a statement of the grounds on which you consider yourself entitled to the Victoria Cross for your services during the American War, and I am to acquaint you in reply that it is not intended that the grant of this decoration shall extend to deeds of gallantry performed prior to the commencement of the present war. His Lordship is unable to advise her Majesty to confer it upon you.[7]

Having disposed of the heroes of the past, the military bureaucracy turned to deal with the heroes of the present. The publication of the warrant and the absence of precedent brought as many contemporary heroes to the fore as those claiming the Cross for previous wars. The War Office quickly established two basic precepts:

> Having laid before Lord Panmure your letter of the 29th ultimo, and its enclosures, recommending that the decoration of the Victoria Cross should be conferred on assistant surgeon O'Callahan, I am directed to

acquaint you in reply that his Lordship finds himself unable to receive any application for this decoration except through the Commander of the Forces in the Crimea.[8]

Only submissions through the established chain of command within the military would be considered:

> I am directed by Lord Panmure to acknowledge the receipt of your letter of the 16th ultimo, requesting to be informed whether, as representing your late son, Lieutenant Godfrey, of the 1st Battalion of the Rifle Brigade, you would be entitled to prefer a claim under the Royal Warrant instituting the decoration of the Victoria Cross; and to acquaint in reply, that this decoration will not be conferred upon the families of deceased officers, and that it is more in the nature of an order like that of the Bath rather than of a medal commemorative of a campaign or an expedition.
>
> In the case of the Crimean medal her Majesty was pleased specially to command that the medals of those who died should be given to their representatives, but it is by survivors only that claims to the Victoria Cross will be able to be established.[9]

The Victoria Cross would not be awarded posthumously.

It took some time to organize a selection board in the Adjutant General's office and establish the basic criteria for selection, but by September 1856 the War Office was ready to entertain official submissions:

> As the Army has now returned from the Crimea, and the officers in command of Divisions and Brigades are within easy reference, I think no time should be lost in ascertaining the names of the officers, non commissioned officers, and privates whose conspicuous gallantry entitles them to be recommended to the Queen for the Victoria Cross.
>
> I enclose to your Royal Highness copies of her Majesty's warrant instituting this decoration and request that you will call on the officers in command of her Majesty's forces, as well as those who have been in command of Divisions and Brigades of the Army to furnish the names of those under their command whom they may consider entitled to this order.[10]

A circular letter was dispatched 20 September 1856, notifying commanding officers to submit the names of officers and men they deemed worthy of consideration.[11] The exact parameters of the award were still under question at this point. The volume of the recommendations apparently surprised the Duke of Cambridge as the first replies to the circular arrived in London. Accordingly, he sought guidance on the matter from the War Office. In reply he was informed:

> his Lordship does not think that this Department is in a position to assign any limit at present to the number of recipients of the decoration of the Victoria Cross.
>
> Lord Panmure is further of opinion that it would be better that H.R.H. in giving the warrant instituting the decoration in question direct respective effect as regards the late war, should be very strict in requiring the rigid compliance with its directions.
>
> His Lordship considers that there should be a personal act of valour in each case so signal as to make evident the propriety of awarding the decoration.[12]

Rather than set a specific number per year or devise a formula to award Crosses on some ratio system, the limiting factor was the valour itself. There was also no definition of heroism, only the admonition that the act be self-evidently worthy of recognition.

Also during this interim period London firmly established that the VC was for persons serving in the British military only. Thus, when a Colonel O'Connor of the 1st West Indian Regiment wrote the War Office recommending a French Captain of Marines, Ducrest de Villeneuve, for valour in the fighting against Muslim rebels in Combo in July and August of 1855, his request was denied. It may very well be that the War Office did not want the Cross to become a diplomatic award granted to make allied officers happy.[13]

The regimental returns to the War Office circular varied widely. Some units did not recommend anyone, officer or enlisted, for the award. Other regiments returned modest numbers of nominees, in some cases artificially limiting the returns to officers only. Still other regiments sent in impressive lists of heroes, some of which were obviously manufactured. The character of the regiment in question or of the recommending officer often shone through the recommendations that arrived at Horse Guards.

The units that reported no recommendations either sent back blank submission forms or curt letters noting the receipt of the circular and that the regiment would not be submitting any heroes. Some of these nil returns can be explained by the resistance felt by some of the older officers to the establishment of a gallantry award. There was an undercurrent of almost puritanical conservatism among the old guard of the officer corps who were outraged at the thought that a British soldier might need or desire an award to proclaim his martial prowess to the rest of the world.[14] Already by the 1850s existing (officer only) gallantry awards had been so cheaply won and widely distributed as to dilute their distinction; many officers saw no need to extend this situation into the other ranks.[15]

This view was also held by some members of parliament. Sir W. Fraser, 1858:

> The great principal advocated by the Duke of Wellington for the English Army, which, he said, would have gone anywhere and done anything, was the principal of duty. Of all the despatches written by that great man there was not one in which the word 'glory' did occur, nor one in which the word 'duty' did not occur. Such was the mode of modern warfare that it was next to impossible for an officer of any rank to attain the Victoria Cross, and he doubted whether its being attainable by subalterns, corporals, and men of the line would not lead them to neglect duty in the pursuit of glory.[16]

Fraser did not know what he was talking about, as Wellington died at least two years before the Cross was even a concept, much less a reality.

Other blank returns represented the opinion of the commanding officer that no man in his regiment had sufficiently distinguished himself as to warrant special recognition:

> On assuming command of the 41st Regiment, I find the circular dated September 20th 1856, relative to the institution of the 'Order of the Victoria Cross' has not been replied to.
>
> I have the honour to state that after making a strict enquiry, I do not find that there are any Officers, Non Commissioned Officers or Soldiers in the 41st Regiment who could be considered eligible to be recommended for that most distinguished decoration.[17]

Still others could be attributed to a staunch sense of regimental pride. Several of the regimental historians consulted in the preparation of this work pointed out that regiments which considered themselves naturally elite tended to shy away from special recognition of individuals within the unit by authority figures outside the unit.[18] The acclaim of the immediate peer group was more important than that of an impersonal War Office. Some of the nil returns reflected this sentiment, in essence replying to the War Office request for the names of distinguished soldiers in such a way as to imply that *all* the soldiers of the regiment were distinguished simply by the fact that they belonged to that particular unit.[19]

The regiments that responded to the circular with modest recommendations did so for two main reasons. Some commanders made an honest appraisal of their men and their actions and recommended those who had indeed performed 'some signal act of valour.' For example, the 89th Regiment nominated only one man, Private John Fisher, who had remained steadfast at his post in a trench fatigue party when his companions retired under fire.[20]

Other regiments limited their recommendations according to much less objective criteria. The 47th Regiment did not return any other ranks for the VC; all four of its Crimean recommendations were for officers, and none of them was below the rank of captain.[21] This may have been a coincidence, that no enlisted soldier had performed any act deemed worthy of the Cross, but it may very well reflect the attitude put forth by Colonel Henry Warre of the 57th regiment:

> and as I am quite ignorant of the extent to which the Government intend to grant the annuity attached to this much coveted and very distinguished Order: I have taken the liberty of submitting the whole of the names of these men, whom upon careful examination . . . distinguished themselves 'above their comrades.'
>
> I do not anticipate that Her Royal Highness will admit the whole of these claims, but it will be a great satisfaction to the claimants to know their gallantry has been made known, as many if not all these soldiers would, I am convinced, have been perfectly satisfied with the Cross, unaccompanied by the pecuniary remuneration, *which must limit its distribution.* [Emphasis added.]
>
> As there is no pecuniary award attached to the Cross to be conferred upon officers I have submitted the names of five (see above) whose conspicuous gallantry on all occasions Entitles them I hope for this distinction – and should His Royal Highness take into consideration my own conduct on the 10th of June – for an account of which I trust I may refer you to [a variety of illegibly scrawled names] or to the officers of my own regiment I should feel gratified . . .[22]

Warre hit precisely on a sinister aspect of the selection process. Under the provisions of the Royal Warrant, enlisted personnel who won the Victoria Cross were to receive an annual pension of £10.[23] The magnanimity of

Queen Victoria would serve in the minds of some as a limiting factor to the number granted to the other ranks.

Despite his disclaimer Colonel Warre submitted a total of 22 privates, three corporals, seven sergeants, one lieutenant, two captains, one major, one lieutenant colonel, and one colonel (Warre himself) for the consideration of the War Office.[24] He was not alone in submitting a glowing account of his regiment's gallantry. Some of these were the result of over-zealous commanders with a low threshold of heroism, while others were intended to salve the wounds of a battered regiment. Still others owed their origins to a romantic desire for glory. Lieutenant Colonel Henry Charles Barnston Daubeney of the 55th Regiment flooded London with a tide of recommendations, naming 26 enlisted men, six officers (including himself), and one civilian as candidates for the Cross.[25]

In the case of Warre, it seems that he was merely anxious to procure a Cross or Crosses for his regiment, and if he could gain one for himself, so much the better. For example, Private Charles McCorrie of the 57th had been recommended and approved for the award, but had died in hospital on Malta (gazetted 24 February 1857, died 9 April 1857), before the first investiture. Warre lost no time, writing on the day of McCorrie's death to his brigade commander General John L. Pennefather, 'being naturally anxious to have a decoration, so much looked up to, in the Corps.' He sounded out the idea that perhaps one of the other men who had been recommended might be reconsidered. The reply was brief, a penciled 'No' on the back of his request.[26] Once his own request had been rejected, however, he made no further attempts to procure a Victoria Cross for himself.

Colonel Daubeney on the other hand was quite shameless in his efforts to garner recognition. He had been originally recommended along with two other officers for the Cross by General Pennefather in October 1856: 'Distinguished for energy and devotion in keeping his men together crossing the river under a terrible fire, setting a cool & glorious example [Battle of the Alma]. Distinguished for gallantry and active zeal & forwardness . . . after Warren was wounded [Battle of Inkerman].'[27]

There is evidence, however, that Daubeney had already been pestering his superiors for some form of recognition. Included in the jacket containing the 55th Regiment's recommendations is a June 1855 letter from Lieutenant General Sir DeLacy Evans, commander of the Second Division in the Crimea, in reply to a letter from Daubeney: 'You are perfectly correct in saying that you were reported to me by General Pennefather & by me to Lord Raglan as having distinguished yourself in the Battle of the Alma – you were similarly mentioned in Division Orders.'[28] This reply was sent well before there was any mention of the existence of the Victoria Cross. It is clear that Daubeney was already trying to turn a mention in dispatches into some form of Order before the possibility of winning a VC appeared on the horizon; once the Cross became a reality, Daubeney focused all his attention on acquiring one for himself.

It is unclear whether or not Daubeney knew he had been recommended. He wrote Pennefather in December 1856, detailing his own heroism in a nine-page letter and enclosed the signed affidavits of seven privates and one sergeant attesting to his valour at Inkerman.[29] On the strength of this new evidence, Pennefather submitted a secondary recommendation on Daubeney's behalf to the War Office in January 1857. It cited Inkerman only, for 'charging a body of Russians which had penetrated his post in the fog – as vouched for by the accompanying papers.' He explained in a separate paragraph that he had already recommended Daubeney before reading these affidavits.[30] Nine days after making sure his own horn had been blown, Daubeney submitted his regimental recommendations.

The regimental returns were somewhat suspicious:

Sgt Patrick Ashe: Valour at Inkerman
Pvt John Prinsinville:         "
Pvt Thomas Layland:            "
Pvt John Stokes:               "
Pvt William King:              "
Pvt Donato McIntosh:           "
Pvt William Smith:             "
Pvt Jeremiah Ready:            "
Pvt Patrick Guering:           "
Pvt James Ryan:                "
Sgt William Jackson:           "
Pvt Bryan Hughes:              "
Pvt Michael Kilbride:          "[31]

Of these men listed under the blanket (and vague) 'valour at Inkerman,' Privates Prinsinville, King, Layland, McIntosh, Smith, Ready, Stokes, and Sergeant Ashe were the eyewitnesses whose affidavits were forwarded to General Pennefather to support Daubeney's claim. The affidavits of the privates were obviously dictated, as they are all written in the same hand. This is not unusual, given the literacy rates in the Army of the mid-nineteenth century, and some of the statements are signed with a witnessed 'X' rather than a signature.

It is nonetheless disturbing that all of the privates' statements are virtually identical, word for word. It is even more disturbing that a comparison with Daubeney's letter shows them to be written in the colonel's own hand. They were not just dictated in his presence, but to him personally. One of two scenarios can explain this irregularity: either Daubeney coerced his subordinates to verify his claim and then recommended them to buy their silence, or Daubeney simply cut a deal with these men, one recommendation for another. In either eventuality, the War Office was having none of it; of the officers and men recommended by Daubeney, only one private, Thomas Beach, and one officer, Brevet Major Frederick Cockayne Elton, received the VC, both gazetted 24 February 1857 in the first group of Cross winners.[32]

A year passed without any reaction by the War Office. Daubeney grew anxious as to his prospects for a Cross, and enlisted the aid of the senior colonel of the 55th, Major General Sir James Holmes Shoedde. In the letter Daubeney wondered if the recommendations originally submitted were 'perhaps either informally drawn up, or not sufficiently particularized' and therefore dismissed out of hand. He reiterated how at the Alma he rallied his troops round the colors under fire. At Inkerman he led the retaking of an enemy-held section of the breastworks and later charged a deploying Russian battalion with about forty men 'and so effectively destroyed its formation that it was compelled to retire.' He cited eyewitnesses to his gallantry and what he terms as 'parallel cases' of similar acts that won VCs by Gazette numbers 1, 2, 3, 9, 11, 12, 13, and 18. He also included affidavits and extracts from letters concerning the events.

It is worth noting that while the extracts from letters written by his superior officers did mention his valour, they said nothing about any recommendations for awarding the same. Essentially, this new packet consisted of his own personal recommendation of himself, some vague references to his heroism by superior officers, and a pair of affidavits from officers under his command, Captains Harkness and Richards. He closed with a plea for personal recommendation:

> I now beg permission to forward through you, as the Colonel of the Regiment, supplementary recommendations for this highly prized Decoration – & request you will be good enough, should you deem them worthy of such attention, to submit them to His Royal Highness the General Comd. in Chief.[33]

Schoedde forwarded the new application and threw his weight behind the Daubeney recommendation in a separate letter to Major General Sir Charles

Yorke: 'which I beg strongly to recommend to His Royal Highness... There are I believe few better or more gallant officers in the service than Col. Daubeney.'[34] According to the tattered manuscript jacket that enclosed the file, this second application was rejected by the board on 30 March 1858.

In addition to the recommendations made by commanding officers, the War Office and Horse Guards also had to sift through a number of personal recommendations. As with the regimental returns, these ran the spectrum from the sincere through the self-seeking to the absurd.

Some men truly believed they had earned the recognition due to a Victoria Cross winner through their services to Queen and country. A lengthy petition was put forward by Lieutenant (then Colour Sergeant) John Brophey of the 63rd Regiment requesting a VC for his services in the Crimea. It included testimonials from no less than three captains, four lieutenant colonels, the regimental surgeon, his commanding officer, Lieutenant Colonel Dabzell, and the regimental chaplain. Also from the 63rd came the self-recommendation of Ensign (then Sergeant) James Slack, with endorsements from Lieutenant Colonel Dabzell (whose life he had saved) and from a Lieutenant Colonel Lindsay, also apparently of the 63rd Regiment.

Both of these claims were denied when they reached the Board of Selection.[35] Although the board did not give any specific reasons for the rejection of the petitions (they rarely did), either of two possibilities could explain their actions. In the clannish atmosphere of the Victorian officer corps there was some resentment at the promotion of sergeants to the rank of officer, and the selection board may have reflected this prejudice. Conversely, that they had been promoted may have been seen as reward enough. The selection board also undoubtedly took note of the fact that while the Commanding Officer of the 63rd passed on a favorable endorsement of the new officers' claims, he did not himself recommend the men for the VC. If he had thought them truly deserving of the award, he would have recommended them.

This latter scenario was certainly the case in the rejection of the petition by Lieutenant D. Sullivan of the 82nd Regiment. His petition did not even make it to the board; the word 'rejected' was scrawled beneath his name on the original submission letter. This was apparently due to a lack of corroboration and the lack of his commanding officer's support for the claim. Sullivan had transferred into the 82nd from the 30th and it was in the latter that he claimed to have shown his valour. His new commanding officer, Lieutenant Colonel E. F. Yates, passed on the petition but in his cover letter honestly told the Adjutant General that he knew nothing about the action in which Sullivan claimed to have been a hero.[36]

There were also those who sought, like Colonel Daubeney, to inflate some mention of their gallantry into official recognition. The 50th Regiment did not recommend anyone in the official reply to the War Office circular announcing the award.[37] The Commanding Officer of the Regiment, Lieutenant Colonel Richard Waddy, did submit himself for the Victoria Cross in a separate letter sent directly to General Yorke. He included a copy of a letter sent by Lieutenant General Richard England, commander of the Third Division in the Crimea to the Quarter Master General of Headquarters, Crimea, in February 1855. The letter detailed the gallantry of Waddy in the holding of the trenches on the night of 20–21 December 1854. England never said anything about recommending Waddy for an award, but did state that 'Colonel Waddy appears to be entitled to my best commendations for the especial gallantry with which he conducted the efforts so forcefully made for the repulse of the enemy.'[38] The War Office and Horse Guards apparently did not approve of Waddy's presumption to the honor, and reasoned that if England had meant the colonel to have a Victoria Cross, he would have recommended the colonel for a Victoria Cross. Waddy's self-seeking request was denied.[39]

The Queen herself was involved in the selection process as the final arbiter. In most instances she was content to trust those to whom selection authority had been delegated, but was occasionally moved to overrule their decisions:

> The selections appear to her very much well-made & with a close regard not to make the distinction too common & not to recognize the mere performance of duty to the satisfaction of superiors, but solely volunteer acts. There is only one case which the Queen thinks had better be omitted, viz. that of private McGuire of the 33rd. This deed, although publicly praised & rewarded by Lord Raglan, was one of very doubtful morality & if pointed out by the Sovereign as praiseworthy, may lead to the cruel & inhumane practice of never seeking prisoners, but always putting to death those who may be overpowered for fear of their rising upon their captors.[40]

Lord Panmure, true to his pledge that the Cross was the sole preserve of the Queen, duly dropped McGuire from the list.[41]

The Adjutant General's office rarely gave reasons for denial of the Cross, understandable from an administrative standpoint, as it would tend to derail any appeal of the rejection. A soldier or an officer might feel justified in appealing a decision if a specific lack or deficiency were pointed out in the rejection. When the Adjutant General spoke with the cold voice of authority, without giving any reason, the aspirant was unable to protest any specific point. In due course the War Office developed a flinty briskness in dealing with denials of VC recommendations. One such rejection, posted during the Mutiny, read in total:

> I have the honour, by the direction of the Commander in Chief in India, to inform you, with reference to your letter of the 10th August, that the recommendations for the decoration of the Victoria Cross in behalf of the Officers and Soldiers named in the Margin, of the Regiment under your command, has not been confirmed by the Board appointed to investigate claims to this distinction.[42]

The letter did not even refer to the commanding officer of the regiment by name.

Despite the chilliness of the rejection notices, some men persisted in pestering the War Office, Horse Guards and even Victoria herself for what they considered their just reward. The 44th Regiment presented Horse Guards with a pair of notable controversies of this kind in the wake of the Crimea.

Corporal William Courtney, who had lost an eye in combat and had been invalided from the service protested the award of the VC to Sergeant William McWheeney shortly after the award was gazetted in *The Times*:

> Sergeant WILLIAM M'WHEENEY (No. 2,802) – Volunteered as a sharp-shooter at the commencement of the siege, and was in charge of the party of the 44th Regiment; was always vigilant and active, and signalized himself on October 20, 1854, when one of his party, private John Keane, 44th Regiment, was dangerously wounded in the Woronzoff road, at the time the sharpshooters were repulsed from the quarries by overwhelming numbers. Sergeant M'Wheeney, on his return, took the wounded man on his back, and brought him to a place of safety. He was also the means of saving the life of Corporal Courtney. This man was one of the sharpshooters, and was severely wounded in the head December 5, 1854. Sergeant M'Wheeney brought him in from under fire and dug up a slight cover with his bayonet, where the two remained until dark, when they retired. Sergeant M'Wheeney volunteered for the advance guard of General Eyre's brigade, in the Cemetery, June 18, 1855, and was never absent from duty during the war.[43]

Courtney claimed that it had been he, not McWheeney, who had saved Private Keane, and that McWheeney had been nowhere near him when he himself was wounded, and thus could not have saved him. He claimed to be the last man out of the quarries, despite his multiple wounds, which supposedly had been the reason McWheeney had carried him out.[44] Upon an inquiry from Horse Guards, the 44th produced a series of witnesses – Lance Corporal (then private) William Doole, Private George Finch, Private Robert Crookshanks – who confirmed the official report and McWheeney's actions as published in the citation. Courtney, they swore, had not even been in the quarries on the day in question, having been shot before they got there and as a result had been out of his head, raving, from the wound.[45]

Colonel Stanley, the commanding officer of the 44th, bundled up all the affidavits, a surgeon's report confirming that Courtney had received only one wound (a shot to the head that cost him his eye, not the multiple wounds he claimed), and his own personal observation that Courtney was 'incorrect' in his recollection of events and passed them on to the Adjutant General.[46] The Selection Board weighed the evidence and promptly rejected Courtney's claim.[47]

Despite the rejection, Courtney maintained his claim that it had actually been himself who had carried wounded Private John Keane through heavy fire to a place of safety, not Sergeant McWheeney. He also claimed that McWheeney lied about saving his [Courtney's] life on 5 December 1854. He continued to write to the Duke of Cambridge to reopen the investigation of his claims. When this did not work he attempted to gain an audience with Victoria herself to present his version of the events.[48] Oddly enough, Courtney was a booster of McWheeney when the latter was initially recommended for the VC by Colonel Stanley. He faded from the files by 1860, apparently convinced he could gain no justice from the system.

Another VC claimant of the 44th was not put off so easily. Private Robert Thimbleby wrote to the Duke of Cambridge requesting special consideration of his claim to the VC for his services in the Crimea:

> Being unable to procure the Commanding Officer's consent to forward my application for the Victoria Cross for distinguished service in the Crimea...I feel myself entitled I beg most respectfully to solicit Your Royal Highness's attention to my claim. Trusting Your Royal Highness will be pleased to cause an enquiry to be made into my conduct [and] as to the cause of my Commanding Officer having refused to recommend me for the Honor with others who have received the Order and whose claims are not considered superior of my own.[49]

Thimbleby based his claim on the statement made by an officer of another regiment who had observed his conduct during the assault on Sebastopol 18 June 1855:

> In the attack that took place yesterday by the 2nd Brigade 3rd Division we especially remarked the conduct of Private Robert Thimbleby No. 3475 44th Regiment who distinguished himself by his gallant conduct while in the most advanced spot. We also know that he attended to the wounded of the several Regiments engaged under a most heavy fire.
>
> His soldierlike behaviour and assistance rendered to the officers during the occupation of the advanced Houses were particularly remarked.
>
> He also volunteered for and was one of the advance guard.[50]

The Duke of Cambridge did 'cause an enquiry to be made' concerning Thimbleby's claims. He contacted the 44th for details and annotation of Thimbleby's reported heroism. Colonel Stanley of the 44th replied that it was possible Thimbleby may have acted with great gallantry, but that he himself had not witnessed any act on the private's behalf. As to the 'attending to the wounded of the several Regiments under a most heavy fire,' witnesses examined within the regiment reported that this had been done under cover inside the aforementioned houses. He concluded his reply by stating that 'there is not a man in the Regiment who considers that he is entitled to the decoration he claims.'[51]

Colonel Stanley also included a copy of Thimbleby's service record for the period in question. He had arrived in the Crimea on 14 September 1854, and had served as orderly to Lieutenant Bradford. He left the Crimea with the wounded Bradford on 23 October, and spent the bitter winter of 1854–55 in sunny Malta. He returned to the Crimea 15 February 1855 and became Brevet Major Fletcher's batman until May 1855. In June he spent three or four days in the trenches before Sevastopol; after this he was put to work building a hut for General Sir William Eyre, but was dismissed from that labor party under strong suspicion of theft. The application was rejected.

Robert Thimbleby was not deterred by this rejection and continued to press his claim for the VC. John Thimbleby (relationship to Robert unclear) wrote the Duke of Cambridge on Robert's behalf, describing in great detail his exploits. He pulled out all the stops, stating that Robert not only deserved a Victoria Cross, but a promotion as well, as it was only a circumstance of education – or the lack thereof – that had kept him a private since he had enlisted in 1848.[52] This did not change the Duke's mind, and Thimbleby was again denied the VC. Undeterred, the private continued writing Cambridge for more than a decade; the last mention of his name in the VC files was a draft of yet another rejection notice, dated 28 February 1869.[53]

The persistence of Courtney and Thimbleby pales in comparison to the audacity of Thomas Morely, a man who made a profession of being a self-proclaimed hero. Morely, late a sergeant in the 17th Lancers, raised the art of self-promotion (or perhaps self-delusion) to new heights. In July 1857 he made his first request, writing directly to Lord Panmure. This initial self-recommendation was parried with an administrative passing of the buck: 'I am directed by Lord Panmure to acknowledge the receipt of your letter and enclosures of the 17th ultimo and in reply to inform you that all communications on the subject of your claim to the Victoria Cross should be addressed to H. R. H. the General Commanding in Chief.'[54] Morely then approached Horse Guards a number of times during the 1850s and subsequent decades inquiring as to the possibility of a VC to back up his claims of virtue. The tales of his exploits grew with each subsequent letter.[55]

Not content to limit his claims to a single war or country, in 1899 he published a booklet detailing his exploits at Balaclava and elsewhere, including his claim to have been instrumental in the Union victory in the American Civil War. He took credit for saving the 12th Pennsylvania Cavalry from capture at the Battle of Bull Run (he did not specify first or second), but as his horse was killed he was taken prisoner. He made no mention of how he managed to escape, only stating that when he 'returned to the regiment I received a commission and back pay and allowances which amounted to some hundreds of pounds.'[56] Given the pay scale for enlisted personnel in the Union Army in 1861, he would have had to have been a prisoner for decades to receive back pay amounting to 'some hundreds of pounds.' But, then, Morely was not a man to allow facts to impede the course of his narrative:

> I was second in command in Dismounted Camp in Pleasant Valley, Maryland to equip all cavalry without horses... I was then appointed Assistant inspector of the Cavalry, with Major Gordon, for the Department of Western Virginia. I was in Libby Prison for twelve months... One of the worst running fights I ever was in was when General Max Weber sent me from Harper's Ferry, Va. to Charlestown to capture fifteen of the enemy's cavalry. I was allowed to pick thirty horses and men. After we had advanced about five miles we saw them and pursued; we found two thousand men and two guns. Two squadrons charged us and we had a fight with revolvers for four miles, till close to the forts I lost twenty-one out of the 30 men. This was on the 29th June, 1864... I am the only officer that knew the plans General Grant used to capture Richmond

in nine days. I also assisted General L. P. D. Cesnola to make out these plans and forward them to President Lincoln. I saved General Cesnola's life... He often writes thanking me for saving his life... On the ninth day of May 1863, I was working in the government building, in which Lincoln was assassinated, when part of the building fell, killing 25 and injuring nearly 200. I was one of the latter and being unable to perform my duties was discharged.[57]

Internal contradictions in his own writing did not seem to bother him much either, although one wonders how he managed to fight off the rebel hordes on 29 June 1864 when he had been invalided out of the Union Army in 1863. It was also somewhat startling to an historian to discover that Ford's Theater was a government building, or that it collapsed on 9 May 1863.

Having received no satisfaction from the War Office or Horse Guards, Morely decided to go straight to the top. On 20 October 1902 he wrote King Edward a long letter describing the particulars of his heroism in the Crimea in 1854. He claimed a Victoria Cross for 'saving the day' at Balaclava 25 October 1854. He claimed a bar to that Cross for recovering the mortally wounded Coronet Cleveland off the field at the Battle of Inkerman 5 November 1854. He claimed a second bar to the VC for rescuing 'part of the Land Transport Corps from the hands of the Russians' on an unspecified date. However, the modest Morely did not want to paint too glorious a picture of himself: 'But as this incident (although proving I was ever brave and ready to die for my country) does not count for anything compared to the others, I am not desirous of troubling your majesty with the particulars but leave my claim based on the other two.'[58] Modesty would have to be its own reward, for the government was not about to give its highest gallantry decoration to a man that was at best deranged and at worst a shameless huckster.

Regardless of the difficulties of selecting the deserving heroes, their presentation to the Empire was a gala event that served all the desired pomp and circumstance to an eager crowd. *The Times* waxed positively republican in extolling the egalitarian virtues of the new award:

A new epoch in our military history was yesterday inaugurated in Hyde Park. The old and much abused campaign medal may now be looked upon as a reward, but it will cease to be sought after as a distinction, for a new order is instituted – an order for merit and valour, open, without regard to rank or title, to all those whose conduct in the field has rendered them prominent for courage even in the British Army. A path is left open to the ambition of the humblest soldier – a road is open to honour which thousands have toiled, and pined, and died in the endeavour to attain; and private soldiers may now look forward to wearing a real distinction which kings might be proud to have earned the right to bear. The old spirit of exclusiveness, which, while limiting the Order of the Bath to field-officers only, yet dissipated its honours on the whole staff, may be considered to have terminated when policemen and parkkeepers, officers and privates, captains and foremost sailors stood side by side as they did yesterday in the presence of their Sovereign to receive at her hands that high reward for deeds which all had earned alike. Let us hope that with this last bright episode of the great Russian war the old regime under which the heroism of the private soldier was ignored is at an end, and that the Victoria Cross will muster among its wearers a glorious roll of rank and file, who have always signalized their bravery, but until now in vain. If the campaign in the Crimea has effected only this, it has done more towards maintaining the high efficiency of our Army than any military distinction founded since the days of Marlborough.[59]

The cases arising out of the Crimean conflict did not resolve all of the potential questions concerning the award. The units involved in the Crimea represented only a fraction of the military establishment of the British Empire and a narrow range of the tasks those forces performed. Even as the Queen made the first presentations of the Victoria Cross on 26 June 1857 a series of events unfolded half a world away that would result in further clarification of what the Cross was and was not.

The Indian Mutiny opened several new controversies and contributed to the further definition of the official boundaries of heroism. For the first time since the inception of the award troops not under the direct control of the Crown were engaged in combat against the foes of the Empire. Also for the first time Clause VII of the warrant, providing for the provisional bestowal of the VC by a commander in the field, came into play. There were opportunities to fine-tune other clauses as well through situations that arose on the subcontinent and elsewhere in connection with the Mutiny.

The main question facing the masters of the armed forces was whether or not to include troops employed by the British East India Company as eligible under the provisions of the warrant, and if so, how and to what extent. The troops in question were a mixed bag of white troops hired directly by the company and native units commanded by white officers. This unusual amalgamation was further complicated by a lack of central control over the armed forces in India, with three separate military commands, or presidencies, operating three distinct military formations.[60]

An additional problem was that not all of the sepoys revolted. Most of the uprising was limited to Bengal; few of the native units in the two other presidencies expressed any form of sympathy with the rebels, much less joined in the rebellion. Even in Bengal a number of units remained true to their salt.[61] Many of the sepoys and sowars that fought alongside the British troops exhibited courage and loyalty far in excess of the value of their pay. If all the Indian troops had risen it would have been simple to deny them access to official recognition of their courage. That most had remained loyal complicated the equation.

The government moved fairly quickly in opening the VC to troops involved in putting down the Mutiny, but with characteristic vagueness. In late October 1857 the Queen signed an amendment to the Warrant of 29 January 1856 that extended the VC to 'be conferred on the officers & men of the Naval and Military Services of the East India Company who may be qualified to receive the same in accordance with the rules and ordinances that govern the Victoria Cross for Royal Troops.'[62] This meant that some recommendations from India for the VC might be entertained, but 'may be' implied a degree of discretion in the final decision on the part of the home authorities as to which they would accept.

The troops in the field were by and large willing to pay tribute to the courage of their native comrades. There is even one (probably apocryphal) story in which the 9th Lancers nominated their *bhisti* for the VC due to the courage the water carrier had shown in tending the wounded at Lucknow.[63] The Governor-General, Viscount Charles Canning (who later got the nickname 'Clemency Canning' for his treatment of former Mutineers), quickly determined to exclude sepoy and sowar from the Victoria Cross:

> I have the honour to acknowledge the receipt of your letter of the 11th instant, with copy therein enclosed of the dispatch from the Governor General in India in Council to the Court of Directors of the East India Company dated the 13th of October last, recommending that the decoration of the Victoria Cross should not be extended to native troops in India; and I have to acquaint you in reply that her Majesty's confidential servants are of opinion that in deference to the Governor General's judgment the native troops should not be considered as eligible for this decoration.
>
> I do not therefore intend to take any steps with regard to the communications of the Governor of Bombay in Council, communicated to me in your letter of the 24th ultimo, that the decoration of the Victoria Cross

be conferred on Duffadar Gunkut Ras Deokur of the Southern Mahratha Irregular Horse.[64]

Despite this definitive pronouncement that native troops would not be eligible, a less arbitrary reason was apparently felt necessary to justify this position. This was provided by the Duke of Cambridge. His staff sifted through the regulations until they came up with a more concrete reason to deny the award to Deokur. The Duffadar was *ineligible* for the Cross because he *was* eligible for the Indian Order of Merit.[65] The decoration was a valour award instituted by John Company in 1837. Issued in three classes, it carried with it both a cash award and the potential for a grant of land upon mustering out of company service.[66] Since the IOM was open only to native troops, the staff officers explained, it was unfair to British troops to allow native eligibility for a Victoria Cross as well. Deokur's recommendation was promptly rejected and the precedent had been set. No further native nominations would be entertained.[67]

The exclusion of native troops appears to a large extent to have stemmed from moral indignation rather than pure racism. Able Seaman William Hall won the VC during the relief of Lucknow on 16 November 1857 as part of the naval gun detachment detailed to breach the walls of the Shah Nujeff mosque. He and Lieutenant Thomas James Young (who also got the Cross) continued to serve the last gun after the rest of the detail had been killed or wounded by the mutineers. Born in Nova Scotia, Hall was black.[68] Nor were there any objections to the bestowal of a Cross on Private Samuel Hodge of the 4th West India Regiment. In 1866 he won the VC at Tubabecelong in West Africa for opening a breach in a village stockade and then accompanying the assault armed only with the axe he had used to chop through the wall.[69]

While the number of men of color who earned the official recognition of a Victoria Cross is statistically insignificant, that these recommendations went through the process proves that the War Office and Horse Guards did not dismiss claims merely on the basis of the melanin content of the man's skin. Given the number of non-white troops and auxiliaries maintained by the Empire during the nineteenth century, the paucity of non-white Victoria Crosses does indicate a degree of latent racism in the administration of the award. In this, the military was simply reflecting the culture that created it, the same imperialist attitude summed up in 'The White-Man's Burden.'

The exclusion of Indian soldiers from eligibility was, by contrast, almost certainly based far more on the fact that some of them had broken their oaths than on their skin tone. The public fed on a steady diet of lurid tales of massacre and rapine perpetrated by the 'dusky heathen,' and the whole of the Indian military establishment was tarred with the same brush:

> Some of the Europeans escaped across the Jumma, and 13 are reported to be now near Bagput, on the left bank, protected by the zemindars; but the rest, it is deeply feared, including the ladies and the children, have been brutally murdered. The mutineers then proceeded to the city, in which are situated the arsenal, the fort, and the King's palace and the civil station, and took unresisted possession of the whole, murdering all the Europeans they could lay their hands on.[70]

It did not matter that the majority of the native troops had remained loyal; from the vantage point of London, all Indians were the same and all Indians had forfeited the right to the distinction of the Victoria Cross. The tragedy was that this attitude and the decisions that flowed from it denied the bravery displayed by the loyal sepoys and sowars. Not until after the turn of the century would native Indian courage receive the same official recognition from the empire they served.

Given the public climate, it was fairly simple to disallow all native eligibility. It was not quite so simple to exclude the white men that commanded them, as the War Office and Horse Guards soon discovered. In November 1857 the Board of Control forwarded recommendations for Lieutenant William Alexander Kerr of the 24th Regiment of Bombay Native Infantry and Commander James Rennie of the Indian Navy made by the governor of the Bombay Presidency.[71]

The initial reaction in London was to lump the company officers with the company soldiers and exclude both. The Board of Control was informed:

> With reference to your letter of the 24th of November last, I have the honour to acquaint you that I have been in communication with the Lords Commissioners of the Admiralty and H.R.H. the General Commanding in Chief on the subject of the recommendations therein made that the decoration of the Victoria Cross be conferred on Commander James Rennie, of the Indian Navy, for distinguished acts of gallantry in the military operations against Persia, and on Lieutenant William Alexander Kerr, of the 24th Regiment of Bombay Native Infantry in an encounter with mutineers at Calapore.
> From the accompanying copies of letters . . . Their Lordships and H.R.H. do not consider the claims of these officers to this high distinction are sufficiently established; and under the circumstances, I find myself unable

to submit the names to her Majesty for this distinguished mark of her Majesty's favour for which they have been recommended in consideration of the acts of gallantry described in the enclosures to your letter.[72]

This prohibition would have remained in effect had Lord Panmure remained in the War Office. In February 1858 the Palmerston Ministry fell and the new government of Lord Derby pitched two new players into the India question. Panmure was replaced as Secretary of State for War by Major General Jonathan Peel, younger brother of Sir Robert Peel, and Edward Law, First Earl Ellenborough, became the new President of the Board of Control. Lord Ellenborough had long opposed the existing administration of British India under John Company and advocated the transfer of the government of India directly to the Crown.[73]

The Kerr recommendation was again submitted on 23 March 1858 with further endorsements, including that of Lord Ellenborough. These were bundled up at the War Office and sent to Horse Guards for reconsideration:

...I am directed by Secretary Major General Peel to transmit to you, for the consideration of H.R.H. the General Commanding in Chief copies of a further letter and of its enclosures from the President of the Board of Control on the subject; & I am to request that, in laying these papers before H.R.H. you will move H. R. H. to inform Major General Peel whether H.R.H. sees any reason to alter the opinion which he has already espoused with regard to this claim.[74]

In addition to repeating the Kerr recommendation, Ellenborough sent a second letter the next day, pressing the claims of a further ten individuals previously denied out of hand as a result of Lord Panmure's position on Indian submissions. This was likewise forwarded for the consideration of the Duke of Cambridge, with a strong hint as to what the Indian political situation demanded:

I am directed by Secretary Major General Peel to transmit to you ... [a] copy of a letter (with its enclosures in original) from the President of the Board of Control, recommending for the distinction of Victoria Cross the several officers, non commissioned officers, and soldiers whose names are stated in the margin, who have distinguished themselves by acts of bravery during the process of the present operations in India ... Major General Peel proposes, in deference to the judgment of the Governor General in Council, to waive on this occasion the rule laid down by Lord

Panmure on the subject . . . and submit at once to Her Majesty the names of the several officers, non commissioned officers, and soldiers referred to in the enclosed papers with the view to this high distinction being conferred upon them.[75]

Two letters were dispatched from the War Office to Lord Ellenborough 16 April 1858. The importance attached to His Lordship's endorsement is evident in the tenor of the reply to his letters. As to Kerr:

. . . I transmit herewith for your Lordship's information a copy of a letter which has been received in reply from H.R.H.'s Military Secretary, and I have to acquaint your Lordship that, as H.R.H. sees no objection to the Victoria Cross being now conferred upon Lieutenant Kerr I propose to take an early opportunity of bringing that officer's name before Her Majesty with a view to his receiving this high distinction.[76]

For the other ten recommendations, eight were accepted and two rejected:

. . . I have to acquaint your Lordship that, in deference to H.R.H.'s judgment I propose to take and early opportunity of submitting to Her Majesty the names of the officers and soldiers in question with the exception of those of Lieutenant Colonel Reid of the Bengal infantry and Lance Corporal William Taylor into order that, should it be Her Majesty's pleasure, this high distinction may be conferred upon them.[77]

The colonial administrators of India had made it quite clear that they expected the European component of the Indian Army's establishment to be treated on the same basis as the regular Army. From this point forward the eligibility of Indian Army officers was not challenged.

In addition to the establishment of guidelines for the inclusion and exclusion of Indian formations, the Mutiny also provided the first test of Clause VII of the warrant, allowing local commanders to confer the Cross on the spot, subject to Crown review of the circumstances. In and of itself the provision was not bad, especially given the size of the British Empire and lack of speedy communications. There were those who received provisional VCs that were richly deserved and dearly won; Lieutenant Frederick Sleigh Roberts, Kipling's immortal 'Bobs Bahadur,' earned his Cross in such a fashion.[78]

The administrative machinery in London quickly developed an unfavorable opinion of the practice. Peel took exception to a General Order issued

21 September 1857 from Headquarters, Delhi City, by Major General Archdale Wilson, detailing the provisional award of the VC to Bugler Robert Hawthorn and Lance Corporal Henry Smith. He sent a directive to Sir Colin Campbell, the Commander-in-Chief, India, to limit the number of Crosses conferred provisionally:

> I am of the opinion that it would be attended by convenience to the interests of the public service that in the case of all claims which may in future arise to the distinction of the Victoria Cross during the progress of the present operations in India, the recommendations in any case should reach me through yourself, as the officer in supreme command; I have accordingly to express to you that it would be advisable that general instructions to this effect should be issued to general & other officers in command, so as to obviate the delay which must take place from the making of a reference back to India before the appointments in any case can be submitted to her Majesty's confirmation.[79]

Peel did not prohibit provisional VCs, as they were statutory law in the warrant. The clause was, though, dangerously open to abuse, as can be seen in the case of Lieutenant Henry Masham Havelock.

Lieutenant Havelock was awarded the VC provisionally in the field by his own father, Brigadier General Henry Havelock. He got it for taking part in the storming of the Char-Bagh Bridge on 16 July 1857 along with a few thousand other officers and men in the process of forcing entry into Lucknow.[80] The reason he was singled out for bravery was that he led his section of infantry whilst mounted, and all the other (cowardly?) officers led their charge on foot. Major General Sir James Outram[81] submitted a glowing report as to what a good officer the younger Havelock had been during the attack. On this basis Havelock senior felt justified in giving his son a Cross on the spot, rather than go through the regular channels of submission. As Havelock senior reported, 'On this spontaneous statement of the Major General, the Brigadier General consents to award the Cross to this officer which act if originating from himself, might from the near relationship Lieutenant Havelock bears to him assume the appearance of undue partiality.'[82]

It certainly did bear that appearance, especially to other officers. Despite the disclaimer, the Havelock VC was widely accepted in India as pure favoritism. The blatant nepotism of the provisional bestowal was only reinforced by Havelock senior's recommendation of a bar for the VC for a later act of heroism by Havelock junior before the original award had been confirmed by the home government. The War Office could not deny the initial provisional bestowal of the Cross without undercutting the authority of a commander in the field, but the bar was another matter entirely, as it had come in as a recommendation through normal channels and was thus subject to review. Peel solicited the opinion of Horse Guards on the question when the bar recommendation reached London. He had not objected to the provisional VCs granted before his instructions to Sir Colin Campbell arrived in India, but this situation merited special attention:

> With regard however to the case of Brevet-Major Sir H. Havelock of the 18th Regiment I should be glad to be favoured with your Royal Highness's opinions, whether, as this officer has already received the Victoria Cross for a previous act of gallantry, the nature of the act of gallantry reported in the papers enclosed in Sir Henry Storks' letter of the 10th instant, was such as would entitle him to the bar to be attached to the ribbon by which the Cross is suspended, in accordance with the fourth clause of the Royal Warrant.[83]

The War Office found itself in agreement with the General-Commanding-in-Chief's solution to the situation: dump it back on Campbell.[84]

Subsequent events offer an insight into the mid-Victorian military mind. There was nothing the Indian Staff could do about the original, but when the opportunity arose for them to quash the bar recommendation, they did. Sir Colin Campbell lost no time convening a board of field officers to review the recommendation. The board condemned the bar recommendation and followed up with a weak explanation that the bar could not be recommended for an award that had not been officially confirmed by Her Majesty.[85]

Campbell was unable openly to criticize a fellow general officer's decision (particularly the now deceased Major General Henry Havelock, promoted for his defense of Lucknow and who died after Campbell's force extricated the besieged Residency defenders) even when he knew it was wrong and dishonorable; only when queried by a higher authority was he able to voice his concerns, and as we can see, he still had to be circumspect. It would still not do to call official attention to a general's blatant act of nepotism to award his own son for an act of questionable extreme valour, and a manufactured technicality had to be produced to cover the denial of the bar.

With the exchange of inquiry and report the true situation was known by everyone that mattered. Havelock junior kept the original VC because the Army did not air its dirty laundry in public – that was the price of maintaining the honor of the Victorian officer corps. The message had been delivered, though. The government would not tolerate nepotism or 'old boy' connections in the granting of the Victoria Cross. As a result of these incidents provisional conferral of the Cross, which had been the expected method,[86] became a rare event, with most recommendations instead going through the War Office/Horse Guards review process.

From the outset the guardians of valour were determined to keep the Cross an exclusive and honorable decoration and avoid the fate of other honors, the wide distribution of which had largely diluted their value. The staff officers who adjudicated the recommendations were aided by the fact that, Havelocks notwithstanding, there was a strong code of honor in the officer corps. This attitude also kept the award from being used to lay a facade of glory over a failed operation or a lackluster campaign ... at least for the time being.

Lieutenant Colonel Weber of the 1st Battalion Royal North British Fusiliers serves as a prime example of this integrity with respect to the award of the VC. Despite the fact that a brace of VCs would have added greatly to his regiment's reputation, he notified the Adjutant General's office that something seemed irregular in a pair of recommendations made by his temporary replacement while he had been on leave. It seemed that Lieutenant Colonel Pratt had recommended Captain Norton and Lieutenant Russell for VCs on 10 August 1859 and followed up with an inquiry on 18 January 1860. Specifically, neither of the official communications had been written up in the Regimental Letter Book as required, nor had a copy of either letter been given to him upon his return in late January 1860. The first he learned that the men had been recommended was in a letter from the Military Secretary concerning the matter that arrived in February 1860.

Further investigation on his part revealed that the act for which they claimed the VC, moving an ammunition wagon under fire, was not particularly valorous for a variety of reasons. The troops were not under heavy fire by any estimation of the term and there was no danger of an explosion. The location of the wagon did not need to be changed as it was in no danger. He went on to report that no casualties had been taken by the party that moved the wagon – as a matter of fact, six companies of the battalion had crossed that same stretch of open ground only moments before, marching in formation, and had taken no casualties. Although the colonel made no direct accusations concerning the honor of the men involved, he clearly believed someone was trying to get a VC on the cheap.[87] Neither of the officers concerned received the award.

There were a few cases in which a man might recommend himself and win through the selection process to receive the Cross. The application for a VC by Private Samuel Morely (no apparent relation to Thomas Morely) of the Military Train was proof that a man could nominate himself for the award and get it, providing he went through proper channels and he had actually done something worthy of recognition. Private Morely had saved the life of the adjutant of a Sikh cavalry unit on 15 April 1858 when the latter had been dismounted, wounded, and surrounded by the enemy. Despite having had his own horse shot from under him, Morely and another man rushed to the aid of the adjutant and shielded him with their own bodies until rescue arrived.[88]

The other man, Farrier Michael Murphy had been severely wounded in the incident and recommended for the VC by the commanding officer of the Military Train. He was gazetted for the award 27 May 1859, which prompted Morely to apply for a Cross for himself.[89] He did so with the permission of his commanding officer and applied through regimental channels rather than approaching the War Office, the Duke, or the Queen directly. The War Office and Horse Guards decided they could hardly award one man and not the other for performing the same deed, and on 7 August 1860 Samuel Morely was gazetted as the newest recipient of the country's highest honor.[90]

The troop commitments required to quell the Mutiny also forced the Army to shuffle its garrisons, which contributed to a major change in the Victoria Cross warrant to include bravery beyond the battlefield as a legitimate reason to award the Cross. The incident that provoked this change was a fire aboard the troop transport *Sarah Sands* on 11 November 1857. As the fire spread from the galley and grew out of control, the women and children accompanying the 54th Regiment were placed in boats and out of immediate danger. In the proud tradition of the troops aboard the stricken *Birkenhead* six years earlier, the men of the regiment remained aboard rather than risk swamping the boats carrying their dependents.[91]

At sea and with no hope of immediate aid, the regiment fought the fire. Foremost among them was Private Andrew Walsh, who helped empty the powder magazine, carrying sacks of black powder through burning companionways to toss them over the side. He also took part in slapping out fires in the rigging with wet blankets atop the burning mainmast. The 54th fought the fire for 16 hours until it was finally extinguished and the women and children could be brought back aboard.

The heroism shown by the 54th in the protection of lives and property prompted a movement within the government to extend the Cross warrant to include noncombat valour. The Duke of Cambridge made the first inquiry on 5 April 1858, suggesting to the War Office that the warrant should be so amended. His suggestion met a sympathetic audience:

> ... Secretary Major General Peel ... entirely concurs with H.R.H. in opinion that the heroism displayed by the officers and men of the 54th Regiment on the 11th November last, on their passage to India on-board the 'Sarah Sands' transport, on the occasion of that vessel taking fire at sea, is deserving of being rewarded by the bestowal of the Victoria Cross on those who have displayed qualities of so Honourable on nature; and Major General Peel accordingly proposes to submit for Her Majesty's gracious consideration, whether it would be desirable to extend the provisions of Her Majesty's Royal Warrant instituting that decoration, so as to include cases of conspicuous courage and bravery of this nature displayed by officers and men of the Army and Navy, under circumstances of extreme danger, such as the occurrence of a fire on-board ship, or the foundering of a vessel at sea, or under other circumstances in which, through the courage and devotion displayed, life and public property may be saved.[92]

Major General Peel lost no time in submitting the proposal to Her Majesty, actually dispatching the letter to the Queen before replying to the Duke's letter.[93]

With the possibility of some of his soldiers being eligible for the Victoria Cross, the lieutenant colonel in charge of the 54th in transit, W. F. Brett, approached his commanding officer, Colonel Charles Mitchell, as to the possibility of submitting some recommendations for the Cross on behalf of his men.[94] Mitchell requested further information from Brett and at the same time inquired as to the possibility of Horse Guards entertaining such recommendations. Upon gaining the assent of the Duke of Cambridge, Mitchell forwarded Brett's recommendations of 25 men and added his own personal recommendation of Walsh.[95]

The powers-that-were agreed that the 54th had exhibited extreme courage in the face of almost certain death aboard the *Sarah Sands*. The new warrant was issued 10 August 1858, and in the process, the men who inspired it were denied recognition by the literal interpretation of the wording:

> By a Warrant under Her Royal Sign Manual August 10, 1858, Her Majesty was pleased to direct that the Victoria Cross should be conferred subject to the rules and ordinances already made on officers and men of Her Majesty's Naval and Military Services who may perform acts of conspicuous courage and bravery under circumstances of extreme danger, such as the occurrence of a fire on board a ship, or the foundering of a vessel at sea, or under any other circumstances in which, through the courage and devotion displayed, life or public property might be saved.[96]

Those 'who *may perform* acts,' not 'those who *have performed* acts' were eligible for the Cross. Despite the fact that the amendment was made *specifically* because of the bravery of the troops in saving the ship, none of them were eligible for the award because the conditions under which they conducted themselves so bravely were not covered in the rules at the time of the act, and as worded, the warrant could not be applied retroactively. Peel had the opportunity to bring up the *Sarah Sands* incident in an address before the House of Commons even before the warrant extension was signed. Parliament itself was not concerned with the extension; the Cross was brought up as an example during the course of a debate over the state of the Order of the Bath. Peel did not press for the antedating of the warrant, and mainly used the extension to noncombat life-saving as proof of his regard for the soldiers under his administration.[97]

Thus, when Walsh, whom all agreed had been the key figure in saving the ship applied for a Victoria Cross, it was denied. Fully 25 men were mentioned by name in the official report of the fire as having distinguished themselves far above and beyond the call of duty. There is a rather sinister marginal note on one of the memos concerning the case that may reveal the true reason the warrant was not antedated: Peel commented to Storks that if all 25 men were given VCs it would cost the government £250 per annum in pensions.[98] The War Office sugar coated the announcement of the denial to Horse Guards:

> Lord Herbert has received with great gratification the favourable testimony which has been borne to the conspicuous courage and Bravery of Private Walsh... his Lordship regrets that the Royal Warrant... will not admit of his being recommended for a distinction which he has so well earned.[99]

This did not resolve the situation; many officers were outraged by the parsimonious attitude of the War Office. Walsh's part was taken up in particular by Lieutenant General H. W. Brereton in 1863, in a strongly worded letter to the War Office. He pointed out that Lieutenant Colonel Brett had followed all the proper procedures and applied through the correct channels, and had shown considerable gentlemanly restraint in not forwarding his own name for a VC, as his own conduct in the 16-hour battle to save the troop ship clearly (in Brereton's estimation) entitled him to do.[100] The War Office stuck to its decision, however and repeated its position that the Cross warrant could not be backdated no matter how brave Walsh had been.[101]

As it turns out, the amendment to the Warrant for noncombat Victoria Crosses was subsequently used on only two occasions. Private Timothy

O'Hea was granted a Cross for extinguishing a fire in a railway carriage containing 2000 pounds of ammunition on 9 June 1866 in Danville, Canada.[102] Five were awarded in one stroke to the 2nd Battalion 24th Regiment, for the rescue of stranded companions on Little Andaman Island in the Bay of Bengal on 7 May 1867. The original party had landed to ascertain the fate of the commander and seven of the crew of the *Assam Valley*, and had lost their longboat in heavy surf. The rescuers braved the surf in reaching the island, as well as the cannibalistic natives that inhabited it.[103] There were no significant questions raised concerning the award of the VCs to the Andaman Island five. They saved 17 officers and men from certain death, making no less than three excursions into the extremely treacherous surf to do so.[104]

Others now saw their own noncombat actions as deserving of recognition; Lieutenant Joseph Bourke of the 29th Regiment recommended himself for the VC for his conduct in fighting a fire on the magazine at Fort Charlotte in the Bahamas, 10 January 1862. He bypassed his commanding officer entirely, writing directly to the War Office himself. The Adjutant General's office examined his statement and the battalion diary and ruled that he had never actually been in any danger, and besides, by his own statement the fire had burned itself out anyway.[105] General Peel considered that awarding the VC in this instance would damage the prestige and integrity of the award. The powers-that-were wanted to keep the VC a distinctive award and avoid establishing any precedent that might endanger that distinction.[106]

The need for the warrant extension covering noncombat VCs was in any event soon obviated by the creation of the Albert Medal in 1866. This award was designed to cover those who 'in saving or endeavouring to save the lives of others from shipwreck or other peril of the sea, endangered their own lives.' It was extended to included life-saving on land in 1877, and was superceded by the George Cross in 1940.[107] The Albert Medal gave the crown the opportunity to return the Victoria Cross to its original distinction as a purely combat award, and also decreased the potential for its abuse. The royal warrant governing the Cross was again modified in 1881 to read 'Our Will and Pleasure is that the qualifications shall be 'conspicuous bravery or devotion to the country in the presence of the enemy.'[108] The noncombat option was thus quietly dropped.

The Victoria Cross had been born in the bungled campaigns of the Crimea, perhaps as an atonement for the wastage of life due to the stupidity of the military high command. It had been tempered in the reconquest of India and many of the rough edges had been worn off in the process. The basic criteria for the institutional determination of heroism were established by

1860, although the actual definition of heroism still eluded the powers-that-were. Their case-law arose from large-scale conflicts, but for all their glory (and all their casualty figures) these major wars were aberrations. It was in the small wars of empire that the Victoria Cross received its final nineteenth-century refinement, and it is to these small wars that our focus must now shift.

# Four

# Big Implications from Small Wars: The Imperial Vision of Heroism, 1860–1911

Large-scale operations of the Crimean and Indian variety were not the normal employment of the British military in the nineteenth century. The Army, and to a lesser extent, the Royal Navy were employed more often in small-scale operations designed to project power in an imperial context. In most cases they encountered a numerically superior but technologically inferior foe, and in so doing further questions as to the nature and limits of the new institutional heroism were raised and resolved. The duties of policing a globe-spanning empire presented a new environment for heroism; facing bodies of disciplined Russians supported by artillery was not the same as facing Maori rebels, cannibalistic Andaman Islanders, or assegai-wielding Zulus. The standard doctrine for mid-nineteenth century colonial warfare placed a premium on implacable aggressiveness as a way of establishing psychological superiority over the enemy.[1] This was reflected in a rash of 'first in' Crosses and recommendations in the 1860s, designed to reward the aggressive bravery of those first to breach an enemy stronghold.

The first of these 'first ins' went to William Odgers, Leading Seaman of HMS *Niger* for being the first man in the rebel *pah*, a wood and earth palisade, and for hauling down the rebel colors on 28 March 1860, during the first Maori War:

> Three flags bearing Maori war-devices were seen waving above the smoke-hazed palisades. 'Ten pounds to the man who pulls down those flags!' shouted [Captain Peter] Cracroft [RN]. Yelling, shooting, slashing, the Navy lads were over the stockade in a few moments 'like a pack of schoolboys', in the phrase of a survivor of Waireka. The first man in was William Odgers, the Captain's coxswain. He charged to the flagstaff and hauled down the Maori ensigns.[2]

His recommendation did not cause any undue controversy in London, other than a brief exchange of memos between Horse Guards and the War Office to determine that the action did come under the provisions of the warrant.[3] It did, however, establish a precedent; it was not long before other recommendations were forwarded to Horse Guards solely on the basis that the candidate had been 'first in.' As early as February 1861 the Odgers VC was used to justify the submission of another 'first in':

> This case is cited by the Commd. Officer of the 65th Regiment, as a ground for conferring the Cross on Lance Corporal Fierock of the regiment 'as being the first man who entered the far more stubbornly defended position of Mahoetahi, which was stormed on the 6th November, last.' The claim is forwarded by the General Commanding without remarks, and H.R.H does not consider the case as one in which the distinction should be conferred. Concur?[4]

The War Office did concur. To institutionalize the practice of granting a VC simply on the grounds that an individual was the first to enter an enemy fortification would have opened the door to widespread abuse of the award. Military Secretary Edward Lugard passed the memo on to the Secretary of State for War Sidney Herbert with his own comment: 'I do not see sufficient grounds for granting this distinction – indeed the practice of giving it on every paltry occasion *lowers* the character of the distinction.'[5]

Thus 'first in' came to occupy a middle ground as far as recommendations went. In some cases it was a valid claim, but was not an automatic cause for the award. This position was put to a test quite rapidly, as the storming of the North Taku Fort in the Third China War, 8 August 1860, produced no less than six recommendations on the basis of being 'first in.' The Theatre Commander – a somewhat lofty title for a general in command of at most 2500 troops – General Sir James Hope Grant, recommended Lieutenant Robert Montresor Rogers, 44th Regiment (who had been promoted by the time of the recommendation to captain and had transferred to the 90th Regiment), Private John McDougall, also of the 44th, and Lieutenant Edmund Henry Lennon, 67th Regiment, for being the first to enter the fort through an embrasure, in that order; Lieutenant Nathaniel Burslem, 67th (now a captain in the 60th), Private Thomas Lane, 67th, for trying to be first in and getting wounded in the process, and Ensign John Worthy Chaplin, 67th (now a lieutenant with the 100th) for planting the colors in a breach in the wall.[6]

The original recommendations from Hope Grant were denied on the grounds that while the actions of these individuals had been commendable, they were not beyond the bounds of simple duty, and thus not VC material. Hope Grant replied to the denial in a snit, declaring that he had promised Lane and Chaplin VCs on the spot for their actions, and under the Clause VII of the warrant, it was within his power as theatre commander to confer VCs provisionally in the field. As it was, he had chosen to go through channels. He wrote Horse Guards requesting a reassessment, as he felt his promise to be binding on himself and the government, 'tantamount to a provisional bestowal.' He went on to state that he felt it would look bad if those two got it and the other five did not.[7]

At the time of the Third China War the Duke of Cambridge was still feeling out the parameters of his office as General Commanding in Chief and was often uncooperative with Lord Herbert of Lea's War Office administration. He had interfered with the command selection process for the expedition, and at one point the War Office complained that all the communiques originating from China were being mailed to Horse Guards and then forwarded to the War Office.[8] Upon receipt of Hope Grant's letter protesting the rejections he reviewed the situation and saw an opportunity to one-up the War Office. He passed it along to the War Office with his hearty approval; the War Office followed his lead and passed all the recommendations to Her Majesty. All of them got it.[9]

Despite the Duke of Cambridge's interference, the precedent was clearly established that merely being first in the van was not enough; the initial penetration had to have concrete merit. A good example of this situation occurred in the process of ferreting out the mad Emperor Theodore from the mountain fortress of Magdala. The fortress presented concentric earthwork ramparts that proved impervious even to the fire of the Armstrong 12-pounders; the gates of the outer ring had been blocked with boulders and rubble and were likewise shell-proof.[10]

A soldier of the 33rd Regiment, James Bergin, managed to hack a hole in the thorn bushes that festooned the palisade and boost drummer Michael Magner on top of the wall. Magner pulled Bergin up beside him and while the latter took potshots at the enemy hoisted several more men over the top. This small force held the breach and more importantly seized the inner gate of the next palisade, opening up the interior of the fortress to assault. An ensign named Wynter arrived carrying the colors and was placed on top of the wall to rally troops to the breach.[11]

In this instance the actions of Bergin and Magner proved the pivotal moment in carrying Magdala by storm. Both were recommended for the

Victoria Cross and both received it without controversy.¹² Unlike Ensign Chaplin, Ensign Wynter was commended but not recommended; the theatre commander in this case, Sir Robert Napier, was interested in results, not theatrics. While there would be other 'first in' VCs, the fad for them had passed by 1870.

The small wars' effect was not limited to finer definitions of administrative policy. Some of the questions raised by these conflicts resulted in changes in the warrant itself in recognition of the broader scope of colonial and imperial warfare. Once again the conflict with the Maoris provided the catalyst for change.

Major Charles Heaphy, Auckland Militia, was originally recommended for the VC by Lieutenant General Duncan Cameron on 14 November 1864, for tending a wounded British regular under fire. The problem, according to Secretary for War Earl de Gray, was that the colonial forces fought in this instance for rewards of land to be granted after the campaign. These rewards were not available to the regular troops, who fought for Queen and country. This was the only reason he was hesitant to rework the rules to allow Heaphy a VC; he considered the act itself worthy, but the rules did not specifically state the award could be given to irregular troopers. As such, he was forced to deny the recommendation, a position that irritated the Colonial Office.¹³

The empire was in the process of transferring responsibility for local defense to the colony in the 1860s, which gave both Heaphy and the Colonial Office some leverage in the pursuit of the award.¹⁴ Heaphy himself wrote a letter to Prime Minister Palmerston, requesting that his recommendation be reconsidered.¹⁵ When that did not provoke a favorable response the Colonial Office got behind the situation, adding its considerable influence to the recommendation. This was in response to an initiative by the New Zealand government, which was quite upset with metropolitan stone-walling. The colonial government left no stone unturned in gathering and transmitting affidavits in Heaphy's favor.¹⁶ It soon became apparent that part of the price for New Zealand's cooperation in accepting greater responsibility in imperial defense was local access to the laurels of heroism.

Under this pressure the government had to extend the warrant, but it did so carefully. The service heads did not trust the colonial irregulars to hold the proper objectivity in recommending VC winners, so they were included as eligible only if serving under the command of regular forces.¹⁷ Military Secretary Edward Pennington drafted a careful assessment of the situation for distribution to the War and Colonial Offices. In it he noted that the Duke of Somerset, First Lord of the Admiralty, proposed either the extension of the VC or the creation of an analogous award for colonial troops.

The Duke of Cambridge endorsed the extension of the VC to colonial troops but was wary of the idea, as it would mean possibly extending the award to militia and volunteer units, measures to which he was decidedly opposed. Pennington also pointed out that there was a definite danger of losing control of the award if colonial governors were allowed to make recommendations. Civilian authorities might not be able to distinguish between simple duty and outright valour. It is interesting to note that Pennington concluded that there were no set guidelines for valour, no official rules to determine if an act was truly heroic.[18]

Pennington's position reveals a basic belief among the military that civilians did not possess the necessary discrimination to determine the valour of an act. Horse Guards had developed its own esoteric criteria for the evaluation of an act, an arcana that the civilian mind could not fathom, and that, as Pennington himself had to confess, defied definition. This unwritten code became a standard feature in the debates surrounding the development of the VC as an institution. Though the officer corps was unable precisely to define the true nature of heroism, they were resolutely opposed to civilians defining it for them.

Horse Guards thus took the lead in formulating the final draft of the amended warrant, imposing some strict conditions on extending the award to colonial formations. There was no provision for election, nor for self-recommendation. It was undertaken with a firm delineation of proper channels. All recommendations had to be submitted through the Theatre Officer Commanding to Horse Guards, not through the Colonial Office, not through the War Office.[19]

The warrant dated 1 January 1867 not only approved the extension of the award to colonial irregulars, but also added the suppression of rebellion as a legitimate class of operations eligible for VC awards. Unlike the Walsh case, Heaphy got his Cross even though he was not covered by the warrant at the time of his act, perhaps the greatest indicator of the influence commanded by the Colonial Office.

Thereafter there were numerous decorations granted to personnel of colonial or irregular forces attached to the British Army with little controversy. What did cause a stir was the question as to whether or not a British officer could receive a VC for gallantry performed under the flag of an allied nation. Captain John Robert Beech, formerly of the 20th Hussars but 'at the time lent for service to H.H. the Khedive,' was recommended for the VC by the Sirdar of the Egyptian Army. On 19 February 1891 at Tokar, Bimbushi[20]

Beech rescued an Egyptian officer under attack by a trio of Dervishes. He killed one outright but got manhandled by the other two until he managed to stab the one strangling him from behind; the third Dervish retreated and Beech helped the Egyptian, Millrezim Awal Ali eff Kamil, back to safety.[21]

The Duke of Cambridge was very impressed by Beech's actions and threw his full weight behind the recommendation, as did Military Secretary Sir George Harman. His actions fit in nicely with the Victorian idea that it was always good to show courage in front of the 'lesser breeds without the law.'[22] The recommendation was forwarded to the Permanent Under-Secretary of State at the Foreign Office, who promptly washed his hands of the matter by bouncing the packet to the War Office and the consideration of Secretary for War Edward Stanhope.

The War Office gave the matter serious contemplation, holding the packet for almost a month before rejecting it. Stanhope himself penned the reply:

> After much consideration with my colleagues I have reluctantly come to the conclusion that this cannot be granted. I am very sorry to have to refuse it after the warm terms in which it is recommended by H.R.H. but I cannot distinguish it from the other decorations sufficiently to say that it might be given to a service performed with the Egyptian Army in an operation in which British Troops were not engaged.[23]

The task of informing Beech of the bad news was delegated to the Military Secretary, who attributed the denial to simple bad luck.[24]

The initial announcement of the Victoria Cross had generated a torrent of recommendations both from the Crimea and the Mutiny with just under 300 Crosses awarded in the 1850s. That torrent dropped to a trickle in the 1860s, with only 39 awards gazetted in that decade. A slight rise in the number conferred, 47, occurred in the 1870s, due to the scale of the Zulu and Afghan Wars. This statistical aberration raised some concerns at Horse Guards that the award might be in danger of losing its distinction if too many were granted.

The incident that provoked the reaction was the number of recommendations generated by the famous defense of Rorke's Drift, 22–23 January 1879. Lieutenant Gonville Bromhead, 24th Regiment of Foot, made the initial recommendations for Private John Williams, Private Henry Hook, Private William Jones, Private Robert Jones, Corporal William Allan, and Private Fred Hitch to his regimental commanding officer. Lieutenants Bromhead and John Rouse Merriott Chard, RE, were recommended by their respective commanding officers. The Duke of Cambridge did not hesitate in confirming their recommendations and forwarding them along with his own endorsement to the War Office.[25]

The problem arose with the continuing trickle of recommendations from the defense of the mission station. Each originated from a different chain of command: Surgeon James Henry Reynolds was nominated by the Army Medical Department; Corporal Ferdnand Christian Scheiss by the Natal Native Contingent; Commissary James Langley Dalton and a soldier named Dunne by Lord Chelmsford and Lieutenant Chard. Dalton in particular was lauded by Chard as the originator of the plan to defend the station rather than try to outrun the impis. Nor was he the passive ammunition bearer portrayed in the movie Zulu: 'the deadliness of his fire did great service and the mad rush of the Zulus met its first check.'[26] At length the Duke felt that the event was being milked for valour: 'We are giving the VC very freely I think, but probably Mr Dalton has as good a claim as the others who have got the Cross for Rourke's Drift defense. I don't think there is a case for Mr Dunne.'[27] Dalton did get the medal. A total of 11 VCs were won at Rorke's Drift. In addition to the three won at Isandhlwana on 22 January, this made a rather high two-day total.

The effect of the Duke of Cambridge's disapproval was a drastic reduction in the number of VCs granted in the 1880s. The British Army was as busy in this decade as it had been in the last, conducting campaigns throughout the empire against both tribal and more settled enemies. Only 21 Crosses were granted. This trend continued into the 1890s, with only 27 VCs won between 1890 and 1898. The scope and scale of the Second Boer War shattered this pattern, and once again raised concerns as to the frequency of bestowal.

In this instance Lord Kitchener served as the filter for recommendations coming out of the field:

> I think that some steps should be taken to discourage recommendations for the Victoria Cross in Civilized Warfare in cases of mere bringing in of wounded or dismounted men. The case of Lt Price, herewith forwarded, well exemplifies my point; his efforts to bring in Lieutenant Delmahay and Private Sheddon resulted in the former being again wounded and the latter killed.[28]

Here Kitchener made the distinction that the nature of the enemy had an impact on the caliber of the heroism. The Boers, a civilized foe, did not carve up wounded survivors as did Pathans or Zulus, thus making the retrieval of the wounded or stranded less of a life-saving imperative. Overall he saw to it that the VC became harder to gain during his tenure as theatre commander. Of the 12 men noted on a War Office minute sheet as nominees for the Cross, only two got it. Three were given the Distinguished Conduct Medal, two the Distinguished Service Order, and one was given consideration for the DSO in place of the VCs for which they had been recommended. The other four claims were dismissed entirely.[29]

Kitchener was one of the few officers who used these lesser awards to his advantage. The Distinguished Conduct Medal (non-commissioned officers and enlisted only, established 1854) and the Distinguished Service Order (officer only, established 1886)[30] gave him the opportunity to recognize deserving services while maintaining the integrity of the VC as a paramount award. The recommendations of two men from the 69th Battery Royal Field Artillery provide a case in point for the Kitchener ideal of heroism.

Major A. J. Chapman, Officer Commanding the troops at Itala Camp, Zululand, recommended Driver 3015 Frederick Henry Bradley and Gunner 14494 W. H. Rabb for their conduct during the Boer attack on the camp on 26 September 1901. He stressed in his recommendation that he gave equal weight to both men. Both had, without hesitation, darted out to recover a wounded mate, Driver Lancashire. Once they had the man under cover, Rabb tended him while Bradley went out to continue Lancashire's task, bringing up ammunition across 150 yards of exposed, fire-swept ground.[31]

Kitchener passed on the recommendation, but only gave his endorsement to Bradley; Rabb he lumped in with three men that Chapman had put forward for the DCM (Driver E. Lancashire, Gunner M. Boddy, and Gunner A. Ball). He included a sequence of events to support his position.

Lancashire and Ball responded to a call for volunteers to carry ammunition to the infantry on the firing line and started up the hill with a case of rifle cartridges. Lancashire was hit by Boer rifle fire, the box was dropped, and Ball took cover. Bradley and Rabb went out to recover Lancashire on their own initiative. While Rabb tended Lancashire Bradley enlisted the help of Boddy to drag the ammunition box out of the line of fire. The two filled their pockets with cartridge packs and ran the gauntlet to the top of the hill, delivering the much-needed ammunition to the infantry. In Kitchener's estimation the only one who had shown both initiative and courage warranting a Cross was Bradley.[32] It is interesting to note that neither Ball nor Lancashire were ever considered for the VC; in the 1850s being 'first to volunteer' for hazardous duty was widely considered grounds for recommendation, but times had clearly changed.

The South African War created two even more lasting changes in the nature of the Victoria Cross: the institutional (but not statutory) elimination of provisional bestowal of the Cross by the theatre commander and the extension of the Cross as a posthumous decoration. Both of these developments were connected to Victorian Britain's most beloved soldier, Lord Roberts of Kandahar.

Sir Redvers Buller had been the initial Theatre Commander for South Africa, but after a series of embarrassing defeats was replaced by Lord Roberts late in 1899. While Roberts exhibited a better grasp of field operations against the Boers than had Sir Redvers, he made some astonishingly bad decisions concerning the Victoria Cross.

On the evening of 30 March 1900 a British column of some 1800 men under the command of Brigadier General Robert George Broadwood bivouacked at Sanna's Post, which guarded the waterworks supplying Bloemfontein. As the force sent out no patrols, they were unaware that Christian de Wet and a force of 1600 commandos with artillery support were in the immediate area. De Wet had not made the same mistake, and was well aware of the British presence; he resolved to drive them into an ambush when they proceeded on toward Bloemfontein in the morning. The spot he chose for the trap was the drift crossing a rivulet called the Korn Spruit.[33]

Despite a report by an early morning patrol that they had been fired on, Broadwood ignored the possibility of a large Boer presence until the first artillery round from across the Modder River landed in his midst at about 0630. As the men were getting their breakfast, considerable chaos ensued. The logical course of action for the British was to move out of the enemy field of fire toward the safety of Bloemfontein. As shells burst about them drivers cursed their mules and horses into harness and began moving out, directly into the ambush at the drift.[34]

First in line were the vulnerable supply wagons; de Wet's Boers captured them without a shot. Scrub brush and the slope of the drift concealed their capture from the rest of the force. Broadwood still had no idea of the proximity of the Boers when he ordered 'U' and 'Q' batteries of the Royal Horse Artillery to follow the supply train and take up positions on the other side of the drift to cover the general retirement of the force.

'U' battery, in the lead, stumbled into the ambush as neatly as had the supply train, but in the confusion of their capture Major Philip Taylor managed to slip away and wave off 'Q' battery. Their sudden wheel about prompted de Wet's riflemen to open fire at last. Pandemonium reigned in Korn Spruit as the now driver-less teams of 'U' battery bolted, some becoming hopelessly entangled, others madly galloping across the plains toward Bloemfontein.[35]

The situation was scarcely better for 'Q' battery; one gun and two ammunition wagons overturned in the violent maneuver and had to be left behind. The survivors retired to the three buildings at Sanna's Post, roughly 1000 yards from the Korn Spruit, unlimbered, and opened a lively, if entirely ineffectual fire on the Boer positions. The drift offered excellent cover from the flat trajectory of the field guns at that range. The guns, lacking splinter shields, offered no shelter from the fire of 350 Mausers.[36]

The gunners of 'Q' battery were caught in the open by a foe who knew their exact range. Casualties steadily mounted until the order to fall back behind the cover of the buildings arrived. The fire was so heavy that Major Edmund Phipps-Hornby ordered the guns run back by hand rather than expose the horses. Assisted by troopers from the Burma Mounted Infantry (their own numbers too depleted by this point) 'Q' battery managed to withdraw four of the five guns to safety; the fifth was abandoned.[37] The day had been an unmitigated disaster: 570 casualties, with seven guns captured by de Wet's partisans.[38]

Amazingly, Lord Roberts conferred a provisional Victoria Cross on Major Phipps-Hornby and directed the battery to elect three members to receive the same decoration as their commanding officer. These three, Gunner Isaac Lodge, Driver Horace Henry Glasock, and Sergeant Charles Edward Haydon, were likewise given provisional VCs on the spot. Roberts also forwarded three more candidates through regular channels for Crosses. The whole packet was presented as a *fait accompli* to the War Office.[39]

That four provisional VCs were awarded on a single engagement raised some eyebrows in London; that it was for a debacle such as Korn Spruit was remarkable; that Lord Roberts further recommended another three candidates was unbelievable. His actions resulted in near censure from the War Office.

London realized it could do nothing about the four VCs already granted. To deny them would undercut Roberts's authority as theatre commander. They could and did quash the three further recommendations. The original draft of the letter informing him of this was quite curt, a rebuke to Roberts: 'The Grant of four Victoria Crosses for an affair, which, taken as a whole, was highly discreditable, is ample recognition of the service rendered; to give seven would be very inexpedient.'[40] The final draft softened the phrasing somewhat to read 'taken as a whole was not of a nature to reflect credit on our army ... ' but the message was clear: Roberts had made a grievous error. Equally clear was the message that provisional conferral of the VC was a thing of the past.

Originally the bestowal of Crosses by the commander on the spot reflected the nature of communications available at the time. The far-flung posts of empire were often weeks, if not months, from contact with the authorities in London. It was therefore thought proper to award the medal in a timely fashion for two reasons. Praise deferred might seem begrudging a hero of his laurels, and thus the award should be given while the deed was still fresh in the minds of the hero's comrades. In addition, a seriously wounded candidate could (and on occasion did) die before the recommendation could be confirmed and the medal awarded.[41] In the initial years of the Cross it was widely assumed that bestowal in the field would become the rule rather than the exception.[42] The experiences of the Mutiny injected a note of caution into the provisional question, but there were still instances in which the clause was cited to justify an award questioned in London.

The Korn Spruit incident, however, put an end to provisional bestowal. While the warrant retained the clause permitting it, no other commander had the temerity to chance granting a Cross in the field after Roberts's experience. When the warrant was redrawn in the wake of the First World War the provisional bestowal clause was quietly omitted, and thereafter only recommendations coming through proper channels were eligible for the award.[43]

Korn Spruit created a further controversy. Late in 1901 Colonel Edward Owen Hay, Assistant Adjutant General for the Royal Horse Artillery, made an astounding request. He argued that as the VCs granted to 'Q' battery for its action at Sanna's Post had been elected by the battery, it was in effect an award to the battery bestowed on individuals. Therefore, the battery itself, an immortal corporate entity, collectively had won the VC and should be allowed to let all of its current and future members wear some form of permanent badge on their uniform to represent this accomplishment. Whether intentional or not, it is interesting that Hay never referred to the action as Korn Spruit, but only as Sanna's Post.[44]

After reviewing all of the cases in which a unit had elected winners under Clause XIII, dating all the way back to the Mutiny, the Adjutant General's Office determined that there was no precedent for a unit citation interpretation of the regulations. 'The V.C. if possible should be a purely personal distinction. I think it would not be anything but misleading to allow staff segts to wear V.C. as a badge.'[45]

Why had Roberts suffered such a severe lapse of judgement concerning the Cross as to provoke such intense criticism from the War Office and

Horse Guards? The answer may lie in the sequence of events leading up to the admission of posthumous VCs. Once again, Roberts was at the heart of the matter, even though he was still in Britain at the time.

Contrary to Victorian military conventions, Frederick Sleigh Roberts had married in 1859 at age 26, while still a lieutenant. Only three of his children, however, survived into adulthood, two daughters and a son. Frederick Sherston Roberts duly followed his father's footsteps into a military career, gaining a commission in the King's Royal Rifle Corps.[46] The winter of 1899 found him in the field against the Boers. Freddy Roberts was a well-liked young officer who tried hard to live up to his father's reputation. He was with General Sir Redvers Buller's staff on 15 December 1899 at the disastrous Battle of Colenso.

Colenso has been rightly condemned as one of the most ineptly conducted actions in the annals of British military history and more generally as a prime example of how not to fight a battle. Its role in the evolution of the Victoria Cross as an institution is less well known. A split-second decision by a lieutenant precipitated a complete reversal in the interpretation of the Victoria Cross warrant, and led to an incident of favoritism unparalleled since the Havelock VC of the Mutiny.

Lack of proper reconnaissance led Buller to believe the town of Colenso was deserted, or at the worst, only lightly defended.[47] When it became apparent that this assumption was wrong, Buller lost control of the battle and instead became obsessed with trying to save the guns of the 14th and 66th batteries.

These guns had become exposed and then had to be abandoned due to the rashness of the battery commander, Colonel Charles Long. His own philosophy was 'the only way to smash those beggars is to rush in at 'em.'[48] Appropriate, perhaps, for a cavalry regiment, recommended, even, when dealing with a savage or aboriginal foe, but hardly sound doctrine when facing an enemy equipped with modern rifles.[49] Buller had given only ambiguous orders for the deployment of the artillery; Long's best judgement was to gallop past the advancing infantry for a full mile and unlimber his guns in a completely exposed position, taking care to dress his formation to parade ground perfection before opening fire.[50] The horses and limbers were sent back to shelter in a large donga (a dry wash) some 800 yards to the rear.

Long's guns fired more than 1000 shells within an hour and ran short of ammunition. The gunners took 25 percent casualties in the process, but managed to silence the Boer artillery across the Tugela. Long was wounded and command devolved to Major A. C. Bailward, who ordered the crews back to the shelter of a smaller donga about 50 yards to the rear of the artillery park to await ammunition resupply.[51] The guns sat deserted while the Boer cannon, now unopposed, returned to action.

Buller and his staff moved forward to oversee the infantry assault on Colenso. While en route they encountered one of the two officers sent to speed the artillery resupply and learned that the guns sat unattended in front of friendly lines. Buller rode immediately for Long's battery to find its commander delirious and raving about his poor brave gunners and the guns themselves exposed and unmanned.[52] Possibly suffering from shell-shock himself, having less than an hour earlier been bruised by the near-miss of a Boer shell that killed his personal surgeon, Buller lost control and focused on recovering the guns to the exclusion of all else.[53]

Buller first ordered Captain Harry Norton Schofield to take some teams and drivers out to recover them, but they were met with such a hail of fire that they were forced to turn back short of the guns. Then, according to Captain Walter Norris Congreve, who won his own Victoria Cross that day:

> Generals Buller and Clery stood out in it [the donga] and said 'some of you go out and help Schofield.' ADC Roberts, myself, and two or three others went to the waggons and we got two waggons horsed up with the help of a corporal and six gunners. I have never seen even at field firing the bullets fly thicker.[54]

Freddy Roberts got about 30 yards from the donga, laughing and twirling his riding crop, before a Boer shell blew his horse to bits and mortally wounded the young officer.[55] Congreve and the others were either wounded or driven to cover, and the attempt to save the guns failed. A further attempt managed to drag two of the guns to safety, but Buller then lost his resolve. Unwilling even to wait for cover of darkness to retrieve the others, he ordered a general withdrawal; the remaining ten guns were handed over to the Boers.[56] Buller had given the order that killed the only remaining son of England's most beloved soldier and had been soundly defeated by the upstart Boers.

Exactly what went through Buller's mind the next day cannot be stated with any certainty; his own recollections of Colenso and the aftermath became thoroughly muddled in the process of explaining what had happened to the War Office. What he did on 16 December 1899 is a matter of official record, however. As Freddy Roberts lay dying, Buller recommended him for the Victoria Cross, and in so doing discarded 42 years of precedent regarding badly wounded heroes.

The VC warrant was vague concerning the nuances of eligibility. Clause V stated that the award was open to any officer or man who had served in the presence of the enemy and had performed some signal act of valour. Clause VI specified that neither rank, nor long service, nor wounds were to enter into the determination of fitness for the award, that it should rest solely on the merit of the action.[57] It did not specifically bar the VC to soldiers killed in the process of serving the Queen. That decision originated in the bureaucracy at the War Office.

The precedent for refusing to consider posthumous recommendations came from Lord Panmure's desk almost before the ink on the original warrant had dried. Queried as to the possibility of granting a VC to the father of a soldier who died in action in the Crimea, he replied that the Cross 'is an *order* for the living.'[58] From the outset it was made clear that submitting the names of dead men for the honor would not be tolerated.

In only six cases before the Boer War had this precedent even been questioned. Private Edward Spence was mortally wounded in an attempt to retrieve the body of a dead lieutenant 15 April 1858. He died two days later. Ensign Everard Aloysius Lisle Phillipps was cited for cumulative bravery during the siege of Delhi, 30 May to 18 September 1857, including the capture of Water Bastion during the assault on the city. He was killed in street fighting 18 September. Two lieutenants of the South Wales Borderers, Teignmouth Melvill and Nevill J. A. Coghill, died together at Isandhlwana, 22 January 1879, trying to spirit away the Queen's Colours from the hands of the Zulus after the day (and the battalion) was lost.

More recently Trooper Frank William Baxter lost his life in the Matabele Rebellion on 22 April 1896, when he gave his horse to a wounded comrade and tried to escape the pursuing Matabele on foot. At the village of Nawa Kili, during the Tirah Campaign in 1897, Lieutenant Hector L. S. MacLean was mortally wounded in an attempt to recover a wounded officer. These six were each gazetted as 'would have been recommended to Her Majesty for the Distinction of the Victoria Cross had he survived,' but no medals were issued.[59] The War Office was careful even of extending recognition to the dead in this fashion:

> I am directed by Secretary Major General Peel to acknowledge the receipt of your letter of the nineteenth ultimo regarding that, in consideration of the deed of gallantry performed by your late brother Captain Howard Douglas Campbell of the 78th Highlanders in India, a notice be published in the London Gazette to the effect that the distinction of the Victoria

Cross would have been conferred upon him had he survived; and I am to acquaint you in reply, that as no distinct recommendation of the late Captain Campbell for this honor was ever made, his death having taken place a few days after the performance of the act of gallantry and question, Major General Peel regrets that he is unable to comply with the request which you have now made as in the absence of such recommendation it has been found impossible to bring under Her Majesty's notice the act of heroism which Her Majesty would no doubt have gladly rewarded had circumstances permitted.[60]

In practice the prohibition against posthumous Crosses evolved into a rough rule of thumb applied by commanding officers. Unscathed heroes could be submitted without reservation. Dead heroes could never be submitted. Wounded heroes could be submitted only if there was a strong chance of their surviving their wounds. Buller, whether motivated by shame, guilt, remorse, or shell-shock, violated the last principle in his recommendation of young Roberts. He did not deserve a Victoria Cross for his actions at Colenso. All he did was get killed, a distinction he shared with a number of individuals in that donga. His final gallop toward the guns was the result of Buller's order, not an impulsive or voluntary act. At the very most he should have been gazetted as 'would have ... had he survived.' Although the general did adhere to the letter of the regulations in recommending the lieutenant before his death, the recommendation was suspect from the moment he set pen to paper.

Buller was, furthermore, transparent in his padding of the account of Colenso to justify the recommendation of Roberts. He detailed the actions of Congreve and Captain Hamilton Lyster Reed[61] in their VC recommendations, but of Roberts he could only report, 'Lieutenant the Honourable F. Roberts, King's Royal Rifles, assisted Captain Congreve. He was wounded in three places.'[62] He did not mention that Roberts was acting in response to his direct order to 'Help Schofield,' nor did he state that Roberts's wounds were mortal. In fact, the report was worded in such a way to suggest he (Buller) was not present at the time of the event. Also interesting was the slant Buller put on his reasons for recommendation of certain individuals while skipping others:

I have differentiated in my recommendations, because I thought that a recommendation for the Victoria Cross required proof of initiative, something more, in fact, than mere obedience to orders, and for this reason I have not recommended Captain Schofield, Royal Artillery, who was acting under orders, though I desire to record his conduct as most gallant.[63]

Oddly enough, Buller recommended only those who had failed to retrieve a gun; he nominated the six drivers who actually accomplished their mission and came back with two guns for the Distinguished Conduct Medal. All in all, it is obvious that he was rushing this report: he closed it with the statement 'several other gallant drivers tried, but were all killed, and I cannot get their names.'[64] It truly seems he was trying to dispatch the letter before Freddy Roberts breathed his last.

His recommendation sailed through the adjudication process without comment, and Lieutenant Roberts was gazetted as a Victoria Cross winner 2 February 1900, along with Congreve, Reed, and Corporal George Edward Nurse. Buller had nominated and had passed four VCs for a dismal failure *that was largely his own fault*. More VCs were to come of Colenso: Major William Babtie, RAMC, who tended Roberts under fire was gazetted 20 April 1900. Captain Schofield received the Distinguished Service Order for his efforts that day as well.

Here the Victorian sense of fair play became part of the process, both inside and outside the administration of the Army. It was hardly proper that Congreve and Roberts got the VC for trying to do the same task as Schofield, who received a lesser award. Buller's argument that Schofield was acting under orders while the others showed initiative was undercut by Congreve's statement to the contrary. It is unclear who initiated the sequence of events, but once Lord Roberts had handed off command in South Africa to Herbert Horatio Kitchener and returned to London as the new Commander-in-Chief, further inquiry was made in the Colenso affair, specifically as to the actions of Schofield. In a letter marked 'secret,' Colonel Ian Hamilton, Military Secretary to Roberts at Horse Guards, asked Captain Congreve for his version of the events at Colenso.[65]

Based on Congreve's account, Roberts pushed for an upgrade in Schofield's reward for gallantry and on 30 August 1901 he was gazetted for the VC. Hamilton wrote the letter informing Buller of this development:

In considering the case of a soldier of the Royal Scots Fusiliers recommended for the V.C. the question of Captain Sc[h]ofield, and his reward came up and was discussed by the Secretary of State and the Comm. in Chief.

Lord Roberts thinks you would like to know that as a result it is now intended to give Captain Sc[h]ofield the Victoria Cross instead of the D.S.O.

This action is taken in assumption that although you did not think you were justified under the terms of the warrant in recommending Captain Sc[h]ofield, you would nevertheless be glad to learn he was going to obtain this great distinction.[66]

The British did not allow stacking awards for the same deed; when Captain Schofield was awarded the VC he had to relinquish the DSO he had already been awarded for the same event. In this instance, he held the DSO for only 30 days before the War Office took it back.[67]

Fair play also dictated a review of cases similar to that of Freddy Roberts. Lord Roberts took the lead in assembling a case for changing the interpretation of the warrant. The long-standing policy of the government concerning the VC was to consider it a hybrid award, combining aspects of both a medal (some of which could be granted posthumously) and an Order (which could not be granted posthumously).[68]

Roberts's staff attacked the latter premise, dredging up instances in which an Order had in fact been granted to the widow of the man who earned it. The strongest case they came up with was that of Lieutenant Colonel A. Ellis, 'who would have been recommended for the dignity of Knight Commander of the Bath (Military Division) had he survived' operations on the West Coast of Africa in 1894. They pointed out, however, 'His widow was granted the Style, Plan and Precedence which she would have been entitled to had her husband survived.'[69]

There were six instances in the Boer War involving great courage with fatal results. Horse Guards made a test case out of the actions of Sergeant Alfred Atkinson of the Yorkshire Regiment. On 18 February 1900 he made repeated trips under heavy fire to bring water to the wounded, and was mortally wounded on his seventh traverse of the fire zone. He died three days later. In April 1902 Lord Roberts gave his endorsement to granting the VC he should have won to Atkinson's mother, and then recommended that the five other dead heroes be given the same.[70] All six were gazetted on 8 August 1902.[71]

This set the precedent that the posthumous award of the Victoria Cross was now an acceptable course of action, but the debate over posthumous awards was not finished. The announcement of the awards prompted a call for fair play from outside the War Office and Horse Guards. Even before the *London Gazette* with their citations left the printers word had leaked, prompting letters from grieving and in some cases irate family members demanding similar treatment for their fallen sons.⁷² Most were easily dismissed, but the six who had been gazetted as 'would have ... if survived' proved to be more difficult, particularly when their proponents were members of the aristocracy. The first blast came from Sir John Joscelyn Coghill, father of one of the fugitive heroes of Isandhlwana. He wrote a threatening letter to the Secretary of State for War on 3 August 1902. When he got no satisfaction, he called on the young officer's uncle, Lord Rathmore, to put further pressure on the administration. Lord Rathmore contacted Secretary of State for War St John Broderick on the subject in mid-September of 1902. He suggested that the government could hardly withhold the Cross from those who would have earned it had they not died, and now that the interpretation of the warrant had been altered, there was no bar to granting it posthumously. It is apparent from the letter that he intended to get a VC for his dead nephew, no matter what the cost. If he had to force the government to grant the award to five other corpses, so be it. It was not, however, as if he were going to bat for the other five specifically.⁷³

Broderick forwarded the letter to Lord Roberts along with a request for information on any other 'would haves.' The C-in-C replied that only six such pre-Boer War cases existed, and voiced his approval of backdating the VCs of the 'would haves,' on the condition that only those already gazetted as such would be considered. It is apparent in the letter that he could not in good conscience refuse the award granted to his dead son to those who had earned it in the past.⁷⁴

Others in the administration did not share his optimism, among them his Military Secretary, Ian Hamilton. Hamilton did not see a problem with granting the VC to men who, like Freddie Roberts, had died of wounds after the fact of their heroism. Where he saw potential problems was with the inclusion of the men killed outright, both the three men of the Boer conflict and the six who had been gazetted as 'would have' in earlier conflicts:

> If we confine this to the above nine all will be well but I must say I have had misgivings about this business –
> Until now it has been the laudable object of a commander to write to the relatives of officers and men who have fallen in terms of unmeasured praise. This could do no harm; could serve as a basis to no claims and was a certain consolation – Now either all this must stop and a dead man must be measured by the same standard as a living one; or else applications for posthumous decorations will be the rule and not the exception –

The impossibility of arguing with the relatives of a dead man is well shown by the intensely disagreeable and threatening tone of Sir J. Coghill in his letter to the S. of S. dated 3rd August 1902.[75]

Broderick shared some of Hamilton's misgivings, but approved the measure: 'Submit to the king and at the same time make it perfectly clear no one will be allowed to participate in the decision who is not one of these nine.'[76] Lord Roberts did not credit their apprehensions; when Hamilton queried him a final time over the proposal he replied with a brief note: 'Carry Out. I confess I do not share your fears . . . .'[77]

Subsequent to the deliberations of Roberts, Broderick, and Hamilton, the proposal to grant the six pre-Boer War VCs was submitted to Edward VII on 2 November 1902. The king refused to approve the measure on the grounds it would provoke a flood of submissions from grieving relatives.[78] It is interesting to note that he had received the rambling and quite mad letter from Thomas Morely, the man who claimed three VCs for his actions in the Crimea and manufactured an entire heroic history of himself spanning three continents, just days before the decision was made. The problem was that his majesty *had* approved the issue of posthumous VCs to the three dead heroes of the Boer War, which left an awkward situation with the War Office caught between the monarch on one side and adamant relatives on the other.

Another reason cited for the King's reluctance to backdate Victoria Crosses was that so much time had elapsed since the original acts. As Lord Knollys later explained: 'H.M. thinks that with 2 exceptions the acts of gallantry were so long ago that it would be hardly understood were the VC to be given to the representatives of the deceased officers and men after a lapse of so many years.'[79] At some point in late 1906, however, the widow of Lieutenant Teignmouth Melvill wrote directly to the King requesting that the VC he should have earned at Isandhlwana be forwarded to her as his next of kin. It was clear that she understood the importance of the award despite the years that had passed since 1879.

Accordingly, the Crown requested further information from the War Office on 3 December 1906 regarding the particulars of Melvill's case. General Sir Arthur Wynne at the War Office used this opportunity to bring up the cases of the other five 'would haves,' pointing out that there was no substantive difference between Melvill and any of the others, and that to grant one and not the others would be a great injustice. Edward VII decided, based on this information, to go ahead and grant the VC to the six – on strict condition that no other pre-Boer War claimants be considered under any circumstances.[80] On Tuesday, 15 January 1907, the six were gazetted. What the reasoning of the War Office, the bombast of Sir J. Coghill, and the influence of Lord Rathmore could not accomplish, a widow's plea made reality.

One final change in the institutional case-law of the Victoria Cross took place just before the First World War. Shortly after his accession to the throne George V added his own mark to the regulations governing the Cross:

> We do by these Presents, for Us, Our Heirs and Successors, ordain and appoint that it shall be competent for the native officers, non-commissioned officers and men of Our Indian Army to obtain the said decoration in the manner set forth in the rules and ordinances referred to, or in accordance with any further rules and ordinances which may hereafter be made and promulgated by Us, Our Heirs and Successors, for the government of the said decoration.[81]

The motivation behind this policy change is unclear, as no official documentation has so far been released to the Public Record Office files on the Victoria Cross. In November 1911, however, the King and Queen made a state visit to India. 'The King had come in person to announce his coronation, and, as is the secular custom of the East on such occasions, to commemorate it by certain marks of especial favour.'[82] These marks of 'especial favour' were the cause of special debate shortly before the King's departure. The viceroy had initially suggested a gift of a crore of rupees (equivalent to £666,666) to the Government of India as an appropriate gesture of imperial largesse, a proposal firmly rejected by the cabinet. As an alternative the abstract boons of reversing the unpopular partition of Bengal and transferring the seat of government from Calcutta to Delhi were accepted.[83] Although the warrant extension was not mentioned in the discussions, it was signed into effect on 21 October 1911, just 21 days before the royal party set sail for the subcontinent. It is likely that the gesture was part and parcel of the King-Emperor's largesse towards his imperial domain.

# Five

# Fifty Years On: A Half-Century of Heroism

The last pre-First World War Victoria Cross was granted in 1904. Thus it is a convenient point, 50 years after the first decoration was won, to examine the statistical trends that evolved in that half-century. Since its creation 521 Crosses had been confirmed by the Crown, enough for a viable statistical universe. For our purposes what is critical are the trends in the types of acts that were winning the VC, the 'cost of courage' in terms of casualties amongst those identified as heroes, and the pattern of distribution of the award throughout the ranks of the military.

The acts winning awards can be divided into four broad categories, two of which bear further subdivision. For the most part, aggressive 'war-winning' acts garnered the lion's share of Victoria Crosses, slightly over 52 percent of the Victorian total. This aspect of courage needs to be differentiated, however, into subcategories. Obviously offensive actions figure into this category, acts that were intended to gain ground, capture a strong point, or break an enemy formation. War-winning can also include acts defending territory, holding a fortification, or in general resisting an enemy attack. In a less concrete sense, certain acts that contributed to victory carried a high symbolic value for the rank and file. Examples of this include rallying troops under fire, saving one's own artillery from capture, or in turn, capturing the enemy's guns. The fourth subcategory deals with acts that 'pave the way' to victory in a secondary sense, through combat engineering, reconnaissance, or resupply. Thus, there are four categories for combat service: War-Winning, Offensive; War-Winning, Defensive; War-Winning, Symbolic; and War-Winning, Secondary.

War-winning was followed closely and sometimes surpassed by 'Humanitarian' valour. Life-saving also bears breaking down, in this case into acts saving enlisted personnel and acts saving the lives of officers. This category also includes disposing live ordnance – shells and grenades – the explosion of which would have caused casualties.

Purely symbolic acts comprised a small percentage of the deeds earning a Victoria Cross, things like saving the colors or retrieving the body of a dead officer. A final category consists of acts that defy categorization, and have been labeled simply as 'Special.'

A certain amount of subjectivity is unavoidable in the categorization of the actions that won the decoration. In many cases multiple acts of valour were cited, some of which fit into more than one of the categories listed above. For example:

> On 5 November 1854 at the Battle of Inkerman, Crimea, Private [Anthony] Palmer with two other men were the first to volunteer to go with a brevet major to dislodge a party of Russians from the Sandbag Battery. The attack succeeded. During this action Private Palmer shot down an assailant who was in the act of bayoneting the brevet major, and so saved his life. He was also one of a small band which, by a desperate charge against overwhelming numbers, saved the Colours of the battalion from capture.[1]

Here we see a soldier who could fit into three categories, War-Winning, Offensive, Life-Saving, Officer, and Symbolic. In this case Private Palmer has been listed as War-Winning, Offensive, on the basis that the assault was the most important aspect of his actions according to the recommending officer, and the other actions were predicated by offensive action on the soldier's part.

The particulars of each citation have been evaluated in Table 5.1 and each has been assigned to a single category with no overlap. With only slightly over 500 units in the survey, all percentages have been rounded to the nearest whole number.

Given the differences in circumstances, theatres of operation, and attitudes of commanders, shifts of less than 10 percent do not constitute a trend or aberration.[2]

The vast majority of the Victoria Crosses won in the nineteenth century were won on land. The Royal Navy accounted for only 44 of the 521 awards, or 8.4 percent of the pre-First World War total. Of those 44, 38 were won by Navy personnel operating on shore; only six (1 percent) were won at sea.[3]

With the exception of the 1880s, offensive war-winning acts remained fairly steady at about 15 to 19 percent of the awards granted. This category includes such acts as capturing a strongpoint or enemy troops, charging an

Table 5.1 Acts winning the Victoria Cross, nineteenth century: winners per decade

| Decade | 1850s 296 | | 1860s 39 | | 1870s 48 | | 1880s 21 | | 1890–1904 117 | |
| --- | --- | --- | --- | --- | --- | --- | --- | --- | --- | --- |
| # Awarded | Raw | % | Raw | % | Raw | % | Raw | % | Raw | % |
| War-Winning | 178 | 60 | 17 | 44 | 29 | 60 | 3 | 14 | 52 | 44 |
| – Offensive | 55 | 19 | 6 | 15 | 9 | 19 | 0 | 0 | 16 | 14 |
| – Defensive | 19 | 6 | 0 | 0 | 14 | 30 | 0 | 0 | 9 | 8 |
| – Symbolic | 76 | 26 | 7 | 18 | 3 | 6 | 2 | 9 | 22 | 19 |
| – Secondary | 28 | 9 | 2 | 5 | 3 | 6 | 1 | 5 | 5 | 4 |
| Humanitarian | 103 | 35 | 18 | 46 | 16 | 33 | 18 | 86 | 63 | 54 |
| – Enlisted | 64 | 22 | 14 | 36 | 13 | 27 | 11 | 53 | 43 | 37 |
| – Officer | 39 | 13 | 4 | 10 | 3 | 6 | 7 | 33 | 20 | 17 |
| Symbolic | 12 | 4 | 6 | 15 | 2 | 4 | 0 | 0 | 2 | 2 |
| Special | 3 | 1 | 0 | 0 | 1 | 2 | 0 | 0 | 0 | 0 |

enemy body, and serving the guns under fire, acts that materially contributed to victory:

> On 5 November 1854 at the Battle of Inkerman, Crimea, Brevet Major [Charles] Russell offered to dislodge a party of Russians from the Sand Bag Battery if anyone would follow him. A Sergeant and two privates (one of whom was subsequently killed) were the first to volunteer. The party met with much resistance and several times seemed to be of the point of a annihilation but their skill, especially with the bayonet, finally brought success. Major Russell himself fought with great valour and in single combat wrenched the rifle out of the grasp of a powerful Russian.[4]

War-winning is not necessarily confined to acts of conquest and capture. Often holding a vital position in the face of a determined attack can be just as decisive as a cavalry charge:

> On 26 September 1857 at Lucknow, India, Private [James] Hollowell was one of a party which was shut up and besieged in one of the houses. He behaved throughout the day in a most admirable manner, encouraging the other nine men, who were in low spirits, to keep going. His cheerful persuasion prevailed and they made successful defence in a burning house with the enemy firing through four windows.[5]

It was not, however, as glorious in the eyes of the War Office. Defensive stands accounted for only about 7 percent in the decades they were recognized at all. True, there is a massive jump in defensive VCs during the 1870s, but this is due to two entirely defensive engagements, Isandhlwana and Rorke's Drift. When the ten defensive awards won in these engagements are subtracted from the total and the percentages refigured, defensive VCs drop back down from 30 percent to a more expected 11 percent. This slight rise can be explained as an effect of the precedent established by the number granted for the above mentioned battles.

Two decades did not produce any defensive Crosses at all, but for two very different reasons. The campaigns of the 1860s were by nature aggressive, taking the war to an enemy who was wedded to a defensive strategy. The majority of the Crosses granted during this decade came from the protracted war against the Maoris, which involved ferreting the rebels out of their fortified *pahs*, or from the China War, which was largely decided by the taking of key Imperial fortresses. The storming of Magdala and the naval action ashore at Shimonosekei were likewise offensive operations. Moreover, the commanders of the 1860s were both aggressive and competent, which kept troops out of desperate defensive situations.

The lack of defensive VCs in the 1880s can be attributed to the Duke of Cambridge's pique at the number of Crosses dropped on the defenders of Rorke's Drift. Fully 35 percent of the Zulu War awards were for the defense of the mission station, or 15 percent of the total awards of the decade. The duke's memo noting that the award was being given too freely carried a lot of weight, and even though British troops fought defensive engagements at Maiwand and Kandahar in Afghanistan and at Laing's Nek and Majuba Hill in South Africa, the laurels went to the relief forces, not the defenders.

This trend continued in the 1890s; despite a war which saw British troops in hard fought defensive situations time and again against the Boers, only 8 percent of the awards went to defensive actions. Buller and Roberts were more likely to forward a recommendation for defensive valour than Kitchener; only one of the six Boer War defensive VCs originated during his tenure in command.

One of the most dramatic changes in distribution of the Cross came in symbolic war-winning. Capturing enemy guns or saving friendly artillery from capture, charging a superior foe; for enlisted men, staying at one's post, and for officers showing 'good form' in the face of overwhelming odds, all carry with them something beyond the concrete value of the moment:

On 9 July 1857, at the siege of Delhi, India, Second Lieutenant [James] Hills most gallantly defended the position assigned to him when attacked by enemy cavalry. Single-handed he charged the head of the enemy's column and fought fiercely – on foot after he and his horse had been ridden down. He was about to be killed with his own sword which one of the enemy had wrested from him, when his senior officer saw what was happening and twice in a short space of time came to the rescue of his subaltern.[6]

In Hills's case it seems to be the thought that counted, as his commanding officer probably had more important things to do than protect a subaltern who could not hang on to his own weapon.

Good form could also be recognized in the rank and file. Lieutenant Luke O'Connor started out in the ranks and in the Crimea, where he:

> was one of the centre sergeants at the battle of the Alma, and advanced between the officers, carrying the colours. When near the redoubt, Lieutenant Anstruther who was carrying a colour, was mortally wounded, and he [O'Connor] was shot into the breast at the same time, and fell; but recovering himself, snatched of the colour from the ground, and continued to carry it to the end of the action, although urged by Captain Granville to relinquish it, and go to the rear, on account of his wound; was recommended for, and received his commission for his services at the Alma.[7]

During the 1850s and 1860s this flavor of valour accounted for over 20 percent of the VCs awarded. The numbers decline in subsequent decades, due partially to the discontinuation of 'first in' Crosses by the authorities in London. Technological changes also had an impact; had Sergeant O'Connor been struck in the chest by a 7.62 x 54R Moisin-Nagant round (the standard Russian rifle ammunition of the First World War) instead of a Cossack's musket ball, he would not have got back up and continued to carry the colors.[8]

Field officers served as the first filter of heroism. As shown in previous chapters it was very difficult for an individual to nominate himself for an award. The recommendation of an officer was vital, and the preconceptions of the officer corps determined what acts were forwarded for consideration by higher authorities. The high number of symbolic war-winning awards at mid-century are a direct manifestation of the preindustrial army of Wellington. Many of the recommending officers clearly valued style over substance.

Although many of these traditions and attitudes carried over into the late Victorian officer corps, this aspect did not. During the 1870s and 1880s symbolic war-winning acts dropped to less than 10 percent as officers who had started their careers under the Iron Duke were replaced by the children of the industrial age. Both Buller and Roberts were of the old school, reaching the end of their respective careers. If the dubious VCs of Colenso and Korn Spruit they put forward are discounted, this trend continued through the turn of the century, with the ratio dropping to under 6 percent of the Crosses awarded between 1890 and 1904.

One factor that remained steady throughout the half-century was the percentage of awards bestowed for what have been categorized as 'war-winning secondary' acts. These medals went to feats that aided success indirectly, such as bringing up fresh ammunition, reconnaissance of enemy dispositions, serving as a courier, or performing operations that today would be termed combat engineering:

> For distinguished conduct on the night of 4 August 1855, when in command of the working party in the advanced trenches in front of the quarries, encouraging and inciting his men by his example, to work under a dreadful fire; and, when there was hesitation shown, in consequence of the severity of the fire, going into the open, and working with pick and shovel, the showing the best possible example to the men. In the words of one of them, 'there was not another officer in the British Army who would have done what Major [Frederick C.] Elton did that night.'[9]

Enlisted personnel were also rewarded for combat engineering. Corporal John Ross displayed:

> Extremely creditable conduct on the 23rd of August 1855, in charge of the advance from the Fifth Parallel Right Attack on the Redan, in placing and filling 25 gabions under very heavy fire, whilst annoyed by the presence of light balls.
> Intrepid and devoted conduct in creeping to the Redan in the night of the 8th September 1855, and reporting its evacuation; on which its occupation by the English took place.[10]

Like the defensive VCs, these functions can be vital to the success of a campaign, but lack the glamor of saving the guns or carrying the enemy breastworks. With the exception of just under 10 percent reported in the 1850s – the Crimean War involved a lot of trench digging under fire – only about 5 percent of the pre-First World War Crosses were bestowed for paving the way for others.

Humanitarian acts comprised the majority of the remaining nineteenth-century Victoria Crosses. Private John J. Sims was one of the early winners

Table 5.2  Enlisted versus officer in life-saving VCs, nineteenth century

| Decade | 1850s 103 | | 1860s 13 | | 1870s 16 | | 1880s 18 | | 1890–1904 63 | |
|---|---|---|---|---|---|---|---|---|---|---|
| # Awarded | Raw | % | Raw | % | Raw | % | Raw | % | Raw | % |
| Enlisted | 64 | 62 | 10 | 77 | 13 | 81 | 11 | 61 | 43 | 68 |
| Officer | 39 | 38 | 3 | 23 | 3 | 19 | 7 | 39 | 20 | 32 |

for retrieving the wounded: 'For having, on 18 June 1855, after the Regiment had retired into the trenches from the assault on the Redan, gone out into the open ground, under heavy fire, in broad daylight, and brought in wounded soldiers outside the trenches.'[11] Overall humanitarian valour accounted for 35 percent of the awards for the 1850s, 38 percent in the 1860s (discounting the noncombat Andaman Island rescue) and 33 percent during the 1870s. Breaking those figures down into saving officers as opposed to saving enlisted shows that saving an officer was more likely to result in an award (see Table 5.2).

Although the numbers of a given battalion varied widely depending on available manpower, a safe estimate of 600 men and 32 officers yields a ratio of 5 percent officers and 95 percent enlisted. Even doubling the officer ratio to account for staff and visiting officers on detached duty would not account for the disparity between population and distribution. Clearly, saving the life of an officer got one noticed:

> On six January 1893, during the Kachin Expedition, Burma, while an attack was in progress on Fort Sima, Surgeon Major Owen Lloyd went, with an Indian NCO, to the assistance of the commanding officer who was wounded. Surgeon Major Lloyd then stayed with the officer while the NCO went back to get further help in carrying the wounded man back to the fort, where he died a few minutes later. The enemy was within 10 to 15 paces during this time, keeping up a heavy fire, and Surgeon Major Lloyd was wounded while returning to the fort.[12]

Another aspect of these humanitarian awards was getting rid of ordnance before it exploded. The first VC earned went for this action by Mate Charles D. Lucas:

> On 21 June 1854 in the Baltic, H.M.S. *Hecla* with two other ships, was bombarding the Bomarsund, a fort in the Aland Islands. The fire was

returned from the shore, and at the height of the action a live shell landed on the *Hecla's* upper deck, with its fuse still hissing. All hands were ordered to fling themselves flat on the deck, but Mr Lucas with great presence of mind ran forward and hurled the shell into the sea, where it exploded with a tremendous roar before it hit the water. Thanks to Mr Lucas's action no one was killed or seriously wounded.[13]

Only 11 'Dispose Ordnance' Crosses were granted in the nineteenth century. Ten of these were earned in combat during the 1850s, with the final noncombat one won in Canada in connection with extinguishing a fire in the ammunition car of a military train. The demise of this category in the later decades of the century is a direct result of technological change. Better fusing methods eliminated the 'hissing fuse' encountered by Mate Lucas and others. There simply was no time to pick up a shell and toss it aside. Not until the reappearance of hand grenades in the First World War did this type of heroism resurface.

Some aspects of heroism were purely symbolic. Unlike the acts noted above under the heading 'War-Winning, Symbolic' these acts are entirely in the abstract realm, acts that do not make a concrete contribution in a material sense. Only 4.2 percent of the Victorian era VCs went to purely symbolic acts, for example, retrieving the body of a dead officer:

On 7 September 1863 near Cameron Town, New Zealand, Lance-Corporal [John] Ryan, with two privates, removed the body of a captain from the field of action after he had been mortally wounded and remained with it all night in the bush, surrounded by the enemy.[14]

The recovery of the officer's body did not, at least according to the citation, materially affect the outcome of the engagement. Such an act by itself holds only an abstract value. Likewise the capturing of the enemy's flag, when the act itself is isolated and not the precursor of subsequent events:

On 21 September 1857 at Mungalwar, India, Sergeant [Patrick] Mahoney, whilst doing duty with the Volunteer Cavalry, helped in the capture of the Regimental Colour of the 1st Regiment Native Infantry.[15]

Given that the 1st Regiment Native Infantry was in rebellion against the government that had given them that set of Colors, the flag probably had more significance to the men who captured it than it did to the native infantrymen.

The colors were important to many, but some commanding officers were more pragmatic. Lieutenant Colonel John Ewart of the 93rd Highlanders led the assault on the Secundra Bagh during the Mutiny and engaged in hand-to-hand combat with saber and revolver. At one point he cut down two Mutineers and seized their colors. By this time the Bagh had been secured and Ewart proudly presented himself and the colors to Sir Colin Campbell.

'Damn your Colours, sir!' Campbell exploded at the astounded Ewart. 'It is not your place to be taking Colours; go back to your Regiment this instant, sir!' Sir Colin later apologized for the outburst, but Ewart never got the VC for which he was recommended.[16] Interestingly enough, Private Peter Grant did get a VC at the Secundra Bagh that day – for saving Ewart's life:

> For great personal gallantry on 16th November 1857 at the Secundra Bagh in killing five of the enemy with one of their own swords who were attempting to follow Lieutenant-Colonel Ewart when that officer was carrying a Colour which he had captured. (Elected by the regiment.)[17]

Campbell was not so much angry at Ewart for displaying the captured colors as he was for Ewart failing to command. As Ian Hamilton later discovered, field officers were expected to command rather than indulge in personal combat, and thus very few colonels got Crosses for physical combat.

There were a very few acts that defy real categorization, and in some cases perhaps reflect a wry bit of humor in the Victorian ranks. An example of one of these 'Special' VCs is the case of Bugler William Sutton:

> His conduct was conspicuous throughout the operations especially on 2 August 1857 on which occasion during an attack he rushed over the trenches and killed one of the enemy's Buglers, who was in the act of sounding. (Elected by Regiment.)[18]

How could soldiers resist giving a medal to the man who killed a bugler?

The cost of courage varied during the nineteenth century. The majority of winners were not wounded in the process, although that figure declined gradually during the period.

This is not surprising, given the policies established by the War Office concerning posthumous Victoria Crosses. Commanders were reluctant to recommend severely wounded men who might die before confirmation of the award, thus depriving the regiment of the honor.[19]

The variations in the 'No Wound' and 'Wounded in Action' (WIA) categories before 1890 can be attributed to the difference in foes faced.

Grapeshot and musket balls tended to produce devastating wounds, whereas an assegai rarely shattered an arm or leg. Thus, when facing the Russians or well-equipped Mutineers, more of the wounded sustained lethal injuries. When facing more primitively armed enemies, the wounded stood a better chance of recovery. Both the Afghans and the Boers had more rifles per capita than the Zulu or Maori, and caused more lethal wounds.[20] The 'Killed in Action' (KIA) and 'Died of Wounds' (DOW) figures represent the men brought in by the revision of the warrant interpretation under Lord Roberts.

The drop in the number of unwounded VC winners in the 1890s was due largely to an increase in the quality of medical care in the field and provision of hospital facilities in the rear areas. During the Crimean War amputation was the standard treatment for shattered limbs, and God help the man with an abdominal wound. By the late 1890s antiseptic surgery and x-ray machines accompanied the troops into the field.[21] More heroes survived their acts of valour to claim their reward; commanders could recommend severely wounded soldiers with greater confidence.

Table 5.3 The cost of courage: casualties among nineteenth-century VC winners per decade

| Quarter | 1850s 296 | | 1860s 39 | | 1870s 48 | | 1880s 21 | | 1890–1904 117 | |
| --- | --- | --- | --- | --- | --- | --- | --- | --- | --- | --- |
| # Awarded | Raw | % | Raw | % | Raw | % | Raw | % | Raw | % |
| No Wound | 226 | 76 | 26 | 67 | 33 | 69 | 16 | 76 | 73 | 62 |
| WIA | 67 | 23 | 13 | 33 | 13 | 27 | 5 | 24 | 35 | 30 |
| DOW | 2 | 0.7 | 0 | 0 | 0 | 0 | 0 | 0 | 4 | 3 |
| KIA | 1 | 0.3 | 0 | 0 | 2 | 4 | 0 | 0 | 5 | 4 |
| Total Casualties | 70 | 24 | 13 | 33 | 15 | 31 | 5 | 24 | 44 | 38 |
| Total Lethal | 3 | 1 | 0 | 0 | 2 | 4 | 0 | 0 | 9 | 8 |

Distribution of the Victoria Cross was heavily biased toward the officer corps in general and the rank equivalent to that of the Army lieutenant in particular. Overall the award was divided almost equally percentage-wise between officers and the other ranks, but once again it must be remembered that officers, including staff, could not have comprised more than 10–12 percent of the military establishment. Thus, just over 46 percent of the nineteenth-century VCs going to officers represented a tremendous bias toward the military elite.

Of the officers the rank of lieutenant and its Navy equivalent took the majority of the awards. Just under 50 percent of all officer VCs went to these junior officers. The obvious reason for this disparity is the potential for valour provided to lieutenants by virtue of being at the sharp end of combat more often than more senior officers. There was also an institutional bias in their favor from the very inception of the award. Lord Panmure, although admitting the award was open to all ranks, inquired of Horse Guards whether or not it should be directed toward the lower ranks.[22] Although never made statutory, the bias is apparent in two cases in point.

On the night of 29/30 October 1863 Major Charles Keyes led an assault to capture a mountain strongpoint called the Crag Piquet during the Ambeyla Campaign in India; his success prompted a recommendation for a Victoria Cross. His recommendation was quashed by the Commander-in-Chief, India, Sir Hugh Rose, with the following explanation:

> Personal gallantry on several occasions during a hard-fought campaign on the part of certain Majors in command of regiments was no more than their duty, and should be recognized by other rewards than the Victoria Cross... A captain or a subaltern might stake his life and lose it for the sake of the decoration without playing with the lives of others, but a field officer in command risked not only his own life, but possibly the success of the operation devolving upon him, by an unnecessary display of personal valour.[23]

Likewise, when then Lieutenant Colonel Ian Hamilton was recommended the second time for a VC in 1899 for his leadership in the assault on Elandslaagte in South Africa, it was denied on grounds of his rank; his notification of this pointed out that the award was meant for younger men.[24] Ironically, Hamilton had been recommended for a Cross on 27 February 1881 as a 28-year-old subaltern for the defense of Majuba Hill. The recommendation was rejected on the grounds that the act was really not quite VC material and as a young man he would have many opportunities in the future to earn recognition.[25] It is evident that even though it was confirmed in statute that all ranks had equal footing, in practice lieutenants had an edge over other ranks.

It is interesting to note that in the second instance that Hamilton was recommended Sir Redvers Buller was the officer who decided not to forward the recommendation to higher authorities. Buller also refused to approve Hamilton's promotion in South Africa.[26] This situation brings up the question of inter-Army politics, as Buller was a member of the Ashanti Ring while Hamilton was a partisan of Roberts. Buller disliked Hamilton, and the two were diametric opposites when it came to style and character. While it would be tempting to link these disservices to 'ring politics,' it appears that in this case it was entirely personal dislike between two officers. There is no evidence other than this series of events to support the idea that the Cross had become a pawn between factions within the Army.

Among the enlisted men the distribution was far more equitable. Privates and their equivalent obviously formed the bulk of the other ranks, and it was to them the majority of the enlisted VCs came. Overall privates accounted for almost 55 percent of all enlisted awards and 29 percent of all pre-First World War VCs.

Only nine of the Victorian-era winners held a local, provisional or brevet rank at the time they won the award. There were four brevet majors, three brevet lieutenant colonels, one local lieutenant colonel and one provisional lance corporal. These nine Crosses represent 1.7 percent of the total pre-1904 awards. This ratio changed dramatically during the First World War.

Only ten nineteenth-century VC winners were members of the nobility at the time the award was won. This includes six with the designation 'the honourable,' two lords, one 'sir,' and one viscount. They represent 1.9 percent of the Victorian era winners. An additional 52 winners were later knighted. Three VC winners rose to the rank of earl after winning the Cross. In total 64 pre-1904 Cross winners were either connected with the nobility at the time they won the VC or were subsequently ennobled. This represents 12 percent of the total nineteenth-century VCs and indicates some influence by an 'old-boy' system, but not as much as might be thought, due to the high ratio of aristocratic officers in the forces. It must be pointed out that the Victoria Cross was not given out as a party favor by the Crown. Unlike the Order of the Bath, which had been conferred so frequently as to greatly dilute the distinction of the award, the Cross remained an exclusive fraternity. Proof of this can be seen in the coronation gala of Edward VII in 1901; of all the notables listed with minor alphabets appended to their names, only two bore the gothic initials 'V.C.' to indicate possession of the award.[27]

Clause XV of the warrant provided for the degradation of Cross winners (and in the case of enlisted men, the suspension of the £10 annual pension) in cases where the winner had been 'convicted of Treason, Cowardice, Felony or of any infamous Crime, or if he be accused of any such offence and doth not after a reasonable time surrender himself to be tried for the same.'[28] The Crown invoked this clause seven times during the reign of Victoria and once in the reign of Edward VII.

Private William Stanlake nearly ran foul of Clause XV in 1857. A sharpshooter, he volunteered to undertake a night reconnaissance of the

Russian positions near Inkerman. The intelligence he brought back allowed a successful surprise attack. However, he had since 'rendered himself unworthy of the honour by commission of theft.' The War Office recommended withholding the award 'until he shall have regained his character' through a course of good conduct.[29]

The Duke of Cambridge notified Panmure that in his – and the Queen's – opinion, the reward should be revoked entirely. The problem with that position was the nature of the legal proceedings in Stanlake's case. His commanding officer had not convened a general court martial, but rather dealt with the issue with company punishment. Thus, although Stanlake was an admitted thief, he had never been convicted of the offense and by the letter of the warrant was still eligible for the Cross. Her Majesty played by the rules and approved the grant of the award, but refused to present it to Stanlake in person as she had done all other winners then in the United Kingdom. The medal was forwarded to his commanding officer with stern instructions from Cambridge to explain why he was getting it from a colonel and not the Queen.[30]

Of the eight cases in which the Cross was revoked, seven were enlisted men. Private Valentine Bambrick won his Cross in the Mutiny for defending himself from the attack of three Ghazees, but lost it when he was convicted of assault and the theft of the medals of another soldier. It didn't help matters that the offense took place in an Aldershot brothel. After a controversial trial he was sentenced to three years penal servitude in December 1863. He hanged himself in his cell at Pentonville Model Prison on 1 April 1864.[31] Gunner James Colliss won his Cross at Maiwand in 1880 for drawing fire away from the wounded. He was convicted of bigamy in 1895 and stripped of the award.[32] Private Frederick Corbett tended a wounded officer under fire at Kafr Dowar, Egypt in 1882 to win his VC, which he sold immediately after his discharge at some point between 1882 and 1884. In 1884 he re-enlisted, joining the Royal Artillery. On 30 July 1884 he was convicted by a District Court Martial of being absent without leave, of theft, and of embezzling money from an officer.[33]

Private Thomas Lane was convicted of desertion, horse theft, and theft of government property and stripped of his medal on 7 April 1881. He had won a 'first in' Victoria Cross at the storming of the North Taku Fort on 8 August 1860 and had been the subject of a heated exchange between Sir Hope Grant and the home government, as he was one of the men to whom Grant had promised the VC on the spot.[34] Sergeant James McGuire won a VC at Kabul Gate in 1857 for quick thinking in an emergency. An artillery round detonated three ammunition boxes and set two more on fire. McGuire and Drummer Miles Ryan quickly tossed the burning boxes over the parapet before they too exploded, thus preventing further casualties among the packed troops at the gate. He was convicted of the theft of a cow back in Ireland, part of a family dispute that resulted in another controversial trial in December 1862.[35] Farrier Michael Murphy, along with Private Samuel Morely, protected a dismounted cavalry officer during the mopping up operations of the Indian Mutiny at Azumgurh, India, in 1858 to win Victoria Crosses. Murphy was also indirectly involved in one of the early test cases of establishing VC procedure and parameters, as Morely petitioned for his own VC shortly after the gazetting of Murphy's award. Murphy was stripped of his award in March 1872 on his conviction of the theft of ten bushels of oats.[36] The final enlisted man degraded from the Cross was Private George Ravenhill, who won his in yet another controversial engagement. He was one of the men recommended for the award by Redvers Buller in connection with the attempts to save Long's abandoned guns on 15 December 1899. The War Office revoked his VC upon his conviction of the theft of iron on 24 August 1908.[37]

Although there are some coincidences – three of the men stripped of the award were Irish, and three were involved in controversial or 'test-case' applications of the VC regulations – there is no evidence of any conspiracy at the War Office or the Palace to single these men out. All had been legally convicted of crimes prohibited in the warrant, and as the case of William Stanlake proves, the government played by the rules even if they didn't like it.

Only one officer recipient of the Victoria Cross has ever been stripped of the award. Midshipman Edward St John Daniel presents a fascinating and in some ways mysterious case. Daniel won his VC in the Crimea as aide-de-camp of Captain William Peel:

Midshipman Daniel was one of the volunteers from HMS *Diamond*, who, under the command of the captain [Peel] brought in powder to the battery from a waggon under very heavy fire, a shot having disabled the horses. On 5 November at the Battle of Inkermann he, as ADC to the captain, remained by his side throughout a long and dangerous day. On 18 June 1855 he was again with his captain in the first scaling party at the assault on the Redan binding up his superior officer's severely wounded arm and taking him back to a place of safety.[38]

Daniel was stripped of the award on 4 September 1861 for desertion and failure to answer court martial charges. The VC Registry being at the War Office, the Admiralty had to write the Secretary of State for War to have his name officially struck from the list. Initially the Navy tried to gloss over the case, stating only that Daniel was a deserter and thus was to be struck. The War Office asked for details of the offense before proceeding with the action, to which the Navy replied that Daniel had deserted rather than face trial on charges of a 'disgraceful offence.' At this point the official communications between the Admiralty and the War Office became quite circumspect. There was one cryptic comment that alluded to the degradation of Sir Eyre Coote from the Order of the Bath, noting that 'His case was like the present, a very bad one.'[39] Coote was degraded from the Order in 1816 on allegations of 'indiscretions' with schoolboys at the Bluecoat School. Here the War Office files at the Public Record Office stop.

Michael Daniels, PhD, a possible collateral relative of Midshipman Daniel, undertook a research project into the young officer's case. He reports the nature of the 'disgraceful offence' was described in a letter from Captain William Clifford of HMS *Victor Emanuel* (Daniel's commanding officer at the time of his desertion) to Rear Admiral Dacres, Captain of the Fleet and senior officer at Corfu, that Daniel had been arrested for 'taking indecent liberties with four of the Subordinate Officers of the *Victor Emanuel*.' His desertion may have been encouraged, as he absconded between the time of his arrest on 28 June 1861 and 10:00 p.m. the following night, when his absence was reported by the *Victor Emanuel*'s Master-At-Arms. In any case, it allowed the Navy to simply mark him down as a deserter and strike his name from the Navy List rather than go through an embarrassing public trial.[40]

The current warrant retains the provision that a winner may be struck from the list for serious offenses, but this clause has not come into play since Ravenhill's case in 1908. Shortly after the publication of the updated, post-First World War warrant in 1920 King George V's private secretary, Lord Stamfordham wrote: 'The King feels so strongly that, no matter the crime committed by anyone on whom the VC has been conferred, the decoration should not be forfeited. Even were a VC to be sentenced to be hanged for murder, he should be allowed to wear his VC on the scaffold.'

One subcategory of heroism does not appear in any of the above tables, perhaps the most difficult to quantify in all but the most blatant cases: Victoria Crosses granted as a result of command blunder. There are many instances in which hindsight reveals a command flaw or a poorly crafted battle plan that results in the men on the sharp end performing Herculean labors to survive the day. The Battles of Balaclava and Isandlwana come to mind without much effort. The phenomenon reached its epitome (or perhaps nadir) during the Boer War with the citation of the Honourable Frederick Sherston Roberts:

> On 15 December 1899 at the Battle of Colenso, South Africa, Lieutenant Roberts, with several others, tried to save the guns of the 14th and 66th batteries, Royal Field Artillery, when the detachment serving the guns had all become casualties or had been driven from their guns. Some of the horses and drivers were sheltered in a donga about 500 yards behind the guns and the intervening space was swept with shell and rifle fire. Lieutenant Roberts with two other officers helped to hook a team into a limber and then to limber up a gun. While doing so, he fell badly wounded and later died of his wounds.[41]

The citation is a direct contradiction of the eyewitness account given by Captain Walter Norris Congreve – for that matter it embellishes substantially Buller's original dispatch on the event. As discussed in the previous chapter, Buller changed official reality to atone for the order that killed Freddy Roberts. This practice was rare during the nineteenth century. The coming Great War would offer more opportunities as the Victorian ideal floundered to its death in 1914 and 1915.

## Six

## 1914: The Last Stand of the Thin Red Line

The ideals of Victorian heroism had been refined facing crazed Ghazis, fanatical Dervishes, and most recently obstinate Boers. Only the last had come close to technological parity, and even they could not hope to match the industrial might of the aroused British Empire. As the First World War began, Britain suddenly found itself propelled into a full-scale continental war against one of the foremost industrial powers of Europe. It was a conflict for which the British military establishment was scarcely prepared.

The British Army that embarked for the front in 1914 was still very much a colonial force. Despite the harsh lessons of the Boer experience, the only substantive changes in equipment and training were the adoption of an improved rifle, the Lee-Enfield Mk III (along with an emphasis on rapid, accurate musketry) for the Infantry, and new quick-firing 13 pr and 18 pr guns for the Artillery.[1] The Haldane reforms had established an Imperial General Staff, revamped the organization of the Territorial and Reserve Forces, and created an Expeditionary Force, but Haldane left the details of training and equipment to the General Staff – which saw to the return of the lance as an active service weapon and training manuals that included cavalry shock charges as a viable tactical alternative. The soldiers themselves had changed little; their officers still came from society's elite and the men from society's dregs. There had been a slight demographic shift in recruitment, with a lower percentage of Irish and a higher percentage of men with an English or Welsh background. The economic origins of the recruits, however, remained fairly consistent with the nineteenth-century pattern, with over 60 percent of the rank and file from the Medical Department's 'labourer' category regardless of geographic origins from 1865 to the turn of the century.[2]

## 1914: THE LAST STAND OF THE THIN RED LINE

The British Expeditionary Force (BEF) was also a pathetically small force in comparison to the juggernauts maneuvering across the fields of France and Belgium. The Haldane reforms had created a strike force for deployment in a European conflict, but it was a mere six divisions of infantry and one of cavalry. At the same time, this small force was thoroughly professional on the regimental level, and man for man had the best riflemen in the world.[3] The BEF proved its mettle in the opening battles of the 1914 campaign, but at a terrible cost in manpower and materiel. The shattered regiments that survived found themselves in an alien environment completely unlike their colonial experience; few of their enemies, from Afridi to Zulu, had ever possessed machine guns – much less artillery. As the winter of 1914 closed in and supplies dried up, the BEF resembled the thin red line of legend, bewildered and battered, but determined to hold fast.

The Victorian Army died in the mud of Flanders.[4] With it died the Victorian ideals of heroism. The survivors melted into the ranks of the citizen soldiers that swarmed the recruiting depots and from that amalgamation and its commanders came a new heroic paradigm, one suitable to the realities of barbed wire and poison gas and an industrial society waging total war. For the time that the thin red line survived, however, the old Victorian heroic standards remained intact.

The initial British war plan was a simple one that took into consideration the size and skill of the BEF. Upon a declaration of war, the BEF was to mobilize in all haste, cross the Channel, and take up a position on the French left. Pre-war projections envisioned a main German thrust along the Franco-German frontier; positioning the small but effective British Army on the flank would allow them the opportunity to deliver the decisive blow at the proper moment.[5] This deployment plan did not envision a German advance through the heart of Belgium. For diplomatic reasons the deployment was carried out despite the change in the strategic situation. The BEF found itself not in a position to outflank the German right, but rather in a position to be steam-rolled by the 300,000 men of General Alexander von Kluck's First Army.[6]

Being hung out to dry for political considerations was nothing new to the British Army. Despite the lackluster leadership of Sir John French, his staff saw to the efficient deployment of the BEF along the line of the Mons Canal by 23 August. The Victorian attitude toward the coming conflict was summed up in the report penned by *The Times* military correspondent, Lieutenant-Colonel Charles Reppington, on the eve of the battle. He described Mons as 'glorious country for fighting in, glorious weather, and a glorious cause. What Soldier could ask for more?'.[7] The ensuing battle and the long retreat from Mons was a different arena for the British regular, but the heroism displayed had direct counterparts in the imperial campaigns of the previous century.

The initial German assault on Mons consisted of five divisions attacking the British II Corps of two divisions commanded by Lieutenant General Horace Smith-Dorrien, an old India hand. The German attack must have seemed quite familiar to him; they advanced in tight ranks across open ground, as ignorant of the effect of concentrated firepower as any tribesman he had faced on the Northwest Frontier. Von Kluck's men suffered heavy casualties and the first assault was thrown back. They regrouped and a more extended order of attack advanced on the British line a half-hour later. This probe managed to find and dislodge the exposed flank of the British 3rd Division and turn the previously defensible perimeter of the British force into a dangerous salient.[8]

Despite the tremendous casualties inflicted by the defenders, the sheer weight of numbers worked against them; what had initially resembled Omdurman was rapidly turning into something more akin to Isandlwana. The point companies holding the bridge approaches suffered what for this early stage of the war were heavy losses, but still managed to hold on. There at the Nimy Bridge Lieutenant Maurice Dease, machine gun officer of the Royal Fusiliers, won the first Great War Victoria Cross. 'The gun fire was intense, and the casualties very heavy, but the lieutenant went on firing despite his wounds, until he was hit the fifth time and was carried away to a place of safety where he died.'[9] The second VC followed in short order, as Private Sidney Frank Godley took Dease's place at the gun and kept it firing until the position was overrun. In a final gesture of defiance, Godley smashed the firing mechanism and tipped the gun into the canal just before retiring:[10]

> We carried on until towards evening when the order was given for the line to retire. I was asked by Lieut. Steele to remain and hold the position while the retirement took place, which I did do, although I was very badly wounded several times, but I managed to carry on. I was on my own at the latter end of the action. Of course, Lieut. Dease lay dead by the side of me, and Lieut. Steele, he retired with his platoon. I remained on the bridge and held the position, but when it was time for me to get away I smashed the machine gun up, threw it in the Canal, and then crawled back on the main road where I was picked up by a couple of Belgian civilians and was then taken to hospital in Mons... I was being attended by the doctors... when the Germans came in and took the hospital.[11]

# 1914: THE LAST STAND OF THE THIN RED LINE 113

Both of these Crosses are reminiscent of those awarded during any number of nineteenth-century engagements – the forlorn hope holding out against overwhelming odds and defying the enemy at the very last by denying him the trophy of his victory:

> On 7 November 1900 in South Africa, Sergeant [Edward James Gibson] Holland kept the Boers away from two 12-pounder guns with his Colt gun. When he saw that the enemy were too near for him to escape with the carriage, as the horse was blown, he calmly lifted the gun off the carriage and galloped away with it under his arm.[12]

Many of the VCs earned in the coming months had nineteenth-century counterparts.

The German crossing of the canal and contact with the exposed flank of 3rd Division made the defensive position at Mons precarious. News that Lanrezac's Fifth French Army had suffered a defeat at Charleroi and commenced a general retirement that would leave the British force alone and completely exposed made the British position untenable. These factors, combined with the sheer numbers the Germans were able to throw into the line, prompted French's decision to pull back and reestablish contact with the French Fifth Army.[13] Two more VCs were won in attempts to blow bridges across the canal before pulling out.[14] Von Kluck's nose had been so thoroughly bloodied that he did not immediately follow up the withdrawal from Mons on 24 August.[15]

The fight at Mons had all the elements of standard Victorian heroism, desperate defense, personal sacrifice, and defiance of the enemy. There was even an opportunity to perform that most holy of preindustrial heroic acts – saving the guns – during the final pull out from the line at Elouges on the right of the II Corps:

> On 24 August 1914... when the flank guard was attacked by a German corps, Major [Ernest Wright] Alexander handled his battery against overwhelming odds with such conspicuous success that all his guns were saved notwithstanding that they had to be withdrawn by hand by himself and volunteers led by a Captain [Francis Grenfell] of the 9th Lancers. This enabled the retirement of the 5th Division to be carried out without serious loss. Subsequently, Major Alexander rescued a wounded man under heavy fire.[16]

Despite the fact that they were giving up ground, the BEF left Mons with its Victorian honor and heroic ideals intact.

The BEF split its route of march to avoid the narrow roads of the Mormal Forest, with I Corps passing to the east and II to the west of the wood.[17] Sporadic contact was maintained with German scouts; one night action at Landrecies resulted in the first VC for a soldier from I Corps. Part of the 3rd Battalion of the Coldstream Guards came under attack in a farmyard and during the firefight several straw sacks in the barnyard caught fire:

> On 25/26 August 1914 at Landrecies, France... The Lance-corporal [George Henry Wyatt] twice dashed out under very heavy fire from the enemy, only 25 yards away, and extinguished the burning straw, making it possible to hold the position. Later, although wounded in the head, he continued firing until he could no longer see owing to the blood pouring down his face. The medical officer bound up his wounds and ordered him to the rear, but he returned to the firing line and went on fighting.[18]

The incident has the same flavor as the VC won by Lieutenant Robert Hope Moncrieff Aitken during the Mutiny:

> On one occasion when the enemy had set fire to the Bhoosa stock in the Garden, the lieutenant, with other officers, cut down all the tents in order to stop the fire from spreading to the powder magazine that was there. This was done close to the enemy's loopholes under the bright light of the flames.[19]

Likewise Victorian in character were the Crosses won by men of the II Corps at Le Cateau. Turning at bay, Smith-Dorrien fought a costly delaying action to set von Kluck's pursuit back on its heels.[20] It also provided for another display of Victorian bravado, as the 37th Battery, Royal Field Artillery won three Crosses in the Korn Spruit tradition by galloping back to within 100 yards of the advancing German infantry to retrieve one of two guns that had been abandoned due to enemy fire.[21] They lost only one desperately needed team of horses and one gun crew in the process.[22]

Less fortunate were two companies of the King's Own Yorkshire Light Infantry. Serving as point defense for the fighting retreat they were cut off. Then:

Major [Charles Alix Lavington] Yate... when all other officers had been killed or wounded and ammunition exhausted... led his 19 survivors against the enemy in a charge in which he himself was severely wounded. He was picked up by the enemy and subsequently died as a prisoner of war.[23]

The government gave him a Victoria Cross for destroying what remained of his command in a pointless and futile gesture of defiance. It was a portent of things to come.

Not all gestures of defiance and perseverance were wasted or futile. A case in point is the action of 'L' Battery, Royal Horse Artillery, at Nery on 1 September. Le Cateau had forced another pause in German First Army operations and the gap between the retreating British and their pursuers had widened, inducing perhaps a hint of complacency in the BEF. Whether it was complacency or exhaustion, 'L' Battery and the 1st Cavalry Brigade were caught by surprise as they broke camp that morning.[24]

The Germans managed to deploy artillery, machine guns, and riflemen on a low ridge about 600 yards away under the cover of darkness. Enemy artillery knocked out three guns before they fired a shot; crews scrambled to control horses and bring the remaining three guns into service. Two managed a few rounds before bullets and shrapnel swept the gunners from their lanyards. The last gun, served by the remaining three gunners (Captain Edward Kinder Bradbury, Battery Sergeant-Major George Thomas Dorrell, and Sergeant David Nelson) maintained a one-sided duel with the 12 Krupp 77mm pieces on the ridge.[25] They fought for nearly an hour before a round finally put them out of commission, killing the captain. Their survival had occupied the attention of the German gunners, however, allowing the cavalry time to assemble and work their way around the German flank. Reinforcements arrived and helped push the Germans off the ridge, capturing all 12 of the abandoned 77s in the process.[26] The three artillerymen received the VC.

The British retreat continued into the first week of September. French's nerve was gone; convinced the BEF was far too damaged to be effective, he astounded his allies by announcing plans to disengage entirely and withdraw behind the Seine. Only the personal intervention of Lord Kitchener prevented the move and kept French in the field.[27]

While the commander of the BEF suffered a crisis of confidence, the same could not be said of the men he commanded. Many of their letters, diaries, and comments would do justice to a Henty hero. Many like Captain Julian

Grenfell, cousin of VC winner Francis Grenfell, fairly bristled to be at the Hun:

> I have not washed for a week, or had my boots off for a fortnight... it is all the best fun. I have never felt so well, or so happy, or enjoyed anything so much. It just suits my stolid health, and stolid nerves, and barbaric disposition. The fighting-excitement vitalizes everything, every sight and word and action. One loves one's fellow man so much more when one is bent on killing him.[28]

Nor was this eagerness confined to the officer corps. Corporal John Lucy recorded the reaction of his company to deployment at Mons: 'Keen as mustard, we set about overhauling our fighting gear, cleaning and re-cleaning our rifles and recently sharpened bayonets, easing up our cartridge clips, and looking forward eagerly to action.'[29]

Others were more philosophical in their approach to war, but every bit as enthusiastic. Rupert Brooke declared:

> Well, we are doing our best. Give us what prayers or cheers you can. It's a great life, fighting, while it lasts. The eye grows clearer and the heart stronger. But it's a bloody thing, half the youth of Europe blown through pain to nothingness, in the incessant mechanical slaughter of these modern battles.[30]

Even the shock of the 'mechanical slaughter' at Mons did little to dampen the spirit of the BEF, either in the field or in those regiments hastily assembled at home and thrust across the Channel:

> All through the night we march, rocking about on our feet from want to sleep, and falling fast asleep even if the halt lasted only a minute. Towards dawn we turned into a farm, and for about two hours I slept in a pigsty. [Later] an order was read to us that the men who had kept their overcoats were to dump them, as we were to advance at any moment. Strangely, a considerable amount of cheering took place then.[31]

Back in Britain news of the reverses in Belgium prompted Captain Lionel Crouch to write a remarkably prescient letter to his father from training camp:

I do think that the English people haven't yet realized the seriousness of this show. Every man of military age ought to be put into training *at once*. We have got to lick these chaps, and we are only playing at it at present. Our Expeditionary Force will be practically wiped out in a month, and more men must be sent. I don't take a pessimistic view of the ultimate result, but by our present shilly-shallying we are likely to keep the war lasting for years.[32]

The spirit of Henty was alive and well even in death. Jack Archer could have spoken the lines penned by Julian Grenfell:[33]

Darling Mother, Isn't it wonderful and glorious that at long last after long waiting the Cavalry have put it across the Boches on their flat feet and have pulled the frying pan out of the fire for the second time ... We are practically wiped out but we charged and took the Hun trenches yesterday. I stopped a Jack Johnson [a variety of German artillery shell] with my head and my skull is slightly cracked. But I'm getting along splendidly. I did awfully well. To-day I go down to Wimereux, to hospital, shall you be there? All all love. Julian of the 'Ard 'Ead.[34]

Grenfell died of infection on 26 May 1915. His account underscored that the dashing cavalry charge was a thing of the Victorian past.

Though the BEF remained in the line, French Marshal Joseph Joffre saw to it they did not face any stiff resistance when the retreat finally ended and they took to the offensive in the Battle of the Marne. Joffre's troop dispositions took into account his distrust of and disdain for Sir John French. The British were to hit the crease that had developed between the German First and Second Armies, a gap occupied only by three under-strength divisions of the German II Cavalry Corps. Even then only an emotional personal appeal from Joffre himself convinced French to turn and fight.[35] The British played only a minor part in turning the German offensive; their next intensive action would come on the River Aisne.

Even at this late stage, in the face of assaulting the prepared German positions on the Chemin des Dames Ridge above the Aisne, the Victorian ideal survived. The citation of Captain William Henry Johnston, Royal Engineers, was strikingly similar to that of Brevet Major Frederick C. Elton in the Crimea. Johnston's citation reads in part: 'On 14 Sep. 1914 at Missy, France, Captain Johnston worked with his own hands on two rafts on the River Aisne ... '[36] while Elton's reported that: ' ... he was command of a working party in the advanced trenches in front of the Quarries, encouraging his men to work under very heavy fire and even used a pick and shovel himself to set an example.'[37] Despite all the hardships of the campaign it was still remarkable for an officer to 'work with his own hands.'

Another Victorian characteristic of heroism was evident in the Army of 1914. During the nineteenth century special distinction was given to the loyal soldier who rescued a fallen officer. This tradition survived into the first years of the Great War:

> On 14 September 1914 at the battle of the Aisne, France, Private [Ross] Tollerton carried a wounded officer, under heavy fire, as far as he was able, into a place of greater safety. Then, although he himself was wounded in the head and hand, he struggled back to the firing line where he remained until his battalion retired. He then returned to the wounded officer and stayed with him for three days until they both were rescued.[38]

The BEF did not take the Chemin des Dames and the line in that sector solidified. Neither the German offensive nor the cobbled-together counter-attack achieved their objectives. French at this point wanted to move his force north-northwest for two main reasons. It was obvious the war was going to settle in for another year at the very least. Moving closer to the Channel ports would shorten and simplify his supply lines, with the additional benefit of denying those ports as bases for German naval operations, a potential that worried the Admiralty. Flanders also seemed to offer the possibility of a clearer field for cavalry maneuvers, which French still believed would be the decisive factor in the war.[39]

This proved to be a fateful decision. With the resignation of General Helmut von Moltke as chief of staff, 14 September 1914, General Eric von Falkenhayn became the top German commander on the Western Front.[40] Von Falkenhayn had three courses of action open to him as he took command: he could use the 6th army to bulk up the open flank of the 1st army on his right, he could push it on to the Channel coast, capturing strategic ports in the process, or he could use it to resume the offensive and attempt to envelope the Entente's left wing. He chose the third option.[41] French's shift placed him directly in the path of this new German offensive, and the place they met was Ypres.

And still the Victorian heroic ideal survived. Soldiers were rewarded for retrieving wounded comrades under fire.[42] Officers were commended for striding up and down the firing line, recklessly exposing themselves to the enemy to encourage and hearten their men.[43] There were some changes in terms of statistical distribution of the Crosses, however. During the last major conflict, the Boer War, roughly 40 percent of the Crosses awarded went to acts that somehow contributed to victory. The tenor of heroism was more aggressive in 1914, with some 56 percent of the medals going to war-winning acts. Whereas 53 percent of the Crosses in the Boer War went for some form of life-saving, only 30 percent of those in 1914 were earned for rescuing or tending the wounded.

Among the officers, captains proved to be the largest group of Cross winners, with just under 20 percent of the total VCs. They were second only to privates, the largest group overall, at 33 percent. During the nineteenth century most officer Crosses were earned by lieutenants. The shift from lieutenants to captains gathering more awards can be explained by the tactical structure of the BEF. In the colonial campaigns organization was looser and formations employed were smaller. In such an environment a subaltern was more likely to exercise greater authority and command responsibility, and thus be in the position to display the initiative required to win a Cross. This was not the case on the Western Front.

Surprisingly, the casualty statistics for the 1914 campaigns easily fall within the range established in the previous century, particularly those of the Boer War era, after posthumous VCs became a reality. Before 1890, 65–70 percent of winners per decade were not wounded in the process of winning the award. During the Boer War that figure dropped to just under 60 percent, with slightly over 30 percent wounded and 8 percent either killed in action or died of wounds. 1914 generated 50 percent unwounded, 24 percent wounded, and 19 per cent killed in action or died of wounds. Twice as many winners died in the process, but it must be remembered that the posthumous option was not available until well into 1900.

While in absolute percentages fewer 1914 heroes got through their exploits unscathed, during the nineteenth century a severely wounded man was unlikely to be recommended at all. With the relaxation of the posthumous restriction at the turn of the century soldiers severely wounded or killed outright could be safely recommended. Thus, the higher percentage of casualties in 1914 is probably a reflection of the administrative changes made in the Boer War rather than an indication of a rising standard of ruthlessness in heroism. That would come later.

This was not the only change in the works during the 1914 campaign. Even as the traditional paradigm of heroism gave a VC to Captain John Franks Vallentin for doing nothing more than getting shot in proper military fashion[44] new ideas about the role of the hero were forming. Officers like Lieutenant James Leach were being awarded for bayoneting the enemy personally, a practice frowned on in the Victorian Officer Corps. The officers in coming years would be expected to get their hands dirty.[45]

From 10 October to 22 November the British doggedly defended the key to the Channel Coast. The BEF had taken heavy casualties in battles of Mons, La Cateau, and the Aisne. The First Battle of Ypres (19 October–15 November 1914) bled it white: 58,155 men were killed or wounded during the defense of the Ypres sector. Many battalions were almost entirely destroyed.[46] In the words of the official history:

> In the British Battalions which fought from Mons to Ypres there scarcely remained with the colours an average of one officer and thirty men who had landed in August 1914. The Old British Army was gone beyond recall.[47]

Vestiges of the nineteenth-century hero still surfaced in 1915 and 1916, with purely symbolic acts winning Victoria Crosses; in the tradition of Piper George Findlater, who at Dargai in 1897 had been wounded in both legs but continued to skirl the troops forward:

> On 25 September 1915 near Loos and Hill 70, France, prior to an assault on enemy trenches and during the worst of the bombardment, Piper [Daniel] Laidlaw, seeing that his company was shaken with the effects of the gas, with complete disregard for danger, mounted the parapet and, marching up and down, played his company out of the trench. The effect of his splendid example was immediate and the company dashed to the assault. Piper Laidlaw continued playing his pipes even after he was wounded and until the position was won.[48]

The Victorian image in this case was a bit tarnished, as the chlorine gas giving so much trouble to Laidlaw's company had been released by the British Army. This attack took place before gas shells were available and the chemical agent had been dispersed from cylinders in the British lines through pipes laid out into no-man's-land. The wind was light and variable and in Laidlaw's sector blew the gas back into the British lines.[49]

The Scots provided one last musical VC in 1916, When on 1 July Drummer Walter Potter Ritchie;

> on his own initiative, stood on the parapet of an enemy trench and, under heavy machine-gun fire and bomb attacks, repeatedly sounded the 'Charge' thereby rallying many men of various units who, having lost

their leaders were wavering and beginning to retire. He also, during the day, carried messages over the fire-swept ground.[50]

Ritchie's last tattoo notwithstanding, the Victorian Army was a thing of the past by the end of 1914:

> There is not much left of the old Army and the new campaign is going to be fought and won by a great half-trained National Army – where you've got to take what you can get and not laugh at people for being a certain class or making fools of themselves. But if the old Army is going to be worth its salt and remain the backbone of the show, it's got without jealousy and in humbleness to allow itself to be absorbed into a less efficient whole, and have amateurs put over them and see daily laughable mistakes and old lessons relearnt in bitterness and go on helping without superior bearing. Anyone who doesn't recognize the above is either not rising to the occasion or anything but a self-satisfied self-seeker. We've all got to simply sacrifice anything for an *esprit d'armee*. The end of the war will depend on it.[51]

As these troops and their commanders floundered toward a new tactical doctrine to deal with the conditions of the Western Front, a new heroic paradigm would be imposed by industrial-scale warfare.

While the Victorian ideal died on the Western Front, it did manage to survive for a time in other arenas of the war. In the Royal Flying Corps and on the fringes of empire the pattern of the past managed to prevail until swept away in the bureaucratic standardization that followed the war. In the air the new technology of flight somehow conferred an almost mystical, romantic aura of heroism on the brave aviator.

The status of the military flier in the public mind was summed up by no less than Herbert George Wells:

> Every aviator who goes up to fight, I don't mean to reconoitre but to fight, will fight all the more gladly with two kindred alternatives in his mind, a knighthood or the prompt payment of a generous life assurance policy to his people. Every man who goes up and destroys either an aeroplane or a Zeppelin in the air should, I hold, have a knighthood if he gets down alive.[52]

Wells and the general public overestimated the offensive capacity of aircraft in the Great War, where the primary contribution of aviation was the very reconnaissance so denigrated by Wells. The ability to range far over enemy lines, photograph trench systems, spot troop concentrations and supply buildups, and later accurately spot for the artillery, proved invaluable during the course of the war, and observer aircraft consistently outnumbered all other types for the duration of the conflict. It was not, however, duty as glamorous as the fighter pilot's.[53]

Wells's statement captures another aspect of the popular conception of the heroic flier. It was appropriate for Wells to mention a knighthood for the successful air warrior, for in the eyes of many the aviator was a modern incarnation of the age of chivalry or the dashing cavalryman of the Victorian era.[54] The mechanics of flight dictated that the fighter pilot, the lone warrior, was to be the hero of the skies. The pilot had to be an individual, fighting an individual duel with another individual. Here was the opportunity for both style and sportsmanship, far above the anonymous squalor of the trench troglodytes.[55] As Billy Bishop observed:

It was the mud, I think, that made me take to flying. I had fully expected that going into battle would mean for me the saddle of a galloping charger, instead of the snug little cock-pit of a modern aeroplane. The mud, on a certain day in July 1915, changed my whole career in the war.[56]

The Crosses conferred on airmen reflect this attitude. Despite the overwhelming usefulness of observation missions, only one VC went solely for reconnaissance The rest went to fighter pilots for showing good form. Some were direct holdovers from the Victorian era:

On 20 March 1917 in Egypt, during an aerial bomb attack, a pilot was forced to land behind enemy lines, with hostile cavalry approaching. Lieutenant [Frank Hubert] McNamara, seeing the situation, came down through heavy fire to the rescue, despite the fact that he himself was wounded. He landed about 200 yards from the damaged plane, and the pilot climbed into his machine, but owing to his injury he did not keep it straight and it turned over. The two officers extricated themselves, set fire to the machine and made their way back to the damaged one, which they succeeded in starting. Finally, Lieutenant McNamara, although weak from loss of blood, flew the machine back to the aerodrome 70 miles away.[57]

# 1914: THE LAST STAND OF THE THIN RED LINE 123

Compare McNamara's act to that of Lord William Beresford:

On 3 July 1879 at Ulundi, Zululand, during the retirement of a reconnoitering party, Captain Lord William Beresford went to the assistance of an NCO of the 24th Regiment, whose horse had fallen and rolled on him. The Zulus were coming in great numbers, but Lord William, with the help from a sergeant of the Frontier Light Horse, managed to mount the injured man behind him. He was, however so dizzy that the sergeant, who had been keeping back the advancing Zulus, gave up his carbine and, riding alongside helped to hold him on. They finally reached safety.[58]

Had McNamara been on horseback his citation could easily have come from the nineteenth century. As it stands, the citation is a bit suspicious: if the 'hostile cavalry approaching' was an immediate threat, how did McNamara and his unnamed companion have time to take off, crash, and then get to and repair the other aircraft and fly away to safety without coming under attack?

Showing 'good form' was an important aspect of the early VCs in the nineteenth century, even if the act did not accomplish much in concrete terms:

On 20 September 1854 at the Battle of the Alma, Crimea, when the shot and fire from the batteries just in front of the battalion threw it into momentary disorder, it was forced out of its formation, becoming something of a huge triangle, with one corner pointing towards the enemy. A captain was carrying the Queen's Colour, which had the pole smashed and 20 bullet holes through the silk. Sergeant [James] McKechnie held up his revolver and dashed forward, rallying the men round the Colours. He was wounded in the action.[59]

The same attention to 'good form' can be seen in some of the early air VCs:

On 7 November 1915, second Lieutenant [Gilbert Stuart Martin] Insall, on patrol in a Vickers fighter, engaged in the enemy machine, the pilot of which was eventually forced to make a rough landing in a plowed field. Seeing the Germans scramble out preparing to fire, the Lieutenant dived to 500 feet and his gunner opened fire, whereupon they fled. After dropping an incendiary bomb on the German aircraft he flew through heavy fire, at 2,000 feet over the enemy trenches. The Vickers' petrol tank was hit, but the Lieutenant managed to land near a wood 500 feet inside Allied lines and he and his gunner, after repairing his machine during the night, flew back to base.[60]

Insall managed to force down one airplane and in turn get shot down himself, but he did so with good form.

These two aerial citations illustrate one of the intrinsic problems of heroism in the air. The aviators of the First World War operated beyond the scope of the traditional command structure and the mechanism for recommendation. In many cases, particularly with the more flamboyant fliers, they flew alone and their exploits lacked any corroboration:

> On 2 June 1917 near Cambrai, France, Captain [William] Bishop, patrolling independently, flew to an enemy aerodrome where several machines were standing with their engines running. One of the machines took off, but Captain Bishop fired at very close range and it crashed. He fired at and missed the second, but his fire made the pilot swerve and hit a tree. Two more aircraft then took off – he emptied his Lewis gun into the forward fuselage of the first and it crashed. He then emptied a full drum into the fourth machine which had come up behind him and it dived away. Captain Bishop then flew back to his station.[61]

This VC was given on the strength of his squadron commander's recommendation; there were no witnesses to the act. At the time there were rumors that Bishop, a Canadian, had inflated his claims of victory, if not manufactured it from the whole cloth. It has been alleged that the Royal Flying Corps was well aware of the rumors of Bishop's fabrications, but turned a blind eye in the interests of maintaining an amicable relationship with the Canadian military establishment.[62] This problem with respect to aerial acts of heroism came under sharp scrutiny at the end of the war.

At the same time that flamboyant fliers like Bishop were rising to do single combat in their airborne steeds, the RFC was in the process of becoming the Royal Air Force and developing a rudimentary tactical doctrine.[63] The later Crosses reflect this shift, as they reward more than a single victory and the actions performed have some concrete military merit:

> During the period 8 August to 8 October 1918 over France, Captain [Andrew Frederick Wheatherby Beauchamp-] Proctor was victorious in 26 air combats, but from his first victory in November 1917 in all he destroyed 22 enemy aircraft, 16 kite balloons and drove down a further 16 enemy machines completely out of control. In addition, his work in attacking enemy troops on the ground and in reconnaissance during the

advance of the Allied armies, commencing on eight August was almost unsurpassed in its brilliancy.⁶⁴

It was not until the final days of the war that a Cross went to a purely reconnaissance mission:

> On 10 August 1918 northeast of Roye, France, Captain [Ferdinand Maurice Felix] West, who had spent the two previous days on reconnaissance patrols and attacking the enemy from tree level, found a huge concentration of troops and transport. He had noted the strength of the enemy formation when he was attacked by several German scouts, receiving five bullets in his left leg which was partially severed. In a rapidly weakening state and in great pain he managed to bring his aircraft back to safety, and on landing, despite waves of unconsciousness, insisted on giving his report before being taken to hospital.⁶⁵

While the air provided an environment for the Victorian ideal to continue past its demise on the ground, only 16 of the 633 Crosses won during the Great War went to aviators. They represent only 2.5 percent of the total, and far too few to preserve the nineteenth-century ideal intact. At any rate, as may be seen from the later citations, the RAF was on its way toward developing a more utilitarian, modern conception of heroism as the war drew to a close.

The Royal Navy, likewise, garnered few VCs during the war. Only 51 of the 633 First World War Crosses went to the Navy, 8 percent of the total. Unlike the nineteenth century, almost half went to actions at sea, with 25 given for maritime combat. Amphibious operations accounted for another 14, and only seven went for combat purely ashore in the tradition of the Naval detachments of the Crimea and the Mutiny. Two naval aviators won Crosses and three more came from river operations in Mesopotamia. In the main the Royal Navy rewarded tenacity and audacity:

> On 31 May 1916, at the Battle of Jutland, Commander [The Honourable Edward Barry Stewart] Bingham of HMS *Nestor*, led his division in their attack, first on enemy destroyers and then on their battle cruisers. He finally sighted the enemy battle group and followed by the remaining destroyer of his division (HMS *Nicator*), he closed to within 3,000 yards of the enemy, in order to attain a favourable position for firing his torpedoes. While making his attack *Nestor* and *Nicator* were under the concentrated fire

of the secondary batteries of the High Seas Fleet. *Nestor* was subsequently sunk.[66]

Like some of the nineteenth-century citations, it seemed not a matter of whether or not Bingham actually accomplished anything, but rather that he did so with style.[67] Some naval citations did not even require that. Petty Officer Ernest Herbert Pitcher, of Q-Ship [68] HMS *Dunraven* was awarded a VC by ballot, apparently for getting blown up:

> He and the rest of the crew waited while the battle went on overhead and all around them. When the magazine below them caught fire they took up cartridges and held them on their knees to prevent the heat of the deck igniting them and when the magazine finally blew up they were all blown into the air.[69]

Victorian sentimentality survived at sea:

> On 31 May 1916, at the Battle of Jutland, Boy First Class [John Travers] Cornwell, of HMS *Chester*, was mortally wounded early in the battle, but remained standing alone at a most exposed post, quietly awaiting orders, until the end of the action, with the gun's crew dead and wounded around him.[70]

The rank of 'Boy First Class' is a bit misleading, as Cornwell was 16 years old at the time. And while the phrase 'quietly awaiting orders' has a sort of noble tragedy to it, he would have been more use had he aided the wounded gunners around him.

The Victorian ideal also survived for a time in the sideshows of the colonial campaigns, but for a different reason. Here the campaigns were of a much smaller scale than those on the Western Front, and owing to the nature of the terrain and the opponents faced, were conducted in a more nineteenth-century fashion. Even here, however, the Great War altered the style of frontier heroism as the fighting continued on into its second and third years. The first 'sideshow' Cross earned went to Lieutenant John Paul Butler of the King's Royal Rifles, attached at the time to the Pioneer Company of the Gold Coast Regiment of the West Africa Field Force:

> On 17 November 1914 in the Cameroons, West Africa, Lieutenant Butler, with a party of 13 men went into the thick bush and attacked a force of about 100 of the enemy, including several Europeans, defeated them

and captured their machine gun and many loads of ammunition. On 27 December when on patrol duty with a few men, Lieutenant Butler swam the Ekam River, which was held by the enemy, alone and in the face of brisk fire. He completed his reconnaissance on the further bank and returned to safety.[71]

It compares nicely, if verbosely, to that of Samuel McGaw, gained in the Ashanti War:

On 21 January 1874 at the Battle of Amoaful, West Africa, Lance-Sergeant McGaw led his section through the bush in a most excellent manner and continued to do so throughout the day, although badly wounded in the engagement.[72]

This style continued into 1915 as the war spread to new environments and theaters of operation. The fringes of empire still had room for exploits impossible in northwestern Europe. Some manifestly carried the echoes of the White Man's Burden:

On 3 September 1915, near Maktau, East Africa, during a mounted infantry engagement, the enemy were so close that it was impossible to get the more severely wounded away. Lieutenant [Wilbur Taylor] Dartnell, who was himself being carried away wounded in the leg, seeing the situation, and knowing that the enemy's black troops murdered the wounded, insisted on being left behind, in the hope of being able to save the lives of other wounded men. He gave his own life in a gallant attempt to save others.[73]

Some directly echoed the Crimean War, particularly a pair coming out of the Mesopotamian campaign of 1915. Although the plan came from London, the troops came from the Indian Establishment, which had been thus far untouched by the momentous changes occurring on the Western Front.[74] The heroic paradigm they brought with them was straight out of the nineteenth century:

On 28 September 1915 during the advance on Kut-el-Amara, Mesopotamia, HMS *Comet*, commanded by Lieutenant-Commander Cookson, and other armed vessels, were ordered, if possible, to destroy an obstruction which had been placed across the river by the Turks. When they approached, very heavy rifle and machine-gun fire was open on them, and an attempt to sink the centre dhow by gun fire having failed, Lieutenant Commander Cookson ran *Comet* alongside and he himself jumped on the dhow with an axe and tried to cut the cables connecting it to the other two craft forming the obstruction. He was shot several times and died within a few minutes.[75]

This is the same idea Seaman Joseph Trewavas had 60 years earlier, although he was successful and survived the attempt:

On 3 July 1855 in the Straits of Genitchi, Sea of Azov in the Crimea. Seaman Trewavas of HMS *Beagle* was sent in a 4-oared gig to destroy a bridge, and so cut the Russians' main supply route. This was his third attempt, the first two having failed. As the gig ground against the bridge, Seaman Trewavas leapt out with an axe and began to hew away at the hawsers holding the pontoons together, and although the enemy kept up a heavy fire, particularly on Trewavas himself, he continued until his task was completed, and the two severed ends of the pontoon began to drift apart. He was wounded as he got back into the gig.[76]

Some were utterly out of place in the twentieth century:

On 12 April 1915 at Shaiba, Mesopotamia, Major [George Godfrey Massy] Wheeler took out his squadron in an attempt to capture a flag which was the centre-point of a group of the enemy who were firing on one of our pickets. He advanced, attacked the enemy's infantry with the lance, and then retired while the enemy swarmed out of hidden ground, and formed an excellent target for the Royal Artillery guns. On 13 April Major Wheeler led his squadron to the attack of the North Mound. He was seen far ahead of his men, riding straight for the enemy standards but was killed in the attack.[77]

Nothing could be more Victorian than trying to capture the enemy's colors, with a squadron of glittering lances at your back, no less!

Also Victorian were the two Crosses of the North West Frontier Province won in 1915:

On 5 September 1915 on the Northwest Frontier province, India, Private [Charles] Hull rescued an officer from certain death at the hands of the tribesmen. The latter's horse had been shot and private Hull took the officer up behind on his own horse, under heavy fire at close range, and galloped away to safety.[78]

Hull's citation is virtually identical to that of then Lieutenant-Colonel Redvers Buller, earned in 1879 at Inhlobana. Captain Eustace Jotham also won a Cross on the Frontier in 1915 for sacrificing his life while trying to rescue one of his men stranded during a skirmish with Khostwal tribesmen.[79]

This Victorian trend continued through 1916, with a special emphasis on lifesaving VCs during the Mesopotamian campaign. The operations in the Tigris-Euphrates basin that year generated 12 Crosses. Eight of them went for rescuing the wounded, and interestingly, in light of later developments on the Western Front, three of those went for recovering officers:

On 5 April 1916, during an attack, an officer was lying out in the open severely wounded about one hundred fifty yards from cover. Two men went out to his assistance and one of them was hit at once. Captain Buchanan immediately went out and with the help of the other man, carried the first casualty to cover under machine-gun fire. He then returned and brought in the other wounded man, again under heavy fire.[80]

The heroism recognized in the 1916 Mesopotamian campaign in general indicates a very colonial, Victorian concept on the part of the recommending officers. Fully 75 percent of the 1916 VCs earned in Mesopotamia went for lifesaving. As will be shown in subsequent chapters, this was more than twice the rate for lifesaving on the Western Front during 1915 and 1916. Defensive actions accounted for 12.5 percent and another 12.5 percent were won in an abortive attempt to resupply the garrison at Kut by river.[81] There were no Crosses won for offensive actions.

This changed in 1917. The humiliating fall of Kut on 29 April 1916 prompted London to take control of the operation and reshuffle the Indian command structure. In the process they promoted divisional commander Major-General Sir Frederick Stanley Maude to overall command.[82] Maude wanted to erase the stain of Kut and managed to convince Sir Charles Munro, the new Commander-in-Chief, India, of the need for aggressive prosecution of the Mesopotamian campaign.[83]

The new standard of aggressive command is reflected in the tenor of the heroism submitted for official endorsement. Ten VCs were won during the 1917 Mesopotamian operations. Seven of these went to war-winning acts. The aggressiveness of the offensive actions could be quite impressive:

> On 21 April 1917, Private [Charles] Melvin's company were waiting for reinforcements before attacking the front line trench, but he rushed on by himself over ground swept by rifle and machine-gun fire. On reaching the trench and having killed one or two of the enemy, he jumped in and attacked the rest with his bayonet. Most of the enemy then fled but not before Private Melvin had killed two more and disarmed eight unwounded and one wounded. He bound up the wounded man and took him and his other prisoners back to an officer before reporting back to his platoon sergeant.[84]

The defensive Crosses won in this phase of the campaign also represented a new standard of aggressive leadership.

> On 22 April 1917, Lieutenant [John Reginald Noble] Graham was in command of a machine-gun section which came under very heavy fire. When his men became casualties he insisted on carrying the ammunition and although twice wounded, he continued in control and with one gun opened accurate fire on the enemy. This gun was put out of action and he was again wounded and forced to retire, but before doing so he disabled his gun and then brought a Lewis gun into action with excellent effect until all the ammunition was expended. He was wounded yet again and was forced again to retire.[85]

Maude clearly wanted soldiers who would take the war to the enemy, and was willing to reward those who did so. That having been said, it must also be noted that fully 30 percent of the Crosses won in Mesopotamia in 1917 went for life saving, far above the 13 percent for 1917 overall. The traditions of earlier eras died more slowly in the fringe campaigns of the war.

Even in 1918 the Crosses won on the periphery, while reflecting the newer attitude of aggressive heroism, often still had a whiff of the nineteenth century about them:

> On 23 September 1918 on the West Bank of the River Jordan, Palestine, when his squadron was charging a strong enemy position, Ressaidar Badlu Singh realized that heavy casualties were being inflicted from a small hill occupied by machine-guns and 200 infantry. Without any hesitation he collected six other ranks and with entire disregard of danger he charged and captured the position. He was mortally wounded on the very top of the hill while capturing one of the machine-guns single-handed, but all the guns and infantry had surrendered to him before he died.[86]

Such an act would have been impossible on the Western Front, and indeed even on the fringes of the war they had developed a high cost, as the ressaidar discovered.

The Victorian ideal of heroism could not survive in the new environment of warfare. Machine guns, barbed wire, and massive troop formations killed the concept quickly on the Western Front. It did manage to survive a bit longer in the more traditional environments of Africa and the Middle East, and remained relatively intact in aerial and naval operations. Even in these arenas the war took its toll, however, and the standards of heroism changed as the war progressed. These changes were not the product of the sideshow campaigns. The war would not be won or lost in Africa, Palestine, or Mesopotamia, in the air or on the sea, but on the Western Front. It is there we must look for the dynamics that shaped the modifications of the heroic ideal and drove the post-war rewriting of the regulations controlling the Victoria Cross.

# Seven

# The Middle Parts of Fortune: Heroism in Evolution, 1915–1916

The campaign of 1914 was a brutal awakening for the BEF. Virtually every pre-war assumption held by even the most dour military savant proved wrong. The manpower needs, material expenditures, and the number of casualties produced by industrial-scale warfare shocked the nation, but at the same time inspired a spirit of national self-righteousness that sent hundreds of thousands to the recruiting stations. The rush of volunteers was gratifying, but it would take more than a year to train, equip, and ship the troops to the front in any appreciable numbers. The campaigns of 1915 were thus fought with the remains of the pre-war standing army, augmented by men of the Territorial Force who had volunteered for service outside the British Isles and bolstered by drafts from all corners of the empire.

These troops, whether regulars, Territorials, or drawn from the Indian establishment, were still part of the old order. Even the new levies arriving from Australia and New Zealand had a disproportionate leavening of 'old sweats' in the ranks; 43 percent of the First Australian Division had seen military service before the war.[1] They correspondingly brought with them the nineteenth-century's ideals of heroism, though circumstances soon dictated its supercession.

The biggest problem on the Western Front was the lack of a tactical doctrine to deal with the stalemate. Both 1915 and 1916 were years of experimentation, adaptation, and reorganization for all the combatants' armies, as the industrial resources of Europe were tapped for manpower and technology. The British Army was no exception. The fighting of 1915 was the last gasp of the Haldane-era army; 1916 was the baptism of Kitchener's New Armies. New commanders floundered toward new doctrines, would-be boffins introduced new gadgets guaranteed to send the Hun reeling, and bewildered clerks learned which end of the rifle was the dangerous part.² The ideal of heroism began evolving from its Victorian roots into a twentieth-century ideal as harsh and ruthless as the war that spawned it.

One aspect of the Victoria Cross that was not exactly new was using the award to atone for a guilty conscience. Redvers Buller had done as much for Freddy Roberts. The command incompetence and consequent wastage of the Great War gave many opportunities for commanders to express remorse through official channels. In March 1915 the lost possibilities of Neuve Chapelle – the lack of coordination and the failure to take Aubers Ridge – provide the starting point for the changes afoot for heroism:

> For three days and nights none of us got a wink of sleep, our nerves strung to the highest pitch waiting to charge every minute. We were in the trenches acting as a covering force to our 'regular' comrades, who attacked the German lines on Thursday morning; the 1st King's Liverpool's in that charge lost 200 men and officers, among the latter archdeacon Madden's son. Other regiments suffered heavily too, yet by their pluck our brave lads achieved their aim. Critics say Mons and Ypres were nothing to it. An inferno of artillery and rifle fire for hours. Our own trench was blown to pieces in parts, we had many wounded, and ten killed, how any of us lived through it is a marvel. We were all praised by the 'Regular Army' officers for our courage and the way we helped bring in the wounded, some of us being specially mentioned for decorations. I did my share in bringing in and succouring the wounded, and earned my Captain's praise. It is impossible to describe the scene, dead piled up in front, men crawling in with limbs blown off, and other horrible wounds. The Germans suffered just as heavily, though. Shall never forget these last few days, never. Every man who took part in it deserves the VC.³

At the Battle of Neuve Chapelle, Corporal Cecil Reginald Noble and Company Sergeant-Major Harry Daniels received Crosses with almost identical citations:

> On 12 March 1915 at Neuve Chapelle, France, when the advance of the battalion was impeded by wire entanglements and by very heavy machine-gun fire, Company Sergeant Major Daniels and another man [Noble] voluntarily rushed in front and succeeded in cutting the wires. They were both wounded at once, and the other man later died of his wounds.⁴

The citations neglected to mention that the entanglement in question was the British barbed wire directly in front of their own trenches. D Company of the 2nd Battalion, Rifle Brigade had been ordered over the top into the teeth of concentrated enemy fire and their own entanglements. Noble and Daniels were not cutting their way through German field fortifications, but rather through the sheer bloody-mindedness of their company commander, Lieutenant Mansel.[5]

One event of 1915 had quite far-reaching Victoria Cross consequences, the 'Six VCs Before Breakfast' awarded to the 1st Battalion of the Lancashire Fusiliers for the Gallipoli landing on 25 April 1915.

The landings at Gallipoli have been almost universally condemned as one of the most poorly executed operations of the war.[6] The spearhead of the landing was the 29th Division, commanded by Major General Sir Aylmer Hunter-Weston. Along with virtually every other unit taking part in the landing at W Beach, the Lancashires took heavy losses (some 50 percent of the battalion were killed or wounded) wading ashore and consolidating a beachhead.[7] At about 1400 hours they were joined by Colonel O. C. Wolley-Dod, a Lancashire officer currently serving as Hunter-Weston's chief of staff. Perhaps at Wolley-Dod's suggestion, a few days later Hunter-Weston directed the 1st Battalion's commanding officer to submit six names for the VC. After consulting with 'the officers who happened to be with him,' Major H. O. Bishop submitted Captains Richard Raymond Willis and Cuthbert Bromley, Sergeants Alfred Joseph Richards and Frank Edward Stubbs, Lance Corporal John Elisha Grimshaw, and Private William S. Keneally.[8]

Hunter-Weston forwarded the recommendations to the theatre commander, General Sir Ian Hamilton, who passed them on to the War Office with his own endorsement.[9] Hamilton was quite taken with the 29th Division, on several occasions remarking his admiration for their exploits and general heroism, going as far as writing up the entire division in dispatches on 12 May 1915.[10]

There were some immediate problems with Hunter-Weston's recommendation. It read as if he himself had accompanied the Fusiliers:

> Their deeds of heroism took place under my own eyes. As we approached the beach in the first light of morning the lines of high barbed wire entanglements could be seen stretched across the beach. From the beach the ground sloped up gradually to the North, very steeply to the right (East) and precipitously to the left (West)....
>
> Where all did so marvelously it is difficult to discriminate, but the opinion of the Battalion is that Captain Bromley and Captain Willis are

the officers, and sergts: Stubbs and Richards, corpl: Grimshaw and private Keneally, are the N.C.O.s and men, to whom perhaps the greatest credit is due. As the representatives therefore of the Battalions as well as for the deeds of great gallantry performed by them themselves under my own eyes, I strongly recommend these Officers, N.C.O.s., and men for the Victoria Cross.[11]

There are some immediate problems with this statement. Hunter-Weston observed the action on W Beach from his command ship HMS *Euryalus*, at least 2000 and more probably about 6000 yards offshore, keen eyesight indeed to pick out and note individual acts of heroism.[12] The letter itself contradicts the opening sentence by attributing the selection of nominees to the consensus of the battalion rather than his own determination.

This is not to say that he had been entirely random, but rather made his nominations according to an investigation of the circumstances surrounding the actions of the battalion. Richards, it was revealed, continued to lead his men forward despite a broken leg. Grimshaw managed to keep control of his section and likewise lead them through the wire. Keneally crawled up and tried to cut a gap in the entanglements, with no report as to his success in the endeavor. Bromley 'perhaps did more than anyone else in getting the men forward through the entanglements and up the cliff,' while Willis 'shouted to the men to get up and rush through the gap a few yards away and they would not move.'[13] Stubbs was not mentioned in the report. It is apparent that the officers and men had been picked by their peers on the basis of existing pre-battle respect and a certain amount of battlefield leadership.

On 11 June 1915 Military Secretary Frederick Spencer Robb kicked the six recommendations back to Hamilton on the grounds that they violated the provisions of Clause XIII of the VC warrant, that of elective recommendations.[14] The clause stipulated that in such cases:

for every Troop or Company of Soldiers one Officer shall be selected by the Officers engaged for the Decoration; and in like manner one Petty Officer or Non-commissioned Officer shall be selected by the Petty Officers and Non-commissioned Officers engaged; and two Seamen or Private Soldiers or Marines shall be selected by the Seamen or Private Soldiers or Marines engaged respectively for the Decoration; and the names of those selected shall be transmitted by the Senior Officer in Command of the Naval Force Brigade Regiment Troop or Company to the Admiral or General Officer Commanding who shall in due manner confer the Decoration as if the acts were done under his own eye.[15]

For Hunter-Weston to forward a total of six VCs was excessive. That he had not submitted one officer, one NCO and two privates violated the elective formula. Hamilton queried Hunter-Weston, who replied by selecting Captain Willis, Sergeant Richards and Private Keneally of those nominated in the original recommendation. He ran into a problem with the naming of a second private; the surviving privates of the battalion still wanted to put forward Corporal Grimshaw instead of a second private. He thus proposed that the War Office accept their evaluation that Grimshaw's 'gallantry is more deserving of the V.C. than that of any private.'[16]

In his decision on the matter, Robb in a sense violated Clause XIII himself. He refused to accept the nomination of Corporal Grimshaw and recommended only Willis, Roberts and Keneally to His Majesty for the award, thus depriving the Lancashire Fusiliers of one elective VC to which they were entitled. Grimshaw eventually got the Distinguished Conduct Medal instead of the VC.[17] There the matter sat until administrative changes altered the environment.

In 1916 O. C. Wolley-Dod was promoted to Brigadier and named Inspector of the Infantry in England. F. S. Robb was replaced as Military Secretary by Lieutenant-General Francis Davies, who had succeeded Hunter-Weston in command of the 29th Division at Gallipoli when the latter collapsed from exhaustion in July 1915. In late 1916 Wolley-Dod approached Davies as to the possibility of reopening the case.[18]

Davies examined the circumstances and advanced the possibility that the wrong clause had come into play in the decision handed down by his predecessor. He pointed out that the phrase 'Their deeds of heroism took place under my very eyes' may have indicated Hunter-Weston's intent to confer the VCs on the spot, as provided in Clause VII of the Warrant – in which case there was no statutory limit to the number of provisional bestowals by the theatre commander, Ian Hamilton. That Hamilton had forwarded the recommendations through formal channels complicated the matter, but it appeared to Davies that there was a case for giving Crosses to Captain Bromley – who had drowned in the *Royal Edward* in August 1915 – and Corporal Grimshaw – who had gotten a DCM in place of the VC.[19]

He ran his idea past the Deputy Chief of the Imperial General Staff, General Sir Robert Dundas Whigham, the Assistant Military Secretary, Colonel Malcolm Graham, and the Permanent Secretary at the War Office, Sir Reginald Brade. All replied in affirmative, with Brade suggesting that since there was more than one company involved, logically there could be more awards. The Military Secretary pointed out that there was an additional soldier, Sergeant Stubbs, in the original recommendation; the Deputy

Chief recommended that all three men get the VC. With the approval of the Secretary of State for War Lord Derby, the names were forwarded to the King, who approved the awards on 15 March 1917.[20] This solved the controversy as far as the Lancashire Fusiliers were concerned, but as we shall see in Chapter 9, the issue had far reaching implications.

The wastage and frustration of Neuve Chapelle and Gallipoli set the pattern for the remainder of 1915. The Gallipoli Campaign by early June bogged down into a Western Front-style trench slugging match, ending any hope of a decisive blow on the Dardanelles.[21] Hope was also dashed in France and Belgium. In April the Germans attacked the Ypres salient using gas for the first time, driving the Canadians and French back after weeks of hard fighting and high casualties.[22] Douglas Haig tried (and failed) again to take Aubers Ridge in mid-May, soaking up 11,629 casualties in the first day's assault alone. Another 16,648 British troops fell in the abortive attack on Festubert near the end of the month.[23] Following an equally futile assault on Givenchy in mid-June, French, Haig, and the BEF went dormant for the summer, having exhausted both their manpower and their munitions.[24] Joffre demanded their cooperation in the French fall push, the British portion of which came to be known as the Battle of Loos.[25] Between late September and early October the BEF lost 50,380 men killed and wounded. Total British casualties to this point in the war were over 512,000, of which some 200,000 were either killed or missing in action.[26]

The British high command had precious little to show for the profligate expenditure of life that accompanied their efforts. Despite some local successes at Neuve Chapelle and Loos, there had been no decisive breakthrough. In 1914 the British soldier had shown an aggressive nature beyond that exhibited in the nineteenth century. This trend continued into the early months of 1915, but it is also evident that the soldiers did not appreciate being spent like water. The aggressiveness of heroism exhibited in the earlier months tapered off as the fruitless offensives continued (Table 7.1). As war-winning acts dwindled, particularly those listed in the offensive category (capture, attack, assault, etc.) the humanitarian categories rose to take up the slack. Although it is probably a statistical anomaly, it is interesting to note that while the percentage of Victoria Cross incidents involving saving the life of an enlisted man rose from 15 percent in the first quarter to 53 percent in the last, saving officers rose only from 0 percent to 13 percent.

While these figures do reflect a higher standard of aggressiveness in the Army as opposed to the nineteenth century, there is a marked decline in the willingness of soldiers to expose life and limb for commanders who had

Table 7.1  Acts winning the Victoria Cross, 1915: winners by quarter

| Quarter<br>Total | Jan.–Mar.<br>13 | | April–June<br>50 | | July–Sept.<br>39 | | Oct.–Dec.<br>15 | | 1915 Total<br>117 | |
| --- | --- | --- | --- | --- | --- | --- | --- | --- | --- | --- |
| # Awarded | Raw | % | Raw | % | Raw | % | Raw | % | Raw | % |
| War-Winning | 11 | 85 | 37 | 78 | 25 | 64 | 5 | 34 | 80 | 68 |
| – Offensive | 8 | 61 | 19 | 38 | 11 | 28 | 4 | 27 | 42 | 36 |
| – Defensive | 1 | 8 | 12 | 24 | 7 | 18 | 1 | 7 | 21 | 18 |
| – Symbolic | 0 | 0 | 2 | 4 | 2 | 5 | 0 | 0 | 4 | 3 |
| – Secondary | 2 | 15 | 6 | 12 | 5 | 13 | 0 | 0 | 13 | 11 |
| Humanitarian | 2 | 15 | 10 | 20 | 13 | 33 | 10 | 66 | 35 | 30 |
| – Enlisted | 2 | 15 | 8 | 16 | 11 | 28 | 8 | 53 | 29 | 25 |
| – Officer | 0 | 0 | 2 | 4 | 2 | 5 | 2 | 13 | 6 | 5 |
| Symbolic | 0 | 0 | 1 | 2 | 1 | 3 | 0 | 0 | 2 | 2 |
| Special | 0 | 0 | 0 | 0 | 0 | 0 | 0 | 0 | 0 | 0 |

demonstrated a willingness to pour them into battle with seemingly little regard to casualty figures. Second Lieutenant Lionel Sotheby was shocked by the attitude that greeted him upon arriving in France in January 1915:

> I boarded a Harfleur train at 7.30 P.M. & had a most interesting talk with some Tommies back from the front. I think they said they were from the Munsters, but am not sure... The stories they had to tell were very interesting & extremely hard to put down on paper. All 6 declared themselves fed up with the war, much to my surprise.[27]

Sotheby was not alone in seeing a great deal of war-weariness among the veterans of the trenches. Robert Graves was worried about the attitude displayed by the old sweats influencing the new levies:

> The few old hands who went through the last show infect the new men with pessimism; they don't believe in the war, they don't believe in the staff. But at least they would follow their officers anywhere, because the officers happen to be a decent lot. They look forward to a battle because that gives them more chances of a cushy one in the arms or legs than trench warfare.[28]

Both of these were either a diary entry or a letter home, not memoirs written after years of reflection on the 'bigger meaning' of the war. In both cases the arriving officers had seen enough lassitude in the ranks to comment on it as a problem early in 1915.

To Sotheby life in the trenches (even before he had experienced it) represented a certain kind of heroism in and of itself. Reflecting on those men who had suffered self-inflicted wounds or purposely exposed an extremity to enemy fire to 'catch a Blighty,' he could not bring himself to class them with the malingerers and deserters who had never seen the front:

> There can be no doubt that it needs & calls for exceptional endurance and fortitude to live through 36 hours & sometimes many days in a trench with mud to your knees, a drenching rain, perhaps a sharp frost, & little or no food, when there is exceptional vigilance on the enemy's part against relief & food supplies coming up. So people in England, if they hear of these people, should not condemn them without giving them a hearing as all people are not blessed with the same endurance & vitality.

The cure for such malaise was, in his opinion, 'an advance & none of this trench warfare.'[29]

The total casualties were on a scale Britain and the empire had never before experienced, but the casualty figures among the VC winners for 1915 were not appalling. In fact, when the advances in medical treatment and inclusion of posthumous recommendations are considered, the injury/death rates of winners are not that far off the nineteenth-century statistics.

The figures for the Boer War round out to 59 percent with no wound reported, 30 percent wounded, and 8 percent either died of wounds or killed in action, for a total casualty rate of 38 percent. Once again, it must be remembered that the posthumous alternative was not a possibility before 1900, and for the remainder of the Boer War it was a limited option. Only in the third quarter of 1915, which included the big push at Loos, did the figures show any real variance from the Boer War statistics (Table 7.2).

While these figures remain fairly close to the parameters established in South Africa they run higher than the casualty rate for the Army as a whole. During the course of the war the British Empire fielded 8,904,000 men. Of those, an average of 78 percent were in the combat arms during the course of the war. These troops sustained 2,174,675 combat casualties, generating a 31 percent casualty rate.[30] Thus, Victoria Cross winners at 47 percent sustained a higher rate than the rest of the combat troops.

The ratio of officer to enlisted Victoria Crosses remained fairly constant, with a brief aberration in the first quarter of 1915. In the nineteenth century the officer class averaged 46 percent of the VCs awarded. For

Table 7.2 The cost of courage, 1915: casualties per quarter

| Quarter<br>Total | Jan.–Mar.<br>13 | | April–June<br>50 | | July–Sept.<br>39 | | Oct.–Dec.<br>15 | | 1915 Total<br>117 | |
|---|---|---|---|---|---|---|---|---|---|---|
| # Awarded | Raw | % | Raw | % | Raw | % | Raw | % | Raw | % |
| No Wound | 8 | 61 | 30 | 60 | 15 | 38 | 9 | 60 | 62 | 53 |
| WIA | 2 | 15 | 9 | 18 | 15 | 38 | 2 | 13 | 28 | 24 |
| DOW | 1 | 8 | 5 | 10 | 2 | 5 | 2 | 13 | 17 | 14 |
| KIA | 2 | 15 | 6 | 12 | 7 | 18 | 2 | 13 | 17 | 14 |
| Total Casualties | 5 | 38 | 20 | 40 | 24 | 61 | 6 | 39 | 55 | 47 |
| Total Lethal | 3 | 23 | 11 | 22 | 9 | 23 | 4 | 27 | 27 | 23 |

the majority of 1915 this varied by no more than 6 percent in either direction. Between 1 January and 31 March officers gathered only 31 percent of the medals confirmed in that quarter. In the absence of declassified documents concerning recommendations there really is no way to explain this aberration; it may just be a statistical fluke.

Eleven percent of the awards earned in 1915 went to men holding a temporary or acting rank. This is significantly higher than the Victorian 1.7 percent, and represents the increased lethality of the battlefield; more units, from squads to battalions, were led by men thrust into a command situation beyond their substantive rank. Most of the awards to temporary ranks in this early stage of the war went to the lower echelons in both the officer and other ranks, with three acting lance corporals and second lieutenants, and two acting lieutenants winning a VC. One acting sergeant, one acting captain, one acting major and one acting lieutenant colonel also earned the award. This pattern changed somewhat in 1916. The third year of the war saw 21 Crosses given to men holding temporary or acting rank, slightly over 25 percent of the year's total. The distribution of these Crosses changed as well, moving up the chain of command: there were three temporary second lieutenants as in 1915, but here there were four acting lieutenants and captains, three acting majors and four acting lieutenant colonels as well. Two acting corporals and one temporary chaplain rounded out the year.

Statistically, however, it is clear that the Army of 1915 was still trying to operate in accord with the Victorian heroic model. Modifications to this model had occurred and the morale of the rank and file was an obvious factor in the decline of aggressiveness, but the basic core remained intact. The problem was that the Army was running out of old sweats at an intolerable rate. The men who entered the Army on the outbreak of war were of a very different mold than the pre-war establishment.

While there were those who anticipated a quick end to the War, the top officers in the field and back in England knew from the outset that the BEF was no more than a token force as it sailed from the Channel ports in the fall of 1914. The War Office itself was vacant at the declaration of war. Despite some ministerial misgivings, the position was offered to Earl Kitchener that very afternoon.[31] Kitchener lost no time in calling for more troops; the next morning, 6 August, he sought and gained parliamentary approval to expand the Army by a further 500,000 men. Newspapers nationwide carried the appeal for volunteers the morning of 7 August.[32]

The young men of England responded admirably to the call for soldiers. At the same time, there was a strange mix of intensity and casualness to the response. Many did hurry off to enlist straightaway, fueled either by patriotic enthusiasm, righteous indignation, or the desire to escape the humdrum life of office or factory. Others hesitated, either due to a moral quandary or to settle business or family affairs before embarking on a new course.[33] In the Dominions, too, young men responded to the call of King and Empire:

When Alf Bastedo left Pembroke [Ontario, Canada] in August 1914 to join his regiment in Milton, Ramsey and Basil [Morris] had already discussed the matter of enlistment with their father. Both wanted to join the overseas army at once. Although sympathetic to his sons' eagerness, his advice was both practical, in terms of the family's well-being, and ironical, as things turned out: as the eldest son, he said, Ramsey should have the privilege of going overseas first; Basil should return to the university to complete his course in engineering.[34]

Those who did enlist swamped the recruiting stations and competition for the 'better' regiments was keen. Fully 300,000 took the shilling before the end of August. Even more signed up in September, with over 450,000 more men responding to the news of Mons and Le Cateau. Although monthly totals dropped below 200,000 for the rest of the year, by 31 December 1,186,357 men had joined the armed forces.[35]

The men who flocked to the recruiting stations in the fall of 1914 were disproportionately middle class in origin.[36] The public school ethos of 'play up and play the game' that inspired them was not limited to the upper class, but rather disseminated widely through the middle class as well. As the Victorian plutocracy grew in strength, increasing numbers of their sons were enrolled in public schools. For those who had not the means to gain admission to a public school, the state secondary school system emulated the public school model, thus hitting the middle-class child with an increasing barrage of nationalist sentiment.[37]

The working-class exhibited a certain amount of internationalism and class consciousness in the immediate wake of the declaration of war. Some Labour organizations denounced the war as 'a war of the rulers and not of the people.' This attitude was quickly subsumed, however (at least on the part of Labour leadership) in the rising tide of patriotism by the end of August.[38]

In addition many of the youth organizations of the late nineteenth and early twentieth centuries developed a distinct paramilitary character, whether it be the Boy Scouts, the Boys' Brigade, or the Church Lads' Brigade.[39] By 1914 working as a part of a team, wearing quasi-military uniforms, and giving and taking orders within a hierarchy of command had been a part of as much as 41 percent of the adolescent male population's growing up.[40]

To many of these young men the war represented an escape, a chance for adventure. Some enlisted to escape the clutches of the law. Others were coerced by employers, or social superiors, or their social equals; the white feather still carried weight in 1914.[41] Some signed up in a fit of alcoholic fervor. At least one did so and 'having never remembered taking the shilling . . . "when the sergeant came and claimed" him next morning he was as surprised as his wife was annoyed.'[42] For whatever reason, they had never seen fit to sign up in the past.

These new men did not begin to arrive in France in any significant numbers until the spring of 1916. The training and equipping of such a massive influx of volunteers was a monumental task.[43] Even after the first New Army finished training, the failures of the first half of 1915 prompted Kitchener to delay its deployment. Only after the defeat at Gallipoli and some intensive French diplomacy did the British government commit to France and Flanders as the main theater of British operations, and even with this decision the government wanted to delay any major operations until at least June 1916 in order to build up manpower.[44] Thus, when they did arrive, Haig, who had replaced French as the Commander-in-Chief of the BEF on 10 December 1915, husbanded them carefully, introducing them to the realities of the front and integrating them into existing formations.[45] The British Army could not afford to waste manpower in the fruitless manner of 1915.

In addition to expanding the ranks of the British and empire forces, much work had to be done to prepare for the big push when it came. Most of the new men found themselves digging trenches, burying communications wire to protect it from shell fire (a total of 50,000 miles of telephone line was buried or strung by the British Army in 1916), building rail lines, and creating new roads. The net result was that most formations only got one week devoted to actual combat training after their arrival in France.[46] By the summer of 1916 fully 60 percent of the men waiting for the next big push were the new recruits of the Kitchener Armies.[47]

The high command had fallen in love with the destructive power of artillery and built a tactical doctrine around it. The theory was that if the artillery preparation of the intended enemy position was intense enough it would cut all enemy wire, kill the defenders, and destroy their trench system.[48] To this end ammunition and artillery were accumulated for the push on the Somme in June 1916 until the British Army boasted 1537 guns and howitzers, one gun for every 21 yards of enemy front, and a stockpile of 1,732,873 shells.[49] In coordination with a French offensive these guns thundered the largest single barrage to date in human history during the last week in June.[50]

The shelling mainly served to alert the Germans where and roughly when the British were going to attack. While it damaged them, it did not destroy the enemy trenches or their defenders; in many areas the wire remained uncut. The staff officers had expected the shell storm to devastate their opponent.[51] The Germans disabused them of this belief in the single darkest day in British military history; 120,000 British troops took part in the opening day of the Battle of the Somme. By nightfall on 1 July 1916 the BEF had taken almost 60,000 casualties, 20,000 killed outright.[52] Before the battle wound down in mid-November the British Army absorbed 420,000 casualties. Between them the British and French operations on the Somme recaptured at most 125 square miles of German lines.[53] They never achieved the fabled breakthrough.

The Kitchener men soaked up casualties on a scale grand even by Great War standards. They lost more men in a single day than the entire Battle of Loos had consumed the previous fall.[54] They were not professionals or even the semi-professional soldiers of the Territorials, and their reaction to the stress of combat was markedly different, if the Victoria Cross statistics are an indicator (Table 7.3). Unlike previous engagements, the percentage of VCs given for aggressive acts *increased* during the course of the battle, despite the mounting casualties.

How could they do it? How could these men, most of whom had no previous military exposure, endure the hottest fighting the British Army had seen to date and soak up casualties that made the bloodletting of previous campaigns pale in comparison, react in such a different way to sustained, futile operations? Was it an expression of the righteous wrath of the British

Table 7.3  Acts winning the Victoria Cross, 1916: Winners by quarter

| Quarter | Jan.–March 7 | | April–June 25 | | July–Sept. 41 | | Oct.–Dec. 10 | | Total 1916 83 | |
|---|---|---|---|---|---|---|---|---|---|---|
| # Awarded | Raw | % | Raw | % | Raw | % | Raw | % | Raw | % |
| War-Winning | 3 | 43 | 14 | 56 | 28 | 68 | 8 | 80 | 53 | 64 |
| – Offensive | 0 | 0 | 4 | 16 | 15 | 37 | 5 | 50 | 25 | 30 |
| – Defensive | 2 | 29 | 4 | 16 | 7 | 17 | 1 | 10 | 14 | 17 |
| – Symbolic | 1 | 14 | 3 | 12 | 4 | 10 | 2 | 20 | 10 | 12 |
| – Secondary | 0 | 0 | 3 | 12 | 2 | 5 | 0 | 0 | 5 | 6 |
| Humanitarian | 4 | 57 | 2 | 8 | 10 | 24 | 2 | 20 | 16 | 19 |
| – Enlisted | 2 | 29 | 1 | 4 | 5 | 12 | 2 | 20 | 8 | 10 |
| – Officer | 2 | 29 | 1 | 4 | 5 | 12 | 0 | 0* | 8 | 10 |
| Symbolic | 0 | 0 | 0 | 0 | 0 | 0 | 0 | 0 | 0 | 0 |
| Special | 0 | 0 | 0 | 0 | 3 | 7 | 0 | 0 | 3 | 4 |

* Once again, while it is probably a statistical fluke, it is interesting to note that the number of VCs given for rescuing officers in 1916 dropped the longer operations continued, just as they had done in 1915.

public? Were these newly trained civilians somehow more adaptable to the rigors of war than their professional predecessors?

At first blush the numbers suggest just that; somehow, the New Armies had a greater dedication to taking the war to the enemy and as they gained experience during the course of the battle they became increasingly aggressive. If this then is the case, why are the total number of VCs confirmed for 1916 so much lower than the total for 1915?

The Battle of the Somme represented the greatest concentration of British troops thus far in the war. If the 'Kitchener Mob' was indeed more aggressive, it stands to reason that more men would generate more VCs. In fact, the quarterly distribution follows the same trend for both years. The commencement of active operations – second quarter for 1915, third for 1916 – saw the greatest concentration of awards, and in both cases as operations continued and casualties mounted the number of awards dropped markedly (Table 7.4).

The New Army of 1916 thus exhibited the same reaction to the futility of prolonged, fruitless frontal attacks on prepared positions as had the regulars and Territorials in 1915. The lower total number of Crosses awarded when in fact greater numbers of men were engaged in active operations argues

Table 7.4  Breakdown of Crosses won, 1915 and 1916 by quarter

| Quarter | Jan.–Mar. | April–June | July–Sept. | Oct.–Dec. | Year Total |
|---|---|---|---|---|---|
| 1915 | 13 | 50 | 39 | 15 | 117 |
| 1916 | 7 | 25 | 41 | 10 | 83 |

against the notion that somehow the Kitchener men were more aggressive. Yet the statistics superficially indicate exactly that.

It is possible that these new troops did not understand the realities of war and were thus prone to some sort of 'heroic idiocy,' rashly pushing forward where more seasoned soldiers would wait for artillery support or reinforcement. If this was the case, they managed to conceal their vigor from their commanding officers. Sir Henry Rawlinson, in charge of the Somme operations, was convinced the unblooded, poorly-trained soldiers would disintegrate into panicked knots of men clinging to what scant cover they could find as soon as they left the trenches.[55] He accordingly issued a tactical directive that the assault forces on 1 July were to cross no-man's-land in line abreast at a steady walk, maintaining an interval of two or three paces from the next soldier.[56] There may have been some VCs originating in ignorance, but they could hardly explain the surge of aggressiveness in the last half of 1916.

The 1916 casualty statistics among VC winners (Table 7.5) certainly do not support the thesis that the aggression level was due to a lack of comprehension of combat danger.

The only quarter that might suggest 'heroic idiocy' is the period from April to June, when the big buildup began for the Somme. Thereafter the

Table 7.5  The cost of courage, 1916: casualties per quarter

| Quarter | Jan.–Mar. 7 | | April–June 25 | | July–Sept. 41 | | Oct.–Dec. 10 | | Total 1916 83 | |
|---|---|---|---|---|---|---|---|---|---|---|
| # Awarded | Raw | % | Raw | % | Raw | % | Raw | % | Raw | % |
| No Wound | 4 | 57 | 10 | 40 | 22 | 54 | 5 | 50 | 42 | 50 |
| WIA | 2 | 29 | 4 | 16 | 10 | 24 | 4 | 40 | 20 | 24 |
| DOW | 1 | 14 | 3 | 12 | 2 | 5 | 0 | 0 | 6 | 7 |
| KIA | 0 | 0 | 8 | 32 | 7 | 17 | 1 | 10 | 16 | 19 |
| Total Casualties | 3 | 43 | 15 | 60 | 19 | 46 | 5 | 50 | 42 | 50 |
| Total Lethal | 1 | 14 | 11 | 44 | 9 | 22 | 1 | 10 | 22 | 26 |

lethality total drops first to a level equal to that of the previous year, and then in the next quarter to less than half of the previous year. If anything, the New Army learned very quickly how dangerous the battlefield was and if these figures are any indication of their attitude, soon became less likely to risk life in the name of glory. Future Prime Minister Harold Macmillan observed that the physical reality of the modern battlefield made the heroism of the past obsolete:

> Perhaps the most extraordinary thing about the modern battlefield is the desolation and emptiness of it all. Nothing is to be seen of the war or soldiers – only the split and shattered trees... The glamour of red coats – the martial tunes of flag and drum – aides-de-camp scurrying hither and thither on splendid chargers – lances glittering and swords flashing – how different the old wars must have been![57]

The new levies were, in fact, far from being as belligerent as the 'war-winning' percentages suggest. Private Arthur Surfleet kept a diary of his experience of the Somme, contrary to Army regulations. His regiment, the East Yorkshires, took part in only two attacks, but the experience traumatized the entire unit. In mid-October the regiment marched back up to the trenches after a rest period in the rear. He described how they swung along the roads singing 'It's a Long Way to Tipperary' and 'There's a Long, Long Trail a-Winding'... until they entered the environs of the Somme. Then:

> The whole lot of us had that characteristic depression which these parts induce. I could not make out exactly where we were, but past, miserable experiences in that sector told us we were too near to the enemy to be pleasant and just about opposite that ominous blackness near Serre.[58]

The training exercises that followed did nothing to inspire confidence. Surfleet and his messmates did not want to be there. 'I know all the lads here will go wherever they are told in spite of the fear we cannot help, but I don't know anyone who would not welcome with open arms news of our departure to some less devastated and dangerous part.'[59]

Surfleet was not alone in dreading combat. According to Denis Winter's survey of the unpublished memoirs of Great War soldiers held by the Imperial War Museum, ten expressed the same fatalism and 'characteristic depression' for every one who embraced the war as a great game or marvelous experience.[60] Nor did a whiff of cordite cure the malaise; two weeks into the battle:

Men spoke in whispers. Their faces were pallid, dirty, and unshaven, many with eyes ringed with fatigue after the night, hot and fetid, gaseous and disturbed by shell fire, in Bazetin. Few there were whose demeanor expressed eagerness for the assault. They were moving into position with good discipline, yet listless, as if facing an inevitable. Their identity as individuals seemed to be swallowed up in the immensity of war: devitalized electrons.[61]

In mid-November Surfleet found himself in the front lines before Serre. A call for volunteers to go over the top generated little enthusiasm among Surfleet's mates, until they were told it was to rescue the helpless wounded, whereupon 'each of us went about that job with real enthusiasm.'[62]

This reaction is far from the aggressiveness the VC statistics indicate. A trip into no-man's-land was dangerous, whether it was an assault or a rescue. Here we see soldiers who were unwilling to volunteer when they thought it was to attack, but eager to risk life and limb when they discovered their risk had the concrete (and achievable) object of recovering the wounded.

As the battle dragged on the futility and waste induced a state of pessimism and fatalism. Private Ivor Gurney echoed the thoughts of Wilfred Owen:

What a life! What a life! My memories of this week will be – Blockhouse; cold; stuffy heat; smashed or stuck Tanks; A gas and smoke barrage put up by us. A glorious but terrifying sight; Fritz's shells; one sunset; two sunrises; Thirst; Gas; Shrapnel; Very H. E.; Our liquid fire;... Does it sound interesting? May God forgive me if I ever come to cheat myself into thinking that it was, and later lie to the younger men of the Great Days. It was damnable.[63]

The fatalism could even take on apocalyptic overtones, as the living began to envy the dead:

I think, too, we are becoming more or less fatalistic; you get like that. I, for one, cannot imagine this blasted war ever ending without most of us being killed or so wounded that we go home to Blighty for good... It boils down to this: we've got to the stage when we don't dare think about the future. If we are alright today – if we are alright this hour, almost – it is enough... Four of the new draft who had only just arrived were killed and some of the new lads wounded... It seemed like fate that those poor lads should be put out of it all so soon; someone said they were lucky.[64]

The Somme was a harsh baptism for the Kitchener soldiers, and it cost the commanders the confidence of the men they led:

> They say we smashed the old German Army there on the Somme, but we smashed something else too. The faith we'd had found its grave there in the nuckly hills and valleys round the Ancre ... Never again was the spirit or the quality so high. After the Somme, the French sneered at the British, and the British at the French, and the Australians and Americans at both. Last sons were called up and the conscripts went forward like driven sheep. I never heard them singing again as I heard them that summer of 1916.[65]

The swing toward more 'war-winning' Victoria Crosses in 1916 cannot be explained by a fundamental difference in the character of the New Army. While its social composition was different from that of the pre-war Army, it did not exist in a vacuum separate from the older institution. The Kitchener men were integrated into the existing system and if anything, their commanders expected a lower level of dash and directness in their battlefield conduct. It was not so much the conduct of the soldiers, but rather the expectations and doctrines of their commanders that created a greater emphasis on equating aggressiveness with heroism. At the core of this change was Field Marshal Sir Douglas Haig.

Douglas Haig took command of the BEF from Sir John French in December 1915. As a subordinate he had been critical of what he perceived as his commander's timidity and failure to commit himself to a decisive blow.[66] Now he had the opportunity to prove his fitness as a theater commander and in the process justify his criticism of French by achieving the breakout.

Haig had long been an advocate of the offensive as the proper means of conducting a war. In a staff study written in 1907 he asserted that 'the real objective in war is the decisive battle.' He expanded on that statement in 1909, declaring 'decisiveness in battle can be gained only by a vigorous offensive.'[67] For Haig there was only one sort of war: offensive, decisive, and mobile. Haig looked for the breakout battle that would sunder the German lines and allow him to end the war in an overwhelming defeat of the enemy in the open field.[68]

A cavalryman first and foremost, he never lost his conviction that the horseman would strike the decisive blow in this war. It is truly amazing that even after well over a year of combat on the Western Front he protested a proposal to reduce his cavalry force as a matter of economy in 1916.[69] For Haig, the infantry was merely the tool to open the breach for his cavalry.

He expected the intense artillery preparation would allow the British Fourth Army to punch through the three lines of the German trenches, at which point he would pour Hubert Gough's Reserve Army, heavy with horse troops, through the breach to capture Arras, 14 miles away.[70]

General Sir Henry Rawlinson, commander of the Fourth Army, was not such a prophet of the great breakout as Haig, and long before the Somme recorded this evaluation of Haig's tactics: 'He expects to get the Cav[alry] through with the next big push but I very much doubt if he will succeed in doing more than lose a large number of gallant men without effecting any great purpose.'[71] This is not to suggest he was not an aggressive commander, however; his tactical doctrine has been described as 'bite and hold,' making an all-out effort to achieve limited advances to secure a strategic objective, reinforcing the gain, and then breaking the enemy's teeth as they try to recapture the lost strong point.[72] Like Haig, however, he placed great faith in the power of the artillery, and in his tactical directive at the Somme, put great emphasis on pressing home the attack.[73]

The shift in the nature of heroism sprang in 1916 from the attitude of the commanders. It has been established in earlier chapters that the commander in the field and the overall commander of the theater served as a lens through which the authorities back in London saw heroism. Kitchener had done so in South Africa, swatting down recommendations he did not consider sufficiently distinguished to merit a Cross, particularly those involving tending the wounded.[74] Given the indications that the troops of the New Army were not intrinsically more aggressive than previous formations, that they reacted to prolonged futile offensives in a similar fashion, and that there was no substantial change in the battlefield environment, command selectivity in endorsing recommendations is the only remaining variable.

The trend toward increased aggressiveness as the Battle of the Somme progressed into its later stages itself supports a command emphasis on rewarding aggressiveness. The bestowal of honors is the opposite side of the coin to enforcing discipline when instilling desired behavior in a military formation.[75] Haig wanted a breakout, and when that goal proved unreachable, he had to take enough ground and inflict enough casualties to justify the casualties his own forces sustained.[76] Neither of these goals required retrieval of the wounded; they needed soldiers that took the bayonet to the enemy. Thus, at the same time as we see the total number of awards dropping in the final quarter, the percentage going for aggressive acts reached its highest point of the year.

There is also evidence that the Army was if not manufacturing, at least laundering heroes in 1916. It is doubtful there was any sort of quota for heroism, some formula that mandated 'x' number of heroes for 'y' number of troops involved.[77] The lower number of VCs awarded in 1916 was unusual, however, and may have contributed to altering the actual circumstances of bravery to make an act more acceptable for public consumption. Such is the case of Thomas Alfred 'Todger' Jones:

> On 25 September 1916 at Morval, France Private Jones was with his company covering the advance in front of a village, when he noticed an enemy sniper 200 yards away. He went out and, although one bullet went through his helmet and another through his coat, he returned the sniper's fire and killed him. He then saw two more Germans firing on him although they were displaying a white flag. Both these he shot. On reaching the enemy trench he found several occupied dug-outs and single-handedly disarmed 102 of the enemy, including three or four officers, and took them prisoner.[78]

Todger Jones actually did venture out into no-man's-land, kill a sniper, and bring back 102 prisoners. But it did not happen quite the way the official citation had it.[79]

Jones was a character in the regiment, and a regular recipient of the nastier work details for disciplinary reasons. As he himself later reported, 'I really did some things I shouldn't have done.'[80] On the day in question he and another soldier, a relative of his from Runcorn, had been detailed to empty the 'honey-tubs' from the company latrine. He 'noticed' the sniper when his kinsman was shot dead and he was drenched with the contents of the tub in the process. He stalked the sniper, disposed of him, and started looking for other Germans to kill in retribution. After killing two more men in no-man's-land, he entered the German trench line. There he discovered a large dugout. He entered, fired a round into the ceiling and shouted 'Hande hoch!' Surprised by the appearance of a British soldier, the inhabitants of the bunker surrendered.

Well over a hundred Germans filed out into the trench. When they realized that there was only one enemy anywhere near their lines, some of them tried to escape. Jones killed two, rapid-firing his rifle from the hip; the rest froze. Jones got them organized and started them back across to the British lines. His mates, who did not even know he was gone, saw a clump of Germans crossing no-man's-land and opened fire, killing many of them before Jones managed to wave them off. One hundred and two survived to be marched off to the rear by Todger Jones.

A photograph was taken of the cocky Cheshire private as he herded his charges into the rear area. Examination of the photo reveals one more thing about the men he captured. They wore a variety of different regimental uniforms, and all of them sported field bandages. Todger Jones had captured a forward dressing station (which does much to explain how one Tommy could 'disarm' well over 100 of the enemy).

That things were not exactly the way they seemed does not detract from the bravery of Jones's action. To venture out into the enemy trench line alone required courage. The motivation (revenge), however, was not acceptable to the higher powers, nor were the actual details. The sight of one man bringing in over a hundred prisoners single-handed was, however, too good an opportunity to pass up. Jones was gazetted, shook hands with King George V, and became a hero, an example of British courage and pluck and aggressiveness.

During the final two years of the war the pattern established on the Somme battlefields solidified into a new type of heroism. In its older conception the heroic ideal had an almost equal measure of belligerence and compassion. Those who exposed themselves to peril to save the life of a comrade or retrieve the wounded (or even the dead) were regarded with the same respect as those who captured strong points or led a blazing cavalry charge. As the war dragged on and casualty figures mounted, commanders shifted the emphasis of the heroic ideal. It is to the commanders that we must now turn to discover the parameters of Victoria Cross heroism. The High Command of the Western Front no longer wanted men who would rush to the aid of the fallen. They wanted killers first and foremost.

# Eight

## 'Courage isn't what it used to be': Heroism Emerges from the Great War, 1917–1918

The British Army survived the dubious victories of the Somme campaign. The Asquith Coalition did not. From its ashes rose the new coalition of David Lloyd George, with the lean and streamlined War Cabinet of five men at its heart. The Welshman was an opponent of Haig and meant to curb what he considered the reckless excesses of the Western Front.[1] Military circumstances, Allied requirements, and the political environment conspired against him, however, placing Haig in an even more autonomous position than he had enjoyed in 1916.

A side-effect of this struggle between field marshal and prime minister was to place an increasing importance on Haig's ideals as regards the nature of the Victoria Cross. His command both became the center of gravity for the winning of the war and generated most of the Crosses won during the war. The primacy of his command gave weight to his pronouncements; the volume of Crosses passing through his vetting process gave him influence over the nature of heroism recognized by the government. Haig understood the usefulness of medals and decorations, that they were not just the rewards of the valiant but also important tools of command and thus had to be awarded carefully.

He deemed some acts, though undoubtedly heroic, counter-productive to the overall war effort and thus refused to recognize them with the Victoria Cross. The result was a new definition of the VC, one that proved virtually devoid of human compassion. The machine age finally, fully caught up with the concept of heroism in 1917, creating a creature very different from its ancestors.

Lloyd George became prime minister on 7 December 1916 and created the War Cabinet two days later. This new cabinet had the self-proclaimed function of taking direct control of the prosecution of the war.[2] Three of the five members – Lloyd George, Lord Curzon, and Lord Milner – saw little value in continuing the slaughter on the Western Front for little result, and advocated a policy of 'knocking out the props' of Imperial Germany by disposing of her allies. Not only would this (they hoped) lower the human costs of the war, but held the added potential of expanding the Empire in the process.[3] Haig disagreed vehemently, as in his estimation the Germans were ready to crack and needed but one more offensive in Flanders to break them. Waiting on the Western Front would only damage Russian and French morale, already tenuous, and allow the Germans to shore up their sagging defenses.[4]

It was not that the War Cabinet wanted to abandon the Western Front; they did not believe that Germany would collapse if the Sultan struck his tents in Palestine and surrendered, nor did they see Bulgaria as a linchpin of the Central Powers. They were worried about the damage that continuing casualty-dense operations on the Western Front would cause to morale at home and to the power of the Army itself. They were looking not just to the end of the war, but to the peace that would follow. If Britain wanted to be a dominant force in forging the treaties that settled the war, they had to survive the war with an intact army. What they hoped for were some morale-building victories in the secondary theaters while husbanding their resources in the West.[5]

Circumstances dashed Lloyd George's hopes. As 1917 progressed, Russia was wracked by Revolution, French commanders demanded British support of their planned offensive operations, and the Italian Chief of Staff, General Cadorna rejected his proposal for a powerful new attack on the Isonzo Front. With these developments he was forced to endorse offensive operations by Haig's command.[6] He tried to place limitations on Haig's options and tie his operations to cooperation with the Nivelle Offensive, but Douglas Haig was not going to take usurpation of his command lightly.

Further frustrating the War Cabinet was a hostile press. Of the major newspapers, most trusted the pronouncements of the military more than those of the politicians. Only the Daily Telegraph and the Daily Chronicle could be said to be friends of Lloyd George, and their combined circulation could not match that of the antagonistic Times or Daily Mail.[7] As a consequence, much of the reading public was treated to a steady diet of pro-military editorials.

The War Cabinet also faced a distrustful monarchy that had personal ties to Haig.[8] It is not an accident that Haig's promotion to field marshal by George V followed close on the heels of Lloyd George's move to Downing Street. The king feared the new prime minister's power; he and court officials repeatedly warned Haig and Robertson not to go too far in provoking the Welshman. Should Haig be forced to resign, 'Lloyd George, in Wigram's opinion, would then appeal to the country, and might possibly emerge as a dictator.'[9] Haig, however, held the king's confidence.

Haig also held a greater degree of the confidence of the general public than Lloyd George. Both official communiques and newspaper coverage of the war tended to build up the case of the soldiers in the public mind, a situation that allowed Asquith and other opposition leaders to use the slogan 'hands off the generals' as an effective tool.[10] The new prime minister stood at the head of a shaky political coalition and had created a lot of opponents during his rise to power.[11] The Conservative Party was still a minority and all the Liberal leadership except Churchill had refused office in Lloyd George's coalition. Almost half of the Liberal members in the Commons had indicated they would support the new government, but how long could they resist the pull of their leadership? Lloyd George had to depend on the support of the Conservative Party, and the elder statesmen of that party stood foursquare behind Haig.[12]

Lloyd George thus could not simply replace Haig or even realistically limit his discretionary powers without eroding his political position in the process.[13] At the same time he could not garner any effective support for shifting the focus of the war to another theater.[14] He tried to subordinate Haig to the French High Command early in 1917, hoping to tie down the commander he considered a loose cannon. The field marshal managed to place so many conditions on the arrangement as to emerge with even more autonomy; in essence, he partially served two masters and could play them against each other to his own advantage. Ultimately, he managed to gain the primacy of British General Headquarters in planning any joint operations with the French.[15]

This gave Haig the opportunity to vindicate his military policies and management of the war effort, and the process had a profound effect on the character of the Victoria Cross. He was pledged to support the French 1917 Spring Offensive under Robert Nivelle, but the actual planning and conduct of the British contribution to the operation remained the province of GHQ.[16] The genesis of the first British offensive of 1917 was thus a diversion on a grand scale to prevent German reinforcement of the Chemin des Dames when Nivelle's attack there commenced. Thus began the Battle of Arras.[17]

For a diversion it was a major production, involving General Sir Edmund Allenby's Third Army, assisted on the left by the Canadian Corps of General Henry Horne's First Army and elements of Sir Hubert Gough's Fifth Army on the right. The main body was to thrust at Cambrai to the southeast while the Canadians stormed Vimy Ridge to secure the left flank of the assault. If all went according to plan, the main element would continue to the southeast, ultimately linking up with Nivelle's push through the Chemin des Dames and pincer off a good portion of German-held France in the process.[18]

The agony of the Somme in 1916 had not been entirely in vain. Some tactical lessons had been learned and were put to use with good effect in the attack of 9 April. Artillery concentration – the weight of shell, the reliability of the fuses, and the accuracy of the barrage – contributed greatly to the successes of the opening two days of the battle.[19] What had not been learned was when to call it quits. The only significant gains made were on the British left and within 48 hours of the first attack. Gough's troops on the right, attacking the northern anchor of the Hindenburg Line, achieved nothing.[20] Even though it was by design a diversion, the early success on the left revived hopes of a breakout at GHQ and the attacks continued until 17 May, resulting in a total of 150,000 casualties.[21]

Eight Victoria Crosses were won on the first day of the Arras offensive, and they indicate the nature of courage expected for the remainder of the war. Seven of the eight were for offensive acts and five of them were for solo attacks against machine-gun posts.

> On 9 April 1917 at Neuville-St-Vaast, France, during an attack on enemy trenches, Lance-Sergeant [Ellis Welwood] Sifton's company was held up by machine gun fire which inflicted many casualties. The sergeant located the gun and charged it all alone, killing the crew. A small enemy party then advanced down the trench but he managed to hold them off with bayonet and clubbed rifle until his comrades arrived and ended the unequal fight, but in carrying out this gallant act he was killed. His conspicuous valour undoubtedly saved many lives and contributed largely to the success of the operation.[22]

The level of aggressiveness achieved during the last quarter of 1916 carried over into 1917 as the new standard to which to aspire:

> On 9 April 1917 near Thelus, France, on approaching the first objective, Private [William Johnstone] Milne noticed an enemy machine gun firing on our advancing troops. Crawling on hands and knees he managed to reach the gun which he captured, killing the crew. Later, he again located a machine gun in the support line, but stalking this gun, as he had the first, he put the crew out of action and captured it. He was killed shortly afterwards.[23]

Note the common factors in these two citations. The hero killed the enemy. The hero contributed to the success of the offensive. The hero faced the new queen of the battlefield, the machine gun, and with raw courage overcame it. The hero was not necessarily expected to survive the act.

The nature of heroism was in transition in 1916 as Haig solidified his control over military affairs and created a GHQ in his own image. The political and diplomatic events of 1917 increased his control of British military affairs and in turn that increased his influence on the ideal of heroism. The trends of 1916 became the reality of heroism in 1917. Aggressiveness became the key factor in determining valour in the third year of the war. On 4 May 1917 a meeting of the Allied commands came to the determination that, given the relative strengths of the opposing sides, a full-scale breakout was unlikely in the near future. The British and French commands agreed that the best course was to pursue a war of attrition, to wear down the enemy to the point that an effective breakout was possible. General Sir William Robertson summarized the sense of the meeting: 'In order to wear him down we are agreed that it is absolutely necessary to fight with all our available forces with the object of destroying the enemy's divisions... by relentlessly attacking with limited objectives while making the fullest use of our artillery.'[24] This meant that the primary virtue of the British soldier was now killing Germans.

This factor is instantly evident in the statistical breakdown of Victoria Cross winners for 1917. War-winning acts resulting in enemy casualties garnered an unprecedented share of the Crosses awarded. Beginning with the active phase of operations in the April 1917 offensive, enemy-killing acts outstripped all other categories combined. Unlike 1915, when offensive acts declined with the continuation of operations and mounting casualty figures, 1917 generated a steady level of aggressive actions. Unlike 1916 when the number of awards steadily declined from the outset of active operations, in 1917 they steadily increased. Both trends are indications that commanders were driving their troops harder and rewarding aggressive actions more frequently.

Not only were more offensive acts getting awarded, these acts were increasing in ruthlessness toward the enemy – and the troops under British command:

On 20 August 1917 near Tower Hamlets, east of Ypres, Belgium, Second Lieutenant [Montague Shadworth Seymour] Moore volunteered to make a fresh attack on a final objective and went forward with some 70 men, but they met with such heavy opposition that when he arrived at his objective he had only one sergeant and four men. Nothing daunted he at once bombed a large dug-out, taking 28 prisoners, two machine guns and a light field-gun. Gradually more officers and men arrived, numbering about 60 and he held the post for 36 hours beating off counter-attacks, until his force was reduced to 10 men. He eventually got away his wounded and withdrew under the cover of thick mist.[25]

Lieutenant Moore was awarded the Victoria Cross for killing Germans; that his actions apparently destroyed almost an entire British company in the process was secondary to that fact.

More ominous are the figures for humanitarian acts of bravery. Even in the most aggressive quarter of 1916, fully 20 percent of the VCs confirmed were for life saving. In 1917 only in the relatively inactive first quarter of the year were there more than 20 percent, and in two quarters (corresponding with the big push at Arras and again with the third phase of Passchendaele) life saving did not even break into double digits. High command clearly indicated that it would reward soldiers who willingly passed by the wounded to kill the enemy.

But to how great a degree was this a reflection of Haig's attitudes? Frank Manning's Great War novel *The Middle Parts of Fortune*, which was firmly grounded in his own experiences, contains an episode in which an order issued before the attack at Arras directed the men to bypass the wounded.[26]

Table 8.1 Acts winning the Victoria Cross, 1917: winners by quarter

| Quarter | Jan.–Mar. 20 | | April–June 47 | | July–Sept. 48 | | Oct.–Dec. 55 | | 1917 Total 174* | |
|---|---|---|---|---|---|---|---|---|---|---|
| # Awarded | Raw | % | Raw | % | Raw | % | Raw | % | Raw | % |
| War-Winning | 13 | 65 | 42 | 89 | 40 | 83 | 49 | 89 | 147 | 84 |
| – Offensive | 7 | 35 | 26 | 55 | 28 | 58 | 31 | 56 | 95 | 55 |
| – Defensive | 4 | 20 | 10 | 21 | 7 | 15 | 13 | 54 | 34 | 19 |
| – Symbolic | 2 | 10 | 2 | 4 | 2 | 4 | 2 | 4 | 8 | 5 |
| – Secondary | 0 | 0 | 4 | 8 | 3 | 6 | 3 | 5 | 10 | 6 |
| Humanitarian | 6 | 30 | 4 | 9 | 7 | 15 | 5 | 9 | 22 | 13 |
| – Enlisted | 4 | 20 | 4 | 9 | 7 | 15 | 5 | 9 | 20 | 12 |
| – Officer | 2 | 10 | 0 | 0 | 0 | 0 | 0 | 0 | 2 | 1 |
| Symbolic | 0 | 0 | 0 | 0 | 0 | 0 | 0 | 0 | 0 | 0 |
| Special | 1 | 5 | 1 | 2 | 1 | 2 | 1 | 2 | 5 | 3 |

* Total includes Crosses awarded for cumulative valour not reflected in quarter figures.

This fictional order was a stark reflection of Haig's vision of warfare. From the outset of the war he disapproved of granting the VC for rescuing the wounded. In part, his view reflected that of Lord Kitchener's policy in South Africa, as the recommendation of Private F. W. Dobson of the Coldstream Guards demonstrates.

On 28 September 1914 private Dobson volunteered to retrieve two men who had fallen wounded in front of the trench line. Under heavy fire he crawled out to find one of the men dead, but managed to bring the other to safety. His commanding officer, Major R. A. Markham and two artillery officers who witnessed the act recommended him to the regimental commander for the VC. Regimental commander Lieutenant-Colonel V. Peretia 'strongly' approved the recommendation and passed it on to Brigade; Brigade commander Earl Cavan approved and passed it on to Division; Division commander Sir Charles Munro concurred and passed it on to Corps[27] ... where I Corps Commander Haig dismissed it out of hand:

> I fully appreciate the bravery shewn by no. 6840 Pte. F. W. Dobson, 2nd Battn Coldstream Guards, who is recommended for the V.C., but I am not in favour of this reward being granted for bringing in wounded officers or men in European warfare & I therefore recommend [he] ... should be granted the D.C. Medal.[28]

Haig was not the final arbiter in the field in 1914, however. Sir John French forwarded the original recommendation with Haig's reservations to the War Office along with a similar recommendation for Lieutenant L. E. O. Davidson of the 121st Battery, Royal Field Artillery (recommended through II Corps chain of command), where they provoked a flurry of activity. The VC committee requested guidance from Lord Kitchener as Secretary of State for War, as they were not sure if he was prepared to accept recommendations for rescuing the wounded. They noted the difference of opinion on the matter among the corps commanders (Haig swatting down field recommendations for life saving, Horace O. Smith-Dorien forwarding such) and the Commander-in-Chief as well as the dangers of a lack of common policy in recommending humanitarian acts. Kitchener was a soldier and understood the importance of the chain of command; he was apparently unwilling to undercut the overall commander in the field and promptly dumped the matter back on Sir John French.[29]

French compromised on the issue, writing the War Office on 25 November:

> ... I am in agreement that the Victoria Cross should not be awarded for the rescue of wounded in the case of officers unless under very exceptional circumstances.
>
> As regards men, I think it should be awarded, but in making the recommendations I have been guided by the facts of the case. For instance, the rescue of a wounded man lying exposed to fire between two trenches, or in a retreat, where a rescue has been made on the sole initiative of the non-commissioned officer or private, are cases in which recommendations would be given.
>
> I am, however, quite willing to be guided by any ruling which may be given, as no doubt the present system tends to lack uniformity.[30]

Dobson got the VC, Davidson did not, and the precedent was set that for an enlisted man, rescuing the wounded still merited a Victoria Cross in the right circumstances.

The setting of precedent did not alter Haig's ideas concerning the VC. On 3 December 1914 he lectured George V:

> He expressed the opinion that the grant of the Victoria Cross for carrying a wounded man out of action was justified and was beneficial. I replied that each case must be judged on its merits but, as a rule, any careless movement did a wounded man much more harm and also tended to increase loss of valuable lives. On the other hand, in the case of a building containing wounded catching fire and troops going forward under fire to remove the wounded from it, they would certainly merit the V.C. As a matter of fact we have to take special precautions during a battle to post police, to prevent more unwounded men than are necessary from accompanying a wounded man back from the firing line![31]

Here he reveals another part of his reasoning: combat on the Western Front was a question of firepower, and he could not afford to lose men from the firing line to rescue or tend the wounded.

While French remained in command the VC retained a place for humanitarian heroism on the part of the combat soldier. Even after Haig replaced French on the eve of 1916 soldiers continued to win VCs for rescuing the wounded, although the numbers began to shift in favor of war-winning Crosses. The statistics indicate that this may be due partially to an unwillingness on Kitchener's part to reverse the precedent set in the opening months of the war. The major shift toward a more aggressive VC paradigm coincides both with the death of Lord Kitchener and the opening of the

Somme campaign, and in the absence of conclusive documentary evidence it is impossible to assign primary responsibility to either event. In either case, the shift is directly linked to Haig assuming command and intensified as his autonomy in that capacity increased. And Haig was far more interested in winning the war than stroking the sentimentality of the Victorian Era. The primary virtue of the soldier on the Western Front was now aggressiveness.

This meant that the primary duty of the soldier was to kill Germans. On the battalion level strict orders were issued to press forward at all costs. 'The Colonel finished with a stony look. "There will be no retiring," he said. "On no conditions whatsoever is any man to turn back. Let them all understand that."'[32] Duty on the individual level also dictated that soldiers had to abandon men to a lingering death:

> A party of 'A' Company men passing up to the front line found a man bogged down above the knees. The united efforts of four of them with rifles beneath his armpits, made not the slightest impression, and to dig, even if shovels had been available, would be impossible, for there was no foothold. Duty compelled them to move on up to the line, and when two days later they passed down that way the wretched fellow was still there; but only his head was now visible and he was raving mad.[33]

A corollary of this shift was a dramatic drop in the number of VCs given for saving officers.[34] This trend that in previous chapters was attributed to a statistical anomaly or coincidence is made painfully clear in the 1917 statistical breakdown: saving officers did not merit a Cross any more. Of the 174 Victoria Crosses won in 1917, exactly two went for saving the lives of officers. It is tempting to surmise that the rank and file were no longer willing to expose themselves to save the men ordering them over the top, but the line officers shared the same privations as the other ranks. The ire of the average Tommy was directed not at the officer that accompanied him into battle, but rather the staff officers that sent them both out into no-man's-land.[35] The reality was that high command wanted soldiers to kill Germans, not rescue the wounded – whatever their rank – and recommended soldiers for the VC accordingly.

The statistics are closer to previous trends in terms of the cost of courage. As offensive operations continued and men saw their mates fall about them, they became more cautious in their valour. The average total casualty rate for the year (Table 8.2) is actually 5 percent lower than that of 1916, indicating that despite the high command's emphasis on aggressive action in 1917 the rank and file were quietly becoming more cautious. The quarterly totals are in line with previous years.

Table 8.2 The cost of courage, 1917: casualties per quarter

| Quarter | Jan.–Mar. 20 | | April–June 47 | | July–Sept. 48 | | Oct.–Dec. 55 | | 1917 Total 174 | |
|---|---|---|---|---|---|---|---|---|---|---|
| # Awarded | Raw | % | Raw | % | Raw | % | Raw | % | Raw | % |
| No Wound | 10 | 50 | 22 | 47 | 29 | 60 | 33 | 60 | 96 | 55 |
| WIA | 5 | 25 | 11 | 23 | 7 | 15 | 5 | 9 | 28 | 16 |
| DOW | 2 | 10 | 2 | 4 | 8 | 17 | 6 | 11 | 18 | 10 |
| KIA | 3 | 15 | 12 | 26 | 4 | 8 | 10 | 18 | 29 | 17 |
| Total Casualties | 10 | 50 | 25 | 53 | 19 | 40 | 22* | 40 | 78 | 45 |
| Total Lethal | 2 | 25 | 14 | 30 | 12 | 25 | 16 | 29 | 18 | 28 |

*Total includes one unwounded soldier taken prisoner.

The statistics for the first quarter of 1918 deviated sharply from the pattern of 1917 (Table 8.3), with a huge spike in the number of Crosses granted for defensive actions, but this does not indicate a change in the concept of heroism. In the first quarter the brunt of the German Spring Offensive fell on the British. For the rest of the year the pattern of 1917 was repeated and intensified.

Table 8.3 Acts winning the Victoria Cross, 1918: winners by quarter

| Quarter | Jan.–Mar. 27 | | April–June 37 | | July–Sept. 86 | | Oct.–Dec. 44 | | 1918 Total 203* | |
|---|---|---|---|---|---|---|---|---|---|---|
| # Awarded | Raw | % | Raw | % | Raw | % | Raw | % | Raw | % |
| War-Winning | 26 | 96 | 29 | 78 | 82 | 95 | 40 | 31 | 182 | 90 |
| – Offensive | 1 | 4 | 15 | 40 | 67 | 78 | 24 | 54 | 110 | 54 |
| – Defensive | 19 | 70 | 7 | 19 | 11 | 13 | 3 | 7 | 41 | 20 |
| – Symbolic | 4 | 15 | 2 | 5 | 2 | 2 | 3 | 7 | 11 | 5 |
| – Secondary | 2 | 7 | 5 | 13 | 2 | 2 | 10 | 23 | 20 | 10 |
| Humanitarian | 0 | 0 | 6 | 16 | 3 | 3 | 2 | 4 | 13 | 6 |
| – Enlisted | 0 | 0 | 6 | 16 | 3 | 3 | 2 | 4 | 13 | 6 |
| – Officer | 0 | 0 | 0 | 0 | 0 | 0 | 0 | 0 | 0 | 0 |
| Symbolic | 0 | 0 | 0 | 0 | 0 | 0 | 0 | 0 | 0 | 0 |
| Special | 1 | 4 | 2 | 5 | 1 | 1 | 2 | 4 | 8 | 4 |

*Total includes Crosses awarded for cumulative valour not reflected in quarter figures.

Once again, the number of Crosses given for taking the war to the enemy far outnumbered those given for saving the life of a comrade. In addition, many of those in the 'War-winning, Symbolic' and 'Special' categories in both 1917 and 1918 came either from the Royal Navy or the Royal Air Force. Gone were the days when the Army gave a VC for inspirational pipe playing. The new symbolism of the Army VC had been set on the first day of Arras. It involved facing machine guns.

The first quarter of 1918 was a dark one for the BEF. Gough's Fifth Army on the Somme bore the brunt of the German Spring Offensive, starting 21 March, giving up 138 square miles of territory and losing 38,500 casualties, of which 21,000 were taken prisoner. Both the Fifth and Third Armies retreated in the face of tremendous German pressure, moving back over land hard won in the Somme Campaign. British and French reinforcements moved in behind them, finally blunting the assault on 5 April. Between them the BEF and French armies lost over 240,000 casualties and 1200 square miles of France.[36]

The next German thrust came against Plumer's Second Army in Flanders. On 10 April it bore the brunt of a German offensive, and was driven back toward the critical rail junction at Hazebrouck.[37] Haig had no reinforcements to send; instead he issued a controversial General Order on 11 April: 'Every position must be held to the last man: there must not be a retirement. With our backs against the wall and believing in the justice of our cause each one of us must fight to the end.'[38] Some commanders refused to publish what they considered an insulting and condescending order. Others attributed it with inspiring a new level of vigor and determination in the troops.[39] If so, it certainly was not reflected in the casualty figures of Cross winners in April 1918 (Table 8.4).

They were even less willing to get killed in the process of doing their duty than those of 1917. Only during opening stages of the *Kaiserschlacht* do the casualty figures of 1918 exceed those of 1917 in any significant way. The reaction of the rank and file to heavy fighting and seemingly pointless casualties was exactly what it had always been: take fewer chances.

> A month of incessant attacks, with little progress, appalling casualties, and severe fighting, was having a bad effect on the morale of everybody concerned. Reinforcements of the new armies shamble past the guns with dragging steps and the expressions of men who knew they were going to certain death. No words of greeting passed as they slouched along; in sullen silence they filed past one by one to the sacrifice.[40]

Table 8.4  The cost of courage, 1918: casualties per quarter

| Quarter | Jan.–Mar. 27 | | April–June 37 | | July–Sept. 86 | | Oct.–Dec. 44 | | 1918 Total 203 | |
|---|---|---|---|---|---|---|---|---|---|---|
| # Awarded | Raw | % | Raw | % | Raw | % | Raw | % | Raw | % |
| No Wound | 11 | 41 | 23 | 62 | 49 | 57 | 41 | 75 | 118 | 58 |
| WIA | 5 | 19 | 8 | 22 | 15 | 17 | 5 | 9 | 35 | 17 |
| DOW | 1 | 4 | 2 | 5 | 5 | 6 | 3 | 5 | 11 | 5 |
| KIA | 10 | 37 | 4 | 11 | 17 | 20 | 6 | 11 | 39 | 19 |
| Total Casualties | 20 | 74 | 14 | 38 | 38 | 44 | 14 | 25 | 85 | 42 |
| Total Lethal | 11 | 41 | 6 | 16 | 22 | 26 | 9 | 16 | 50 | 25 |

Once they got to the Front they were not as likely to stand in a desperation defense as the VC statistics indicate:

> When the Jerries came towards our line in large numbers, they were firing from the hip and I thought, Tosh. Do what some of the others are doing. Hop it back. So I did . I was not alone, I can assure you, otherwise I don't think I should be able to write this.[41]

During the last 42 days of the war the total casualty figure dropped markedly and perfectly understandably; why get killed being a hero just as the Big Show was winding down?

The trend of 1916 in terms of men earning the Cross while holding a temporary or acting rank continued in 1917 and 1918. Fully 20.6 percent of the winners in 1917 and 23.6 percent of the winners in 1918 did so, but with a broader distribution across the rank spectrum than in 1917. In 1917 the greatest concentration of awards went to acting captains, with 13 Crosses, followed by acting lieutenant colonels at six Crosses. Every commissioned and non-commissioned officer rank except colonel was represented, from brigadier to lance corporal. The same held true for 1918, but the greatest concentration of awards went to acting lieutenant colonels with 15 Crosses.

The Great War forever changed the nature of warfare among industrialized nations. With it changed the nature of heroism. War on an industrial scale demanded heroes that were as implacable as the machines they used to fight. True, the Poor Bloody Infantry still looked roughly the same as their ancestors at Mons, but they had become the cutting edge of a vast system for the production, supply, and distribution of wholesale slaughter. A machine pays little attention to hot or cold, dry or wet, unless those conditions impede its function. A machine does not feel compassion or remorse. Neither did the heroic ideal that emerged from the Western Front in 1917:

> A consumptive machine gunner, too scared in an attack to bolt, can sit in a lucky hole and scupper a company of the best as they advance. Courage isn't what it used to be. The machine runs over us and we can't stop it.[42]

The scale of warfare and the range of the new weapons of war created a new environment for the hero, and potentially opened their ranks to some who had never been considered in the past. The British government and the armed services realized these changes as they occurred and as the war entered its final phase an interservice panel was convened on the subject of valour. Its purpose was two-fold: to institutionalize the new heroic environment and to restandardize the qualifications of the hero. As the next chapter will reveal, the committee decisions reached as the war ended in the autumn of 1918 had far-reaching implications on the nature of heroism in the future.

# NINE

## The Hero Comes Home from the War: The Institutionalization of Modern Heroism

The Great War was a watershed for society, politics, and the military, and in many ways set the pattern for the rest of the twentieth century. And the modern concept of heroism in its institutional form was created during the war. As the final battles played out, the powers-that-were recognized the need to bring the official parameters of ultimate heroism in line with the new reality of industrial-scale warfare. Accordingly, a panel was convened to examine the existing Victoria Cross warrants in the fall of 1918. From that commission came the new paradigm embodied in the current VC warrant. Haig's vision of the aggressive hero, forged on the Somme, tempered at Arras, and burnished during the 1918 campaigns, became the new standard of British heroism and has carried on through the Second World War and to the far islands of the South Atlantic.

The first official consideration of the need to reexamine the existing regulations came in the summer of 1918 when Naval Secretary Sir Oswyn Murray contacted the War Office concerning the Elective and Provisional Clauses of the VC Warrant. The Navy dealt with a situation similar to that of the Lancashire Fusiliers at Gallipoli in the form of recommendations generated by the raid on Zeebrugge 22/23 April 1918. In the process of sorting through and resolving the group recommendations, the Navy noted ambiguities of Clause VII (Provisional Bestowal) and Clause XIII (Elected Selection) and inquired if the Army had any thoughts on the subject or archived documents that might shed light on the origins and intent of the clauses.[1]

At the War Office Sir Reginald Brade passed the request on to Deputy Military Secretary Colonel Malcolm David Graham. Graham burrowed into the files and produced a brief that noted three possibilities of the intentions of the original framers of the warrant as to the conditions under which a commander could recommend an individual for a Cross or confer it provisionally, noting none of which were possible in modern warfare. He didn't see a problem with the wording of Clause VII, but noted the ambiguities of Clause XIII. More than anything else, his research revealed that the Army's records on the creation of the Victoria Cross were 'defective,' consisting of the signed 1856 Warrant and two undated, unsigned minute sheets that were little more than fragmentary notes. He and Brade concluded that they dated possibly from 1852, as one set of initials could be read as 'J.P.,' which they took to mean 'Sir J. Pakington,' the Secretary of State in that year.[2] Brade sent a copy of Graham's brief to Murray, along with his observation that since the warrant would need to be amended in the near future to recognize the existence of the Royal Air Force, it might be time to convene a general committee to rewrite the warrant entirely.[3]

The idea was kicked back and forth between the War Office and the Admiralty for the rest of July, with various deficiencies of the existing warrant discussed. At length the Navy let the Army take the lead on approaching King George V for permission to convene a committee to rewrite the warrant, perhaps on the grounds that the majority of VCs had been won by Army personnel over the years. On 30 July 1918 Bertram Blakiston Cubitt wrote the Admiralty on behalf of the War Office to indicate that the Army Council had made a formal request of His Majesty and they would be informed of the decision. The next day Graham wrote to Sir Frederick Ponsonby, the Keeper of the Privy Purse, to brief King George V on the proposed committee.[4] It is at this point that a highly controversial issue entered the discussion.

Ponsonby replied on 3 August that the King approved of the revision and had named him (Ponsonby) as chair of the committee. But there was a specific issue His Majesty wanted clarified:

> There is one point the King wishes you to have discussed privately before the meeting is held, and that is whether or not women should be eligible for the V.C. It is conceivable that a woman driving a motor car, or a nurse, might possibly perform sufficiently gallant services to merit the V.C., but according to the Statutes at present she would not be eligible. The fact that women were eligible for the V.C. might be resented in the Army, and it would be best to go carefully in this matter before any decision is arrived at. On the other hand, if civilians are made eligible according to the new Warrant, the question may be asked why should not women be equally considered. On a matter of this sort, it would perhaps be best for you to ask the opinion of the different offices concerned confidentially.[5]

Technological changes and the concept of total war had made these considerations necessary. On 4 March 1918 the supplement to the *London Gazette* carried the following citation for three recipients of the Military Medal: 'For bravery, coolness, and conspicuous devotion displayed in the performances of their duties on occasions when the Casualty Clearing Station had been under hostile shell fire and bombed by enemy aircraft.'[6] This citation is entirely normal except for one minor detail: the persons cited were Acting Sister Maud Alice Abraham, Civil Hospital Reserve, Sister Florence Broome, Civil Hospital Reserve, and Sister Anna Georgina Boyd, Queen Anne's Imperial Military Nursing Service (Reserve). For the first time in British history, women were winning military gallantry decorations.

The need for manpower drained the resources of the nation. The women of Britain stepped in to fill the gap. Of course, the vestiges of Victorian propriety did not allow them to be placed in a combat role, but they could and did fill the roles of drivers, clerks, and nurses. While they were not carrying weapons, some of their duties did carry risks:

> Soon after 10 o'clock this morning he began putting over high explosive. Everyone had to put on tin-hats and carry on. He kept it up all the morning, with vicious screams. They burst on two sides of us, not fifty yards away – no direct hits on to us but streams of shrapnel, which were quite hot when you picked them up. No one was hurt, which was lucky, and they came everywhere, even through our Canvas Huts in our quarters. Luckily we were so frantically busy that it was easier to pay less attention to it.[7]

By 1917 over 100,000 women had volunteered to fill positions in the service branches.[8] They, too, could display courage in the face of the enemy:

> The nurses' rest hut was blown in, one sister being killed outright and two mortally wounded; amidst the horror of it all shone the glory of greater courage. Light-duty patients risked their lives to drag the orderlies from the burning huts – 32 of them died in the attempt. They spoke, too, of the Ambulance Girls – 'the pluckiest of the lot' – out in the thick of it, picking up the wounded.[9]

These uniformed women were uniformly anonymous unless they left behind an illegal diary or personal memoir; they could not count on anyone actually mentioning them by name unless that name was already well-known. Even acknowledged heroines remained nameless in print:

Three nurses recently received the Military Medal 'for conspicuous bravery under fire, on No. 27 Ambulance Train'. The train was carrying a full load of nearly five hundred sick and wounded away by night from a town in the vicinity of the Somme front, when an aeroplane attack began. Five bombs fell in the immediate neighbourhood of the train. The windows were smashed and the lights went out. The train gave a heave which threw some of the patients out of their cots. One of the sisters is reported to have called out to the men in her coach: 'Now, be quiet and good, boys, till I light a lamp.' This she managed to do, and the men declared that her hand never trembled. The commanding officer reports that 'the sisters went about their work coolly, collectively, and cheerfully, and that by their magnificent conduct they not only allayed the alarm among the helpless patients, and those suffering from shell shock, but caused both patients and personnel to play to the standard which they set.'[10]

Women accompanying the Army were not the only noncombatants facing danger from enemy actions. Submarines lurked off the coast while Zeppelins and Gothas droned through the skies, constant reminders that the enemy could strike areas that traditionally never felt the touch of war. All created new potential scenarios for heroism.[11]

With the King's approval in hand, the question of warrant revision achieved a higher level of significance and moved a rung further up on the bureaucratic ladder. Military Secretary Lieutenant-General Sir Francis Davies sent a formal announcement of the impending redraft to the various service branches and appropriate government offices. Having notified them to nominate a representative to the Warrant Committee, he then dropped the bombshell concerning the possibility of including women as eligible for the VC, using Ponsonby's examples and reasoning as to why this was a question of necessity.[12]

It is interesting to note that in addition to the War Office, the Admiralty, The Colonial Office and the Air Office, Davies also sent a copy of the circular to GHQ in France. Davies informed Ponsonby, 'I have also invited the opinion of Sir Douglas Haig and have suggested that he consult his Army commanders. Their opinion should, I suggest, carry great weight as the number of V.C. awarded outside the Army during the present war is very small in proportion.'[13] This reinforces the argument raised in previous chapters as to the influence of Haig on what the VC was and was not.

Responses to the Davies circular ranged from the rational to the apoplectic. Neither the Air Ministry nor the India Office had any philosophical objection to the inclusion of women, although both stressed in their short replies that it would be important to insure that high standards were maintained governing the bestowal of the award.[14]

Rear Admiral Allan Frederic Everett, Naval Secretary to the First Lord of the Admiralty, however, fired off an angry two-page, single-spaced reply condemning the idea on a number of grounds.

> At first blush, it seems logically indefensible to bar the fair sex from being awarded the V.C. provided of course that they 'have performed some signal act of valour or devotion to their country'.
>
> But there are other considerations, both concrete and abstract, which, it is thought, render the idea impracticable, although it is certainly quite possible that a woman could under certain conceivable conditions earn one.
>
> It must be fully realized that the standard of 'valour and devotion to duty' for the Victoria Cross is now very much higher than it was in the earlier years of its introduction. In fact, it may be said that the standard now required for the award of a V.C. is far, far higher than the actual words express.
>
> Literally, the Victoria Cross could be awarded for any signal act of valour and devotion to duty, and if women are to be eligible, will not the ordinary gallantry of man render his judgment lenient; will he not be soft-hearted towards the woman (marriage proves this) and give her the benefit of the loosest interpretation of a female act of valour or devotion to duty; will he not be inclined to say 'By Jove (or Mars or Venus), for woman that was a splendid deed', and assess her award by virtue of being influenced by her sex? Will not, therefore, the traditional interpretation of the signal act of valour and devotion to duty be elastically applied to the so-called frail sex?
>
> I believe these are practicable considerations which must be taken into serious consideration.
>
> Again, let us suppose that women are eligible, let us hypothecate a retreat where some bloody-minded Virago W.A.A.C. is overtaken by a Hun, might she not be the more induced to take up a bundook and battle with the Hun, might she not be all the more tempted to take some very unladylike action or conduct herself in such an unseemly manner from the universal standard expected of the fair sex that the enemy would proclaim all women combatants and shoot them on sight?
>
> To my mind, it may be a narrow masculine one, it would be a dangerous measure to include females into the V.C. area. There are enough bickerings in the masculine line as to whether this man or that should or should

not have been awarded a V.C., but if the hysterical female world is to be allowed in, God help the poor devils who have to make the decisions.

Until the time comes when man and women are treated alike, when chivalry is dead and buried, when the natures of man and women are identical (which, thank God, is a natural impossibility) then, and not until then, will it be wise to artificially place women on the same rude footing as men.

Them's my sentiments, but what you want is the opinion of the official Admiralty. That I will obtain as soon as possible and let you know.[15]

Everett then proceeded to write the official Navy position, which was almost identical to his initial tirade.[16] A few days later he wrote a much more sedate official reply to the original request, noting that the Admiralty formally opposed the notion (for reasons outlined in his earlier private letter) and that he wanted to address the Navy's concerns over the status of the Merchant Marine in the warrant and a desire to eliminate the provisional bestowal of the award. He closed by reporting that he was writing Ponsonby to outline the Navy's position.[17]

The Davies circular was designed as both a sounding board for a couple of controversial proposals and a suggestion that an interservice panel convene to hammer out a blanket resolution.[18] That proposed committee's role was expanded during the second week of August, with King George V's approval, to examine the entire concept of the Cross with the aim of writing a new warrant incorporating the new realities of warfare and discarding Victorian holdovers that no longer applied. The concerned offices were notified on 26 August that the committee would meet at 2:45 p.m. on Friday 30 August in Room 152 at the War Office.[19]

A number of loose ends needed tying up. Some were mere housekeeping formalities: the inclusion of the Royal Air Force by statute as opposed to practice, the standardization of the ribbon color for all service branches, and official recognition of posthumous awards in the warrant, formalizing a practice that during the Great War had become standard. Others were fairly straightforward: updating Clause VII (provisional bestowal in the field), Clause VIII (mechanism of recommendation), and Clause XII (delayed action recommendations) to reflect modern battle conditions and communications. Also due for discussion was Clause XIII, concerning the elective principle, as well as a precise definition of the eligibility of Indian Imperial Service formations. The final provision of the commission was to address 'any further question which may be laid before the Committee.'[20] It was from these 'further questions' that the controversy would arise.

When the 'Committee on Co-Ordination etc. of Warrants Relating to the V.C.' convened its first meeting, Lieutenant-Colonel the Right Honorable Sir Frederick Ponsonby served as chairman. The other members understood that Ponsonby, as Keeper of the Privy Purse and an intimate of George V, represented His Majesty and spoke for the King.[21] The Army tapped Deputy Military Secretary Colonel Graham as its representative; Admiral Everett, as Naval Secretary, spoke for the Admiralty. Colonel Robert Henry More and Colonel S. D. Gordon represented the Air Ministry and the India Office, respectively. The Colonial Office had two officials present, Lieutenant-Colonel Alexander Elder Beatie and the Assistant Under-Secretary of State, Henry Charles Miller Lambert. Although Robert U. Morgan of the War Office served as Secretary, the actual minutes of the meeting were taken in shorthand by a civilian clerk from the firm of W. B. Gurney and Sons. None of the representatives held a Victoria Cross, and of the military officers, only Lieutenant-Colonel Beatie had a gallantry award (the Military Cross) listed among the honors recorded in the roll of representatives.[22]

That the debate over the controversial aspects of the day's work had become heated since Davies's original letter was reflected in Ponsonby's opening remarks: 'We have got a lot of very simple work in front of us, and a certain amount of rather intricate work. I do not think, however, there is anything that requires any acrimonious discussion.'[23] His hope was apparently to begin with one of the innocuous housekeeping tasks, that of how to word the warrant to bring in the RAF. Should there be separate paragraphs for each service, or could they all be included in one blanket qualifying clause? He turned to Colonel Graham for the Army's thoughts on the matter. He discovered that the Army was thinking about women.

Graham quickly turned the discussion of how to include the RAF into a discourse on the possibility of a woman being in a position to win the VC:

> The only objection I see to that [writing a separate clause for each branch] is that we rather have an advantage in redrafting the warrant by ignoring the status of the individual, and laying down what the decoration can be won for. If we were to determine the specific qualifications under each Service of the State it would be rather complicated. I therefore rather favour the idea that we should say what action can get the V.C. in the Navy, Army and Air Force, and then the question arises, can women and civilians get it? If the answer is Yes, then we can say 'The following shall be the qualifications for which the award can be given.' Then if you take the Navy you have got the side issue of the Mercantile Marine, and if you go to the Army you have the side issue of the nursing services, Queen

Mary's Army Auxiliary Corps, and all these auxiliary departments which, behind the lines from time to time, or it might be in the circumstances of air raids, might possibly win the V.C., although, up to date, there has never been a case approaching it. Still it might happen....[24]

Ponsonby ignored the rambling collection of non-sequiturs and dragged the debate back to the point. He had asked for the Army's opinion on how to rewrite the regulations: were the services to be combined or separated in the warrant? Both Admiral Everett and Colonel Gordon thought it advisable to combine them if possible; Colonel More of the RAF agreed and stated it would be a simple matter to add 'Air Force with the General Officer Commanding it' to the existing litany of qualifying formations and solve the debate. Lambert made it clear that the Colonial Office had no views on this point.[25]

With that point partially resolved Everett finally seemed to realize that Graham's rambling discourse had raised the possibility of including women in the warrant, and took exception to it. This exception had far-reaching implications:

> If we are here to discuss the wording of the Royal Warrant, we think that the words 'some signal act of valour or devotion to their country' as a matter of fact should be very severely interpreted. It is only artificially that the V.C. has reached the very high standard it has reached at present and if you are going to bring women in that particular definition would cover all sorts of petty things.[26]

With that statement he opened the door to a tightening of the limits of heroism with the express purpose of raising the criteria to the point where a woman could never qualify. It was agreed that the requirements for winning a Cross needed to be clarified and strengthened for the twentieth century and the chair, sensing the question of including women might derail the discussion, tried to table the matter. Ponsonby once again felt control of the meeting slipping away as the members then started batting about possible phrases and qualifications, including a suggestion from Graham that starkly reflected the coldness of the new industrial heroism:

> That [tightening the regulations] would cover those cases where a man gets an arm or leg blown off in picking up a bomb, or loses his life by throwing himself upon a bomb. That is pure self sacrifice, and not really valour, I mean.[27]

Sergeant John Carmichael's squad mates would have disagreed with him:

> We were on Hill 60, digging a communication trench, and I was detailed off with a party of men to get it done quick. I was supervising the job. We had men working in the trench and men working outside of it as well. One of the chaps was deepening the trench when his spade struck an unexploded grenade, just lodged there in the side of this trench, and it started to fizz. I was an instructor in bombing, so, knowing a bit about explosives, I knew that there would be seven seconds before it went off unless I did something. I couldn't throw it out, because there were men working outside the trench as well as the blokes in it. So I shouted at them to get clear and I had some idea of smothering it, to get the thing covered, keep it down until they were out of range. All I had was my steel helmet. So I took it off my head, put it over the grenade as it was fizzing away, and stood on it. It was the only way to do it. There was no thought of bravery or anything like that. I was there with the men to do the job, and that's what mattered.
>
> Well, it did go off. They tell me it blew me right out of the trench, but I don't remember that. The next thing I remember was being carried away. That's how I got this thing ... [The Victoria Cross][28]

Carmichael suffered two shattered legs and injuries to his right arm. His mates escaped unscathed.[29]

The chair once again ignored the Army representative and more forcefully brought the meeting back on track by insisting they stick to the outline of the commission that convened them. Neither the issue of including women nor the new guidelines for the official recognition of heroism were settled, and would be revisited.

The committee managed to resolve the issue of provisional Crosses bestowed in the field quickly enough. Given the speed of modern communications, it was no longer necessary to allow that power to the commanding officer in the field. Colonel Graham maintained that there had never been an instance in which a VC had been given in such a manner, but there are actually at least three such incidents: Henry Havelock's Cross granted by his own father in the Mutiny, as well as some of the Crosses given for the storming of the Taku Forts and the disaster at Korn Spruit. Even without these caveats the danger of abuse of this clause was obvious and it was dropped from the warrant draft entirely.[30]

The question of tightening the regulations appeared again on the next point. In considering the standardization of the mechanism of recommendation,

Graham proposed that the Army practice of requiring the written attestation of two eye-witnesses for any act of heroism to win a VC be adopted for all services.[31] The Air Force objected to a two-witness standard, perhaps mindful that many air actions happened very quickly and often quite alone.[32] The committee settled for rewording the clause to require 'conclusive proof,' a phrase stronger than the former proof 'to the satisfaction' of the recommending officer in the field. Ponsonby proposed that the phrase 'backed by two witnesses' be included after 'conclusive proof,' but it is not to be found in the approved draft.[33] Regardless, the intent of the rewording was to force field officers to vet their recommendations more thoroughly before forwarding them.

Not all of the committee's decisions narrowed the distribution of the Victoria Cross. An extensive discussion took place concerning the official inclusion of Dominion and colonial forces. The question here was not so much whether such forces would be eligible, but rather the exact circumstances under which, say, troops from the Union of South Africa or the Togoland Expeditionary Force could win one. Obviously Dominion troops should get it – they had been winning Crosses since the Boer War – but would it be only when acting on behalf of the United Kingdom, or fighting directly alongside British troops, or under British command, or when on their own, or what?

Graham stated that it had become standard practice to consider any colonial or Dominion force under imperial orders eligible for Crosses. Other formations, such as the Indian Imperial Service Battalions who drew their wages from other sources, were qualified only when serving alongside regular forces. He noted that the King's African Rifles and the Punjab Frontier Force were not eligible prior to 1911 (apparently he meant the white officers of the latter of these formations) and would have been eligible on an 'alongside' basis only. They were brought in (apparently in theory, as they are not mentioned in the warrant) by the Indian extension of that year. That no case had ever arisen in which a member of these formations was recommended meant that there had never been an official determination of their status 'although I daresay if a case had arisen it would have been given.'[34]

Lambert of the Colonial Office was adamant that the Dominion forces be included without the necessity of acting alongside British regulars or under the command of British officers. This had been a point of contention for the Colonial Office during the war. Lambert cited a War Office reply to a query on the subject dated 21 March 1916, stating that the Warrant of 1867 (generated in response to the Heaphy case) included all native troops forming part of a Dominion or colonial force regardless of race or color.[35] The chair cut short discussion by simply stating that Dominion troops were eligible without restriction.[36]

Ponsonby was equally accommodating to the Admiralty on the question of including the Merchant Marine in the new warrant. Admiral Everett cited the case of the merchantman SS *Otaki* and the conduct of her captain, Archibald Bissett Smith, in a losing fight with the German raider *Moewe* in 1917. Smith went down with his ship after a gallant defense. All at the Admiralty considered him well deserving of a Victoria Cross, but hesitated to submit the recommendation on the grounds that making civilian crews eligible for military awards would cause the Germans to treat them all as combatants and shoot them on sight.[37]

His argument for the Admiralty's failure to recommend Smith is a bit odd, as the *Otaki* was, in fact, a combat vessel. Although not a commissioned warship, she carried a 4.7-inch gun and engaged the much heavier armed German vessel in a duel before being sunk.[38] Be that as it may, the Germans had proved they would shoot on sight (and in the case of submarine warfare, often without warning) both armed and unarmed vessels, which rendered classing merchantmen as noncombatants a moot point. No one raised any objection to the inclusion of the Merchant Marine, although there was some discussion of 'camouflaging' the gazetting of such awards by listing the winner with a postdated commission in the Naval Reserve, both to give some protection to the merchant vessels and to avoid tipping the Germans to any shipping intelligence.[39] It also served to place the Merchant Marine under Admiralty control as far as awards were concerned.

Including the Merchant Marine opened the question of the status of the civilian in general. There had been four civilian Crosses won during the course of the Mutiny, but those had been brought in by a special warrant of 6 July 1859, which was limited to services performed only during the Indian conflict. There had also been a civilian VC during the Second Afghan War, in which a civilian chaplain, James William Adams, rescued some trapped troopers under fire. He also was brought in under a special amending warrant on 6 August 1881; it was limited to members of the Indian Ecclesiastical Establishment.[40]

That civilians were capable of meeting the military standards of heroism was amply demonstrated by existing cases. What was needed was a simple blanket statement covering all civilians in all circumstances, tying up the loose ends of the question. The main concern was controlling submissions. If it were open to any civilian for any act they might consider courageous the government would be swamped with self-recommendations every time a zeppelin crossed the coastline. The decision was therefore made to make 'acting under the authority' of one of the service branches or specifically denoted government department (such as an Indian Political Officer) the basic qualification.[41] As it turns out, the civilian provisions of the new warrant were never put to the test, in no small part due to the creation of the George Cross during the Blitz in 1940 to reward civilian bravery.

Everett also pressed Ponsonby for the King's pleasure regarding the bestowal of the DSO, DSC, and CB on deserving merchant officers. The chairman approved the distribution of all three awards and assured Everett that the King endorsed the existing Navy practice of issuing an antedated commission for such awards as required the recipient to be a commissioned military officer.[42]

The committee were also of a single mind in the decision to drop the 1858 amendment to the original warrant, extending the Cross to noncombat situations (the *Sarah Sands*/Walsh case). Even back in the nineteenth century this had been a controversial provision because it was seemingly so open to abuse. Colonel Graham cited a note penned during the consideration of the Andaman Islands Victoria Crosses that wondered if it was safe to revive the 'very dangerous Warrant that has remained dormant for 9 years.' Admiral Everett pointed out that the 1858 warrant held the added danger of diluting the military character of the award.[43] Oddly enough, not a single member of the panel seemed aware of the amending warrant of 1881, which dropped the noncombat qualification from the Cross.

The creation of the Albert Medal in 1866 to reward those who risked their lives in saving lives at sea and its extension in 1877 to life saving on land gave the committee an honorable means of disposing of the problem. The Albert Medal was open to all subjects of the Crown, military and civilian, and did not carry the intrinsic military baggage of the Victoria Cross.[44] Thus, the committee was able to divorce the VC from noncombat incidents and the clause was dropped from the new warrant.

Having knocked the already dead warrant of 1858 on the head entirely, Ponsonby decided to postpone the question of posthumous awards and attack the sticky proposal of incorporating women and civilians into the warrant. The first order of business was to establish for the record the official position of the various services branches and offices on the subject. It is worth quoting the minutes of the meeting verbatim at this point, to give the flavor of the moment:

MR MORGAN: On the question of awarding the Victoria Cross to women I have received the opinions of various Government Departments. Shall

I read those out? 'Rear Admiral Everett, Admiralty, considers it logical to award the V.C. to women, but is adverse to the adoption as too much sentiment would enter into and induce recommendations. Will send further opinion.' Lieut. General Sir Herbert Cox, India Office: 'There should be no objection to award to women provided that the standard of merit is not lowered in any sense.' Sir G. Fiddes, Colonial Office: 'It would look better and be more in accordance with public opinion to make women eligible for the V.C. provided always that the standard of the decoration is not lowered.'

MR LAMBERT: That was his own personal view; he was not expressing the Departmental opinion and I do not think the Colonial Office has any definite opinion on the subject.

CHAIRMAN: Major General Sir Godfrey Paine, Air Ministry: 'With regard to the question as to the inclusion of women in the V.C. Warrant, it is only logical that they should be included subject to precise definitions as to eligibility.' The Naval Secretary to the Admiralty notifies officially that the Admiralty do not favour extension of V.C. to women. Mr Delevingne, Home Office, remarks that there are precedents for the award of the Albert and Edward Medals to women. General Ruggles-Brise, G.H.Q., France, 'states that it is difficult to conceive that a woman could perform services sufficient to merit as award of the V.C. at the present standard. The Army Commanders, however, are generally of the opinion that there is no objection to civilians, and therefore women, being eligible for the Victoria Cross, so long as the present high standard is maintained and any tendency to forward recommendations for sentimental reasons is sternly repressed. The Field Marshal Commanding-in-Chief concurs with the above opinions.'[45]

Having read off the official opinions, Ponsonby then opened the floor for debate by declaring his own personal opposition to the proposal on the grounds that it would make women combatants in the eyes of the enemy. He was in this sense a creature of Haig's heroic ideal:

> a civilian or a man of any sort might become a combatant and take the fight to the enemy, but women could never be in a position to fight under any conditions. A woman might save a life, might possibly bring a man back or anything of that sort but the idea the V.C. is now given for, exceptional service in the presence of the enemy, means that women will have in future to be considered as combatants.[46]

A hero does not save the wounded; he kills the enemy. Nurses do not kill the enemy. Therefore, nurses could not be heroes.

Morgan asked who had raised the question of female eligibility. Nobody came forward with an author of the idea, and Ponsonby simply replied by calling it a logical necessity. The ensuing debate spoke much as to the attitude of established authority toward the new role of women in society and serves as further evidence of the hardening of the heart of heroism. It was a logical necessity that women had entered the war effort, but their inclusion was something to be endured rather than cherished.

Both the chair and the India Office agreed that the Victoria Cross was exclusively a combat award: 'The V.C. means that you have to do a bit of fighting – you have to shoot somebody.'[47] Colonel More pointed out that active offensive conduct was not necessary to win a VC; chaplains and doctors won it for noncombat operations. Everett acridly pointed out that it was the business of doctors and chaplains 'to go into the firing line and be in the fighting,' supporting the chair's assertion that they became in essence 'combatants for the moment.' It was not the business of women to do so. When Colonel Gordon suggested they might be there helping, Everett sniped back that 'they ought to clear out.'[48]

At the heart of the issue was the fact that modern weapons extended the danger zone of war far beyond the traditional bounds of the battlefield. While no VC had yet been won during the course of an enemy air raid, the possibility did exist, and while women were not taking official part in active frontline operations, that they served on the staff of rear area establishments placed them in harm's way. As Colonel Graham pointed out:

> It is hard to say what the proper definition is for the V.C.; it is arrived at by a comparison of acts in the field which are well known to the individuals who have the power to recommend, but when you come to the case of the nurse, recently, who received the Military Medal, it was sailing very close to the wind. She was wounded three times, and in spite of that she carried on right through the bombing, and went across the bombed area to look after the other nurses, and having got them under shelter, she went back to her ward, and if she had not fainted they would not have found out that she was hit at all.[49]

Despite the admiral's curt suggestion that they should not be there, they *were* there, and subject to the discipline of the King's Regulations. It was necessary to bring them under the provisions of the warrant, no matter how unseemly or unlikely it was that a woman would ever win a Victoria Cross.

Admiral Everett fought a desperate rearguard action against the consensus of the committee in an effort to exclude women. He constantly broke in on the other members as Ponsonby polled them for their official departmental positions. When Colonel Graham reported that the War Office supported the position of Sir Douglas Haig, Everett interrupted to insist that the field marshal had qualified his approval with the requirement that sentimentality not be allowed to enter into the recommendation process, which 'as long as we are men and women you cannot do it.'[50] That argument was shot down by the RAF representative, who pointed out that the award passed through a hefty approval process which would serve to eliminate any sentimentality on the part of the recommending officer.

Ponsonby tried to get the meeting back on track; in his estimation they were beating a dead horse, as the possibility of a woman ever performing an act heroic enough to win a VC was highly unlikely. Everett shot back that the mere mention of them in the warrant would induce women to go out and try to commit some daring deed, which simply was not their place. It was the proper avocation of the male to seek glory, but an aberration for a woman to do so. Ponsonby managed to break in long enough to ask Graham if the War Office was in favor of the proposal and get an affirmative.

Once Everett had given the expected Admiralty disapproval, Colonel Gordon indicated the India Office's support of the idea. Everett turned his ire on Gordon: 'Do you not see any danger of lessening the high standard for the V.C. if you apply it to women?'[51] Colonel Graham answered that question with the same response More had used to knock down the sentimentality objection: the selection process would insure the rejection of spurious or undeserving recommendations and guard the standards of the award. Temporarily out of ammunition, Everett held his tongue while the chair finished the polling and announced the result that women would be eligible and included in the warrant.[52]

Once the decision to include women had been taken, it was necessary to establish exactly how their inclusion would be worded in the warrant. The ultimate decision was to mention them in the preamble along with the other qualified groups and modify the gender-specific clauses in the body of the document to a gender-neutral phrasing. Everett fired off his last salvo, a request that the preamble carry a disclaimer that the Admiralty did not approve of their inclusion. The request was denied and the issue was resolved.[53]

The remaining business before the committee was the formalization of the posthumous Victoria Cross. Here the debate revealed some surprising misconceptions. Graham opened the issue with a recitation of the development of the posthumous principle that more than anything else revealed his ignorance on the subject. He managed to promote Freddy Roberts to captain in citing the first posthumous award, and offered no explanation as to why he got it when so many others had not. Nor did he cite any of the early queries to Lord Panmure, which had established the precedent that the Cross was an order for the living rather than a decoration for the dead.[54] This exchange illustrates the gulf that had grown between the reality of heroism and the perceptions of the masters of the military. Here they sat in judgment of the heroic ideal, yet they had no concrete history of the Cross to work with.

The chairman was scarcely better in his assertion that 'no man can get the V.C. when he gets killed during the action in which he earns the distinction.' The committee then argued pointlessly as to the precise moment a dead man was actually dead for bureaucratic purposes, completely disregarding the fact that dead men had been winning VCs since 1914 on a fairly regular basis. At length Ponsonby concluded the debate by deciding everyone was in favor of the addition of a paragraph specifically allowing posthumous awards of the medal.[55]

After a short further debate on the subject of civilian eligibility, the committee adjourned on the proposal that Morgan prepare a new draft of the warrant incorporating the changes decided during the meeting. This would be distributed to the concerned departments for internal discussions on approval or amendment. A tentative second meeting of the committee was scheduled for 'about three weeks later' to hammer out any fine points, after which the draft would be submitted to the Army Council and the Admiralty Board for final approval before sending it to his majesty for signature.[56]

September and October 1918 came and went without the panel reconvening. The momentous events in France of those months overshadowed the need to revamp the parameters of the Victoria Cross. When the committee did meet again on 12 November 1918, it was flushed with the news of the Armistice. The service branches had been given sufficient time thoroughly to examine the proposals and come to grips with the changes, as opposed to the first meeting, called less than a fortnight after the initial broaching of the subject. The two most vociferous members of the panel, the misogynistic Everett and the rambling Graham, were replaced; the Admiralty sent Naval Secretary Commodore Sir Rudolf (Walter) Bentinck and the Army spoke its will through Lieutenant-Colonel Lord Herbert A. Montague-Scott.[57] These circumstances combined to make the second meeting flow much more smoothly than the first.

## THE INSTITUTIONALIZATION OF MODERN HEROISM    181

The meeting moved fairly quickly through the changes embodied in the new draft. The rewriting of the introductory clause was approved without comment; it was merely a modernization of the old substance. The Clause II, relating to the design of the ribbon, was called into question as an unnecessary point to make in a warrant, and was bracketed for possible removal (it appears in the final warrant). The committee finally got to the meat of the day with the discussion concerning Clause III, governing the circumstances meriting the award of the Cross.[58]

The clause was extensively reworked and tightened, narrowing the defined limits of Victoria Cross heroism and reflecting the new, aggressive style of the Western Front. The new wording:

> It is ordained that the Cross shall only be awarded for conspicuous bravery or some daring or pre-eminent act of valour or self-sacrifice or extreme devotion to duty in the presence of the enemy.[59]

Replaced the less forceful Victorian:

> It is ordained that the Cross shall only be awarded to those Officers or Men who have served Us in the presence of the enemy, and shall have then performed some signal act of valour or devotion to their country.[60]

The new framing made it clear that the award was for combat; as Morgan carefully pointed out, all was keyed to the final phrase 'in the presence of the enemy.' The qualification had also been moved up in the document from Clause V to Clause III to indicate an increase in importance. The discussion on this topic indicated that there were those of the committee who wanted an even tighter regulation of heroism, cutting out noncombatants entirely; there were other awards for life saving that should suffice to recognize such acts. Given that the only two men to have won bars to the Cross by 1918 had done so in a noncombatant medical capacity,[61] and that the most-decorated other rank in the Army, Lance Corporal William Harold Coltman, won all of his gallantry awards as a stretcher-bearer,[62] the position was untenable. The desire, however, was evident.[63]

Also reflecting the aggressive nature of modern warfare was the injection of Clause IV, covering posthumous VCs. It was passed without debate or comment, as the lethality of the modern battlefield had been burned into the collective conscious of all those present.

Clause VI, delineating those eligible for the award was the longest in the new warrant. The idea in this instance was to produce a definitive list of those who were eligible for the award, closing off any other possible claimants. It passed with little discussion. Lambert requested adding the phrase 'marine services' to the Navy subclause to bring in the units operating on African lakes and out of Hong Kong. He also made sure that the various service branch references included all forces of the Dominions, Colonies, Dependencies, and Protectorates. The inclusion of women, civilians, and the Merchant Marine passed without discussion, an indication of some informal communications in the interim between the meetings. All were included subject to the condition that they were at the time of the act under the authority of one of the regularly constituted armed services.[64]

Clause VIII reworked and streamlined the mechanism of recommendation and approval. The provisional bestowal allowed under the original warrant was quietly dropped, and the suggestion from the first meeting of requiring conclusive proof was incorporated. As a sop to the RAF and the Navy Ponsonby's original suggestion that the Army requirement of two witnesses become standard was not included. Instead, the veracity of the claim was to be determined 'according to the customs of the recommending authority.'[65]

The elective principle was retained in modified and standardized form in Clause IX. The primary fear was giving Crosses too freely; under the original proposal up to eight per 100 men was possible, depending on which service branch was involved, far above the ratio generated by single awards. Colonel Montague-Scott reported that in a campaign the Army generally expected a ratio of one in 5000. To have the possibility of a single engagement of a half-company create eight VCs was unacceptable. After a lengthy debate it was resolved to set the rate at three for actions involving up to 100 men, four for any action involving up to 300 men, and cases where more than 300 were involved would receive 'special consideration.' The election was to be made by secret ballot.[66]

Quite some time was spent discussing the subject of pensions, but this involved little more than crossing t's and dotting i's. The final aspect addressed was the question of forfeiture, which translated to the new warrant with nothing more than a modernization of the language. Having reached a consensus on this draft, it was resolved to print up a new copy and circulate it for a final time to the various departments for final approval. That having been accomplished, it would be sent to the Secretary of State for War, Lord Milner, for submission to the king.[67]

Everett had lost in his opposition to the inclusion of women, but the subsequent decision to tighten the regulations achieved his ends. By linking the Cross even more tightly to aggressive combat actions where 'you have to do a bit of fighting – you have to shoot somebody,' the committee made it impossible for a woman to qualify. Everett and the other misogynists of the panel may have lost by the letter of the warrant, but in practice their desire to exclude women from the exclusive fraternity of the VC has lasted to the present. In the process, however, many men who would have won the Cross under the previous interpretation were excluded as well.

The cessation of hostilities and the needs of hammering out a peace settlement placed the new warrant on the back burner of state affairs. King George's reservations also delayed the publication of the new warrant. The final draft arrived at Buckingham Palace at the end of 1918, but was not signed until 7 March 1919. The King had reversed his position on the inclusion of women; despite his initial instructions to Ponsonby to address the subject in committee, he now delayed signing the new regulations until Privy Secretary Lord Stamfordham and Winston Churchill, who had replaced Lord Milner as Secretary of State for War, convinced him of the necessity of their inclusion. Having signed the warrant, he forced the delay of its publication 'until we are no longer in a state of war.'[68] It may very well be that he feared an avalanche of female recommendations if the warrant was published before the official end of the war and the signing of the peace. By holding the new rules until the present conflict ended there could be no question of retroactive recommendation. Thus, George V did not give permission to publish the warrant until 22 May 1920.

It was in a way appropriate that Churchill was the 'principal minister of state' to countersign the warrant that married the Victorian to the Industrial age. He himself was an incarnation of that union, with a romantic streak dating from his earliest childhood tempered with an uncanny insight into the nature of warfare between mature industrial powers.[69] In a philosophical moment he pondered the changes created by the new military technology:

> The heroes of modern war lie out in the cratered fields, mangled, stifled, scarred; and there are too many of them for exceptional honours. It is mass suffering, mass sacrifice, mass victory. The glory which plays upon the immense scenes of carnage is diffused. No more the blaze of triumph irradiates the helmets of the chiefs. There is only the pale light of a rainy dawn by which forty miles of batteries recommence their fire, and another score of divisions flounder to their death in mud and poison gas.[70]

Churchill presided over the next world war, and although it did not degenerate into the massive stalemate of the first nor see the use of poison gas, it was a time of mass suffering, mass sacrifice, and mass victory. The pace of the war would be far different, but the Victoria Crosses earned would be won by Haig's rules.

The warrant signed into effect in 1920 was modified in subsequent years, including a full rewrite in 1931. The changes made were quite minor: the width of the suspender ribbon was specified, the new extensions of air power in the form of the Royal Air Force Reserve and Auxiliary Air Force were included as eligible, and a special half-size replica of the Cross for dress occasions was authorized. Further amendments were made in 1938 and 1939, recognizing the administrative separation of Burmese Forces from the Indian Establishment and including their eligibility, and recognizing a new definition of the rank of Warrant Officer as eligible. Likewise, the creation of the Indian Air Force provoked an amendment specifying its inclusion in January 1941. An additional amendment was made in 1942, including the Home Guard and Women's Services (a reflection of the Blitz) and allowing Dominion governments to make direct submissions to the Crown (a reflection of the new relationship between Britain and the former colonies).

The final changes to the regulations governing the Cross came in 1961, but once again the modifications were in terms of administration rather than the character of heroism. Clauses VI (what formations are eligible), VIII (process of recommendation), and XV (conditions and procedure of forfeiture) were modified to give almost full autonomy to Dominion governments, subject only to royal consent. Clauses X through XIII were changed to provide a £100 sterling pension per annum to all winners. The warrant's definition of heroism remained precisely the same as the Warrant of 1920.[71]

There was one final and subtle nuance hidden within the rewording of the VC warrant. The fifth clause quietly dropped the Royal plural, 'Us.' The Victoria Cross had grown beyond its original concept of a personal bond between sovereign and soldier. It was now understood to be a tool of command, and as we shall see in the next chapter, a tool of politics as well.

# Ten

# Conclusion: The New Hero in Action, 1940–2006

The Great War killed the Victorian ideal of heroism along with the Victorian Army. Four years of total war created a heroic concept that was lean and merciless. The nature of warfare had changed, and continued to change during the interwar period as weapons and ideas cobbled together in the dark days of the stalemate were refined into systems and doctrines by the survivors. More important, the war had brutalized society, or at the very least numbed it to the magnitude of losses generated by industrial-scale warfare. Nineteenth-century colonial concepts of warfare simply did not apply any more: the death of 35 sepoys from the Kapurthala Imperial Service Infantry killed in 1897 was officially a 'disaster'. In 1919, the loss of 113 dead and 200 wounded in a single day's work on the Northwest Frontier was recorded with as much passion as a laundry report might arouse.[1] As a result of these changes and the decisions of the VC committee at the end of the First World War the cost of heroism increased for the remainder of the century and the nature of the hero became something very different from that of his nineteenth-century ancestor. The heroism of the frontier had also paled in comparison to the sacrifices of the Great War. With the exception of a half-dozen Crosses won in 1919–20 in connection with tying up the loose ends of the war, only three VCs came out of the entire interwar period. The full effect of the new paradigm of heroism established by the interservice meeting had to wait for the next great war to take effect.

It may seem strange that a book dealing with the Victoria Cross that has spent so much ink on the nineteenth century and the First World War sums up the remainder of the history of the Cross in a single chapter encompassing the Second World War and all of the Crosses granted since. A few things must be taken into account at this point. The basic parameters of the Victoria Cross were established during the nineteenth century, with the majority of the test cases that defined the nature of heroism taking place in the first 50 years of the Cross's existence. During this period 521 Crosses were bestowed. The new paradigm of heroism was created during the First World War and set into statute during the interservice conference at the end of the war. During the four years of the First World War and in operations connected with mopping up the aftermath, 634 Crosses were granted. Between 1940 and 2006 only 196 Victoria Crosses were granted, and no significant changes in the statutory parameters of the award were made. Thus, the heavy concentration on the formative phases of the Cross. The decisions reached by the committee in 1918 still govern the VC to this day.

Oddly enough, one of the hypothetical problems discussed in the committee meetings that had generated the most debate never materialized in the Second World War. Admiral Everett was adamant that the Merchant Marine be included, but not a single VC went to the Merchant Marine during the entire course of the war. While several members of the Royal Naval Reserve did receive Crosses, all of them were on active duty at the time:

> On 14 February 1942 in the Java Sea, HMS Li *Wo*, a patrol vessel, formerly a passenger steamer, commanded by [Temporary] Lieutenant [Thomas] Wilkinson, sighted two enemy convoys, one escorted by Japanese warships. The Lieutenant told his crew he had decided to engage the convoy and fight to the last in the hope of inflicting some damage – this decision drew resolute support from the whole ship's crew. In the action which followed a Japanese transport was set on fire and abandoned, and Li *Wo* stayed in action against a heavy cruiser for over an hour before being hit at point-blank range and sunk. Lieutenant Wilkinson ordered his crew to abandon ship, but went down with the Li *Wo*.[2]

A reserve lieutenant in command of a reserve patrol craft was as close as the Admiralty got to a Merchant Marine Victoria Cross. None of the thousands of merchant crewmen who braved the U-boat menace out in the cold Atlantic apparently merited consideration. It may very well be that the sole reason Everett was so adamant was the Navy, knowing that the warrant amendment was to include civilian eligibility, wanted to make sure that any such claims arising at sea were kept firmly under Royal Navy guidelines.

Part of the committee's commission had been to update the warrant in light of the new methods of warfare. Tanks made their first substantial appearance in 1916, and were gradually integrated into the tactical doctrine of the British Army. It is interesting to note that while the forces moved toward mechanization between the World Wars and came to depend on

CONCLUSION: THE NEW HERO IN ACTION, 1940-2006

it during the Second World War, mechanized forces garnered only a small share of the VCs given in either war, four in the First, six in the Second.[3] Even more interesting is the fact that of the Crosses conferred on members of armored units in either war, not a single one went to an act performed while inside a tank. This is phenomenal, given the number of armored vehicles used by the British Army during the Second World War, especially considering the relative vulnerability of Allied armor to that of the Germans.[4] No matter how bravely or recklessly a tanker operated his machine, he had to dismount to receive the highest institutional recognition of his heroism.

One of the most immediate and disturbing effects of the committee's changes in the warrant came, predictably, from the formalization of the posthumous Victoria Cross. Comparing the casualty figures between the two world wars suggests that Ponsonby was not alone in his interpretation of the regulations regarding dead heroes. It was his understanding during the debate on the subject that the individual had to survive the action long enough for his name to be submitted as a recommendation.[5]

Apparently some field officers had the same notion, as the total number of heroes killed in action or died of wounds during the Great War ranged from about 20 to 30 percent per year of the Crosses approved. This figure jumped drastically during the Second World War (Table 10.1).

The higher lethality rate can be attributed to two main factors. Clearing up the regulations concerning posthumous awards probably resulted in more 'killed on the spot' candidates getting submitted for consideration. There was less confusion concerning the letter of the law regarding this aspect of heroism, leaving recommending officers free to recognize the sacrifice of their men.

Table 10.1 The cost of courage, the Second World War: casualties per year

| Year | 1940 16 | | 1941 22 | | 1942 33 | | 1943 25 | | 1944 52 | | 1945 34 | |
|---|---|---|---|---|---|---|---|---|---|---|---|---|
| # Awarded | Raw | % | Raw | % | Raw | % | Raw | % | Raw | % | Raw | % |
| No Wound | 4 | 25 | 5 | 23 | 10 | 30 | 11 | 44 | 13 | 25 | 8 | 24 |
| WIA | 4 | 25 | 6 | 27 | 11 | 33 | 5 | 20 | 12 | 23 | 7 | 21 |
| DOW | 2 | 13 | 6 | 27 | 0 | 0 | 2 | 8 | 10 | 19 | 9 | 26 |
| KIA | 6 | 38 | 5 | 23 | 12 | 36 | 7 | 28 | 17 | 33 | 10 | 29 |
| Total Cas. | 13 | 81 | 13 | 77 | 23 | 70 | 14 | 56 | 39 | 75 | 26 | 76 |
| Total lethal | 8 | 50 | 11 | 50 | 12 | 36 | 9 | 36 | 27 | 52 | 19 | 56 |

The other factor reflected the tightening of the regulations. Instigated in part by Admiral Everett's desire to make sure sentimentality did not induce male officers to recommend 'undeserving' female candidates, tightening the regulations meant that fewer borderline incidents got recommended. Getting killed in the commission of an heroic act was certainly proof of 'extreme devotion to duty,' whereas survival might not be. Thus, a higher proportion of those recommended would be the honored dead, for whom a stronger case could be made under the tighter regulations.

The lethality rate is even more impressive when improvements in the medical services are taken into consideration. The speed with which casualties were transported to medical attention increased with advances in mechanization. Once the wounded soldier arrived at the aid station advances in techniques, equipment, and pharmacology resulted in a greater chance of survival.[6] During the First World War 10 percent of the British Forces mobilized were either killed in action or died of wounds.[7] During the Second, this figure dropped to 4.5 percent.[8] During the First World War, VC winners experienced a lethality rate at most three times greater than that of the rest of the military establishment as a whole. In the Second World War, the lethality rate among Cross winners was over ten times greater than that of the armed forces as a whole. The cost of courage had risen indeed .

In some instances there was no need to make a stronger case. The actions ranged beyond the heroic into the fantastic:

> On 25 March 1945 near Meiktila, Burma, during an attack, Naik Fazal Din's section was held up by fire from enemy bunkers, whereupon he personally attacked the nearest bunker and silenced it, then led his men against the other. Suddenly six Japanese, led by two officers wielding swords rushed out and Naik Fazal Din was run through the chest by one of them. As the sword was withdrawn the naik wrested it from the hands of its owner and killed him with it. Having killed another Japanese with the sword he waved it aloft, continuing to encourage his men before staggering back to make his report and collapsing.[9]

Amazingly, Fazal Din was not the first man to perform such an act; just over a year earlier Lieutenant George Albert Cairns of the Somerset Light Infantry had an arm lopped off by a Japanese officer's sword. He killed the officer, took the sword, and used it to kill several more of the enemy before falling due to blood loss and shock.[10]

Tightening the regulations meant the figures for those wounded in action also increased, although not with the same severity as the lethality rate.

CONCLUSION: THE NEW HERO IN ACTION, 1940–2006   189

During the Great War the overall average of VC winners wounded in action ran at just over 20 percent. Raising the threshold of heroism increased that figure by 5 percent during the Second World War. Overall the cost of courage increased dramatically during the course of the Second World War, with total casualties among VC winners running about 20 percent higher than in the previous world war.[11]

Perhaps the most telling figure is the most basic of all: the raw number of awards given. Rewriting the warrant and tightening the interpretation of the regulations concerning the Victoria Cross resulted in fewer awards being granted. In general the British military was more frugal than its counterparts in any official recognition of heroism. For example, British aircrews sported far fewer ribbons and decorations than their American allies.[12] The Victoria Cross was no exception. During the First World War the Crown confirmed 634 VCs. The Second World War generated 182.

The attitude of the committee toward the nature of heroism shines through in the types of heroism awarded. The figures speak for themselves (Table 10.2). A hero does not save the wounded. A hero does not engage in meaningless acts of a symbolic nature. The hero kills the enemy.

There was little room for humanitarian awards, with even fewer Crosses for life saving than had been seen in the First World War. Haig's vision of the aggressive, remorseless soldier had become the official interpretation of the highest form of heroism. The statistics remain remarkably constant throughout the war. Although it looks like a substantial difference in 1941 with fully 14 percent of the Crosses granted for life saving, it must be pointed out that had just one of the humanitarian VCs of that year been for war winning instead, 1941 would have been statistically identical to 1942.

Table 10.2  Acts winning the Victoria Cross, the Second World War: winners per year

| Year | 1940 16 | | 1941 22 | | 1942 33 | | 1943 25 | | 1944 52 | | 1945 34 | |
|---|---|---|---|---|---|---|---|---|---|---|---|---|
| # Awarded | Raw | % | Raw | % | Raw | % | Raw | % | Raw | % | Raw | % |
| War-winning | 15 | 94 | 19 | 86 | 30 | 91 | 23 | 92 | 48 | 92 | 31 | 91 |
| – Offensive | 7 | 44 | 12 | 56 | 23 | 70 | 23 | 92 | 37 | 71 | 23 | 68 |
| – Defensive | 6 | 37 | 4 | 18 | 5 | 15 | 0 | 0 | 10 | 19 | 6 | 18 |
| – Symbolic | 2 | 12 | 1 | 5 | 2 | 6 | 0 | 0 | 0 | 0 | 1 | 3 |
| – Secondary | 0 | 0 | 1 | 5 | 0 | 0 | 0 | 0 | 1 | 2 | 1 | 3 |
| Humanitarian | 1 | 6 | 3 | 14 | 3 | 9 | 2 | 8 | 3 | 6 | 3 | 9 |

The majority of the Second World War VCs – 107 – went to forces originating in the United Kingdom, and of those 55 percent went to land forces. In the Army the distribution is what might be expected, with the infantry taking 80 percent of the VCs granted. Armored units won four medals, but as noted above, none while actually in a tank. Artillery units and Airborne Infantry won three awards each.

The Royal Air Force and Royal Navy won 23 Crosses each. In the RAF all but one went to bomber crews and of those 18 went to aircrew members whose act allowed the plane to continue missions despite damage – RAF VCs will be discussed in greater detail below. For the Royal Navy 39 percent went to special operations. Four Crosses went to the crews of miniature submarines who attacked the German *Tirpitz* and the Japanese *Takao*, while five went for harbor raids, such as the 27/28 March 1942 operation at St Nazaire to scuttle the *Camperdown* at the lock gates. The Navy still valued 'good form,' as 13 percent of RN Crosses went to commanders who attacked a superior foe, generally with fatal results. Both Navy and Air Force granted awards recognizing cumulative command accomplishment, but very sparingly.

The First World War ratio of awards earned by men holding a temporary or acting rank remained constant in the Second, with 22.5 percent of the awards thus won. The distribution was similar to that of 1917, with minor variations – a couple more majors, a couple fewer lieutenant-colonels.

In terms of other national formations involved, Indian troops collected the second largest number of Crosses; their 31 awards represent 17 percent of the war's total. That fully 97 percent of the Indian Establishment's awards went to infantry is a reflection of the difference in force composition as opposed to that of the British Army. Of the Indian awards only three went to White officers of Indian units. Units from Australia and New Zealand garnered 14 percent of the overall total, or 27 medals. Theirs and the Indian VC statistics follow closely the overall distribution by type of act, with slightly over 90 percent given for war-winning acts. The 13 Canadian VCs – 7 percent of the overall number – vary from this pattern, with 31 percent granted for life-saving acts. The Second World War also saw three South African VCs and the first and only VC conferred upon a Fijian.

It is possible that a new use of the Victoria Cross emerged during the First World War, awards granted for political or doctrinal purposes. Statistical analysis of the frequency and timing of VCs on the Western Front suggest that Douglas Haig may have given Crosses more liberally for actions that confirmed his tactical doctrines and supported his strategy. In the absence of concrete documentary evidence this must remain a mere suspicion in

## CONCLUSION: THE NEW HERO IN ACTION, 1940–2006 191

the case of Haig, but during the Second World War this became standard practice for the Royal Air Force.

The youngest of the service branches was still in its infancy in the Great War, with nothing approaching a concrete doctrine for most of the conflict.[13] The VCs won by pilots for the duration of the First World War reflected the romantic reputation of the flyer. All but one were either for aerial combat or rescuing a downed comrade from possible capture.[14]

Between the wars, however, the RAF developed a new doctrine of strategic bombardment.[15] The bomber, not the fighter, was the savior of the nation:

> It was definitely Bomber Command's wholesale destruction of the invasion barges in the Channel ports that convinced the Germans of the futility of attempting to cross the Channel, especially as Fighter Command's victory meant that our bombers could have fighter cover over the Channel if necessary . . . Our attacks on the barges began in July of 1940, well before the main air Battle of Britain developed, and were highly successful.[16]

Not surprisingly, Arthur Harris, the author of the above assessment of the Battle of Britain (that Bomber Command had it won before Fighter Command got decently engaged with the enemy) got the nickname of 'Bomber.'

The RAF had staked its future as an independent service on the doctrine of strategic bombing.[17] Here Arthur Harris had the chance to prove that an air force could fight and win a war from the skies, and proudly boasted that the RAF was the first force to conceive the concept and build itself around it.[18] As a consequence, the Victoria Cross was used to validate the strategic vision of Bomber Command. Only one VC of the Second World War was awarded to a fighter pilot:

> On 16 August 1940 near Southampton, Flight Lieutenant [Eric J. B.] Nicolson's Hurricane was fired on by a Messerschmitt 110, injuring the pilot in one eye and one foot. His engine was also damaged and the petrol tank set alight. As he struggled to leave the blazing machine he saw another Messerschmitt, and managed to get back into the bucket seat, pressed the firing button, continuing firing until the enemy plane dived away to destruction. Not until then did he bale out, and when he landed in a field, he was unable to release his parachute owing to his badly burned hands.[19]

Every other aerial Cross went to bomber missions, either for cumulative command achievement, striking a high-profile target, or in connection with actions that allowed crippled aircraft or wounded bomber crews to continue their mission, thus validating the maxim that the bomber would always get through.

Typical of the RAF Victoria Cross for the Second World War is the citation of Squadron Leader Arthur Stewart King Scarf, including the posthumous notation:

> On 9 December 1941 in Malaya, near the Siam border, all available aircraft had been ordered to make a daylight raid on Singora, in Siam. Squadron Leader Scarf, as leader of the raid, had just taken off from the base at Butterworth when enemy aircraft swept in destroying or disabling all of the rest of the machines. The Squadron Leader decided nevertheless to fly alone to Singora. Despite attacks from roving fighters he completed his bombing run and was on his way back when his aircraft became riddled with bullets and he was severely wounded. He managed to crash-land the Blenheim at Alor Star, without causing any injury to his crew, and was rushed to hospital where he died two hours later.[20]

Even more to the point is the Victoria Cross granted to Squadron Leader John Dering Nettleton for the 17 April 1942 daylight raid on the Maschinenfabrik Augsburg Nuremberg Gesellschaft – the famed Augsburg Raid.[21] Soon after taking over Bomber Command, Harris was eager to prove that Britain could best be served by bombing the means of production rather than sending his planes after the products themselves. The proper role of Bomber Command in the war effort was under debate in the spring of 1942. On 16 April the War Cabinet appointed an independent arbiter to evaluate the RAF's potential based on past experience with both German and British aerial operations. Harris needed to demonstrate Bomber Command's ability to strike targets deep in enemy territory precisely and effectively. He sorted through available high-profile targets and decided to hit Augsburg.[22] In this instance, he wanted a surgical strike against the engine assembly building where U-boat diesels were put together rather than continuing the coastal raids on the U-boat bases.[23] The target was far beyond the range of a fighter escort, but the operational order cheerfully explained that the new Lancasters should expect little trouble:

> The heavy bomber carries a powerful defensive armament, it is capable of comparatively high speeds, and it has a long range. Operating in

daylight the fire-power of a section of three heavy bombers is such as to deter all but the most determined of enemy fighters. Its speed provides the enemy with a difficult interception problem. Its range enables it to outflank the enemy defences and to strike deep into the southern interior of Germany.[24]

Two flights of six Lancasters each made the raid on Augsburg. Nettleton's six got chopped up by German fighters near Beaumont-le-Roger, four destroyed and the other two badly damaged. Nettleton proceeded on to the target where the two aircraft ran a withering flak gauntlet, costing him a fifth airplane. The other flight, commanded by Squadron Leader John Seymour Sherwood, managed to arrive unscathed at Augsburg, but fierce anti-aircraft fire knocked his and another aircraft down. The raid did manage to place seventeen 1000-lb bombs on target, five of which failed to explode. This did considerable structural damage to the assembly plant, but little to the machinery inside.[25] The raid cost seven of Britain's newest bombers and their irreplaceable aircrews.

Harris nominated Nettleton and Sherwood for VCs. Nettleton was recommended without reservation; he had penetrated, struck the target, and returned. Sherwood was recommended in the same document, but a marginal note on his portion of the paperwork directed that his recommendation should be reduced to a Distinguished Service Order if it was later learned that he had survived the crash of his aircraft. He did survive bailing out and was taken prisoner, and consequently received the DSO.[26]

The raid on Augsburg was not particularly effective. It did close down the motor works for a few days, but Germany had many other plants manufacturing U-boat engines. The losses, while proportionally large for a single mission, were not numerically abnormal for RAF bomber operations. Bomber Command lost 1716 aircraft during 1942, an average of just under five per day. By November 1942 Air Ministry figures showed that a bomber crew had only a 44 percent chance of surviving its first tour of duty.[27] Even during the more limited operations in 1940–41 single-raid losses exceeded those of Augsburg. For example, a daylight raid on Brest on 24 July 1941 cost 12 aircraft.[28] The factor that generated a VC in this case was neither a spectacular success nor a horrendous loss; it was Harris's need to vindicate deep penetration raids into German airspace. Nettleton was gazetted just 11 days after the raid.

By the Second World War it is clear that the speed with which a recommendation passed through the vetting process was an indicator of the political or doctrinal importance of certain targets or actions. Every large organization develops a certain amount of bureaucratic inertia that must be overcome before anything gets accomplished. Military formations are no exception. The speed with which any single task moves through a bureaucratic process is an indicator of that task's relative importance. If it happens abnormally fast, it is a safe bet that the high command is interested in its rapid processing. The RAF offers six cases in point that bear examination.

There were 182 VCs awarded in the Second World War. For each one a certain amount of time passed between the commission of the act and the official gazetting of the award. This 'lag-time' between act and gazette date varied from as low as eight days to as high as 2084 days. The median average of lag-time was 90 days.[29] Eighty-six (47.7 percent) had a lag-time between 60 and 120 days. One hundred and thirty of the awards (72 percent) were gazetted between 30 and 150 days after the act. Of the medals that fall outside this majority, only 13 Crosses (7.2 percent) were published in less than 30 days. Thirty-seven VCs (20.5 percent) were granted following a lag-time of more than 150 days.

These long lag-times for the latter category can be explained in a variety of ways. In some cases the individual was either killed or taken prisoner, as were the witnesses to the act. In such cases the recommendation could not be made until the release of the eyewitnesses at the end of the war. Thus the heroism of Honorary Captain John Weir Foote, Canadian Chaplain's Service during the raid on Dieppe, 19 August 1942, was not gazetted until 14 February 1946:

> Captain Foote coolly and calmly during the eight hours of the battle walked about collecting the wounded, saving many lives by his gallant efforts and inspiring those around him by his example. At the end of this gruelling time he climbed from the landing craft that was to have taken him to safety and deliberately walked into the German position in order to be taken prisoner so that he could be a help to those men who would be held in captivity until the end of the war.[30]

Not until the release of POWs at the end of the war could the true intentions of his actions be determined from the accounts of the men he accompanied into captivity.

In some instances the recommendation might be held up by circumstances beyond anyone's control. Such was the situation for Lieutenant Cairns, the officer who had disarmed a sword-wielding Japanese officer in March 1944. His recommendation was in the dispatch pouch accompanying General Orde Wingate when he died in an air crash. Consequently, the particulars of the recommendation were not obtained until well after the end of the war; Cairns was not gazetted until 20 May 1949, the last of the Second World War's awards.[31]

The quick vetting of some of the recommendations cannot be attributed to some force of fate or enemy action. Speeding the wheels of bureaucratic entropy required pressure from above. Thirteen Crosses were gazetted in under 30 days. For some reason these awards were hurried through an adjudication process that was normally slow and deliberate.

Seven of those 13 went for air operations; six of those seven were generated by Bomber Command. Five of those six went to missions against high-profile targets. Flight Lieutenant Roderick A. B. Learoyd bombed the Dortmund-Ems Canal, one of the highest- priority targets mentioned in Harris's memoirs, and in the process demonstrated Bomber Command's proficiency in precision bombing.[32] Nettleton's raid on Augsburg was the trial by fire for unescorted bombers. Likewise was the daring daylight raid on the port of Bremen, led by Wing Commander Hughie I. Edwards on 4 July 1941.[33]

Wing Commander Guy Gibson got a Cross for dam-busting. The large dams at Mohne, Sorpe and Eder were tempting targets. As 'Mutt and Jeff' [Captain 'Mutt' Summers and 'Jeff' – Barnes Wallis, the creator of the dambuster bomb] explained in Gibson's initial briefing, these dams supplied water for drinking and industrial uses and generated electrical power for a large portion of the heavily industrialized Ruhr River Valley. Not only would their destruction reduce the Reich's power production and industrial output, but the flood damage resulting from their sudden rupture had the potential to do 'more damage to everything than has ever happened in this war.'[34] Massive destruction of enemy production, power generation, and civilian workforce from a single air strike would vindicate Harris's position on the effectiveness of strategic bombing

Bomber Command's salvation of England in destroying the invasion barges won a VC for Sergeant John Hannah, whose efforts to extinguish a fire aboard his aircraft allowed the pilot to bring the crippled aircraft to a safe landing. Harris saw these barges as a distinct threat to British security, but 'the War Office seems to have lacked appreciation of how they could be used to put troops across the Channel or of the enormous number of them available.'[35] The gun is not smoking, but the barrel is warm and there is a scent of cordite in the air. It appears the RAF was using the VC to validate the high command's doctrine.

This having been said, it is necessary to point out that the political steering of the types of heroism granted official recognition does not detract from the heroism displayed by the winners. Each of the 'quick' RAF winners displayed extreme valour and courage. In some instances, such as with the sixth of the quick winners, it was nothing less than phenomenal:

> The sergeant [James Allen Ward, Royal New Zealand AF] crawled out through a narrow astro-hatch, scrambled onto the back of the starboard engine which was alight, and smothered the flames with an engine cover. His crawl back over the wing in which he had previously torn hand and foot-holes, was more dangerous than the outward journey, but he managed it with the help of the aircraft's navigator. The bomber was eventually landed safely.[36]

Unfortunately, Ward did not live to receive the Cross he won the night of 7 July 1941. He died in a raid on Hamburg ten weeks later, before the official award ceremony.[37]

The RAF was not the only service that generated VCs for political or doctrinal purposes. A case can also be made for operations centered on German heavy warships. In August 1940 Churchill categorized *Scharnhorst*, *Gneisenau*, *Bismarck*, and *Tirpitz* as 'targets of supreme consequence' in a memo to the RAF.[38] The emphasis on the cruisers intensified after the costly destruction of *Bismarck* on 27 May 1941 through a combination of surface and air action.[39]

German success on the Continent had given the *Kriegsmarine* access to a variety of Atlantic ports. During the last seven months of 1940 U-boats, aircraft, and surface raiders sank an average of 450,000 tons per month, losses the British Merchant Marine could not afford. It only got worse in 1941, with totals topping a half million tons sunk in both March and April.[40] Such losses prompted Churchill to declare that the 'Battle of the Atlantic' had begun in a directive issued on 6 March 1941.[41] Although most of the losses came from U-boat action, the very visible German cruisers stationed in French ports loomed large in the public mind. In the spring and summer of 1941 the Admiralty rated the surface raiders as a greater threat to British survival than the U-boat menace.[42]

A protracted naval stalemate developed in 1941, with the German heavies lurking in Brest and other Atlantic ports and both the Royal Navy and Royal Air Force unable to inflict any serious damage on them. Churchill's directive had in part refocused RAF efforts on pounding these ships.[43] By 7 July over 1400 sorties had flown against them. Flying Officer Kenneth Campbell managed to hit *Gneisenau* with a torpedo on the night of 4/5 April 1941, at the cost of his life, aircraft, and crew.[44] A subsequent raid on 10/11 April

## CONCLUSION: THE NEW HERO IN ACTION, 1940–2006

inflicted four more hits on the battle cruiser, killing many of her crew and putting her out of action for a few months. The rest of the sorties missed entirely.[45]

The RAF kept up pressure on the port throughout the summer of 1941. *Scharnhorst* relocated to the port of La Pallice, where two late July raids scored hits. *Prinz Eugen* suffered serious damage during a night raid by 52 Wellington bombers in July as well.[46] A host of light raids took place in the fall of 1941, but failed to inflict any further damage. Between 1 December 1941 and 12 February 1942 a further 1922 sorties struck at the German warships, all without scoring a hit.[47]

On 12 February 1942 the battle cruisers *Gneisenau* and *Scharnhorst*, accompanied by the cruiser *Prinz Eugen*, broke out of the port of Brest and steamed north up the Channel for German waters. They made the passage in the face of an incoherent, almost entirely ineffectual defense of home waters.[48] The only group that even came close to striking the fugitive warships was 825 Squadron, Fleet Air Arm, a flight of hopelessly outclassed Swordfish torpedo bombers.[49]

> On 12 February 1942 in the Straits of Dover, Lieutenant Commander [Eugene] Esmonde led his squadron of six Swordfish to the attack of two German battle cruisers and the cruiser *Prinz Eugen*, which were entering the Straits strongly escorted by surface craft. Detached from their escorting fighters (just 10 in number) by enemy fighters, all the aircraft of the squadron were damaged, but even after Lieutenant-Commander Esmonde's plane sustained a direct hit he still continued the run-in towards the target until it [his aircraft, not the *Prinz Eugen*] burst into flames and crashed into the sea. The squadron went on to launch a gallant attack, but none of the six aircraft returned.[50]

Esmonde's citation failed to mention that 825 Squadron was blown from the sky without scoring a single hit on any of the three ships. All of the Swordfish were shot down and Esmonde was killed. Only five men were recovered from the waters of the Channel.[51]

Interestingly enough, the same squadron led the aerial attack on *Bismarck* on 25 May 1941, flying from the deck of HMS *Victorious*. There were no VCs given in connection with sinking *Bismarck* – to 825 Squadron or any other entity.[52] Nor had any Crosses come to the aircrews that actually sank the German commerce raider *Kongisberg* on 10 April 1940. *Konigsberg* was a light cruiser, mounting 5.9 inch guns and capable of 32 knots, just the kind of commerce raider the Admiralty was worried about. She was sunk at anchor in Bergen Harbor by Skua dive bombers. The squadron leaders, Captain R. T. Partridge (Royal Marines) and Lieutenant W. P. Lucy (Royal Navy) both received the DSO.[53] Why, then, did a futile gesture in February 1942 win the highest accolades of heroism? The answer may lie in the political response to the cruiser sortie from Brest.

The winter of 1941–42 was a rough time for the Churchill War Cabinet. Criticism of the Churchill government had been growing throughout 1941, although initially most had been directed at allegedly incompetent lesser lights in the administration. After the fall of Crete, however, criticism became increasingly focused on the prime minister himself.[54]

Japanese entry into the war provided the opportunity for both friends and foes of the government to re-examine the management of the war effort to date. Chamberlainite backbenchers rallied around Alexander Erskine Hill, Tory MP for Edinburgh North, demanding reform of the government's structure.[55] The center of discussion was the amount of authority in the hands of the prime minister. At this same time the government was in the midst of reorganization, contemplating the creation of a new cabinet-level position for a Minister of Production. Churchill responded to the military reverses and the criticism stemming from them by turning parliamentary debate at the end of January on the management of the war into a vote of confidence in the ministry. He was vindicated after three days of debate with a substantial division in favor of the government.[56]

With the vote of confidence won, Churchill reshuffled his ministry. In the midst of this process, however, word arrived of reverses in North Africa and the Far East. Before the month was out Singapore fell, Auchinleck was pushed back to Gazala, and, embarrassingly close to home, the *Kriegsmarine* sailed three capital ships the length of the English Channel apparently unscathed.[57] Public confidence in the ministry wavered, despite its official endorsement by the House of Commons.[58]

A storm of criticism washed over the ministry for the apparent impotence of the British response to the enemy trailing its coat along the coast.[59] Both in the streets and in the House of Commons angry questions were asked.[60] Sir Alexander Cadogan, Permanent Under-Secretary at the Foreign Office despaired to his diary:

> So far I have been unable to hear that we have been able to knock any paint off of them. We are nothing but failure and inefficiency everywhere and the Japs are murdering our men and raping our women in Hong Kong . . . I am running out of whisky.[61]

## CONCLUSION: THE NEW HERO IN ACTION, 1940-2006

In a confidential communique to President Roosevelt, Churchill pointed out that it was probably to the Allied advantage to have the German ships concentrated in northern ports as it limited their deployment options. The public mood of the day was succinctly summed up by the prime minister, however: 'it looked very bad at the time to everyone in the Grand Alliance outside our most secret circles.'[62] In fact, both *Scharnhorst* and *Gneisenau* had suffered damage from air-dropped mines during the dash. Churchill knew this through an Ultra intercept of *Kriegsmarine* signals, but was unable to release this information for public consumption without revealing that he was reading German communiques.[63]

In the midst of a potential ministerial crisis, the government badly needed some abstract good news for official report to the Commons. The failure to destroy any of the ships as they lay in port was embarrassing. Allowing them to escape by running up the Channel was unacceptable. Lieutenant Commander Esmonde was gazetted a VC on 3 March 1942, just 19 days after dying while failing to inflict any damage on the enemy. This is a suspiciously short lag time, and well off the 90-day median average. Also well off the median was Flying Officer Kenneth Campbell, who had damaged *Gneisenau* in April of the previous year. Ten days after Esmonde's award he received a posthumous VC on 13 March 1942, 341 days after the act.[64] The only two individuals who could be singled out as having inflicted any damage or had at least died trying to do so were gazetted as heroes.[65] Thus, an incident that was politically embarrassing had been sheathed with a veneer of glory.

It was an unspoken argument. Churchill did not specifically mention the two Cross winners in any subsequent address on the subject. The basic question was whether or not the ministry had failed in its duty in allowing the ships' escape. Had the maximum effort been put into effect? The blood of the courageous lent an aura of glory to failure. Dead heroes meant that every effort had been made to strike a blow at the enemy. While the circumstances surrounding the recognition of the acts do not lessen their heroism, it is obvious that, given the lack of similar recognition for similar action against similar targets, had there not been a political need these acts would not have won the Victoria Cross.

The pattern established on the Western Front and confirmed in the Second World War has remained true to the end of the century. Eleven Victoria Crosses were granted between the end of the Second World War and the end of the century, some in connection with United Nations obligations, some to Dominion forces in a conflict entirely divorced from the mother country, and some resulting from the last gasps of imperial bravado. In each environment, the 1950s, the 1960s, and in 1982 the factor in common was that the hero killed the enemy.

During the Korean War four men earned Victoria Crosses.[66] In each instance the Cross winner engaged in personal combat with the enemy; three of the four died in the performance of the heroic act. A prime example of the Haig-driven idea was exhibited by Major Kenneth Muir in 1950:

> On 23 September near Songju, Korea, there was difficulty in evacuating the wounded after a position had been captured, until Major Muir arrived with a stretcher party. When the enemy started to launch a series of attacks on the positions, the major took command and after a direct hit from a fire-bomb, causing further casualties, he led a counter-attack and the crest of the position was regained. He was determined to hold until all the wounded had been evacuated and moved about his small force shouting encouragement and firing a 2-inch mortar himself until he was mortally wounded.[67]

Muir's VC came not due to his arrival to evacuate the wounded, nor even to his taking command during the enemy counterattack, but rather to his personal manning of a weapon and inflicting casualties on the enemy until he himself was killed. In addition, Muir's case bears a resemblance to that of Daniel Laidlaw, piping encouragement through a cloud of British chlorine at the Battle of Loos: the 'direct hit from a fire-bomb' was an incident of friendly fire, an air-dropped napalm strike.[68]

Australian involvement in the Vietnam conflict also generated four Victoria Crosses. The involvement of Australian forces was initially confined to providing advisors to the Army of the Republic of Vietnam. Although the Australian presence eventually grew to 50,000 men and included combat troops as well as advisors, the four VCs won went to members of the Australian Army Training Team.[69]

Despite the origins through the Australian chain of command, these Southeast Asian VCs maintained a modified version of the tradition of the First World War. Three of the four went to personal actions inflicting casualties on the enemy. For example:

> On 23 February 1967 in Vietnam, Major [Peter John] Badcoe rescued, under heavy fire, a United States Medical Adviser. On 7 March he led his company in an attack and turned what seemed to be certain defeat into a victory. Again, on 7 April he attempted to lead his company against more powerful opposition. This final act of bravery resulted in his death.[70]

# CONCLUSION: THE NEW HERO IN ACTION, 1940–2006

The fourth Vietnam VC was earned for leadership in conducting a fighting withdrawal. While the aggressive heritage of the Western Front Cross was evident in the Australian awards, there was a divergence from the British tradition. In each case the citation pointed out that part of the action was taken to defend or extract wounded or cut-off troops.

Three Victoria Crosses were won in the small battles in the twilight of empire. These VCs were earned through post-war imperial commitments, and in each instance the heroism displayed conformed to Haig's vision.[71] All three winners made single-handed assaults on enemy machine-gun emplacements; two did not survive their attempts:

On 12 June 1982 on Mount Longdon, East Falkland, Sergeant [Ian John] McKay was in command of his platoon, its commander having been wounded in the leg. They were pinned down by heavy enemy fire and several of the men had been either killed or wounded. Sergeant McKay realized that something must be done and he charged the enemy alone. He was killed at the moment of his victory, but his action enabled his comrades to extricate themselves from a most dangerous situation.[72]

Had McKay carried a Lee-Enfield Mk III bolt-action instead of an L1A1 rifle, his citation could have been for action at Arras.

As of this writing (February 2007) the Victoria Cross has entered the twenty-first century with a pair of Crosses won in connection with British operations in Iraq and Afghanistan. They split the divide between life saving and war winning exactly.

Private Johnson Beharry of the Princess of Wales's Royal Regiment won his VC for life saving in Al Amarah, Iraq. On 1 May 2004 his Warrior armored fighting vehicle (AFV) was hit by multiple rocket-propelled grenades, knocking out communications, wounding the platoon commander, the gunner and a number of other men in the vehicle, and setting the vehicle on fire. Beharry accelerated out of the ambush, leading five other AFVs to safety. Once he stopped at the Clinic House outpost he dismounted and while still under small-arms fire climbed the burning AFV to remove his wounded commander from the turret, returned under fire a second time to do the same with the gunner, and then led the disoriented and wounded men from the troop compartment to safety. On 11 June 2004 he was again at the controls of a Warrior when it came under attack. In the initial volley of rocket grenades one hit the frontal armor six inches from his head, resulting in severe injuries. Despite the wounds, he reversed the vehicle out of the ambush before losing consciousness, which allowed his platoon mates to extract him and the rest of the crew in relative safety.[73]

The second VC won in the twenty-first century went to Corporal Bryan James Budd of the 3rd Battalion of the Parachute Regiment for actions in Afghanistan in the summer of 2006. On 27 July Corporal Budd led an attack on an Afghan strong point after two of his squad mates had been hit and were lying exposed to further small-arms fire. His leadership flushed the snipers out of cover and allowed the survivors to be evacuated and saved. On 20 August during a sweep through Sangin District Center, Corporal Budd led his section through heavy brush in an attempt to surprise a group of enemy fighters. Surprise was lost when the enemy caught sight of an armed Land Rover supporting the operation. Corporal Budd attempted to seize the initiative by conducting an all-out assault, ordering his men to follow him. As they moved forward heavy fire knocked down three of his men and forced the rest to take cover. Corporal Budd continued the assault alone, killing the enemy as he rushed their position, continuing the attack after being wounded. The rest of his platoon reorganized and pushed forward. When they recovered Budd's body he was surrounded by three dead Taliban.[74]

In the history of the Victoria Cross we see a momentous transformation in the nature of institutional heroism. In the Victorian period the VC encapsulated and reified a romantic military ideal with a strong humanitarian component. The same officials responsible for evaluating heroic deeds were, in addition, unable to offer a definition of heroism; like art, like beauty, it was in the eye of the beholder.[75] This changed forever during the First World War as the Cross became inextricably linked to aggressive, enemy-killing actions. By the end of the war military officials could state with confidence that winning the VC meant that you had to shoot someone.

The Cross was initially a product of a social climate that was receptive, even eager for a national, egalitarian gallantry award. It reflected the growing importance of middle-class cultural values, especially the ideals of personal responsibility, self-improvement as a virtue, and the recognition of individual accomplishment. It was a reflection of a jingoistic attitude in a nation at war after decades of peace. It also reflected the desire of the British to be as progressive as their French ally in the recognition of the individual hero: certainly if a French soldier was recognized in the press and by the government for gallantry, there had to be equally deserving British warriors.

The political climate was responsive to this social mood, and the creation of the award could serve political needs on both sides of the political equation. There was a call within Parliament for an egalitarian award for

## CONCLUSION: THE NEW HERO IN ACTION, 1940–2006

the individual hero. The Queen and Prince Consort wanted a new link to the Army to replace their perceived loss of influence within it. The award represented cheap balm to mend fences between the Palmerston government and Queen Victoria. All parties concerned had something to gain from the institutionalization of the abstract ideal.

The award inaugurated by the 1856 warrant was quite Victorian in its application. It was egalitarian – to a point. By statute and Lord Panmure's ruling, all personnel were to be considered equally, regardless of rank at the time of the act. In practice the award was slanted toward the lower echelons of the officer corps, particularly the rank equivalent to that of the Army lieutenant. This was due in part to the nature of nineteenth-century warfare, with many actions involving small units and lower ranking officers detailed off in independent command situations. Heroism by senior officers was increasingly deemed inappropriate. Sir Colin Campbell cursed a colonel who neglected commanding his unit to capture an enemy standard. Ian Hamilton, recommended and denied a second time as a lieutenant colonel, was told his place was to command, not to gallop off in some stunt worthy of a subaltern. The Victorian concept of heroism valued dash and impetuosity in youth, but required sober reserve from age and experience.

The heroism deemed worthy of the Victoria Cross was fairly broad in its nineteenth-century definition, and to a certain extent was concerned more with style over substance. While 'war-winning' acts more often than not gathered the lion's share of awards in each decade, actions saving the life of a comrade always garnered a respectable percentage, and in some decades actually surpassed acts that took the war to the enemy. The military establishment was willing to recognize the gallantry in retrieving a wounded man. Paternalistic, romantic class relationships were further sanctified in the awards given to loyal soldiers who rescued a living officer or risked their lives to retrieve the body of a dead one.

The Victorian Victoria Cross was, for most of its incarnation, an award for the living. On numerous occasions the War Office repeated that point, denying all claims to posthumous Crosses. In instances of extreme though fatal valour or an especially sentimental circumstance, such as Melvill and Coghill, the War Office grudgingly gazetted the hero as 'would have been recommended to Her Majesty had he survived.' Only as a result of the Victorian sense of fair play did this posthumous prohibition change at the very end of the Victorian/Edwardian era with the granting of the Roberts posthumous VC. While there was some evidence of nepotism and favoritism – the Havelock provisional bestowal, the Roberts case – the War Office and Horse Guards were meticulous in maintaining the integrity of the award. Only 12 percent of the pre-war Crosses had any connection with the aristocracy (surprisingly, given the proportion of the officer corps with aristocratic connections), and as the circumstances of the posthumous Cross for Lieutenant Coghill demonstrate, aristocratic influence did not guarantee the bestowal of the award.

The romantic conception of heroism and warfare could not survive on the Western Front. Warfare had become an industrial process, a vast corporate effort to slaughter the enemy in the most efficient manner possible. The nature of the war was summed up in the machine gun – a device, a machine designed to kill people with production-line speed and precision without a hint of individual distinction, its victims as faceless and nameless as the lock-stepping proletarians of Fritz Lang's *Metropolis*. Soldiers became nothing more than another statistic in an economy of scale, a combat consumable to be processed from the raw material of the civilian, stockpiled along with the boots and artillery shells, and expended as dispassionately as a rifle cartridge.

The human cost of industrial-scale warfare exceeded the wildest dreams and darkest nightmares of the Victorian concept. The magnitude of the bloodletting made all previous wars pale in comparison. The futility of a war effort in which 'battles' lasted months on end and 'advances' were measured in yards per offensive in return for casualty lists larger than the Army's pre-war establishment muted the significance of individual feats of heroism. The capture of a single machine-gun emplacement, while a tremendous accomplishment on the company level, did not break the enemy's position in the same fashion as breaching a gate or carrying an embrasure had in the nineteenth century.

This new type of warfare, with anonymous death and seemingly futile individual sacrifices, bred a new command concept of heroism. Once the stalemate of the Western Front fully developed, the war became a contest of attrition. Attrition merely required soldiers who killed the enemy in a positive ratio to their own losses. Soldiers killed or wounded recovering casualties did not contribute to this goal, and in the minds of the high command, they therefore did not deserve the highest accolades of heroism. Thus the belief arose that to win the VC 'you have to do a bit of fighting – you have to shoot somebody.' By the end of the war Haig's Western Front concept of the aggressive, man-killing hero had become the British paradigm, and has remained in effect to the end of the century and beyond.

With this new concept of heroism came new uses of heroism. The hero was used as an example of desired behavior. This is not exactly a new idea, as the recognition of virtue as much as its counterpart, delinquency, was a regular feature of military discipline from the institution of the Good

## CONCLUSION: THE NEW HERO IN ACTION, 1940-2006

Conduct Medal under Lord Howick in 1837. In this instance, however, the desired behavior was not showing good form or self-sacrificing compassion. The desired behavior was that of a homicidal maniac, eager to kill until killed himself. The hero also developed significance as a tool of politics and doctrine; the VC may have been used to validate Haig's strategic vision and protect his control of military affairs.

These changes in practice became the institutional standard in the wake of the war. In their effort to exclude women from the Victoria Cross the committee members tightened the standards for the award, intrinsically linking it with aggressive combat operations. This new institutional standard, combined with the official endorsement of posthumous awards had two powerful effects. Fewer Crosses were granted during the Second World War because of the tighter regulations. The cost of VC-caliber heroism increased dramatically; whereas Cross winners in the First World War experienced a casualty rate three times greater than the military establishment as a whole, those of the Second World War suffered a casualty rate ten times greater than the rest of the military at a time when overall casualties had dropped to a rate less than half that of the Great War.

The Cross has been quietly divorced from its formal Crown connection, with the royal 'Us' dropped from the current warrant governing the award. It has been transformed into a political tool rather than a romantic supra-political and institutional ideal. Bomber Command used the VC to promote the doctrine of strategic bombing. The Churchill government probably used the VC to deflect criticism over the Channel dash of the German cruisers. The use of the Cross for political purposes continued into the 1980s: when Margaret Thatcher took her seat on the platform at the 1983 Conservative Party Congress it was beside Sara Jones, the widow of Lieutenant-Colonel Herbert Jones, VC, the Falklands War hero of Goose Green.[76] At the same time, there is little evidence at the time of this writing that the most recent winners of the VC have been used for political purposes; British operations in Afghanistan and Iraq are exceptionally divisive and controversial, yet little controversy has been attached in the popular press and in less formal arenas to the heroism of Beharry and Budd.

The Victoria Cross has endured many environmental changes since its inception. The political arena that spawned it has long since passed away; the popular matrix that demanded it no longer exists; the very nature of warfare in which its standards were set has changed, leaving no place for private Tommy Atkins to seize the enemy's colors or young Lord William Publicschool to rally the broken square armed with nothing more than a swagger-stick. The usefulness of the Cross itself has changed from connecting the monarch to the rank and file of the military to a being a tool of command and party politics. Yet regardless of the machinations of the masters of the military, both civilian and in uniform, it does not tarnish the acts of the winners. There remains one constant at the core of the Cross: It takes a hero to win one.

# Appendix: The Victoria Cross Warrants

## I THE ORIGINAL WARRANT INSTITUTING THE VICTORIA CROSS, 29 JANUARY 1856

Victoria by the Grace of God of the United Kingdom of Great Britain and Ireland Queen Defender of the Faith &c. To all to whom these Presents shall come Greeting! Whereas We taking into Our Royal consideration that there exists no means of adequately rewarding the individual gallant services either of Officers of the lower grades in Our Naval and Military Service or of Warrant and Petty Officers Seamen and Marines in Our Navy and Non-commissioned Officers and Soldiers in Our Army. And Whereas the third Class of Our Most Honourable Order of the Bath is limited except in very rare cases to the higher ranks of both Services and the granting of Medals both in Our Navy and Army is only awarded for long service or meritorious conduct, rather than for bravery in Action or distinction before an enemy, such cases alone excepted while [sic] a general Medal is granted for a particular Action or Campaign or a Clasp added to the Medal for some special engagement, in both of which cases all share equally in the boon and those who by their valour have particularly signalized themselves remain undistinguished from their comrades. Now for the purpose of attaining an end so desirable as that of rewarding individual instances of merit and valour We have instituted and created and by these Presents for Us Our Heirs and Successors institute and create a new Naval and Military Decoration, which We are desirous should be highly prized and eagerly sought after by the Officers and Men of Our Naval and Military Services and are graciously pleased to make ordain and establish the following rules and ordinances for the government of the same which shall from henceforth be inviolably observed and kept.

*Firstly* It is ordained that the distinction shall be styled and designated the 'Victoria Cross' and shall consist of a Maltese Cross of Bronze with Our Royal Crest in the centre and underneath which an Escroll bearing this inscription 'For Valour'.

*Secondly* It is ordained that the Cross shall be suspended from the left breast by a Blue Riband for the Navy and by a Red Riband for the Army.

*Thirdly* It is ordained that the names of those upon whom We may be pleased to confer the decoration shall be published in the *London Gazette* and a registry thereof kept in the office of Our Secretary of State for War.

*Fourthly* It is ordained that anyone who, after having received the Cross, shall again perform an Act of bravery which, if he had not received such Cross would have entitled him to it, such further act shall be recorded by a Bar attached to the riband by which the Cross is suspended and for every additional act of bravery an additional Bar may be added.

*Fifthly* It is ordained that the Cross shall only be awarded to those Officers or Men who have served Us in the presence of the Enemy and shall then have performed some signal act of valour or devotion to their Country.

*Sixthly* It is ordained with a view to place all persons on a perfectly equal footing in relation to eligibility for the Decoration that neither rank nor long service nor wounds nor any other circumstance or condition whatsoever save the merit of conspicuous bravery shall be held to establish a sufficient claim to the honour.

Seventhly It is ordained that the Decoration may be conferred on the spot where the act to be rewarded by the grant of such Decoration has been performed under the following circumstances:

I. When the Fleet or Army in which such Act has been performed is under the eye and command of an Admiral or General Officer commanding the Forces.

II. Where the Naval or Military Force is under the eye and command of an Admiral or Commodore Commanding a Squadron or detached Naval Force or of a General Commanding a Corps or Division or Brigade on a distinct and detached Service when such Admiral Commodore or General Officer shall have the power of conferring the Decoration on the spot subject to confirmation by Us.

Eighthly It is ordained where such act shall not have been performed in sight of a Commanding Officer as aforesaid then the claimant for the honour shall prove the act to the satisfaction of the Captain or Officer Commanding his Ship or to the Officer Commanding the Regiment to which the Claimant belongs and such Captain or such Commanding Officer shall report the same through the usual channel to the Admiral or Commodore Commanding the Force employed on the Service or to the Officer Commanding the Forces in the Field who shall call for such description and attestation of the act as he may think requisite and on approval shall recommend the grant of the Decoration.

Ninthly It is ordained that every person selected for the Cross under rule seven shall be publicly decorated before the Naval or Military Force or body to which he belongs and with which the act of bravery for which he is to be rewarded shall have been performed and his name shall be recorded in a General Order together with the cause of his especial distinction.

Tenthly It is ordained that every person selected under rule eight shall receive his Decoration as soon as possible and his name shall like-wise appear in a General Order as above required, such General Order to be issued by the Naval or Military Commander of the Forces employed on the Service.

Eleventhly It is ordained that the General Orders above referred to shall from time to time be transmitted to our Secretary of State for War to be laid before Us and shall be by him registered.

Twelfthly It is ordained that as cases may arise not falling within the rules above specified or in which a claim though well founded may not have been established on the spot We will on the joint submission of Our Secretary of State for War and of Our Commander-in-Chief of Our army or on that of Our Lord High Admiral or Lords Commissioners of the Admiralty in the case of the Navy confer the Decoration but never without conclusive proof of the performance of the act of bravery for which the claim is made.

Thirteenthly It is ordained that in the event of a gallant and daring act having been performed by a Squadron Ship's Company a detached body of Seamen and Marines not under fifty in number or by a Brigade Regiment Troop or Company in which the Admiral General or other Officer Commanding such Forces may deem that all are equally brave and distinguished and that no special selection can be made by them, Then in such case the Admiral, General or other Officer Commanding may direct that for any such body of Seamen and Marines or for every Troop or Company of Soldiers one Officer shall be selected by the Officers engaged for the Decoration; and in like manner one Petty Officer or Non-commissioned Officer shall be selected by the Petty Officers and Non-commissioned Officers engaged; and two Seamen or Private Soldiers or Marines shall be selected by the Seamen or Private Soldiers or Marines engaged respectively for the Decoration; and the names of those selected shall be transmitted by the Senior Officer in Command of the Naval Force Brigade Regiment Troop or Company to the Admiral or General Officer Commanding who shall in due manner confer the Decoration as if the acts were done under his own eye.

Fourteenthly It is ordained that every Warrant Officer Petty Officer Seaman or Marine or Non-Commissioned Officer or Soldier who shall have received the Cross shall from the date of the act by which the Decoration has been gained be entitled to a Special Pension of Ten Pounds a year; and each additional bar conferred under rule four on such Warrant or Petty Officers or Non-Commissioned Officers or Men, shall carry with it an additional pension of Five Pounds per annum.

Fifteenthly In order to make such additional provision as shall effectually preserve pure this Most Honourable distinction it is ordained that if any person on whom such distinction shall be conferred be convicted of Treason, Cowardice, Felony or of any infamous Crime, or if he be accused of any such offence and doth not after a reasonable time surrender himself to be tried for the same his name shall forthwith be erased from the Registry of Individuals upon whom the said Decoration shall have been conferred by an especial Warrant under Our Royal Sign Manual, and the pension conferred under rule fourteen shall cease and determine from the date of such Warrant. It is hereby further declared that We Our Heirs and Successors shall be the sole judge of the circumstances demanding such expulsion; moreover We shall at all times have power to restore such persons as may at any time have been expelled, both to the enjoyment of the Decoration and Pension.

Given at Our Court at Buckingham Palace this twenty-ninth day of January in the Nineteenth Year of Our Reign and in the Year of Our Lord One Thousand Eight Hundred and Fifty Six.

By Her Majesty's Command
Panmur

## II  AMENDING WARRANT: ELIGIBILITY OF INDIAN ESTABLISHMENT (WHITE ONLY), 29 OCTOBER 1857

Victoria, by the Grace of God, of the United Kingdom of Great Britain and Ireland, Queen, Defender of the Faith, To all to whom these Presents shall come, Greeting! Whereas by a Warrant under Our Royal Sign Manual, countersigned by one of Our Principal Secretaries of State, and bearing date at Our Court at Buckingham Palace, the twenty ninth day of January, 1856, in the Nineteenth year of Our Reign, constitute & create a new Naval & Military decoration, to be styled & designated the 'Victoria Cross', which decoration We expressed the desire should be highly prized & eagerly sought after by the Officers & Men of Our Naval & Military Services, & did also make, ordain & establish the rules & ordinances therein set forth for the Government of the same to be thenceforth inviolably observed & kept.

And whereas for divers reasons Us thereunto moving, We are desirous of rewarding the individual gallant services of Officers & Men of the Naval & Military Service of the East India Company, by the bestowal of the said decoration which We are desirous shall be highly prized & eagerly sought after by the Officers & Men of the said Service.

Now know Ye that We, of Our especial grace, certain knowledge, & mere motion have thought fit hereby to signify Our Royal Will & Pleasure that the said Decoration shall be conferred on the Officers & Men of the Naval & Military Service of the East India Company who may be qualified to receive the same in accordance with the rules & ordinances made, ordained, & established by Us for the Government thereof, by Our said recited Warrant, and We do by these Presents for Us, Our Heirs & Successors, ordain & appoint that it shall be competent for the Officers & Men of the said service to obtain the said decoration in the manner set forth in the rules & ordinances referred to, or in accordance with any further rules & ordinances which may hereafter be made & promulgated by Us, Our Heirs & Successors, for the Government of the said decoration.

Given at Our Court at Windsor, the Twenty ninth day of October 1857, in the Twenty first year of Our Reign.

By Her Majesty's Command,
Panmure

## III AMENDING WARRANT: NON-COMBAT OPERATIONS, 10 AUGUST 1858

Victoria, by the Grace of God, of the United Kingdom of Great Britain and Ireland, Queen, Defender of the Faith, To all to whom these Presents shall come, Greeting!

Whereas by a Warrant under Our Royal Sign Manual, countersigned by one of Our Principal Secretaries of State, and bearing date at Our Court at Buckingham Palace the Twenty-ninth day of January, 1856, in the nineteenth year of Our Reign, We did constitute and create a new Naval and Military Decoration, to be styled and designated the 'Victoria Cross', which decoration We expressed Our desire should be highly prized and eagerly sought after by the Officers and men of Our Naval and Military Services, and did also make, ordain, and establish the rules and ordinances therein set forth for the government of the same, to be then henceforth inviolably observed and kept,

And whereas by another Warrant, under Our Royal Sign Manual, countersigned by one of Our Principal Secretaries of State, and bearing date at Our Court at Windsor, the Twenty-ninth day of October 1857, in the Twenty first year of Our Reign, We thought fit to signify Our Royal Will and Pleasure that the said decoration shall be conferred on the Officers and men of the Naval and Military Services of the East India Company, who may be qualified to receive the same, in accordance with the rules and ordinances made, ordained, and established by Us for the government thereof by Our said first recited Warrant,

And Whereas by the rules and ordinances established by Our said Warrant, it is, amongst other things, ordained that the Victoria Cross shall only be awarded to those Officers or men who have served Us in the presence of the Enemy, and shall have then performed some signal act of valour or devotion to their country, and that with a view to place all persons on a perfectly equal footing in relation to eligibility for the decoration, neither rank, nor long service, nor wounds, nor any other circumstance or condition whatsoever, save the merit of conspicuous bravery shall be held to establish a sufficient claim to the honour,

And, Whereas, for divers reasons Us thereunto moving, We are desirous of rewarding individual instances of conspicuous courage and bravery which may be displayed by Officers and men in Our Naval and Military Services, and in the Naval and Military Services of the East India Company, under circumstances of extreme danger, such as the occurrence of a fire on board Ship, or of the foundering of a vessel-at Sea, or under any other circumstances in which through the courage and devotion displayed, life or public property may be saved.

Now know Ye, that We, of Our especial Grace, certain knowledge, and mere motion, have thought fit hereby to signify Our Royal Will and Pleasure that the said decoration shall be conferred on the Officers and men in Our Naval and Military Services and in the Naval and Military Services of the East India Company, who may perform acts of conspicuous courage and bravery under the circumstances referred to in this Our Warrant. Provided, nevertheless, and We do hereby, for Us, Our Heirs and Successors, declare, ordain, and appoint that nothing herein contained shall be deemed or construed to have the effect, of altering, abrogating, or dispensing with the rules and ordinances set forth in Our said just recited Warrant, or any of them, except so far as may be necessary for the purpose of enabling Us to confer the said decoration on the Officers and men of Our Naval and Military Services or of the Naval and Military Services of the East India Company in conformity with the provisions of this Our Warrant.

Given at Our Court at Buckingham Palace, this Tenth day of August, 1858 in the Twenty second year of Our Reign.

By Her Majesty's Command
J. Peel

## IV  AMENDING WARRANT: CIVILIAN SERVICE DURING THE MUTINY, 13 DECEMBER 1858

Victoria, by the Grace of God of the United Kingdom of Great Britain and Ireland, Queen, Defender of the Faith, To all to whom these Presents shall come, Greeting! Whereas by a Warrant under Our Royal Sign Manual, countersigned by one of Our Principal Secretaries of State, and bearing date at Our Court at Buckingham Palace the 29th day of January 1856, in the nineteenth year of Our Reign, We did constitute and create a new naval and military decoration to be styled and designated the Victoria Cross, which decoration We expressed Our desire should be highly prized and eagerly sought after by the Officers and men of Our Naval and Military services and did also make ordain and establish the rules and ordinances therein set forth for the Government of the same, to be henceforth inviolably observed and kept.

And Whereas by another Warrant under Our Royal Sign Manual countersigned by one of Our Principal Secretaries of State and bearing date at Our Court at Windsor, the 29th day of October 1857, in the Twenty first year of Our Reign, We thought fit to signify Our Royal Will and Pleasure, that the said decoration shall be conferred on the Officers and men of the Naval and Military Service of the East India Company – now Our Indian Naval and Military Forces who may be qualified to receive the same in accordance with the rules and ordinances made ordained and established by Us for the Government thereof by Our first recited Warrant aforesaid.

And Whereas during the progress of the operations which We have undertaken against the Insurgent Mutineers in India, it has not infrequently happened that non military persons who have borne arms as volunteers against the mutineers both at Lucknow and elsewhere have performed deeds of gallantry in consideration of which they are not according to the strict provisions of Our first recited Warrant eligible for this high distinction.

Now know ye that We of Our especial grace, certain knowledge and mere motion, have thought fit hereby to signify Our Royal Will and Pleasure that the said decoration shall be conferred on such non military persons as aforesaid, who may be qualified to receive the same in accordance with the rules and ordinances made ordained and established by Us for the Government thereof by Our said first recited Warrant, and We do by these presents for Us, Our Heirs and Successors, ordain and appoint that it should be competent for such non military persons as aforesaid to obtain the said decoration in the manner set forth in the rules and ordinances referred to, or in accordance with such further rules and ordinances as may hereafter be made and promulgated by Us, Our Heirs and Successors for the Government of the aforesaid decoration provided that it be established in any case that the person was serving under the orders of a General or other Officer in Command of Troops in the Field.

Given at Our Court at Osborne House Isle of Wight, the 13th day of December 1858, in the Twenty second year of Our Reign.

By Her Majesty's Command,
J. Peel

## V AMENDING WARRANT: COLONIAL AND IRREGULAR FORCES, 1 JANUARY 1867

Victoria, by the Grace of God, of the United Kingdom of Great Britain and Ireland, Queen, Defender of the Faith. To all to whom these Presents shall come, Greeting!

Whereas, by a Warrant under Our Royal Sign Manual, counter-signed by one of Our Principal Secretaries of State, and bearing date at Our Court at Buckingham Palace, the 29th day of January, 1856, in the Nineteenth year of Our Reign, We did constitute and create a new Naval and Military decoration, to be styled and designated the 'Victoria Cross,' which decoration We expressed Our desire should be highly prized and eagerly sought after by the Officers and men of Our Naval and Military Services, and did also make, ordain, and establish the rules and Ordinances therein set forth for the government of the same, to be thenceforth inviolably observed and kept.

And whereas, during the progress of the operations which We have undertaken against the Insurgent Native tribes in Our Colony of New Zealand, it has happened that persons serving in the local forces of Our said Colony, have performed deeds of gallantry in consideration of which they are not, according to the strict provisions of Our said recited Warrant, eligible for this high distinction, Now know ye, that We, of Our especial grace, certain knowledge, and mere motion, have thought fit hereby to signify Our Royal Will and Pleasure that the said decoration may be conferred on such persons aforesaid, who may be qualified to receive the same in accordance with the rules and Ordinances made, ordained, and established by Us for the government thereof, by Our said recited Warrant, and We do by these Presents for Us, Our Heirs and Successors, ordain and appoint that it shall be competent for such persons aforesaid to obtain the said decoration in the manner set forth in the rules and Ordinances referred to, or in accordance with such further rules and Ordinances as may hereafter be made and promulgated by Us, Our Heirs and Successors, for the government of the said decoration, provided that it be established in any case that the person was serving with Our Troops, under the orders of a General or other Officer, under circumstances which would entitle an Officer or Soldier of Our Army to be recommended for the said decoration, in accordance with the rules and Ordinances prescribed in Our said recited Warrant, and provided also that such person shall be recommended for it by such General or other Officer.

And We do further, for Us, Our Heirs and Successors, ordain and appoint that the said decoration may also be conferred, in accordance with the rules and Ordinances prescribed in Our said recited Warrant, and subject to the provisos aforesaid, on such persons who may be qualified to receive the same, in accordance with the said rules and Ordinances, as may hereafter be employed in the local Forces raised, or which may be raised in Our Colonies and their dependencies, who may be called upon to serve in co-operation with Our Troops, in military operations which it may be necessary to undertake for the suppression of Rebellion against Our authority, or for repelling invasion by a Foreign enemy.

Given at Our Court at Osborne House, Isle of Wight, this First day of January, 1867, in the Thirtieth year of Our Reign.

By Her Majesty's Command
J. Peel

## VI AMENDING WARRANT: ELIMINATING THE NON-COMBAT PROVISO; EXTENSION OF ELIGIBILITY TO AUXILIARY SERVICES, 23 APRIL 1881

Whereas doubts have arisen as to the qualification required for the decoration of the Victoria Cross, and whereas the description of such qualification in Our Warrant of 29th January 1856 is not uniform,

Our Will and Pleasure is that the qualification shall be 'conspicuous bravery or devotion to the country in the presence of the enemy,' and that Our Warrant of 29th January 1856 shall be read and interpreted accordingly.

It is Our further Will and Pleasure that Officers and men of Our Auxiliary and Reserve forces (Naval and Military) shall be eligible for the decoration of the Victoria Cross under the conditions of Our said Warrant, as amended by this Our Warrant.

Given at Our Court at Osborne this 23rd day of April 1881, in the forty fourth year of Our reign.

By Her Majesty's Command,
Hugh C. E. Childers

## VII AMENDING WARRANT: INDIAN ECCLESIASTICAL ESTABLISHMENT, 6 AUGUST 1881

Victoria by the Grace of God of the United Kingdom of Great Britain and Ireland Queen, Defender of the Faith, Empress of India, To all to whom these Presents shall come, Greeting!

Whereas by a Warrant under Our Royal Sign Manual countersigned by one of Our Principal Secretaries of State and bearing date at Our Court at Buckingham Palace the 29th day of January 1856 in the Nineteenth year of Our Reign, We did constitute and create a new Naval and Military decoration to be styled and designated the 'Victoria Cross', which decoration We expressed Our desire should be highly prized and eagerly sought after by the Officers and Men of Our Naval and Military services, and did also make, ordain, and establish the rules and ordinances therein set forth for the Government of the same to be thenceforth inviolably observed and kept;

And Whereas, by another Warrant under Our Royal Sign Manual, countersigned by one of Our Principal Secretaries of State and bearing date at Our Court at Windsor the Twenty-ninth day of October 1857 in the Twenty first year of Our Reign, We thought fit to signify Our Royal Will and Pleasure that the said decoration shall be conferred on the Officers and Men of the Naval and Military services of the East India Company who may be qualified to receive the same in accordance with the rules and ordinances made, ordained, and established by Us for the government thereof by Our first recited Warrant aforesaid,

And Whereas it has been represented to Us that the Members of the Indian Ecclesiastical Establishments, although not receiving Military Commissions, are liable to be attached to an Army in the field and are then required to perform the same duties as the Commissioned Chaplains of Our Army, who are eligible for this decoration,

Now know ye that We of Our especial grace, certain knowledge, and mere motion have thought fit hereby to signify Our Royal Will and Pleasure that the said decoration shall be conferred on such persons as aforesaid who may be qualified to receive the same, in accordance with the rules and ordinances made, ordained, and established by Us for the Government thereof by Our said first recited Warrant and We do by these Presents for Us, Our Heirs and Successors, ordain and appoint that it shall be competent for such persons as aforesaid to obtain the said decoration in the manner set forth in the rules and ordinances referred to, or in accordance with such further rules and ordinances as may hereafter be made and promulgated by Us, Our Heirs and Successors, for the Government of the said decoration provided that it be established in any case that the person was serving for the time being under the orders of a General, or other Officer, in Command of Troops in the Field.

Given at Our Court at Osborne House, Isle of Wight, this Sixth day of August 1881, in the Forty fifth year of Our Reign.

By Her Majesty's Command.
Hugh C. E. Childers.

## VIII AMENDING WARRANT: NATIVE TROOPS OF THE INDIAN ESTABLISHMENT, 21 OCTOBER 1911

GEORGE, by the Grace of God, of the United Kingdom of Great Britain and Ireland, and of the British Dominions beyond the Seas, King, Defender of the Faith, Emperor of India, to all to whom these presents shall come, Greeting!

WHEREAS Her Majesty, Queen Victoria, by a Warrant under her Royal Sign Manual, countersigned by one of Her Principal Secretaries of State, and bearing date at Her Court at Buckingham Palace, the twenty-ninth day of January, one thousand eight hundred and fifty-six, in the nineteenth year of Her reign, did institute and create a new naval and military decoration, to be styled and designated the 'Victoria Cross', which decoration She expressed Her desire should be highly prized and eagerly sought after by the officers and men of Her

Naval and Military Services, and did also make, ordain, and establish the rules and ordinances therein set forth for the government of the same, to be thence-forward inviolably observed and kept.

And whereas for divers reasons Us thereunto moving, We are desirous of rewarding the individual gallant services of native officers, non-commissioned officers and men of Our Indian Army by the bestowal of the said decoration, which We are desirous shall be highly prized and eagerly sought after by the said native officers, non-commissioned officers and men.

Now know ye that We, of Our especial grace, certain knowledge, and mere motion, have thought fit hereby to signify Our Royal Will and Pleasure that the said decoration shall be conferred on the native officers, non-commissioned officers and men of Our Indian army who may be qualified to receive the same in accordance with the rules and ordinances made, ordained and established for the government thereof by the said recited Warrant, and We do by these Presents, for Us, Our Heirs and Successors, ordain and appoint that it shall be competent for the native officers, non-commissioned officers and men of Our Indian Army to obtain the said decoration in the manner set forth in the rules and ordinances referred to, or in accordance with any further rules and ordinances which may hereafter be made and promulgated by Us, Our Heirs and Successors, for the government of the said decoration.

And We do further, for Us, Our Heirs and Successors, ordain and appoint that in place of the special pension conferred by the fourteenth rule of the said recited Warrant, every native officer who shall have received the Cross shall from the date of the act by which such decoration has been gained be entitled to a special pension of five hundred and twenty-five rupees a year, and each additional bar conferred under the fourth rule on such native officer shall carry with it an additional pension of one hundred and fifty rupees a year. In the case of a warrant or non-commissioned officer or soldier the special pension shall be one hundred and fifty rupees, with seventy-five rupees additional for each additional bar. On the death of a recipient of the Cross these pensions shall be continued to his widow until her death or remarriage.

Given at Our Court at St. James's this 21st day of October, in the second year of Our Reign, and in the year of Our Lord one thousand nine hundred and eleven.

By His Majesty's Command,
HALDANE OF CLOAN

## IX NEW WARRANT: SUPERCEDING ALL PREVIOUS REGULATIONS, 22 MAY 1920

WHEREAS Her late Majesty Queen Victoria, by a Warrant under Her Royal Sign Manual dated 29th January, 1856, did create a Naval and Military Decoration to be styled and designated 'The Victoria Cross', and did express Her desire that this decoration should be highly prized and eagerly sought after by the Officers and Men of Her Naval and Military Services.

AND WHEREAS by divers subsequent Warrants other Officers and Men were admitted to and made eligible for the decoration, and certain amendments were made to the Rules and Ordinances attaching thereto.

AND WHEREAS We deem it expedient that the said Warrant and subsequent Warrants before referred to, as also the Rules and Ordinances affecting the same, shall be consolidated, varied and extended.

NOW, THEREFORE, We do hereby declare that the said Warrants, and the Rules and Ordinances heretofore in force for the Government of the said Decoration, shall for that purpose be amended, varied, modified and extended; and in substitution thereof We by these presents, for Us, Our Heirs and Successors, are graciously pleased to make, ordain and establish the following Rules and Ordinances for the Government of the same which shall from henceforth be inviolably observed and kept:

Firstly, it is ordained that the distinction shall as heretofore be styled and designated 'The Victoria Cross', and shall consist of a Maltese Cross of bronze with our Royal Crest in the centre and underneath it an escroll bearing this inscription: 'For Valour'.

Secondly, it is ordained that the Cross shall be suspended from the left breast by a red riband, and on those occasions when only the riband is worn a replica of the Cross in miniature shall be affixed to the centre of the riband.

Thirdly, it is ordained that the Cross shall only be awarded for most conspicuous bravery or some daring or pre-eminent act of valour or self-sacrifice or extreme devotion to duty in the presence of the enemy.

Fourthly, it is ordained that the Cross may be awarded posthumously.

Fifthly, it is ordained that the names of all those persons upon or on account of whom We may be pleased to confer or present the decoration shall be published in the *London Gazette*, and a Registry thereof kept in the Office of Our Secretary of State for War.

Sixthly, it is ordained that:-

(1) Officers, Warrant Officers and subordinate Officers hereinafter referred to as Officers, Chief Petty Officers and Petty Officers hereinafter referred to as Petty Officers, men and boys hereinafter referred to as Seamen, serving in - (a) our Navy or in ships of any description for the time being under Naval Command; (b) our Indian Marine Services; (c) Navies or Marine Services of our Dominions, Colonies, Dependencies or Protectorates; and (d) our Mercantile Marine whilst serving under Naval or Military Authority, or who in the course of their duties may become subject to enemy action;

(2) Officers, Warrant Officers, Non-Commissioned Officers, men and boys hereinafter referred to as Marines, serving in our Marines;

(3) Officers, Warrant Officers (Classes I. and II.), Non-Commissioned Officers, men and boys hereinafter referred to as Privates, of all ranks serving in our Army, our Army Reserve, our Territorial or other forces, and the Forces of our Dominions, Colonies, Dependencies or Protectorates;

(4) Officers, Warrant Officers, Non-Commissioned Officers, and Airmen in the ranks of Our Air Force, or the Air Forces of our Dominions, Colonies, Dependencies or Protectorates;

(5) British and Indian Officers and men of all ranks of Our Indian Army, the Imperial Service Troops of Native States of India, or any other Forces there serving under the Command, guidance, or direction of any British or Indian Officer, or of a Political Officer attached to such Forces on Our behalf, and

(6) Matrons, sisters, nurses and the staff of the Nursing Services and other Services pertaining to Hospitals and Nursing, and civilians of either sex serving regularly or temporarily under the Orders, direction or supervision of any of the above mentioned Forces shall be eligible for the decoration of the Cross.

Seventhly, it is ordained that if any recipient of the Cross shall again perform such an act of bravery, as would have made him or her eligible to receive the Cross, such further act of bravery shall be recorded by a Bar to be attached to the Riband by which the Cross is suspended, and for every such additional act of bravery, an additional Bar shall be added, and any such Bar or Bars may be awarded posthumously. For every Bar awarded a replica of the Cross in miniature shall be added to the riband when worn alone.

Eighthly, it is ordained that every recommendation for the Award of the decoration of the Cross shall be made and reported through the usual channel to the Senior – Naval, Military or Air Force Officer Commanding the Force, who shall call for such description, conclusive proof as far as the circumstances of the case will allow, and; attestation of the act as he may think requisite, and if he approve he shall recommend the grant of the decoration to Our Lords Commissioners of the Admiralty, Our Secretary of State for War and the Royal Air Force as the case may be, who shall submit to Us the names of every one so recommended whom they shall consider worthy: in the case of there being no British or Indian Officer, then the Political Officer attached to the Force shall, after obtaining conclusive proof of the act of bravery as far as is possible, if he approve, submit the recommendation to Us through the proper channels.

Ninthly, it is ordained that in the event of any unit of our Naval, Military or Air Forces, consisting in the case of our Navy of a squadron, flotilla or ship's company, or of a detached body of seamen or marines; or in the case of our Army of a regiment, squadron, battery or company, or of a detached body of soldiers; or in the case of our Air Force of a squadron or other body of airmen, having distinguished itself collectively by the performance of an act of heroic gallantry or daring in the presence of the enemy in such a way that the Admiral, General or other Officer in Command of the Force to which such an unit belongs, is unable to single out any individual as specially pre-eminent in gallantry or daring, then one or more of the officers, warrant officers, petty officers, non-commissioned officers, seamen, marines, private soldiers or airmen in the ranks comprising the unit shall be selected to be recommended to Us for the award of the Victoria Cross in the following manner:

(a) When the total personnel of the unit does not exceed 100, then one officer shall be selected for the decoration by the officers engaged; and in like manner one warrant officer or petty officer, or non-commissioned officer of the unit shall be selected by the warrant officers, petty officers or non-commissioned officers engaged, and one seaman, marine, private soldier, or airman in the ranks shall be selected by the seamen, marines, private soldiers or airmen in the ranks engaged.

(b) When the total personnel of the unit exceeds 100 but does not exceed 200, then the number of seamen, marines, private soldiers or airmen in the ranks to be selected in the manner described in (a) shall be increased to two.

(c) When the total personnel of the unit exceeds 200 in number, the number of Crosses to be awarded in accordance with these provisions shall be the subject of special consideration by Our Lords Commissioners of the Admiralty or by one of Our Secretaries of State for submission to Us.

(d) The selection to be by a secret ballot in such manner as shall be determined in accordance with the foregoing provisions by the Officer directing the selection to be made.

(e) The death of any person engaged shall not be a bar to his selection. The names of the persons recommended in accordance with these provisions shall be submitted to Us in the manner laid down in Rule 5.

Tenthly, it is ordained that every recipient of the Cross, not being nor ranking as a Commissioned Officer nor in the case of Our Navy, being or ranking with a warrant officer, nor coming within Rule 11, shall from the date of the act by which such decoration has been gained, be entitled to a special pension of Ten Pounds a year, and each additional Bar conferred under Rule 7 on such recipient shall carry with it an additional pension of Five Pounds per annum.

Eleventhly, every Indian Officer of Our Indian Army of rank junior to that of Second Lieutenant who shall have received the Cross shall, from the date of the act by which such decoration has been gained, be entitled to a special pension of Five hundred and twenty-five rupees a year, and each additional Bar conferred on such Indian Officer shall carry with it an additional pension of One hundred and fifty rupees a year. In the case of a Warrant or Non-Commissioned Officer or soldier of Our Indian Army aforesaid We ordain and award a special pension of One hundred and fifty rupees, with Seventy-five rupees additional for each additional Bar. On the death of these recipients of the Cross these pensions shall be continued to his widow until her death or remarriage.

Twelfthly, in order to make such additional provision as shall effectually maintain pure this most honourable distinction, it is ordained that if any person on whom such distinction shall be conferred be convicted of treason, cowardice, felony, or of any infamous crime, or if he or she be accused of any such offence and doth not after a reasonable time surrender himself or herself to be tried for the same, his or her name shall by an especial Warrant under Our Royal Sign Manual forthwith be erased from the registry of individuals upon whom the said decoration shall have been conferred and the pension conferred under Rules 10 and 11 shall cease and determine from the date of such Warrant. It is hereby further declared that We, Our Heirs and Successors, shall be the sole judges of the circumstance demanding such expulsion; moreover, We shall at all times have power to restore such persons as may at any time have been expelled, both to the enjoyment of the decoration and pension, and notice thereof of expulsion or restoration in every case shall be published in the London Gazette.

Given at Our Court at St. James's this 22nd day of May, in the eleventh Year of Our reign, and in the year of Our Lord one thousand nine hundred and twenty.

By His Majesty's Command,
WINSTON S. CHURCHILL

## X  NEW WARRANT: SUPERCEDING ALL PREVIOUS REGULATIONS, 5 FEBRUARY 1931

GEORGE THE FIFTH, by the Grace of God, of Great Britain, Ireland and the British Dominions beyond the Seas, King, Defender of the Faith, Emperor of India; to all to whom these Presents shall come, Greeting!

WHEREAS Her late Majesty Queen Victoria, by a Warrant under Her Sign Manual dated the 29th day of January, 1856, did create a Naval and Military Decoration to be styled and designated 'The Victoria Cross', and did express Her desire that this Decoration should be highly prized and eagerly sought after by the Officers and Men of Her Naval and Military Services.

AND WHEREAS by divers subsequent Warrants other Officers and Men were admitted to and made eligible for the Decoration, and certain amendments were made to the rules and ordinances attaching thereto.

AND WHEREAS the said Warrant and subsequent Warrants before referred to, as also the rules and ordinances affecting the same, were consolidated, varied, and extended by a Warrant under Our Sign Manual dated the 22nd day of May 1920.

NOW, THEREFORE, We do hereby declare that the rules and ordinances contained in Our said Warrant heretofore in force for the governance of the said Decoration, shall be abrogated, cancelled and annulled; and in substitution thereof We by these Presents, for Us, Our Heirs and Successors, are graciously pleased to make, ordain and establish the following rules and ordinances for the governance of the same which shall from henceforth be inviolably observed and kept:

Firstly: It is ordained that the distinction shall as heretofore be styled and designated 'The Victoria Cross', and shall consist of a Maltese Cross of bronze with Our Royal Crest in the centre and underneath it an escroll bearing this inscription: 'For Valour'.

Secondly: It is ordained that the Cross shall be suspended from the left breast by a red riband of one inch and a half in width, and on those occasions when only the riband is worn a replica of the Cross in miniature shall be affixed to the centre of the riband.

Thirdly: It is ordained that the Cross shall only be awarded for most conspicuous bravery or some daring or pre-eminent act of valour or self-sacrifice or extreme devotion to duty in the presence of the enemy.

Fourthly: It is ordained that the Cross may be awarded posthumously.

Fifthly: It is ordained that the names of all those persons upon or on account of whom We may be pleased to confer or present the Decoration shall be published in the *London Gazette*, and a Registry thereof kept in the Office of Our Principal Secretary of State for War.

Sixthly: It is ordained that:-

(1) Officers, Warrant Officers and subordinate Officers hereinafter referred to as Officers, Chief Petty Officers and Petty Officers hereinafter referred to as Petty Officers, men and boys hereinafter referred to as Seamen, serving in – (a) Our Navy or in ships of any description for the time being under Naval Command; (b) Our Indian Marine Service; (c) Navies or Marine Services of Our Dominions, Colonies, Dependencies or Protectorates; and (d) Our Mercantile Marine whilst serving under Naval, Military or Air Force Authority, or who in the course of their duties may become subject to enemy action;

(2) Officers, Warrant Officers, Non-Commissioned Officers, men and boys hereinafter referred to as Marines, serving in Our Marines;

(3) Officers, Warrant Officers Classes I and II, Non-Commissioned Officers, men and boys hereinafter referred to as Privates, of all ranks serving in Our Army, Our Army Reserve, Our Territorial or other Forces, and the Forces of Our Dominions, Colonies, Dependencies or Protectorates;

(4) Officers, Warrant Officers, Classes I and II, Non-Commissioned Officers, and other Airmen serving in Our Air Force, Our Air Force Reserve, Our Auxiliary Air Force, or the Air Forces of Our Dominions, Colonies, Dependencies or Protectorates;

(5) British and Indian Officers and men of all ranks of Our Indian Army, the Imperial Service Troops of Native States of India, or any other Forces there serving under the command, guidance, or direction of any British or Indian Officer, or of a Political Officer attached to such Forces on Our behalf, and

(6) Matrons, Sisters, Nurses and the Staff of the Nursing Services and other Services pertaining to Hospitals and Nursing, and Civilians of either sex serving regularly or temporarily under the orders, direction or supervision of any of the above mentioned Forces shall be eligible for the Decoration of the Cross.

*Seventhly*: It is ordained that if any recipient of the Cross shall again perform such an act of bravery, as would have made him or her eligible to receive the Cross, such further act of bravery shall be recorded by a Bar to be attached to the riband by which the Cross is suspended, and for every such additional act of bravery, an additional Bar shall be added, and any such Bar or Bars may be awarded posthumously. For every Bar awarded a replica of the Cross in miniature shall be added to the riband when worn alone.

*Eighthly*: It is ordained that every recommendation for the award of the Decoration of the Cross shall be made and reported through the usual channel to the Senior Naval, Military or Air Force Officer Commanding the Force, who shall call for such description, conclusive proof as far as the circumstances of the case will allow, and attestation of the act as he may think requisite, and if he approve he shall recommend the grant of the Decoration to Our Lords Commissioners of the Admiralty, Our Principal Secretary of State for War or Our Principal Secretary of State for Air as the case may be, who shall submit to Us the names of every one so recommended whom they shall consider worthy: in the case of there being no British or Indian Officer, then the Political Officer attached to the Force shall, after obtaining conclusive proof of the act of bravery as far as is possible, if he approve, submit the recommendation to Us through the proper channels.

*Ninthly*: It is ordained that in the event of any unit of Our Naval, Military or Air Forces, consisting in the case of Our Navy of a squadron, flotilla or ship's Company, or of a detached body of seamen or marines; or in the case of Out Army of a regiment, squadron, battery or company, or of a detached body of soldiers, or in the case of Our Air Forces of a squadron or other body of airmen, having distinguished itself collectively by the performance of an act of heroic gallantry or daring in the presence of the enemy in such a way that the Flag, General, Air or other Officer in Command of the Force to which such an unit belongs, is unable to single out any individual as specially pre-eminent in gallantry or daring, then one or more of the personnel comprising the unit shall be selected to be recommended to Us for the award of the Victoria Cross in the following manner:-

(a) When the total personnel of the unit does not exceed 100, then one officer shall be selected for the Decoration by the officers engaged; and in like manner one warrant officer or petty officer or non-commissioned officer of the unit shall be selected :by the warrant officers, petty officers or non- commissioned officers engaged, and one seaman, marine, private soldier, or aircraftsman shall be selected by the seamen, marines, private soldiers or aircraftsmen engaged;

(b) When the total personnel of the unit exceeds 100 but does not exceed 200, then the number of seamen, marines, private soldiers or aircraftsmen to be selected in the manner described in (a) shall be increased to two;

(c) When the total personnel of the unit exceeds 200 in number, the number of Crosses to be awarded in accordance with these provisions shall be the subject of special consideration by Our Lords Commissioners of the Admiralty or by one of Our Principal Secretaries of State for submission to Us;

(d) The selection to be by a secret ballot in such manner as shall be determined in accordance with the foregoing provisions by the Officer directing the selection to be made;

(e) The death of any person engaged shall not be a bar to his selection; The names of the persons recommended in accordance with these provisions shall be submitted to Us in the manner laid down in the Eighth Clause of this Our Warrant.

*Tenthly*: It is ordained that every recipient of the Cross, not being or ranking as a Commissioned Officer and in the case of Our Navy and Our Marines, not being or ranking with a warrant officer, and not coming within the Eleventh Clause of this Our Warrant, shall from the date of the act by which the decoration has been gained, be entitled to a special pension of ten pounds a year, and each additional Bar conferred under the Seventh Clause of this Our Warrant on such recipient shall carry with it an additional pension of five pounds a year.

*Eleventhly:* Every Indian Officer of Our Indian Army of rank junior to that of Second Lieutenant who shall have received the Cross shall, from the date of the act by which such Decoration has been gained, be entitled to a special pension of five hundred and twenty-five rupees a year, and each additional Bar conferred on such Indian Officer shall carry with it an additional pension of one hundred and fifty rupees a year, In the case of a Warrant or Non-Commissioned Officer or Soldier of Our Indian Army aforesaid We ordain and award a special pension of one hundred and fifty rupees a year with seventy-five rupees a year additional for each additional Bar. On the death of a recipient of the Cross to whom this clause applies the pension shall be continued to his widow until her death or remarriage.

*Twelfthly:* It is ordained that a reproduction of the Cross known as a Miniature Cross which may be worn on certain occasions by those to whom the Decoration is awarded shall be half the size of The Victoria Cross and that a Sealed Pattern of the said Miniature Cross shall be deposited and kept in the Central Chancery of Our Orders of Knighthood.

*Thirteenthly:* It is ordained that it shall be competent for Us, Our Heirs and Successors, by an Order under Our Sign Manual and on the recommendation to that effect by or through Our First Lord of the .Admiralty or one of Our Principal Secretaries of State to cancel and annul the award of The Victoria Cross to any person, together with any pension appertaining thereto not already paid, and that thereupon his or her name in the Register shall be erased; but that it shall be competent for Us, Our Heirs and Successors, to restore the Decoration when such recommendation has been withdrawn and with it such pension as may have been forfeited.

*Fourteenthly:* It is ordained that notice of cancellation or restoration in every case shall be published in the *London Gazette.*

*Lastly:* We reserve to Ourselves, Our Heirs and Successors full power of annulling, altering, abrogating, interpreting or dispensing with these regulations, -or any part thereof, by a notification under Our Sign Manual.

Given at Our Court at St. James's, this 5th day of February, in the 21st year of Our Reign, and in the Year of Our Lord one thousand nine hundred and thirty-one.

By His Majesty's Command,
T. SHAW

## XI AMENDING WARRANT: ELIGIBILITY OF BURMESE FORCES, 9 MAY 1938

GEORGE THE SIXTH by the Grace of God, of Great Britain, Ireland and the British Dominions beyond the Seas, King, Defender of the Faith, Emperor of India; to all to whom these Presents shall come, Greeting!

WHEREAS His late Majesty King George V, by a Warrant under His Royal Sign Manual dated the 5th day of February, one thousand nine hundred and thirty one, was pleased to make, ordain and establish rules and ordinances for the governance of the Decoration of the Victoria Cross reserving to Himself, His Heirs and Successors full power of annulling, altering, abrogating, augmenting, interpreting or dispensing with these rules and ordinances, or any part thereof, by a notification under Royal Sign Manual;

AND WHEREAS on 1st April, 1937, Burma ceased to be part of India, and We are desirous that Officers, Non Commissioned Officers and Men of Our Burma Army and other Military Forces in Burma shall be considered eligible for the award of the Decoration;

NOW THEREFORE WE do by these Presents for Us, Our Heirs and Successors ordain and appoint that the Fifth Paragraph of the Sixth Clause and the Eighth and Eleventh Clauses of the said Warrant shall be cancelled and annulled and the following substituted therefore:-

(5) British, Indian or Burman officers and men of all ranks of Our Indian and Burma Armies, the Indian States' Forces of Indian States or any Forces serving in India or Burma under the command, guidance or direction of any British, Indian or Burman Officer, or of a Political Officer attached to such Forces on Our Behalf and

*Eighthly*: It is ordained that every recommendation for the award of the Decoration of the Cross shall be made and reported through the usual channels to the Senior Naval, Military or Air Force Officer Commanding the Force, who shall call for such description, conclusive proof, as far as the circumstances of the case will allow, and attestation of the act as he may think requisite, and, if he approve, he shall recommend the grant of the Decoration to Our Lords Commissioners of the Admiralty, Our Principal Secretary of State for War or Our Principal Secretary of State for Air, as the case may be, who shall submit to Us the names of every one so recommended whom they shall consider worthy; in the case of there being no British, Indian or Burman Officer, then the Political Officer attached to the Force shall, after obtaining conclusive proof of the act of bravery as far as is possible, if he approve, submit the recommendation to us through the proper channels.

*Eleventhly*: Every Indian Officer of Our Indian Army and Burman Officer of Our Burma Army of rank junior to that of Second Lieutenant who shall have received the Cross shall, from the date of the Act by which such Decoration has been gained, be entitled to a special pension of five hundred and twenty five rupees a year, and each additional Bar conferred on such Indian Officer or Burman Officer shall carry with it an additional pension of one hundred and fifty rupees a year. In the case of a Warrant or Non-Commissioned Officer or soldier of Our Indian or Burma Armies aforesaid We ordain and appoint a special pension of one hundred and fifty rupees a year, with seventy-five rupees a year additional for each additional Bar. On the death of a recipient of the Cross to whom this clause applies, the pension shall be continued to his widow until her death or remarriage.

Given at Our Court of St. James's, this 9th day of May, 1938, in the Second Year of Our Reign, in the Year of Our Lord one thousand nine hundred and thirty-eight.

By His Majesty's Command,
LESLIE HORE-BELISHA

## XII AMENDING WARRANT: NEW OFFICER GRADES, 21 AUGUST 1939

GEORGE THE SIXTH by the Grace of God, of Great Britain, Ireland and the British Dominions beyond the Seas, King, Defender of the Faith, Emperor of India; to all to whom these Presents shall come, Greeting!

WHEREAS His late Majesty King George V, by a Warrant under His Royal Sign Manual dated the 5th February 1931, was pleased to make, ordain and establish rules and ordinances for the governance of the Decoration of the Victoria Cross reserving to Himself, His Heirs and Successors full power of annulling, altering, abrogating, augmenting, interpreting or dispensing with these rules and ordinances, or any part thereof, by a notification under Royal Sign Manual;

AND WHEREAS by a Warrant under Our Sign Manual dated the 9th day of May 1938, We did ordain that Officers, Non Commissioned Officers and Men of Our Burma Army and other Military Forces in Burma should be considered eligible for the award of the Decoration;

AND WHEREAS by a Warrant under Our Sign Manual dated the 14th day of September, 1938, We did deem it expedient to introduce into Our Regular Army a new class of Warrant Officer;

AND WHEREAS We deem it expedient that the said Warrant dated the 5th day of February, 1931, should be amended to provide for the award of the Decoration to all classes of Warrant Officers;

NOW THEREFORE WE do by these presents for Us, Our Heirs and Successors ordain and appoint that the Sixth Clause, sub-paragraphs (3) and (4) shall be altered by the deletion of the words 'Classes I and II', and that the said alterations shall have effect from the 14th day of September, 1938.

Given at Our Court of St. James's, this 21st day of August, in the 3rd year of Our Reign, and in the year of Our Lord one thousand nine hundred and thirty nine.

By His Majesty's Command,
KINGSLEY WOOD.

## XIII   AMENDING WARRANT: INDIAN AIR FORCE, 25 JANUARY 1941

GEORGE THE SIXTH by the Grace of God, of Great Britain, Ireland and the British Dominions beyond the Seas, King, Defender of the Faith, Emperor of India; to all to whom these Presents shall come, Greeting!

WHEREAS His late Majesty King George V, by a Warrant under His Royal Sign Manual dated the 5th February 1931, was pleased to make, ordain and establish rules and ordinances for the governance of the Decoration of the Victoria Cross reserving to Himself, His Heirs and Successors full power of annulling, altering, abrogating, augmenting, interpreting or dispensing with these rules and ordinances, or any part thereof, by a notification under Royal Sign Manual;

AND WHEREAS by a Warrant under Our Royal Sign Manual dated the 9th day of May 1938, We did ordain that Officers, Non Commissioned Officers and Men of Our Burma Army and other Military Forces in Burma should be considered eligible for the award of the Decoration;

AND WHEREAS by a Warrant under Our Sign Manual dated the 14th day of September, 1938, We did deem it expedient to introduce into Our Regular Army a new class of Warrant Officer;

AND WHEREAS by a Warrant under Our Sign Manual dated 21st August, 1939, We did ordain that all classes of Warrant Officers shall be eligible for the Decoration;

AND WHEREAS we are desirous that Officers, Warrant Officers, Non Commissioned Officers and Airmen of Our Indian Air Force shall be eligible for the award of the Decoration;

NOW THEREFORE We do by these Presents for Us, Our Heirs and Successors ordain and appoint that the Sixth Clause, sub paragraph (4) of the Warrant dated 5th February, 1931, as amended by the Warrant dated 21st August, 1939, shall be cancelled and annulled and the following substituted therefore:-

(4) Officers, Warrant Officers, Non Commissioned Officers and other Airmen serving in Our Air Force, Our Air Force Reserve, Our Auxiliary Air Force, Our Indian Air Force, or the Air Forces of Our Dominions, Colonies, Dependencies or Protectorates;

AND WE DO FURTHER ordain and appoint that the Eleventh Clause as ordained in the Warrant dated 9th May, 1938, shall be cancelled and annulled, and the following substituted therefore:-

*Eleventhly:* Every Indian Officer of Our Indian Army and Burman Officer of Our Burma Army of rank junior to that of Second-Lieutenant and every Indian Officer of Our Indian Air Force of rank junior to that of Pilot Officer who shall have received the Cross shall, from the date of the act by which such Decoration has been gained, be entitled to a special pension of five hundred. and twenty-five rupees a year, and each additional Bar conferred on such Indian Officer or Burman Officer shall carry with it an additional pension of one hundred and fifty rupees a year. In the case of a Warrant or Non-Commissioned Officer or soldier of Our Indian Army, Our Indian Air Force or Burma Army aforesaid We ordain and award a special pension of one hundred and fifty rupees a year, with seventy-five rupees additional for each additional bar. On the death of a recipient of the Cross to whom this clause applies the pension shall be continued to his widow until her death or remarriage.

Given at Our Court at St. James's this 25th day of January, 1941, in the 5th Year of Our Reign.

By His Majesty's Command,
DAVID MARGESSON.

## XIV  AMENDING WARRANT: HOME GUARD AND WOMEN'S SERVICES, DOMINION SUBMISSIONS, AND EXTENSION OF PENSION BENEFITS TO NATIVE TROOPS, 31 DECEMBER 1942

GEORGE THE SIXTH, by the Grace of God, of Great Britain, Ireland, and the British Dominions beyond the Seas, King, Defender of the Faith, Emperor of India, to all to whom these Presents shall come, Greeting!

WHEREAS His late Majesty King George V, by a Warrant under his Sign Manual, dated 5th February, 1931, was pleased to make, ordain and establish rules and ordinances for the governance of the Decoration of the Victoria Cross, reserving to Himself His Heirs and Successors full power of annulling, altering, abrogating, augmenting, interpreting or dispensing with those rules and ordinances, or any part thereof, by a notification under Royal Sign Manual;

AND WHEREAS WE are desirous that persons of any rank in Our Home Guard and any lawfully constituted force corresponding thereto shall be eligible for the award of the Decoration; that the position of Our Women's Auxiliary Services in the matter shall be regularized; that provision shall be made for direct submission to Us in the case of any of Our Dominions, the Government whereof shall so desire; and that eligibility for monetary awards shall be extended to all Our Indian and Burma Forces within the limits of rank to be laid down;

NOW THEREFORE WE do by these Presents for Us, Our Heirs and Successors ordain and appoint that the Sixth Clause of the said Warrant, as amended by Our Warrants dated 9th May, 1938, 21st August, 1939 and 25th January, 1941, the Eighth Clause as ordained in Our Warrant dated 25th January, 1941, shall be *cancelled and annulled* and the following *substituted* therefore:-

Sixthly: It is ordained that the persons eligible for the Decoration of *following substituted* therefore:-

(1) Persons of any rank in the Naval, Military and Air Forces of Our United Kingdom of Great Britain and Northern Ireland, of India, of Burma, of Our Colonies and of territories under Our suzerainty, protection or jurisdiction or under Our jurisdiction jointly with another power, or belonging to any other part of our Dominions, Our Government whereof has signified its desire that awards of the Cross shall be made under the provisions of this Our Warrant, or belonging to any Territory under Our protection administered by Us in such Government, including the Home Guard and any lawfully constituted force corresponding thereto, and, in India, members of the Frontier Corps and Military Police, and members of the Indian States' Forces, and, in Burma, members of the Burma Frontier Force and Military Police, and including also members of the Naval, Military and Air Force Nursing Services and of the Women's Auxiliary Services;
(2) Members of Our Merchant Navy;
(3) Our faithful subjects and persons under Our protection in civil life, male and female, serving regularly or temporarily under the orders, directions or supervision of any of the above- mentioned Forces or Services;

*Eighthly*: It is ordained that every recommendation for the award of the Decoration of the Cross shall be made or reported through the usual channel to the Senior Naval, Military or Air Force Officer Commanding the Force, who shall call for such description, conclusive proof as far as the circumstances of the case will allow, and attestation of the act as he may think requisite, and if he approve he shall recommend the grant of the Decoration to Our Lords Commissioners of the Admiralty, Our Secretary of State for War or Our Secretary of State for Air as the case may be, or, in the case of any of Our Dominions, the Government whereof shall so desire, the appropriate Minister of State for the said Dominion, who shall submit to Us the names of every one so recommended whom they shall consider worthy;

*Eleventhly*: In the case of Our Indian and Burma Forces, a recipient of the Cross or bar, within the limits of rank to be laid down, and, on the death of such recipient, his widow, shall be entitled to receive under regulations to be issued by Our Governor-General of India and Our Governor of Burma such special pension or additional pension as may be provided out of the revenues of India or the revenues of Burma, as the case may be.

AND WE do ordain and appoint that the Ninth Clause of the Warrant dated 5th February, 1931, shall be amended by the relettering of sub-paragraph '(f)' *as* '(g)' and by the insertion of the following sub-paragraph:-

Reference in this Clause to male members of Our Forces shall be deemed to include the equivalent ranks of Our Women's Auxiliary Services.

AND WE do further ordain and appoint that sub-paragraph (c) of the Ninth Clause, and the Thirteenth Clause of the Warrant dated 5th February, 1931, shall be amended by the insertion after 'Secretaries of State' of the words 'or, in the case of any of Our Dominions, the

Government whereof shall so desire, the appropriate Minister of State for the said Dominion', in each case.

Given at our Court at St. James's, this 31st day of December, 1942, in the 7th year of Our Reign.

By His Majesty's Command,
P. J. GRIGG.

## XV NEW WARRANT: SUPERCEDING ALL PREVIOUS REGULATIONS, 30 SEPTEMBER 1961

ELIZABETH THE SECOND, by the Grace of God, of the United Kingdom of Great Britain and Northern Ireland, and of Her other Realms and Territories Queen, Head of the Commonwealth, Defender of the Faith: to all to whom these Presents shall come, Greeting!

WHEREAS His late Majesty King George V, by a Warrant under His Royal Sign Manual dated the 5th day of February 1931, was pleased to make, ordain and establish rules and ordinances for the governance of the Decoration of The Victoria Cross reserving to Himself, His Heirs and Successors full powers of annulling, altering, abrogating, augmenting, interpreting or dispensing with those rules and ordinances or any part thereof, by a notification under Royal Sign Manual;

AND WHEREAS the provisions of the said Warrant were amended by Warrants under the Royal Sign Manual of His late Majesty King George VI, dated the 9th day of May 1938, the 21st day of August 1939, the 25th day of January 1941 and the 31st day of December 1942;

AND WHEREAS We deem it expedient that the provisions of the said Warrant be further amended and augmented;

NOW, THEREFORE, WE do hereby declare that the rules and ordinances contained in the said Warrant heretofore in force for the governance of the said Decoration, shall be abrogated, cancelled and annulled; and in substitution thereof We by these Presents, for Us, Our Heirs and Successors, are graciously pleased to make, ordain and establish the following rules and ordinances for the governance of the same which shall from henceforth be inviolably observed and kept:-

*Firstly:* It is ordained that the distinction shall as heretofore be styled and designated 'The Victoria Cross', and shall consist of a Maltese Cross of bronze with Our Royal Crest in the centre and underneath it an escroll bearing this inscription: 'For Valour'.

*Secondly:* It is ordained that the Cross shall be worn on the left breast pendant from a red riband of one inch and a half in width, and on those occasions when only the riband is worn a replica of the Cross in miniature shall be affixed to the centre of the riband.

*Thirdly:* It is ordained that the Cross shall only be awarded for most conspicuous bravery, or some daring or pre-eminent act of valour or self-sacrifice or extreme devotion to duty in the presence of the enemy.

*Fourthly:* It is ordained that the Cross may be awarded posthumously.

*Fifthly:* It is ordained that the names of all those persons upon or on account of whom We may be pleased to confer or present the Decoration shall be published in the *London Gazette*, and a Register thereof kept in the office of Our Principal Secretary of State for War.

*Sixthly:* It is ordained that the persons eligible for the Decoration of the Cross shall be:-

(1) Persons of any rank in the Naval, Military and Air Forces of Our United Kingdom of Great Britain and Northern Ireland, of Member Countries of the Commonwealth overseas, the Governments whereof have signified their desire that awards of the Cross shall be made under the provisions of this Our Warrant, of Our Colonies or Our other Territories or of the Territories under Our Protection or Administration, (including members of the Home Guard and any lawfully constituted Force corresponding thereto), and including also members of the Naval, Military and Air Force Nursing Services and of the Women's Auxiliary Services;

(2) Members of Our Merchant Navy;

(3) Our faithful subjects and persons under Our protection in civil life, male and female, serving regularly or temporarily under the orders, directions or supervision of any of the above-mentioned Forces or Services.

*Seventhly:* It is ordained that if any recipient of the Cross shall again perform such an act of bravery as would have made him or her eligible to receive the, Cross, such further act of bravery shall be recorded by a Bar to be attached to the riband by which the Cross is suspended, and for every such additional act of bravery, an additional Bar shall be added, and any such Bar or Bars may be awarded posthumously. For every Bar awarded a replica of the Cross in miniature shall be added to the riband when worn alone.

*Eighthly:* It is ordained that every recommendation for the award of the Decoration of the Cross shall be made and reported through the usual channel to the Senior Naval, Military or Air Force Officer Commanding the Force, who shall call for such description, conclusive proof as far as the circumstances of the case will allow, and attestation of the act as he may think requisite, and if he approve he shall recommend the grant of the Decoration to Our Lords Commissioners of the Admiralty, Our Secretary of State for War or Our Secretary of State for Air as the case may be, or, in the case of any Member Country of the Commonwealth Overseas, the Government whereof shall so desire, the appropriate Minister of State for the said Member Country, who shall submit to Us the names of every one so recommended whom they shall consider worthy.

*Ninthly:* It is ordained that in the event of any unit of the Naval, Military or Air Forces mentioned in the Sixth Clause of this Our Warrant, consisting in the case of a unit of Naval Forces of a squadron, flotilla or ship's company, or of a detached body of seamen or marines; or in the case of a unit of Military Forces of a regiment, squadron, battery or company, or a detached body of soldiers; or in the case of a unit of Air Forces of a squadron or other body of airmen, having distinguished itself collectively by the performance of an act of heroic gallantry or daring in the presence of the enemy in such a way that the Flag, General, Air or other Officer in Command of the Force to which such a unit belongs, is unable to single out any individual as specially pre-eminent in gallantry or daring, then one or more of the personnel comprising the unit shall be selected to be recommended to Us for the award of the Victoria Cross in the following-manner:-

(a) When the total personnel of the unit does not exceed 100, then one officer shall be selected for the Decoration by the officers engaged; and in like manner one warrant officer or petty officer or non-commissioned officer or leading rating of the unit shall be selected by the warrant officers, petty officers or non-commissioned officers or leading ratings engaged, and one seaman, marine, private soldier or aircraftman shall be selected by the seamen, marines, private soldiers or aircraft-men engaged;

(b) When the total personnel of the unit exceeds 100 but does not exceed 200 then the number of seamen, marines, private soldiers or aircraftmen to be selected in the manner described in (a) shall be increased to two;

(c) When the total personnel of the unit exceeds 200 in number, the number of Crosses to be awarded in accordance with these provisions shall be the subject of special consideration by Our Lords Commissioners of the Admiralty or by one of Our Principal Secretaries of State or, in the case of any Member Country of the Commonwealth overseas, the appropriate Minister of State for the said Member Country, for submission to Us;

(d) The selection is to be by a secret ballot in such a manner as shall be determined in accordance with the foregoing provisions by the Officer directing the selection to be made;

(e) The death of any person engaged shall not be a bar to his selection; Reference in this Clause to male members of any Forces shall be deemed to include the equivalent ranks of the Women's Auxiliary Services of such Forces;

(g) The names of the persons recommended in accordance with these provisions shall be submitted to Us in the manner laid down in the Eighth Clause of this Our Warrant.

*Tenthly*: It is ordained that every recipient of the Cross, not coming within the provisions of the Eleventh Clause of this Our Warrant, to whom the Cross may be awarded after the 31st day of July 1959 shall from the date of the act by which the Decoration has been gained, be entitled to a special pension of one hundred pounds a year.

*Eleventhly*: It is ordained that, subject to such exceptions as We, Our Heirs and Successors may ordain, a member of the Forces of a Member Country of the Commonwealth Overseas to whom the Cross or bar may be awarded after the 31st day of July 1959, shall receive such special pension or pensions as may be provided from the revenues of that Country, under regulations made by the said Country.

*Twelfthly*: It is ordained that, as from the first day of August 1959, every recipient of the Decoration:-

(a) who was then receiving from moneys provided by Our Parliament of the United Kingdom of Great Britain and Northern Ireland a special pension awarded under the rules and ordinances relating to the Decoration in force from time to time, or

(b) who would then have been so receiving such a special pension if he had not been or ranked as a Commissioned Officer or in the case of Our Navy and Marines he had not been or ranked with a Warrant Officer, or

(c) in respect of whom such a special pension would have been currently in issue on the 31st day of March 1955, if he had not been or ranked as a Commissioned Officer and would, if it had been so in issue, have fallen within any of the descriptions of pensions in the annexe contained in the First Schedule to The Pensions (India, Pakistan and Burma) Act, 1955, shall receive a special pension of one hundred pounds a year, which in cases coming within category (a) above shall be in substitution for any special pension in respect of the Decoration which was previously in issue to him.

*Thirteenthly*: It is ordained that where a recipient of the Decoration coming within the provision of (a) of the Twelfth Clause of this Our Warrant was a Gurkha Commissioned Officer or a soldier of Our Brigade of Gurkhas, his widow shall receive, with effect from the date of his death and until her remarriage or death, a special pension equal to the special pension which was in payment to him immediately before the first day of August, 1959.

*Fourteenthly*: It is ordained that reproductions of the Cross known as a Miniature Cross which may be worn on certain occasions by those to whom the Decoration is awarded shall be half the size of The Victoria Cross and that a Sealed Pattern of the said Miniature Cross shall be deposited and kept in the Central Chancery of Our Orders of Knighthood.

*Fifteenthly*: It is ordained that it shall be competent for Us, Our Heirs and Successors, by an Order under Our Sign Manual and on the recommendation to that effect by or through our First Lord of the Admiralty or one of Our Principal Secretaries of State or, in the case of any Member Country of the Commonwealth Overseas, the Government whereof shall so desire, the appropriate Minister of State for the said Member Country, to cancel and annul the award of The Victoria Cross to any person, together with any pension appertaining thereto not already paid, and that thereupon his or her name in the Register shall be erased; but that it shall be competent for Us, Our Heirs and Successors, to restore the Decoration when such recommendation has been withdrawn and with it such pension as may have been forfeited.

*Sixteenthly*: It is ordained that notice of cancellation or restoration in every case shall be published in the *London Gazette*.

*Lastly*: We reserve to Ourself, Our Heirs and Successors full power of annulling, altering, abrogating, augmenting, interpreting or dispensing with these regulations, or any part thereof, by a notification under Our Sign Manual.

Given at Our Court at St. James's, this 30th day of September, in the 10th year of Our Reign and in the year of Our Lord One thousand nine hundred and sixty-one.

By Her Majesty's Command,
JOHN PROFUMO

# Notes

## INTRODUCTION

1. PRO File WO/32/9394. Letter from Colour Sergeant Harry Hampton to the Private Secretary of King George V, 30 September 1920.
2. John Keegan and Richard Holmes, *Soldiers: A History of Men in Battle* (New York: Viking Penguin, 1986).
3. John Keegan, *The Face of Battle* (London: Cox & Wyman, 1976).
4. Patrick M. Regan, *Organizing Societies for War* (Westport, CT: Praeger, 1994); Hew Strachan, *European Armies and the Conduct of War* (London: George Allen & Unwin, 1983).
5. Lord Moran, *The Anatomy of Courage* (London: Constable, 1945; reprint: Garden City Park, NY: Avery Publishing Group, 1987).
6. Le Roy Eltinge, *Psychology of War* (Fort Leavenworth, KS: Press of the Army Service Schools, 1915).
7. Plinio Prioreschi, *Man and War* (New York: Philosophical Library, 1987).
8. For example, see David Harvey, *Monuments to Courage* (n.p.: Kevin & Kay Patience, 1999), a compilation of VC grave sites; *The Illustrated Handbook of the Victoria Cross and the George Cross* (London: Imperial War Museum, 1970); *The Register of the Victoria Cross*, ed. Nora Buzzell (Cheltenham, UK: This England Books, 1988). Cited hereafter as *Register*.
9. For example, see A. L. Hayden, *The Book of the V. C.* (London: Pilgrim Press, 1906); J. E. Muddock, *'For Valour' the 'V. C.'* (London: Hutchinson, 1895); D. H. Parry, *Britain's Roll of Glory* (London: Cassell, 1906); D. H. Parry, *The VC: Its Heroes and Their Valour* (London: Cassell, 1913); T. E. Toomey, *Heroes of the Victoria Cross* (n.p.: Newnes, 1895); P. A. Wilkins, *History of the Victoria Cross* (London: Constable, 1904)
10. Sir O'Moore Creagh and E. M. Humphries, *The Victoria Cross, 1856–1920* (reprint: London: J. B. Hayward & Son, 1985).
11. For example, see N. McCrery, *For Conspicuous Gallantry – A Brief History of the Recipients of the VC from Notts and Derbyshire* (n.p.: n.p., 1990); see also I. S. Uys, *For Valour: The History of South Africa's Victoria Cross* (Johannesburg: Uys, 1973).
12. Examples of this genre can be found in F. J. Blatherwick, *1000 Brave Canadians* (Toronto: The Unitrade Press, 1991), which details the exploits of other decoration winners in addition to the Victoria Cross; G. Machum, *Canada's VCs* (Toronto: McClelland & Steward, 1956); Graham Ross, *Scotland's Forgotten Valour* (Maclean Press, 1995); L. Wigmore and B. Harding, *They Dared Mightily* (Canberra: Australian War Memorial, 1963); W. Alister Williams, *The VCs of Wales and the Welsh Regiments* (Wrexham: Bridge Books, 1984).
13. For example, see Chaz Bowyer, *For Valour: The Air VCs* (Kimber, 1978); W. J. Elliot, *The Victoria Cross in Zululand and South Africa* (London: Dean & Son, 1982); W. S. James, *Submariners VC* (London: Peter Davis, 1962); W. E. Johns, *The Air VCs* (London: Hamilton, 1935); Roger Perkins, *The Kashmir Gate – Lieutenant Home and the Delhi VCs* (Chippenham: Picton Publications, 1983); J. F. Turner, *V. C.'s of the Air* (London: Harrap, 1960); J. Winton, *The Victoria Cross at Sea* (London: Michael Joseph, 1978).
14. John Laffin, *British VCs of World War 2* (London: Alan Sutton, 1997).

15. Mark Adkin, *The Last Eleven?* (London: Leo Cooper, 1991).
16. Titles published in the *VCs of the First World War* series include three by Gerald Gliddon: *1914* (London: Alan Sutton, 1994), *The Somme* (London, Alan Sutton, 1994), and *Arras and Messines – 1917* (London: Alan Sutton, 1998); and one volume by Peter Batchelor and Chris Matson, *The Western Front – 1915* (n.p.: Wrens Park Publishing, 1999).
17. The spectrum of biographies are represented by Robert A. Bonner, *'Here We Fight, Here We Die!'* (n.p.:R. A. Bonner, 1998); Mary Gibson, *Warneford, VC* (Chippenham: Picton Publishing, 1984); Peter D. Mason, *Nicolson, VC* (Ashford: Geerings, 1991); Ann Clayton, *Martin-Leake, Double VC* (London: Leo Cooper, 1997); and Richard Morris, *Cheshire: The Biography of Leonard Cheshire* (New York: Viking, 2000).
18. M. J. Crook, *The Evolution of the Victoria Cross: A Study in Administrative History* (Tunbridge Wells: Midas Books, 1975).
19. Ibid., pp. 81, 83, 84, 143, to give four examples of this problem.
20. Ibid., pp. 93–4. See Chapter 3 of this work for the entire story.

# CHAPTER 1

1. Leonard M. Ashley, *George Alfred Henty and the Victorian Mind* (San Francisco: International Scholars Publications, 1999), 327–42. This point is extrapolated from Ashley's evaluation of G. A. Henty's influence on the cultural ideology of Victorian Youth. See also James Bowen, 'Education, Ideology and the Ruling Class: Hellenism and English Public Schools in the Nineteenth Century', in G. W. Clarke, ed., *Rediscovering Hellenism* (Cambridge: Cambridge University Press, 1989), 179–80.
2. Patrick Brantlinger, *Rule of Darkness: British Literature and Imperialism* (Ithaca, NY: Cornell University Press, 1988), 47–9. See also W. L. Burn, *The Age of Equipoise* (New York: W. W. Norton, 1969), 78–80. The novels of Captain Frederick Marryat were pioneering works of the genre.
3. Richard P. Martin, *The Language of Heroes: Speech and Performance in The Iliad* (Ithaca, NY: Cornell University Press, 1989), 89–91, 97–8.
4. Christopher Gill, *Personality in the Greek Epic, Tragedy, and Philosophy: The Self in Dialogue* (Oxford: Clarendon Press, 1996), 74–5.
5. Maurice B. McNamee, S.J., *Honor and the Epic Hero: A Study of the Shifting Concept of Magnanimity in Philosophy and Epic Poetry* (New York: Holt, Rinehart & Winston, 1960), 1–3.
6. Homer, *The Iliad*, A. T. Murray, trans. (Cambridge, MA: Harvard University Press, 1999), 2:341–5.
7. Homer, *The Odyssey*, A. T. Murray, trans. (Cambridge, MA: Harvard University Press, 1995), 1:350–5; 1:451–3.
8. Gregory Nagy, *The Best of the Achaeans* (Baltimore, MD: Johns Hopkins University Press, 1999), 115–16.
9. Richard Jenkyns, *The Victorians and Ancient Greece* (Cambridge, MA: Harvard University Press, 1980), 167–8; Frank M. Turner, *The Greek Heritage in Victorian Britain* (New Haven, CT: Yale University Press, 1981), 172–5.
10. Norman Vance, *The Victorians and Ancient Rome* (Oxford: Blackwell, 1997), 199–202.
11. McNamee, *Honor and the Epic Hero*, 40–3.
12. Henry Newbolt, Untitled invocation at the beginning of *Admirals All and Other Verses* (London: Elkin Mathews, 1908).

13. McNamee, *Honor and the Epic Hero*, 51–3.
14. Julius (Publius?) Cornelius Tacitus, *Life of Gnaeus Julius Agricola* Herbert W. Bernario, trans., *Tacitus' Agricola, Germany, and Dialogue on Orators* (Norman, OK: University of Oklahoma Press, 1991), 28.
15. Gildas, *The Ruin of Britain and Other Works*, Michael Winterbottom, ed., trans., (London: Phillimore, 1978), 18.
16. Charles Kightly, *Folk Heroes of Great Britain* (London: Thames & Hudson, 1983), 53.
17. John Milton, *The History of Britain, That Part especially now call'd England, From the first Traditional Beginning Continu'd to the Norman Conquest* (London: Ri. Chiswell, 1695), 79–80.
18. Antonia Fraser, *The Warrior Queens* (New York: Vintage Books, 1990), 297–9, 324–5. The £3,800 necessary to cast the statue and provide the plinth on which it stands were raised by public subscription, an indication of public popularity. Boudicca also proved to be a favorite of the suffragette movement.
19. Graham Webster, *Boudica: The British Revolt Against Rome, AD 60* (Totowa, NJ: Rowman and Littlefield, 1978), 86–101.
20. Denis Judd, *Empire: The British Imperial Experience, From 1765 to the Present* (London: HarperCollins Publishers, 1996), 155.
21. See Mark Girouard, *The Return to Camelot: Chivalry and the English Gentleman* (New Haven, CT: Yale University Press, 1981), ch. 12, 'The Return of Arthur,' *passim*. See also Donald S. Hair, *Domestic and Heroic in Tennyson's Poetry* (Toronto: University of Toronto Press, 1981), 136–7, for the paucity of martial exploit in the Victorian treatment of the Arthurian cycle.
22. Norman Vance, *The Sinews of the Spirit: The Ideal of Christian Manliness in Victorian Literature and Religious Thought* (Cambridge: Cambridge University Press, 1985), 98–101. Not all Victorian authors and philosophers had such a profound respect of 'Saxon Liberalism.' Carlyle dismissed such aspirations toward a rude democracy as merely a lot of barbarians 'lumbering about in pot-bellied equanimity.'
23. Alfred, Lord Tennyson, *The Best of Tennyson*, Walter Graham, ed. (New York: The Ronald Press Company, 1930), 9. This earlier estimation of Tennyson remains current in modern critique; see Marion Shaw, 'The Contours of Manliness and the Nature of Woman', in *Critical Essays on Alfred Lord Tennyson*, Herbert F. Tucker, ed. (New York: G. K. Hall, 1993), 220.
24. Tennyson, 'Ulysses,' *Best Of*, 115.
25. Thomas Babington, Lord Macaulay, 'Horatius at the Bridge,' quoted in J. E. Pournelle, ed., *There Will Be War, Volume IX: After Armageddon* (New York: Tom Doherty Associates, 1990), 181.
26. Michael K. Goldberg, 'Introduction to Thomas Carlyle', in *On Heroes, Hero-Worship, and the Heroic in History* (Berkeley, CA: University of California Press, 1993), xxxiv.
27. Henry Newbolt, 'Vitaï Lampada', in *Admirals All and Other Verses*, 22.
28. G. A. Henty, *One of the 28th: A Tale of Waterloo* (New York: Hurst, 1890?), 254.
29. G. A. Henty, *With Moore at Corunna* (New York: Charles Scribner's Sons, 1897), 13.
30. Arthur Kerr Slessor, *The 2nd Battalion Derbyshire Regiment in Tirah* (London: Swan Sonnenschein, 1900), 67.
31. Byron Farwell, *Queen Victoria's Little Wars* (New York: W. W. Norton, 1972), 132.
32. G. A. Henty, *Facing Death, or, The Hero of the Vaughan Pit* (New York: Hurst, n.d.).
33. G. A. Henty, *A Final Reckoning* (New York: Hurst, n.d.).
34. G. A. Henty, *Jack Archer: A Tale of the Crimea* (New York: Hurst, n.d.), 63.
35. For example, see Natascha U. Haghofer, *The Fall of Arthur's Kingdom: A Study of Tennyson's 'The Holy Grail'* (Salzburg: University of Salzburg Press, 1997), 74.

36. Tennyson, 'Sir Galahad,' *Best Of*, 94.
37. Henty, *One of the 28th*, 249–50.
38. Rudyard Kipling, 'With the Main Guard,' *Soldiers Three: The Story of the Gadsbys in Black and White* (New York: Doubleday, Page, 1914), 60, 62, 66, 70.
39. Henty, *One of the 28th*, 372, 376. See also Henty, *With Moore at Corunna*, 94–7 for an almost identical philosophic treatment of serious maiming.
40. Henty, *Jack Archer*, 103–4.
41. G. A. Henty *For Name and Fame, or, Through Afghan Passes* (New York: Hurst, n.d.), 253. This volume proves once again that you cannot judge a Henty work by the cover; the troops depicted marching through the Afghan Passes carry the US flag.
42. Henry Newbolt 'Craven (Mobile Bay, 1864),' in *Poems: Old and New* (London: John Murray, 1912), 38–9. Italics as in original.
43. G. A. Henty, *Beric the Briton* (New York: Charles Scribner's Sons, 1896), 178–9.
44. Hector Bolithio, ed., *Letters of Queen Victoria From the Archives of Brandenburg-Prussia* (New Haven, CT: Yale University Press, 1938), 50. Letter from Queen Victoria to Princess Augusta, 23 October 1854.
45. Rudyard Kipling, 'With the Main Guard,' 63.
46. Rudyard Kipling, 'The Ballad of Boh Da Thone' in *Kipling: A Selection of His Stories and Poems*, John Beecroft, ed., (Garden City, NY: Doubleday & Co., n.d.), 496–503.
47. Henty, *One of the 28th*, 332. See also Henty, *The Bravest of the Brave, or, With Peterborough in Spain* (New York: Hurst, n.d.), 119.
48. Thomas Babington Macaulay, *Macaulay's Essays on Clive and Hastings*, Charles Robert Gaston, ed. (Boston: Ginn, 1910), 26.
49. Rudyard Kipling, 'The Young British Soldier,' *Rudyard Kipling's Verse, Inclusive Edition, 1885–1918* (Garden City, NY: Doubleday, Page, 1920), 475–6.
50. Kipling, 'That Day,' *Verse*, 497.
51. Henty, *With Moore at Corunna*, 269–70.
52. Rudyard Kipling, 'The Taking of Lungtungpen,' *Kipling Stories: Twenty-Eight Exciting Tales by the Master Storyteller* (New York: Platt & Munk,, 1960), 300.
53. Henty, *The Bravest of the Brave*, 29.
54. Kipling, 'Lord Roberts,' *Verse*, 234.
55. Kipling, 'The Taking of Lungtungpen,' *Kipling Stories*, 300; 'Bobs,' *Verse*, 450.
56. G. A. Henty, *Held Fast for England: A Tale of the Siege of Gibraltar* (New York: Charles Scribner's Sons, 1902), 237.
57. Henty, *One of the 28th*, 135.
58. G. A. Henty, *In Greek Waters: A Story of the Grecian War of Independence* (New York: Charles Scribner's Sons, 1902), 141.
59. Heather Elizabeth Gillis Streets, ' "The Right Stamp of Men:" Military Imperatives and Popular Imperialism in Late Victorian Britain' (PhD diss., Duke University, 1998).
60. Henry Newbolt, 'The Guides at Cabul,' in *The Island Race* (London: Elkin Mathews, 1902), 61–4.
61. Henty, *In Greek Waters*, 120.
62. Ibid., p. 136.
63. Tennyson, 'Maud,' *Best Of*, 312.
64. Henry Newbolt, 'Hymn in the Time of War and Tumults,' in *The Island Race*, 112.
65. Rudyard Kipling, 'The White Man's Burden,' in *Kipling: A Selection of His Stories and Poems*. John Beecroft, ed. (Garden City, NY: Doubleday, n.d.), 444.

66. Macaulay, *Lord Clive*, 76–7. During the course of the negotiations with Mir Jaffar, Clive found it expedient to forge the name of Admiral Charles Watson to a false treaty, which was used to deceive one of the Hindu intermediaries in the discussions who had threatened to betray the plot to Siraj-ud-daula unless he were paid £300,000 for his silence. Watson willingly signed the correct treaty, but refused to do so for the other. Clive believed that his actions were correct and necessary, on the grounds that the dishonorable treaty was used only to counter the efforts of a dishonorable man.
67. Ibid., p. 3.
68. Henty, *Jack Archer*, 74.
69. *Register*, 82, 252.
70. PRO File WO/32/7358, Documents relating to the Forfeiture of Edward St John Daniel.
71. Byron Farwell, *Queen Victoria's Little Wars* (New York: W. W. Norton, 1972), 72–5, 132–3, 193–8. PRO file WO/98/3. Letter from B. Hawes to Sir John Page Wood, 1 May 1857. Henty never mentioned the midshipman in question's first name, but it is interesting to note that there was in fact a midshipman named Wood in the Queen: Midshipman Evelyn Wood, the future Field Marshal, who did indeed accompany Captain Peel and Daniel in the Crimea. Wood was recommended for a VC in the Crimea, but did not receive it. He did receive the VC for chasing bandits in India in 1859. He was later a part of the Ashanti campaign, and Henty served as a war correspondent with him.
72. PRO File WO/32/7358; Henty, *Jack Archer*, 73–93, passim, 225.
73. H. Woosnam Mills, *The Tirah Campaign, Being the Sequel to the Pathan Revolt in Northwestern India Compiled from the Telegrams and Special Correspondence of the Civil and Military Gazette Press* (Lahore, India: Civil and Military Gazette Press, 1898), 73–77. This sort of journalism had been going on for a couple of decades by the turn of the century: see also, for example, 'Afghanistan,' *Times*, 24 December 1879, 10; and 25 December 1879, 8; 'The Zulu War,' *Times* of London, 12 February 1879, 10, and subsequent issues.
74. Gordon Highlanders Museum File PB1215. Telegram from Lord Wolseley to 'the Colonel of the Gordon Highlanders,' 26 October 1897. Telegram from Sir George Wolseley to Colonel Henry Matthias. Assorted telegrams from the 'Durban Fellow Scotchmen,' the Caledonian Society of Johannesburg, ex-officers of the Regiment, and officers of other regiments.
75. Lieutenant Colonel A. D. Gardyne, *The Life of a Regiment, 1816–1898* (London: Medici Society, 1929), 293–4, 307. Piper George Findlater, Lieutenant Henry Singleton Pennell, Private Edward Lawson, and Lieutenant Colonel Henry Matthias. Colonel Matthias, although recommended by the campaign commander General Sir William Lockhart himself, did not receive the Victoria Cross, possibly due to a command failure later in the Tirah Campaign that resulted in the loss of several lives.
76. Guy Arnold, *Held Fast for England: G.A. Henty, Imperialist Boys' Writer* (London: Hamish Hamilton, 1980), 22–3.

## CHAPTER 2

1. John D. Clarke, *Gallantry Medals & Awards of the World*, (Sparkford, Nr Yeovil, Somerset, UK: Patrick Stephens, 1993), 163–4, 39–41.
2. Jay Luvaas, *The Education of an Army: British Military Thought, 1815–1940* (Chicago: University of Chicago Press, 1964), 3.

3. Data on these awards come from their appropriate national entries in Clarke, *Gallantry Medals*.
4. Leading story, *Times*, 3 November 1855, 6–7.
5. Clarke, *Gallantry Medals*, 59–60.
6. Ibid., pp. 54–5.
7. Data on these awards come from their appropriate national entries in Clarke, *Gallantry Medals*.
8. Hew Strachan, *Wellington's Legacy: The Reform of the British Army, 1830–54* (Manchester: Manchester University Press, 1984), 101. Strachan reports that Napier claimed to be the first officer to mention the deeds of specific enlisted men in an official dispatch.
9. Edward M. Spiers, *The Army and Society, 1815–1914* (London: Longman, 1980), 2–3.
10. Spiers, *Army and Society*, 3–6; Strachan, *Wellington's Legacy*, 98–101.
11. Jonathan Philip Parry, *The Rise and Fall of Liberal Government in Victorian Britain* (New Haven, CT: Yale University Press, 1993), 168.
12. John Fletcher Clews Harrison, *The Early Victorians, 1832–1851* (London: Weidenfeld & Nicolson, 1971), 139–40.
13. Oliver MacDonagh, *Early Victorian Government, 1830–1870* (New York: Holmes & Meier, 1977), 9.
14. Theodore K. Hoppen, *The Mid-Victorian Generation, 1846–1886* (Oxford: Clarendon Press, 1998), 513–14.
15 Correlli Barnett, *Britain and Her Army, 1509–1970: A Military, Political and Social Survey* (New York: William Morrow, 1977), 285; Hoppen, *The Mid-Victorian Generation*, 388; Donald Southgate, *The Passing of the Whigs, 1832–1886* (Basingstoke: Macmillan, 1962), 148; see also Harrison, *The Early Victorians*, 135–8. Ramsay Skelley reported 58.5 percent of recruits as being able to read and write as of 1861. This increased to just under 90 percent by 1899. See Ramsay Skelley, *The Victorian Army at Home: The Recruitment Terms and Conditions of the British Regular, 1859–1899* (London: Croom Helm, 1977), 310.
16. Mary Poovey, *Making a Social Body: British Cultural Formation, 1830–1864* (Chicago: The University of Chicago Press, 1995), 4, 8.
17. Harrison, *The Early Victorians*, 144–5.
18. Parry, *Rise and Fall*, 16; see also British Broadcasting Company, *Ideas and Beliefs of the Victorians* (London: Sylvan Press, 1949), 56.
19. Geoffrey Francis Andrew Best, *Mid-Victorian Britain, 1861–1875* (New York: Shocken Books, 1972), 230–1.
20. Spiers, *Army and Society*, 99–100, 106.
21. Letter from 'A Civilian' to the Editor of *The Times*, 11 January 1855, 5. Chosen as an example of many similar letters published. See also an untitled editorial criticizing the command of Sir Richard England, 11 December 1854, 6, and Letter from 'An Old Soldier' to the Editor, 20 December 1854, 8, condemning the staff in the field for aggrandizing themselves with meaningless brevet promotions while combat officers went without notice in promotion and dispatches, quoting the statistic that of 52 captains promoted to the rank of major, 40 were staff officers. Actual combat soldiers (officers) were quickly forgotten and went unrewarded. The issue of 26 December 1854 devoted all of page 9 to letters from men in the Crimea reporting the lack of action, the lack of proper facilities, the lack of proper equipment, and of growing malaise.
22. Anderson, *A Liberal State at War*, 55–6.
23. Untitled Lead Story, *Times*, 3 January 1855, 6.

24. J. B. Conacher, *The Aberdeen Coalition: A Study in Mid-Nineteenth-Century Party Politics* (London: Cambridge University Press, 1968), 364–5.
25. John Sweetman, *War and Administration: The Significance of the Crimean War for the British Army* (Edinburgh: Scottish Academic Press, 1984), 93.
26. Fox Maule, 2nd Baron Panmure, *The Panmure Papers* (London: Hodder & Stoughton, 1908), 149, 194, 267; Richard Mullen and James Munson, *Victoria: Portrait of a Queen* (London: BBC Books, 1987), 32, 49; Richard Williams, *The Contentious Crown: Public Discussion of the British Monarchy in the Reign of Queen Victoria* (Aldershot, UK: Ashgate Publishing, 1997), 82.
27. Monica Charlot, *Victoria, The Young Queen* (Oxford: Basil Blackwell, 1991), 189, 217; Carolly Erickson, *Her Little Majesty: The Life of Queen Victoria* (New York: Simon & Schuster, 1997), 194; Mullen and Munson, *Victoria*, 85–6; James Stokesbury, *Navy and Empire* (New York: William Morrow, 1983), 240; Sweetman, *War and Administration*, 11.
28. Frank Eyck, *The Prince Consort: A Political Biography* (London: Chatto & Windus, 1959), 232–3; Sweetman, *War and Administration*, 11, 84, 91–2, 131.
29. Strachan, *Politics*, 53; For the scope of the direct authority of the Commander-in-Chief, see Sweetman, *War and Administration*, frontispiece diagram.
30. Spiers, *Army and Society*, 16, 90–1.
31. John B. Hattendorf et. al., eds., *British Naval Documents, 1204–1960* (Aldershot: Scolar Press, 1993), 646–50.
32. Darrell F. Munsell, *The Unfortunate Duke: Henry Pelham, Fifth Duke of Newcastle, 1811–1864* (Columbia, MO: University of Missouri Press, 1985), 147–8.
33. Conacher, *Aberdeen*, 394–5.
34. Gwyn Harries-Jenkins, *The Army in Victorian Society* (London: Routledge & Keegan Paul, 1977), 86; Sweetman, *War and Administration*, 84.
35. Conacher, *Aberdeen*, 394–5, 401; Sweetman, *War and Administration*, 84.
36. Munsell, *The Unfortunate Duke*, 148; Conacher, *Aberdeen*, 398–400.
37. John Prest, *Lord John Russell* (Columbia, SC: University of South Carolina Press, 1972), 366.
38. Southgate, *The Passing of the Whigs*, 255.
39. Conacher, *Aberdeen*, 402–3, 409, 450.
40. Alan Palmer, *The Banner of Battle: The Story of the Crimean War* (London: Weidenfield & Nicolson, 1987), 177; Sweetman, *War and Administration*, 91.
41. Conacher, *Aberdeen*, 547.
42. Charlot, 300–1, 313–15, 320, 322–4; Eyck, 234–5; Robert Rhodes James, *Prince Albert: A Biography* (New York: Alfred A. Knopf, 1984), 217; Stanley Weintraub, *Uncrowned King: The Life of Prince Albert* (New York: The Free Press, 1997), 292.
43. J. B. Conacher, *Britain and the Crimea, 1855–6: Problems of War and Peace* (Basingstoke: Macmillan, 1987), 3–4. Cited hereafter as 'Conacher, Britain.' Muriel Chamberlain, *Lord Aberdeen: A Political Biography* (London: Longman, 1983), 512.
44. Mandell Creighton, *Memoir of Sir George Grey* (London: Longmans, Green, 1901), 95; Prest, *Lord John Russell*, 371; Southgate, *The Passing of the Whigs*, 261–2
45. Palmer, *The Banner of Battle*, 178; Royal Historical Society, *The Letters of the Third Viscount Palmerston to Laurence and Elizabeth Sulivan, 1804–1863*, Kenneth Bourne, ed., Camden Fourth Series XXIII (London: Royal Historical Society, 1979), 309. Letter from Palmerston to the Sulivans, 4 February 1855.
46. Conacher, *Britain*, 8–9.
47. Ibid., p. 80.

48. Southgate, The Passing of the Whigs, 284.
49. Palmer, The Banner of Battle, 178–80; Anderson, A Liberal State at War, 62–3.
50. Conacher, Britain, 15, 80–2.
51. Anderson, A Liberal State at War, 53–4.
52. Albert's refusal was based on the fact that the Army was often used to quell civil unrest, and that it would be detrimental to the Queen's public reputation if her husband was the commander of the forces coercing her subjects. Strachan, Politics, 61–2; Williams, The Contentious Crown, 95; See also the Crown reaction to the McNeill and Tulloch report in Spiers, Army and Society, 113–14.
53. Conacher, Aberdeen, 403–4.
54. Giles St Aubyn, Queen Victoria: A Portrait (New York: Atheneum, 1967), 220.
55. Giles St Aubyn, The Royal George (New York: Alfred A. Knopf, 1964), 117. See also Strachan, Politics, 64, for the Queen's desire to maintain a personal link to Army command.
56. Prest, Lord John Russell, 204–5; Sweetman, War and Administration, 91–2.
57. Sweetman, War and Administration, 91–2. Further evidence that the Queen was primarily concerned with maintaining Crown influence can be seen in that she did not raise a similar objection to the appointment of her cousin George, Duke of Cambridge to the position of Commander-in Chief two years later.
58. Ibid., p. 92.
59. Anderson, A Liberal State at War, 66–7; Sweetman, War and Administration, 95.
60. Erickson, Her Little Majesty, 129; Munsell, The Unfortunate Duke, 206; Palmer, The Banner of Battle, 246; Weintraub, Uncrowned King, 298–300, 325.
61. Letter from 'J. C.' to the editor, Times, 3 December 1854, 8.
62. 'Parliamentary Intelligence, Tuesday 19 December: Order of Merit,' Times, 20 December 1854, 3.
63. 'Military and Naval Intelligence,' Times, 3 November 1855, 10; Clarke, Gallantry Medals, 85–6.
64. Unsigned letter to the editor, Times, 8 January 1855, 5.
65. Letter from 'A Civilian' to the editor, Times, 27 December 1854, 5.
66. Royal archives, Windsor Castle: RA VIC /E5/16. Letter from the Duke of Newcastle to the Prince Consort, 20 January 1855.
67. Royal archives, Windsor Castle: RA VIC /E5/18. Letter from the Prince Consort to the Duke of Newcastle, 22 January 1855.
68. Ibid.
69. Ibid.
70. Ibid.
71. Royal Archives, Windsor Castle: RA VIC/E5/30. Letter from the Duke of Newcastle to Queen Victoria, 27 January 1855; RA VIC/E5/31. Letter from Queen Victoria to the Duke of Newcastle, 28 January 1855. Request and approval of a public announcement of the intent to create a 'Cross of Military Merit.'
72. Daphne Bennett, King Without a Crown: Albert, Prince Consort of England, 1819–1861 (New York: J. B. Lippincott, 1977), 259. Bennett does not give an exact date for Albert's inspiration.
73. Sarah A. Tooley, The Personal Life of Queen Victoria (London: Hodder & Stoughton, 1896), 3–4.
74. Erickson, Her Little Majesty, 130–2.

75. Cecil Woodham-Smith, *Queen Victoria: From Her Birth to the Death of the Prince Consort* (New York: Alfred A. Knopf, 1972), 150.
76. Queen Victoria's Journal, 12 November 1854, quoted in Charlot, *Victoria, The Young Queen*, 352.
77. Leading story, *Times*, 3 November 1855, 6–7.
78. Royal Archives, Windsor Castle: RA VIC/E6/69. Memorandum on Proposed Victoria Cross, 2 December 1855; *Panmure Papers*, Letter from Prince Albert to Lord Panmure, 28 December 1855; RA VIC/E6/70. Letter from Lord Panmure to Prince Albert, 30 December 1855.
79. Anderson, *A Liberal State at War*, 65.
80. Royal Archives, Windsor Castle: RA VIC/G42/65. Letter from Lord Panmure to Queen Victoria, 3 January 1856; RA VIC/E6/71. Letter from Queen Victoria to Lord Panmure, 5 January 1856.
81. Royal Archives, Windsor Castle: RA VIC/E6/78. Letter from Lord Panmure to Prince Albert, 14 January 1856.
82. Royal Archives, Windsor Castle: RA VIC/E5/29. Letter from Queen Victoria to Lord Panmure, 17 February 1857.
83. See appendix for full text of the Victoria Cross Warrants.
84. *Panmure Papers*, Letter from Prince Albert to Lord Panmure, 28 January 1856.

# CHAPTER 3

1. See appendix for the full text of the royal warrants governing the Victoria Cross.
2. PRO File WO/98/3. Letter from Godfrey Charles Mundy to Major General Sir Charles Yorke 25 February 1856.
3. PRO File WO/98/2; PRO File WO/98/3. Letter from Godfrey Charles Mundy to Major General Sir Charles Yorke, 20 March 1856.
4. The title of the top soldier in the Victorian Army was altered slightly with the accession of the Duke of Cambridge from 'Commander-in-Chief' to 'General Commanding in Chief.' Although unfamiliar to some readers, it was none-the-less the title by which he was addressed in formal correspondence and the title over which he signed his name, so I have chosen to trust him to know who he actually was and use the title accordingly.
5. St. Aubyn, *Royal George*, 112–14, 332.
6. PRO File WO/98/2. Letters from Lieutenant Colonel MacDowell to War Office; C. J. Bourke to War Office, 29 February 1856; Colonel Jonathan Peel, Military Secretary, to Msr. le Baron Despiaux, 17 March 1856; Untitled memorandum directing complete denial of all pre-Crimea claims.
7. PRO File WO/98/3. Letter from Jonathan Peel to Colonel McDowell, C. B. 26 February 1856.
8. PRO File WO/98/3. Letter from Godfrey Charles Mundy to Dr Smith, Army Medical Department, 8 April 1856.
9. PRO File WO/98/3. Letter from Jonathan Peel to John Godfrey, 13 May 1856.
10. PRO File WO/98/3. Letter from Lord Panmure to the Duke of Cambridge, 5 September 1856.
11. PRO File WO/98/2. Letter from Colonel William Denny, Officer Commanding, 41st Regiment to Adjutant General, 8 December 1856.

12. PRO File WO/98/3. Letter from Jonathan Peel to Major General Sir Charles Yorke, 29 September 1856.
13. PRO File WO/98/2, Letter from G. C. Mundy to Colonel O'Connor, 16 October 1856.
14. J. W. Fortescue, *A History of the British Army* (London: MacMillan, 1899–1930), XIII, 232–3.
15. Ibid., pp. 231–2.
16. 'Army Regulations,' *Times* 31 July 1858, 8.
17. PRO File WO/98/2. Letter from Colonel William Denny, Officer Commanding 41st Regiment, to Adjutant General, 8 December 1856. Of similar flavor were the 66th Regiment's returns for Crimea: 'I have the honor to forward blank reports of soldiers recommended for the Order of the Victoria Cross as under the terms of the Warrant I do not feel justified in recommending any officer or soldier for that distinction.' Letter from F. I. Argyll, 66th Regiment, to Adjutant General 1 January 1857.
18. Interview with Lieutenant Colonel Angus Fairrie, Cameron Barracks, Inverness, 26 July 1995.
19. PRO File WO/98/2. Letter from Lieutenant Colonel Richard Waddy, Officer Commanding, 50th Regiment to Adjutant General Gen. 26 October 1856; Letter and enclosure from Major Frederick Wilkinson, 42nd Regiment, to Adjutant General, 6 December 1856.
20. PRO File WO/98/2. Letter from Colonel A. H. Ferryman, Officer Commanding 89th Regiment to Adjutant General, 26 November 1856. Fisher did not receive the VC.
21. PRO File WO/98/2. Regimental VC forms, 47th Regiment.
22. PRO File WO/98/2. Letter from Colonel Henry Warre, Officer Commanding 57th Regiment, to War Office, 24 October 1856.
23. See appendix for full text of the Victoria Cross Warrants.
24. PRO File WO/98/2. Official Recommendation from 57th Regiment, Malta, to War Office, London, 24 October 1856. Enclosures for Officers missing.
25. PRO File WO/98/2. Letter from Lieutenant Colonel Henry Daubeney to Adjutant General 25 December 1856; Recommendation form for George Fair, MD, 11 March 1858, signed Lieutenant Colonel Henry Daubeney; Letter from Lieutenant Colonel Henry Daubeney to Major General Sir J. H. Shoedde, KCB, undated.
26. PRO File WO/98/2. Letter from Colonel Henry Warre to Lieutenant General John L. Pennefather, 9 April 1857; Letter from Colonel Warre to Lieutenant General Love, 16 April 1857; Letter from Lieutenant General John L. Pennefather to Adjutant General, 12 April 1857.
27. PRO File WO/98/2. Letter from Lieutenant General John L. Pennefather to Horse Guards, 16 October 1856.
28. PRO File WO/98/2. Letter from Lieutenant General Sir DeLacy Evans, GCB, to Colonel Henry Daubeney, ? June 1855.
29. PRO File WO/98/2. Letter from Lieutenant Colonel Henry Daubeney to Lieutenant General John L. Pennefather, 16 December 1856.
30. PRO File WO/98/2. Letter from Lieutenant General John L. Pennefather to War Office, ? January 1857.
31. PRO File WO/98/2. Letter from Lieutenant Colonel Henry Daubeney to Adjutant General, 25 December 1856.
32. *Register*, 24, 103.

33. PRO File WO/98/2. Letter from Lieutenant Colonel Henry Daubeney to Major General Sir J. H. Shoedde, KCB, 6/7 January, 1858.
34. PRO File WO/98/2. Letter from Major General Sir J. H. Shoedde to Major General Sir Charles Yorke, 16 January 1858.
35. PRO File WO/98/2. Petition of John Brophey, received 4 June 1857 by the Commander-in-Chief's office; Petition of James Slack, received 1 May 1857 by the Commander-in-Chief's office.
36. PRO File WO/98/2. Letter from Lieutenant D. Sullivan to Lieutenant Colonel E. F. Yates, Officer Commanding 82nd Regiment, 8 December 1856; Letter from Lieutenant Colonel E. F. Yates to Adjutant General, 12 December 1856.
37. PRO File WO/98/2. Letter from Lieutenant Colonel Richard Waddy, Officer Commanding 50th Regiment to Adjutant General, 26 October 1856.
38. PRO File WO/98/2. Copy of letter from Lieutenant General Sir Richard England to Quarter Master General, Headquarters Crimea, 21 February 1855.
39. PRO File WO/98/2. Memo from Major General Sir Charles Yorke to Adjutant General, 14 October 1856.
40. Royal Archives, Windsor Castle: RA VIC/E5/29. Letter from Queen Victoria to Lord Panmure, 17 February 1857.
41. Royal Archives, Windsor Castle: RA VIC/E9/30. Letter from Lord Panmure to Queen Victoria.
42. PRO File WO/98/2. Letter from Colonel W. L. Parkenham, Adjutant General, Her Majesty's Forces in India to the Officer Commanding, Her Majesty's 1st Battalion, 23rd Regiment, 4 October 1859.
43. 'The Victoria Cross,' *Times*, 26 February 1857, 6.
44. PRO File WO/98/2. Letter from Corporal William Courtney to the Duke of Cambridge, 19 April 1857.
45. PRO File WO/98/2. Undated Affidavits of Lance-Corporal William Doole, Private George Finch, and Private Robert Cruikshanks.
46. PRO File WO/98/2. Letter from Colonel Stanley to Adjutant General, 9 March 1857.
47. PRO File WO/98/2. Notation on Courtney Case file jacket dated 4 July 1857.
48. PRO File WO/98/2. Letter from William Courtney to the Duke of Cambridge, 29 April 1858.
49. PRO FILE WO/98/2. Letter from Private Robert Thimbleby to the Duke of Cambridge, 18 March 1857.
50. PRO File WO/98/2. Affidavit of Lieutenant Colonel C. A. Edwards, Officer Commanding, 18th R. I. Irish, 19 June 1855; Certified as a true copy & signed by Lieutenant Colonel U. M. MacMahan, Officer Commanding 44th Regiment, no date.
51. PRO File WO/98/2. Letter from Colonel Stanley to Horse Guards, 2 May 1857.
52. PRO File WO/98/2. Letter from John Thimbleby, Hertesfordshire, to Duke of Cambridge, n.d. (received 20 March 1857).
53. PRO File WO/98/2. Draft of denial of request to Private Robert Thimbleby, 28 February 1869.
54. PRO File WO/98/3. Letter from Sir Henry Storks to Sergeant Thomas Morely, 13 August 1857.
55. PRO File WO/32/7483. Various claims and denials of Sergeant Thomas Morely.
56. Thomas Morely, *The Cause of the Charge of Balaclava, Oct. 25th 1854 by the 'Man of the Hour'* (Nottingham: Arthur Jackson, 1899), 23.

57. Ibid., *passim*.
58. PRO File WO/32/7483. Letter from Thomas Morely to 'His Majesty the King' 20 October 1902.
59. 'Distribution of the Victoria Cross,' *Times*, 26 June 1857, 7. Not everyone was happy with the arrangements of the day; one spectator wrote *The Times* complaining that he was forced to stand behind the cavalry, where he couldn't see and was constantly assailed by bursts of equine flatulence.
60. Byron Farwell, *Armies of the Raj: From the Mutiny to Independence, 1858–1947*, (New York: W. W. Norton, 1989), 26–7.
61. Ibid., p. 44.
62. PRO File WO/98/2. Draft of Warrant Amendment, dated 29 October 1857.
63. Argyll and Sutherland Highlanders Museum Mss 15012. 'For Valour;' Farwell, *Queen Victoria's Little Wars*, 100.
64. PRO File WO/98/3. Letter from Lord Panmure to the President of the Board of Control, 23 December 1857.
65. PRO File WO/32/7310, Inter-Office Memoranda, Horse Guards, Summer, 1858.
66. Farwell, *Armies of the Raj*, 174.
67. PRO File WO/32/7310. Interoffice Memoranda, Horse Guards, Summer, 1858.
68. *Register*, 135.
69. Ibid., p. 151.
70. 'Calcutta,' *Times*, 27 June 1857, 9. See also 'The Massacre at Cawnpore,' *Times*, 2 September 1857, 5, and 'The Indian Mutinies,' *Times*, 6 October 1857, 9. These stories were standard features of *The Times* for an extended period, as the interval between the dates of the first story and the last indicate.
71. PRO File WO/98/3. Letter from Sir Henry Storks to Major General Sir Charles Yorke, 23 December 1857; Letter from Sir Henry Storks to the Secretary of the Admiralty, 23 November 1857.
72. PRO File WO/98/3. Letter from Lord Panmure to the President of the Board of Control, 6 January 1858.
73. George Smith, ed., *The Dictionary of National Biography* (London: Oxford University Press, 1968), Entry of Edward Law, Third Baron Ellenborough.
74. PRO File WO/98/3. Letter from Sir Henry Storks to Major General Sir Charles Yorke, 30 March 1858.
75. PRO File WO/98/3. Letter from Sir Henry Storks to Major General Sir Charles Yorke, 31 March 1858. The communication cited in the extract, detailing the 'rule laid down by Lord Panmure' on 11 December 1857, is not included in the Victoria Cross Files held in PRO series WO/32 or WO/98, nor does it appear in the published correspondence of Lord Panmure.
76. PRO File WO/98/3. Letter from Major General Jonathan Peel to the Right Honourable the Lord of Ellenborough, G.C.B., 16 April 1858.
77. PRO File WO/98/3. Letter from Major General Jonathan Peel to the Right Honourable the Lord of Ellenborough, 16 April 1858.
78. Byron Farwell, *Eminent Victorian Soldiers Seekers of Glory* (New York: W. W. Norton, 1982), 157–8; *Register*, 273.
79. PRO File WO/98/3. Letter from Major General Jonathan Peel to General Sir Colin Campbell, 17 March 1858.
80. The 'siege, reinforcement/relief, siege, actual evacuation' of Lucknow is a story unto itself and cannot be presented here.

81. Major General Sir James Outram outranked Brigadier General Havelock at the time but had voluntarily subordinated himself to the latter for the relief of Lucknow. This accounts for the seeming contradiction of ranks in Havelock's quoted report. According to the 1911 *Encyclopedia Britannica*, Outram's own men nominated him for the VC for his actions in the battle, which he declined on the grounds that it would not be proper for him to accept it as the general under whom they served.
82. PRO File WO/32/7317. Extract of Field Force Orders issued by Brigadier General Henry Havelock 17 October 1857.
83. PRO File WO/98/3. Letter from Major General Jonathan Peel to His Royal Highness the General Commanding in Chief, 1 June 1858.
84. PRO File WO/98/3. Letter from Major General Peel to His Royal Highness the General Commanding in Chief, 17 June 1858.
85. PRO File WO/32/7317. Letter from Sir Colin Campbell to the Military Secretary, Horse Guards, 17 September 1858; Letter from Duke of Cambridge to Major General Jonathan Peel, 7 June 1858; Follow up on letter mentioned by Sir Colin Campbell to parliament May or June 1858.
86. 'Distribution of the Victoria Cross,' *Times*, 26 June 1857, 7.
87. PRO File WO/98/2. Letter from Lieutenant Colonel Weber, Officer Commanding 1st Battalion Royal North British Fusiliers to Adjutant General, Her Majesty's Forces, India, ? February 1861.
88. *Register*, 230.
89. Ibid., p. 233.
90. PRO File WO/32/7346. The Claim of Private Samuel Morely, Second Battalion, Military Train.
91. Clarke, *Gallantry Medals*, 12.
92. PRO File WO/98/3. Letter from Sir Henry Storks to Major General Sir Charles Yorke, 21 April 1858.
93. PRO File WO/32/7345. Letter from War Office to Queen Victoria, 20 April 1858.
94. PRO File WO/98/2. Letter from Brevet Lieutenant Colonel W. F. Brett, Officer Commanding 54th Regiment in Transit, to Colonel Charles E. Mitchell, 16 July 1860.
95. PRO File WO/98/2. Letter from Brevet Lieutenant Colonel W. F. Brett, Officer Commanding 54th Regiment in Transit, to Colonel Charles E. Mitchell, 15 August 1860; Letter from Colonel Charles E. Mitchell to Adjutant General, 16 August 1860.
96. See appendix for full text of warrant and all amendments.
97. 'Army Regulations,' *Times*, 31 July 1858, p. 8.
98. PRO File WO/32/7345, Inter-Office Memoranda pertaining to the Walsh Case; PRO File WO/98/2, Letter from Edward Luggard to Military Secretary, 9 February 1861.
99. PRO File WO/98/2, Letter from Edward Luggard to Military Secretary, 9 February 1861.
100. PRO File WO/98/2, Letter from Lieutenant General H. W. Brereton to Adjutant General, 1 October 1863.
101. PRO File WO/98/2, Unsigned copy of letter to Lieutenant General H. W. Brereton, 8 October 1863.
102. *Register*, 243.
103. Ibid., p. 26.
104. PRO File WO/32/7373. Andaman Island Rescue, 24th Regiment.
105. PRO File WO/32/7345. Letter from Lieutenant Joseph Bourke to the Secretary of State for War, 21 February 1862.

106. PRO File WO/32/7345. Memo from Edward Pennington to Edward Luggard, War Office, 25 July 1862.
107. Clarke, *Gallantry Medals*, 75, 84–5.
108. See appendix for full text of the royal warrant and amendments.

## CHAPTER 4

1. Charles E. Callwell, *Small Wars: Their Principle and Practice* (London: HMSO, 1906; reprint, Greenhill Books, 1990), 78–84.
2. James Cowan, *The New Zealand Wars: A History of the Maori Campaigns and the Pioneering Period* (Wellington, NZ: n.p., 1922; reprint, New York: AMS Press, 1969), 179. His recommendation did not include the detail of the motivating factor of a ten pound gratuity.
3. PRO file WO/32/7354. Cover Memo of Recommendation Packet, Edward Pennington to Edward Lugard, 14 July 1860; Memo, Edward Lugard to Secretary of State For War, 17 July 1860.
4. PRO File WO/32/7354. Letter from Edward Pennington to Edward Lugard, 23 February 1861.
5. PRO file WO/32/7354. Letter from Edward Lugard to the Secretary of State For War, 25 February 1861.
6. The storming of the Taku Fort was also noteworthy as it produced one of the two contenders for the youngest VC winner, Hospital Apprentice Andrew Fitzgibbon, aged 15 years 3 months at the time of the act. The other contender, Drummer Thomas Flinn, won his Cross three years earlier at Cawnpore during the Mutiny. Flinn was unable to give an exact date of birth, so neither man can claim being the youngest.
7. PRO File WO/32/7356. Letter from Lieutenant General Sir James Hope Grant to the Military Secretary, 22 June 1861.
8. John Selby, 'The Third China War, 1860,' in Brian Bond, ed., *Victorian Military Campaigns* (New York: Frederick A Praeger, 1967), 76–7.
9. PRO File WO/32/7356. Undated Memo from Horse Guards to War Office.
10. D. G. Chandler, 'The Expedition to Abyssinia,' in Brian Bond, *Victorian Military Campaigns* (New York: Frederick Praeger, 1967), 145.
11. Ibid., p. 148.
12. *Register*, 29, 213.
13. PRO File WO/32/7370. Letter from Edward Lugard to Under-Secretary of Colonial Affairs, 26 April, 1865.
14. Geoffrey W. Rice, ed., *The Oxford History of New Zealand* (Oxford: Oxford University Press, 1992), 101; Peter Burroughs, 'An Unreformed Army?', in David Chandler and Ian Beckett, eds, *The Oxford Illustrated History of the British Army* (Oxford: Oxford University Press, 1994), 176
15. PRO File WO/32/7370. Letter from Major Charles Heaphy to Prime Minister Lord Palmerston, 28 August 1864.
16. PRO File WO/32/7370. Letter from Colonial Office to War Office 22 November 1865, including affidavits gathered by the New Zealand Government.
17. PRO File WO/32/7370. Letter from the Duke of Somerset, Admiralty, to Lord Hartington, Secretary at War, 23 April 1866.

18. PRO File WO/32/7370. Edward Pennington's Position Paper, 5 October 1866.
19. PRO File WO/32/7370. Letter from Edward Pennington to be appended to Draft of Warrant Amendment, 13 December 1866; Official recommendation to amend Warrant, 22 December 1866.
20. 'Bimbushi:' Egyptian rank roughly analogous to that of a major in the British Army.
21. PRO File WO/32/7414. Letter from Major General [?] Watkins to Military Secretary at Horse Guards, 9 March 1891; Enclosed Affidavits with Watkins Letter; Letter from Horse Guards to Permanent Under-Secretary of State, 1 April 1891.
22. PRO File WO/32/7414. Letter from Horse Guards to Permanent Under-Secretary of State, 1 April 1891.
23. PRO File WO/32/7414. Memo initialed by Edward Stanhope, Secretary of State for War, to Horse Guards, 1 May 1891.
24. PRO File WO/32/7414. Military Secretary Sir George Harman to General Officer Commanding the Forces in Egypt, 4 June 1891.
25. PRO File WO/32/7390. Letter from Lieutenant Gonville Bromhead to Officer Commanding, 2nd Battalion 24th Regiment 15 February 1879; Letter (personally signed) from Duke of Cambridge to Secretary of State, 29 March 1879.
26. PRO File WO/32/7386. Letter from Lieutenant John Rouse Merriott Chard, Durban, to Sir Edward Strickland, 20 May 1879; Letter from Sir Edward Strickland to Lord Chelmsford, October 1879; Letter from Lord Chelmsford to Military Secretary, War Office, 17 October 1879. Likewise, the film portrayal of Henry Hook was distorted; by all accounts Hook was a model soldier in South Africa.
27. PRO File WO/32/7386. Extract No. 1, His Royal Highness the Duke of Cambridge's Schedule, 18 October 1879.
28. PRO File WO/32/7463. Letter from Lord Kitchener, General Commanding in Chief, South Africa, to War Office, 26 June 1901.
29. PRO File WO/32/7463. War Office Minute Sheet 012/1963 (undated).
30. Clarke, *Gallantry Medals*, 76, 85.
31. PRO File WO/32/7473. Undated Recommendation for the VC for Rabb and Bradley by Major A. J. Chapman, Officer Commanding, Itala Camp.
32. PRO File WO/32/7473. Letter from Kitchener to Under Secretary of State for War, 15 November 1901; Undated Recommendations for the Distinguished Conduct Medal for Lancashire, Boddy and Ball by Major A. J. Chapman.
33. Byron Farwell, *The Great Anglo-Boer War* (New York: Harper & Row, 1976), 257.
34. Louis Creswicke, *South Africa and the Transvaal War*, vol. 5 (New York: G. P. Putnam's Sons, 1900), 34.
35. Farwell, *Anglo-Boer War*, 259.
36. Ibid., p. 259.
37. Creswicke, *Transvaal War*, 6:8.
38. Horace Smith-Dorien, *Memories of Forty-Eight Years' Service* (London: John Murray, 1925), 179.
39. PRO File WO/32/7878. Memorandum from the War Office to Her Majesty, 12 June 1900.
40. PRO File WO/32/7878. Draft of letter 079/2536 War Office to Lord Roberts, Commander-in-Chief, South Africa, June 1900.
41. PRO File WO/98/2. Letter from Colonel Henry Warre to Lieutenant General John L. Pennefather, 9 April 1857.

42. 'Parliamentary Intelligence, Distribution of the Victoria Cross,' *Times*, 26 June 1857, 7.
43. Clause eight of the 1920 warrant; see appendix for full text of all warrants.
44. PRO FileWO/32/7474. Memo from Colonel Edward Owen Hay, Assistant Adjutant General Royal Artillery to Adjutant General's Office, 9 December 1901; Memo from Adjutant General to the General Commanding in Chief, 29 January 1902.
45. PRO File WO/32/7474. Letter from Adjutant General to Colonel Edward Owen Hay, 1 February 1902, with admonition: 'please note, this ends this matter.'
46. Byron Farwell, *Eminent Victorian Soldiers*, 159–60.
47. Creswicke, *Transvaal War*, 2:189.
48. Farwell, *Great Anglo-Boer War*, 127.
49. Callwell, *Small Wars*, 429–32.
50. William Baring Pemberton, *Battles of the Boer War* (London: B. T. Batsford, 1964), 138; Farwell, *Great Anglo-Boer War*, 128.
51. Pemberton, *Battles of the Boer War*, 139.
52. Farwell, *Great Anglo-Boer War*, 133.
53. Pemberton, *Battles of the Boer War*, 141.
54. Statement of Captain Walter Norris Congreve concerning Colenso, quoted in Creswicke, *Transvaal War*, 2:200.
55. Farwell, *Great Anglo-Boer War*, 135; Creswicke, *Transvaal War*, 2:193, 200.
56. Pemberton, *Battles of the Boer War*, 142.
57. Victoria Cross warrant of 1856; for full text see appendix.
58. PRO File WO/32/7300. Letter from Lord Panmure to Edward Pennington, ? April 1856.
59. PRO File WO/32/7498. Memorandum from the War Office to His Majesty, 20 October 1902.
60. PRO File WO/98/3. Letter from Sir Henry Storks to Captain Colin Yorke Campbell, Royal Artillery, 6 May 1858.
61. 'Shortly afterwards Captain H. L. Reed, 7th Battery, Royal Field Artillery, who had heard of the difficulty, brought down three teams from his battery to see if he could be of any use. He was wounded as were five of the thirteen men who rode out with him; one was killed, his body was found on the field, and thirteen out of the twenty-one horses were killed before he got half-way to the guns, and he was obliged to retire'
62. General Sir Redvers Buller, General Commanding in Chief, South Africa, to the Secretary of State for War, 16 December 1899. Quoted in Creswicke, *Transvaal War*, 2:199.
63. Ibid., p. 200.
64. Ibid.
65. PRO File WO/32/7470. Letter from General Sir Ian Hamilton to Captain William Norris Congreve, 7 June 1901.
66. PRO File WO/32/7470. Letter from General Sir Ian Hamilton to General Sir Redvers Buller, 22 May 1901. Hamilton had twice been recommended for the Victoria Cross himself, and on the second occasion his nomination had been denied by Buller as theatre commander. It can only be assumed that he thoroughly enjoyed writing this letter reversing Buller's decision.
67. PRO File WO/32/7470. War Office Memorandum, 18 May 1901.
68. PRO File WO/98/2. Letter from Major General Jonathan Peel to John Godfrey, 13 May 1856.
69. PRO File WO/32/7478. Documents related to the extension of the posthumous Victoria Cross. 'Explanatory Memoranda A.'

70. PRO File WO/32/7478. Memo from Lord Roberts to Secretary of State St John Broderick, 7 April 1902.
71. Lieutenant Gustavus Coulson, DOW 18 May 1901, Lambrechtfontein; Trooper Herman Albrecht and Lieutenant Robert Digby-Jones, KIA 6 January 1900, Ladysmith; Private John Barry, KIA 8 January 1901, Monument Hill; Captain David Younger, DOW 11 July 1900, Krugersdorp.
72. PRO File WO/32/7498. Memo from General Sir Ian Hamilton, 8 October 1902.
73. PRO File WO/32/7498. Letter from Lord Rathmore to St. John Broderick, 17 September 1902.
74. PRO File WO/32/7498. Undated Letter from St John Broderick to Lord Roberts, assumed to be mid-September 1902; Letter from Lord Roberts to St John Broderick, 27 September 1902.
75. PRO File WO/32/7498. Memo from General Sir Ian Hamilton, 8 October 1902.
76. PRO File WO/32/7498. Memo from St John Broderick, 9 October 1902.
77. PRO File WO/32/7498. Lord Roberts, Instructions to Military Secretary (Hamilton), 12 October 1902.
78. PRO File WO/32/7499. Undated Memo of J. S. Ewart, Military Secretary.
79. PRO File WO/32/7500. Memo from Lord Knollys to War Office, ? November 1906.
80. PRO File WO/32/7500. Query from Colonel Sir Arthur Davidson to the War Office, 3 December 1906; Letter from Sir Arthur Wynne to Davidson, 6 December 1906; Letter from Davidson to Wynne, 8 December 1906.
81. See appendix for the full text of all warrants.
82. John Buchan, *The King's Grace* (London: Hodder & Stoughton, 1935), 57.
83. Harold Nicolson, *King George the Fifth: His Life and Reign* (London: Constable, 1952), 169.

# CHAPTER 5

1. *Register*, 246.
2. The author is indebted to Dr Melvin W. Smith, Professor of Marketing and Statistics, Stamford University (retired) for guidance in preparing the statistical analysis of the Victoria Cross winners.
3. Andrew Lambert, 'The Shield of Empire,' in J. R. Hill and Bryan Ranft, *The Oxford Illustrated History of the Royal Navy* (Oxford: Oxford University Press, 1995), 184, pointed out that between 1856 and 1914 the British battle fleet saw action only once, at Alexandria in 1882.
4. *Register*, 279.
5. Ibid., p. 153.
6. Ibid., p. 150.
7. PRO File WO/98/3. Copy of Gazette entry of Lieutenant Luke O'Connor.
8. Keegan, *The Face of Battle*, 265.
9. PRO File WO/98/3. Copy of Gazette entry of Brevet Major Frederick C. Elton.
10. PRO File WO/98/3. Copy of Gazette entry of Corporal John Ross.
11. PRO File WO/98/3. Copy of Gazette entry of Private John J. Sims
12. *Register*, 194.
13. PRO File WO/98/3. Recommendation of Mate Charles D. Lucas; *Register*, 196.
14. *Register*, 281.

15. Ibid., p. 213.
16. William Forbes-Mitchell, *Reminiscences of the Great Mutiny* (n.p., 1893), 42–3; Farwell, *Queen Victoria's Little Wars*, 126.
17. *Register*, 44.
18. Ibid., p. 306.
19. PRO File WO/98/2. Letter from Colonel Henry Warre, Depot Malta, to Lieutenant General John L. Pennefather, 31 October 1857.
20. W. J. Reader, *At Duty's Call: A Study in Obsolete Patriotism* (Manchester: Manchester University Press, 1988), 10.
21. H. D. Hutchinson, *The Campaign in Tirah, 1897–1898* (London: Macmillan, 1898), 242–5.
22. PRO File WO/98/2. Letter from G. C. Mundy to Major General Sir Charles Yorke, 25 February 1856.
23. General Sir Ian Hamilton, *Listening for the Drums* (London: Faber & Faber, 1944), 91–2.
24. Ian B. M. Hamilton, *The Happy Warrior: A Life of General Sir Ian Hamilton, GCB, GCMG, DSO* (London: Cassell, 1966), 41–6, 134–5, 145. (The author is the nephew of Sir Ian.)
25. Hamilton, *Listening For the Drums*, 93.
26. Ibid., p. 145–6.
27. PRO File WO/32/7489. Special Coronation Supplement to *The London Gazette*.
28. See Appendix for full text of all VC Warrants.
29. PRO file WO/32/7313. Documents related to the case of Wm Stanlake. Letter from Sir Henry Storks to Lord Panmure, n.d., 1857.
30. PRO file WO/32/7313. Documents related to the case of Wm Stanlake.
31. *The Hampshire Chronicle*, 5 December 1863; 'The End of A Victoria Cross Man' *United Services Gazette*, 9 April 1864.
32. Imperial War Museum. Lummis File of Gunner James Colliss.
33. Information from victoriacross.org.uk website, accessed 25 August 2004.
34. See Chapter 4 for details of Lane's VC. Imperial War Museum Lummis File of Private Thomas Lane.
35. Imperial War Museum. Lummis File of Sergeant Thomas McGuire.
36. PRO File WO/32/7346. The Claim of Private Samuel Morely, Second Battalion, Military Train; Imperial War Museum. Lummis File of Private Michael Murphy. Lummis incorrectly identifies the individual as 'private' rather than 'farrier.'
37. Imperial War Museum. Lummis File of Private George Ravenhill.
38. *Register*, 82.
39. PRO file WO/32/7358. Letters from Admiralty to War Office and War Office to Admiralty, 29 July 1861, 2 August 1861, 5 August 1861; Letter from Edward Pennington to Edward Lugard, 27 August 1861.
40. Michael Daniels, 'Midshipman Edward St. John Daniels' http://www.mdani.demon.co.uk/esjd/esjdweb.htm. Copyright 1999–2001.
41. *Register*, 272.

## CHAPTER 6

1. Alan Shepperd, *Sandhurst: The Royal Military Academy Sandhurst and its Predecessors* (London: Country Life Books, 1980), 84, 92–3. The cadets at Sandhurst were so keen on riflery during the 1880s that they purchased their own ammunition to supplement that

provided by the school's budget for the Cadet's Rifle Club. The initial issue for the club was 6000 rounds; the cadets bought an additional 14,000 rounds. Riflery, however, was not part of the Sandhurst curriculum until after 1902, while the cadets still spent three hours a day on riding and sword drills. See also Major Darrell D. Hall, 'Field Artillery in the British Army, 1860–1960: Part II 1900–1914', Military History Journal, vol. 2 no. 5 (June 1973); Hubert C. Johnson, Breakthrough! Tactics, Technology, and the Search for Victory on the Western Front (Novato, CA: Presidio Press, 1994), 4–6, and Spiers, Army and Society, 247.

2. Ian Beckett, 'The British Army, 1914–1918: The Illusion of Change,' in John Turner, ed., Britain and the First World War (London: Unwin Hyman, 1988), 101–2; Skelley, The Victorian Army at Home, 287, 297.
3. Malcolm Brown, The Imperial War Museum Book of the Western Front (Osceola, WI: Motorbooks International, 1994), 9; Luvaas, Education of an Army, 313.
4. Ernest W. Hamilton, The First Seven Divisions (New York: E. P. Dutton, 1916), 10.
5. William James Philpott, Anglo-French Relations and Strategy on the Western Front (London: Macmillan, 1996), 11–12. This role was more or less stumbled upon as a result of incoherent pre-war planning on the part of both government and military leadership. French leadership was far less sanguine concerning the combat effectiveness of the BEF, considering its initial contribution more of a morale boost than anything else.
6. J. M. Bourne, Britain and the Great War, 1914–1918 (London: Hodder & Stoughton, 1989), 13–15.
7. 'Mons,' Times, 22 August 1914, p. 5.
8. David Ascoli, The Mons Star: The British Expeditionary Force, 5th Aug.–22nd Nov. 1914 (London: Harrap, 1981), 62–5; Hamilton, First Seven, 15–27. For a much more colorful account of the Battle of Mons, see A. Corbett-Smith, The Retreat From Mons by One Who Shared in it (London: Cassell, 1916), 69–87.
9. Register, 87.
10. Ibid., p. 121.
11. John Terraine, Mons: The Retreat to Victory (London: B. T. Batsford, 1960), 99.
12. Register, 152.
13. Terraine, Mons, 108.
14. Brigadier General James Edward Edmonds, ed., Military Operations, France and Belgium, 1914 (London: Macmillan, 1922), 77. Lance-Corporal Charles Alfred Jarvis and Captain Theodore Wright both won Crosses for their efforts to destroy the bridges.
15. Daniel David, The 1914 Campaign: August–October, 1914 (New York: Military Press, 1987), 125.
16. Register. 11, 130.
17. Hamilton, First Seven, 44–6; Terraine, Mons, 125.
18. Register, 341.
19. Ibid., pp. 11, 341.
20. Terraine, Mons, 141.
21. Peter Liddle, The Soldier's War, 1914–1918 (London: Blandford Press, 1988), 32–3.
22. Ascoli, The Mons Star, 108–9.
23. Register, 342.
24. Edmonds, Military Operations, 236–7.
25. Terraine, Mons, 192.
26. Ascoli, The Mons Star, 133–5.

27. Brown, Book of the Western Front, 17; Philpott, Anglo-French Relations and Strategy, 25–6; Terraine, Mons, 183–4.
28. Ernest Sanger, Letters From Two World Wars: A Social History of English Attitudes to War, 1914–45 (Stroud: Alan Sutton, 1993), 13. Letter from Captain Julian Grenfell, 1st Royal Dragoons, to his parents, 3 November 1914.
29. Trevor Wilson, The Myriad Faces of War (New York: Basil Blackwell, 1986), 53. Corporal John Lucy, 22 August 1914.
30. Sanger, Letters From Two World Wars, 10. Letter from Sub-Lieutenant Rupert Brooke to Leonard Bacon, 11 November 1914.
31. Wilson, Myriad Faces of War, 46. Statement of Corporal B. J. Denore, 3–5 September 1914.
32. Captain Lionel William Crouch, Duty and Service: Letters From the Front (London: Hazell, Watson & Viney, 1917), 27. Letter from Captain Lionel Crouch to his Father, 29 August 1914.
33. Hamilton, First Seven, 38. Julian Grenfell was the cousin of Captain Francis Grenfell, who won the VC at Elouges, 24 August 1914.
34. Sanger, Letters From Two World Wars, 14. Letter from Captain Julian Grenfell to his mother, 14 May 1915.
35. Corelli Barnett, The Sword Bearers: Supreme Command in the First World War (Bloomington, IN: Indiana University Press, 1963), 76, 92; Philpott, Anglo-French Relations and Strategy, 27–8.
36. Register, 169.
37. Ibid., p. 103.
38. Ibid., p. 312.
39. Philpott, Anglo-French Relations and Strategy, 31–5; Wilson, Myriad Faces of War, 47–8.
40. Barnett, The Sword Bearers, 94–5.
41. Hew Strachan, The First World War, Volume I: To Arms (Oxford: University Press, 2001), 264.
42. Register, 91. Private Frederick Dobson.
43. Ibid., p. 42. Lieutenant William Arthur McCrae Bruce.
44. Vallentin was leading an attack at Zillebeke, Belgium on 7 November 1914 when he was knocked down by a bullet. He got back to his feet and was immediately shot dead. The justification for his award was 'the capture of the enemy's trenches which immediately followed was in great measure due to the confidence which the men had in their captain, arising from his many previous acts of great bravery and ability.'
45. Register, 189, 319; Barnett, Britain and Her Army, 343–5.
46. Robin Prior and Trevor Wilson, Command on the Western Front: The Military Career of Sir Henry Rawlinson (Oxford: Blackwell, 1992), 12–15; William Dilworth Puleston, The High Command in the World War (New York: Charles Scribner's Sons, 1934), 100–5; Peter Slowe and Richard Woods, Fields of Death: Battle Scenes of the First World War (London: Robert Hale, 1986), 28.
47. Official History of the Great War (London: HMSO, 1925), 2: 235.
48. Register, 185.
49. Johnson, Breakthrough!, 89; Slowe and Woods, Fields of Death, 87–9; Wilson, Myriad Faces of War, 256–8.
50. Register, 271.
51. Brown, Book of the Western Front, 33. Letter from Captain E. W. S. Balfour, Adjutant, 5th Dragoon Guards, to ?, 3 December 1914.
52. Lee Kennett, The First Air War, 1914–1918 (New York: The Free Press, 1991), 153.

53. Richard Townshend Bickers, *The First Great Air War* (London: Hodder & Stoughton, 1988), 202–3; Wilson, *Myriad Faces of War*, 363.
54. 'Wing Adjutant,' *Plane Tales From the Skies* (London: Cassell, 1918), *passim*. The title alone speaks volumes of the Victorian connection.
55. Denis Winter, *The First of the Few: Fighter Pilots of the First World War* (Athens, GA: The University of Georgia Press, 1983), 132–3.
56. William Avery Bishop, *Winged Warfare: Hunting Huns in the Air* (London: Hodder & Stoughton, 1918), 1.
57. *Register*, 210.
58. Ibid., p. 29.
59. Ibid., p. 206.
60. Ibid., p. 162.
61. Ibid., p. 31.
62. Bruce Lewis, *A Few of the First: The True Stories of the Men Who Flew in and before the First World War* (London: Leo Cooper, 1997), 230; Kennett, *First Air War*, 164.
63. John H. Morrow, *The Great War in the Air: Military Aviation from 1909 to 1921* (Washington: Smithsonian Institution Press, 1993), 320–1.
64. *Register*, 259.
65. Ibid., p. 330.
66. Ibid., p. 30.
67. The role of *Nestor* appears only in the most detailed accounts of Jutland; in most, Bingham's command appeared only as an icon on a chart, noting where the ship was sunk.
68. Submarine commanders often preferred to surface and sink an unarmed target with the deck gun and thus conserve expensive torpedoes for more dangerous targets. Q-Ships were freighters equipped with hidden guns to deal with this threat.
69. *Register*, 254.
70. Ibid., 71.
71. Ibid., p. 47
72. Ibid., p. 202.
73. Ibid., p. 83.
74. Wilson, *Myriad Faces of War*, 276.
75. *Register*, 70.
76. Ibid., p. 315.
77. Ibid., p. 331.
78. Ibid., p. 159.
79. Ibid., pp. 45, 172.
80. Ibid., p. 43.
81. Rescue Wounded: 2nd Lieutenant Myles Edward Kinghorn, Reverend William Addison, Private James Henry Fynn, Corporal Sidney William Ware, Captain Angus Buchanan, Lance-Naik Lala, Captain John Alexander Sinton, Sepoy Chatta Singh; Defense: Naik Shahamad Khan, Private George Stringer; Resupply: Lieutenant Commander Charles Henry Cowley, Lieutenant Hunphrey Obaldson Brooke Firman.
82. William Robertson, *From Private to Field Marshal* (Boston: Houghton Mifflin, 1921), 273–5. Robertson was influential in nominating Maude for the Mesopotamian command.
83. Paul K. Davis, *Ends and Means: The British Mesopotamian Campaign and Commission* (London: Associated University Presses, 1994), 230–1; Puleston, *The High Command*, 264–5; Wilson, *Myriad Faces of War*, 380–1.

84. *Register*, 222.
85. Ibid., p. 126.
86. Ibid., p. 19.

## CHAPTER 7

1. Eric Montgomery Andrews, *The ANZAC Illusion: Anglo-Australian Relations During World War I* (Cambridge: Cambridge University Press, 1993), 44.
2. John Gooch, 'The Armed Services,' in Stephen Constantine, Maurice W. Kirby and Mary B. Rose, eds, *The First World War in British History* (London: Edward Arnold, 1995), 187–90; Johnson, *Breakthrough!*, 116–18.
3. Brown, *Book of the Western Front*, 70–1. Letter from Second Lieutenant Gordon Bartlett, 1/5th King's Liverpool Regiment, to his parents, 13 March 1915.
4. *Register*, 83, 240.
5. Lyn Macdonald, *1915: The Death of Innocence* (London: Headline Books, 1993), 134.
6. Edward Spiers, 'Gallipoli,' in Brian Bond, ed., *The First World War and British Military History* (Oxford: The Clarendon Press, 1991), 165–88. Spiers examines four periods of interpretation. The initial wartime and immediate aftermath assessments were highly critical of the cost of the modest achievements of the campaign as well as the high command decisions of Kitchener, Churchill, and Hamilton. The initial condemnation of the operations generated a series of rebuttals during the 1920s; including from the official history Brigadier General C. F. Aspinal-Oglander's multi-volume *Military Operations Gallipoli* (1929–32), Winston Churchill's *The World Crisis, 1915* (1923), and Sir Ian Hamilton's two-volume *Gallipoli Diary* (1920). These works tended to take a position defending the campaign in initial conception and then offered a variety of excuses as to why it failed. Another wave of Gallipoli revision took place after the Second World War, beginning with Alan Moorehead, *Gallipoli* (1956) and J. F. C. Fuller, *The Decisive Battles of the Western World and Their Influence Upon History* (1956) and Maurice Hankey's devastating insider report of the management of the war effort, *The Supreme Command, 1914–1918* (1961). The general trend in this period was to blame the failure on incompetence at the highest levels of both civilian and military authority. More recently authors have centered their attacks on local command ability as the primary deficiency in the campaign. Both Peter Liddle in *Men of Gallipoli* (1976) and John Laffin, *Damn the Dardanelles!* (1989) blamed Hamilton for the failure of the venture. The one common thread through all interpretations is that the campaign failed to accomplish any of its objectives, and wasted a lot of lives in the process.
7. John Laffin, *Damn the Dardanelles!* (Gloucester: Alan Sutton, 1989), 49–50.
8. Geoffrey Moorehouse, *Hell's Foundations: A Social History of the Town of Bury in the Aftermath of the Gallipoli Campaign* (New York: Henry Holt, 1992), 65, 129–30.
9. PRO File ADM 1/8528/176. Letter from Major-General A. Hunter-Weston to D.A.G., General Headquarters, 15 May 1915; Undated endorsement of recommendations signed by General Ian Hamilton, General Officer Commanding, Mediterranean Expeditionary Force.
10. Ian Hamilton, *Gallipoli Diary* (London:Edward Arnold, 1920), 222–3.
11. PRO file ADM 1/8528/176. Letter from Major-General A. Hunter-Weston to D.A.G., General Headquarters, 15 May 1915.

12. Denis Winter, *25 April 1915: The Inevitable Tragedy* (St Lucia, Queensland: University of Queensland Press, 1994), 87–8. Winter reported a variety of estimates for the distance between the beach and the big ships, ranging from one to four miles. Winter also reported a transit time of 40 minutes for tow vessels ferrying troops ashore at a rate of six knots. This means these boats were covering one nautical mile every ten minutes. Thus, a 40-minute trip indicates a distance of about four nautical miles, or over 6000 yards. Eyewitness Major John Gillam in his *Gallipoli Diary* (n.p.: n.p., 1918; reprint, Stevenage, Herts.: The Strong Oak Press,1989), 31–2, reported that the shore was just barely visible due to mist as the first wave embarked from the transport *Arcadian*. Later, at 0830 hours he reported 'It is quite clear now, and I can just see through my glasses the little khaki figures on shore at 'W' Beach.'
13. PRO File WO/32/4994. Unsigned Report dated 13 May 1915.
14. Moorehouse, *Hell's Foundations*, 130–1.
15. See appendix for full text of all VC Warrants.
16. PRO file ADM 1/8528/176. Letter from Lieutenant-General Aylmer Hunter-Weston to A.M.S., GHQ., 14 July 1915.
17. PRO file WO/32/4995. Letter from Military Secretary Lieutenant-General Sir Francis Davies to D.C.G.I.S., 26 February 1917.
18. Moorehouse, *Hell's Foundations*, 132.
19. PRO file WO/32/4995. Letter from Military Secretary Lieutenant-General Sir Francis Davies to D.C.G.I.S., 26 February 1917.
20. PRO file ADM 1/8528/176. Memoranda related to the Lancashire Fusiliers' Victoria Cross Claims, February/March 1917; Letter from Lord Derby to King George V, ? March 1917; War Office announcement of Victoria Crosses for Captain Cuthbert Bromley, Sergeant Frank Edward Stubbs and Corporal John Grimshaw, 15 March 1917.
21. Laffin, *Dardanelles*, 87–91.
22. Bill Rawling, *Surviving Trench Warfare: Technology and the Canadian Corps, 1914–1918* (Toronto: University of Toronto Press, 1992), 29–35. The Canadians suffered just over 33 percent casualties during this, their first major engagement of the Great War.
23. David F. Burg and L. Edward Purcell, *Almanac of World War I* (Lexington, KY: The University of Kentucky Press, 1998), 62, 67.
24. Prior and Wilson, *Command on the Western Front*, 96–9.
25. Liddle, *Soldier's War*, 52–5.
26. Carver, *Seven Ages*, 171–4.
27. Lionel Sotheby, *Lionel Sotheby's Great War: Diaries and Letters from the Western Front*, Donald C. Richter, ed.(Athens, OH: Ohio University Press, 1997), 7.
28. Robert Graves, *Good-bye to All That* (Garden City, NY: Doubleday, 1929), 110–11. Letter from Captain Robert Graves to his parents, 24 May 1915.
29. Sotheby, *Diaries and Letters*, 16.
30. Chris Cook and John Stevenson, *The Longman Handbook of Modern European History, 1763–1985* (London: Longman, 1987), 133; Beckett, 'British Army,' 113. The figure of 78 percent was derived by averaging the percentage of the establishment in the combat elements of the military on 1 September of each year; Geoffrey Noon, 'The Treatment of Casualties in the Great War,' in Paddy Griffith, ed., *British Fighting Methods in the Great War* (London: Frank Cass, 1996), 88.
31. David A. French, 'A One-Man Show? Civil-Military Relations in Britain during the First World War,' in Paul Smith, ed., *Government and the Armed Forces in Britain* (London: The Hambledon Press, 1996), 91–2.

32. Peter Simkins, *Kitchener's Army: The Raising of the New Armies, 1914–16* (Manchester: Manchester University Press, 1988), 31–9.
33. Ibid., 168–9; Bernard Waites, *A Class Society at War: England, 1914–1918* (Leamington Spa: Berg, 1987), 188.
34. Grace Morris Craig, *But this is Our War* (Toronto:University of Toronto Press, 1981), 29.
35. Denis Winter, *Death's Men: Soldiers of the Great War* (London: Penguin Books, 1978), 27–9.
36. John Gooch, 'Armed Services,' in Stephen Constantine, Maurice W. Kirby, and Mary B. Rose, eds, *The First World War in British History.* (London: Edward Arnold, 1995), 188.
37. Peter Parker, *The Old Lie: The Great War and the Public School Ethos* (London: Constable, 1987), 50–3, 126–9.
38. Bernard Waites, *A Class Society at War: England, 1914–1918* (Leamington Spa: Berg, 1987), 184–7.
39. J. A. Morgan, ' "The Grit of Our Forefathers:" Invented Traditions, Propaganda and Imperialism,' in John M. Mackenzie, ed., *Imperialism and Popular Culture* (Manchester: Manchester University Press, 1986), 127; see also Reader, *At Duty's Call,* 77–8.
40. Simkins, *Kitchener's Army,* 56.
41. David Mitchell, *Monstrous Regiment: The Story of the Women of the First World War* (New York: Macmillan, 1965), 39–40; See also Reader, *At Duty's Call,* 119–20.
42. Sidney Rogerson, *Twelve Days* (London: Arthur Baker, 1933), 40.
43. For the difficulties and delays in providing training facilities and equipment, see Peter Simkins's chapters on Training Camps and Billets, Uniforms and Equipment, and Arms and Ammunition in *Kitchener's Army.* See also Brown, *Book of the Western Front,* 115.
44. Philpott, *Anglo-French Relations and Strategy,* 77, 83–5.
45. Douglas Haig, *The Private Papers of Douglas Haig* (London: Eyre & Spottiswoode, 1952), 116, 121. In his initial orders to Haig upon assuming command of the BEF Kitchener cautioned him that 'in minor operations you should be careful that your subordinates understand that risk of serious losses should only be taken where such risk is authoritatively considered to be commensurate with the objective in view.'
46. Prior and Wilson, *Command on the Western Front,* 155–6.
47. Wilson, *Myriad Faces of War,* 316.
48. Jonathan Bailey, 'British Artillery in the Great War,' in Paddy Griffith, ed., *Fighting Methods in the Great War* (London: Frank Cass, 1996), 31–2.
49. Peter Liddle, *The 1916 Battle of the Somme* (London: Leo Cooper, 1992), 23.
50. John Laffin, *On the Western Front: Soldiers' Stories from France and Flanders, 1914–1918* (Gloucester: A. Sutton, 1985), 67.
51. Tim Travers, *The Killing Ground: The British Army, the Western Front and the Emergence of Modern Warfare, 1900–1918* (London: Allen & Unwin, 1987), 136–41. GHQ was so convinced of the efficacy of the guns that first-hand intelligence that the wire was uncut and the observers were taking small-arms fire in the forward trenches was either discounted or outright ignored.
52. Burg and Purcell, *Almanac of World War I,* 127–8.
53. John Laffin, *British Butchers and Bunglers of World War One* (London: Alan Sutton, 1988), 21.
54. Michael Carver, Field Marshal Lord, *The Seven Ages of the British Army* (New York: Beaufort Books, 1984), 173, reported a total of 50,380 casualties for Loos.
55. Prior and Wilson, *Command on the Western Front,* 155–7.
56. Laffin, *Soldiers' Stories,* 75–6; Wilson, *Myriad Faces of War,* 318.
57. Sanger, *Letters From Two World Wars,* 23. Letter from Harold Macmillan to his mother, 13 May 1916.

58. Arthur Surfleet, 'Blue Chevrons: An Infantry Private's Great War Diary' (Imperial War Museum Collections); Quoted in Wilson, *Myriad Faces of War*, 358.
59. Ibid.
60. Denis Winter, *Death's Men*, 225–6.
61. Wilson, *Myriad Faces of War*, 333. Statement of Graham Seton Hutchison, 15 July 1916.
62. Surfleet, 'Blue Chevrons,' quoted in Wilson, *Myriad Faces of War*, 356.
63. Sanger, *Letters From Two World Wars*, 31. Letter from Private Ivor Gurney to Marion Scott, 7 August 1916.
64. Surfleet, 'Blue Chevrons,' early October, 1916, quoted in Wilson, *Myriad Faces of War*, 359; Surfleet, 'Blue Chevrons,' incident during the battle of the Somme, quoted in Wilson, *Myriad Faces of War*, 356.
65. R. H. Haigh and P. W. Turner, *World War One and the Serving British Soldier* (Manhattan, KS: Military Affairs/Aerospace Historian, 1979), 15.
66. Haig, *Private Papers*, 70, 72; Carver, *Seven Ages*, 170–3.
67. Wilson, *Myriad Faces of War*, 315.
68. Travers, *Killing Ground*, 87–8, 130.
69. Haig, *Private Papers*, 147.
70. Prior and Wilson, *Command on the Western Front*, 147–8; see also Carver, *Seven Ages*, 178–9.
71. Prior and Wilson, *Command on the Western Front*, 78. Diary entry of Sir Henry Rawlinson, 14 March 1915.
72. Ibid., 77–80; Wilson, *Myriad Faces of War*, 317.
73. Travers, *Killing Ground*, 160.
74. See PRO File WO/32/7463 for examples of Kitchener filtering recommendations.
75. Desmond Morton, *When Your Number's Up* (Toronto: Random House of Canada, 1993), 246–7.
76. Travers, *Killing Ground*, 154, 166–7.
77. PRO File WO/32/3443. Minutes to the Second Meeting of the Victoria Cross Commission. During the discussion concerning the elective principle, the Army representative, Lieutenant-Colonel Lord Herbert Douglas-Scott, reported that 'in a campaign the Army works out roughly at one [Victoria Cross] in 5,000 [men]' but he did not cite any formula for determining the number of Crosses granted as a hard ratio of the number of troops involved.
78. *Register*, 172.
79. The following 'True Tale of Todger Jones' comes from a 31 July 1995 interview with Major (ret) Tony Astle, Acting Regimental Historian of the 22nd (Cheshire) Regiment; as a young officer with the regiment, he knew Jones, and heard a very different version of the deed from the man who did it.
80. Chester Regiment Museum File.Jones, T. A. VC, DCM, Pvt.

# CHAPTER 8

1. David R. Woodward, *Lloyd George and the Generals* (East Brunswick, NJ: Associated University Presses, 1983), 91, 142, 224–5. Lloyd George's disapproval of Haig's command abilities predated his assumption of the premiership and continued to the end of the war.
2. The War Cabinet consisted of Lloyd George, Lord Curzon, Sir Austen Chamberlain, Lord Robert Cecil, and Walter Long. For an insider appraisal of the creation of the

new ministry, see Lord Beaverbrook's two-volume *Politicians and the Great War, 1914–1918* (London: Butterworth, 1928, 1932; reprint, London: Archon Books, 1968), especially 494–533. For a more recent critique of the rise of the War Cabinet, see John Turner, *British Politics and the Great War: Coalition and Conflict, 1915–1918* (New Haven, CT: Yale University Press, 1992), 142–8. See also John Turner, 'Cabinets, Committees and Secretariats: The Higher Direction of the War,' in Kathleen Burk, ed., *War and the State: The Transformation of British Government, 1914–1918* (London: George Allen & Unwin, 1982).
3. David French, *The Strategy of the Lloyd George Coalition, 1916–1918* (Oxford: Clarendon Press, 1995), 156–7; Paul Guinn, British Strategy and Politics, 1914 to 1918 (Oxford: The Clarendon Press, 1965), 191, 196–7; Woodward, *Lloyd George and the Generals*, 134–5, Turner, *Coalition and Conflict*, 124–5; Haig, *Private Papers*, 31–2.
4. French, *Lloyd George Coalition*, 110–12.
5. Ibid., 6–9.
6. Wilson, *Myriad Faces of War*, 439–40.
7. Ibid.; French, *Lloyd George Coalition*, 290; Guin, *British Strategy and Politics*, 207; Woodward, *Lloyd George and the Generals*, 133.
8. Haig, *Private Papers*, 20.
9. Guin, *British Strategy and Politics*, 201; Haig, *Private Papers*, 208–9. 'Wigram' is Sir Clive Wigram, Privy Secretary to King George V.
10. John Turner, 'British Politics and the Great War,' in John Turner, ed., *Britain and the First World War* (London: Unwin & Hyman, 1988), 128; Woodward, *Lloyd George and the Generals*, 223.
11. Harvey A. DeWeerd, 'Churchill, Lloyd George, Clemenceau: The Emergence of the Civilians,' in *Makers of Modern Strategy: Military Thought from Machiavelli to Hitler*, Edward Meade Earle, ed. (Princeton: Princeton University Press, 1943), 298–300.
12. French, *Lloyd George Coalition*, 58–9; Guin, *British Strategy and Politics*, 200–1.
13. Woodward, *Lloyd George and the Generals*, 232, 245–7.
14. Turner, *Coalition and Conflict*, 158, 162.
15. Robin Prior and Trevor Wilson, *Passchendaele: The Untold Story* (New Haven, CT: Yale University Press, 1996), 29–31; Philpott, *Anglo-French Relations and Strategy*, 101–2; Turner, *Coalition and Conflict*, 155; Wilson, *Myriad Faces of War*, 444–5.
16. Gerard de Groot, *Douglas Haig, 1861–1928* (London: Unwin & Hyman,1988), 312; Johnson, *Breakthrough!*, 190; Prior and Wilson, *Passchendaele*, 31–3; Philip Warner, *Passchendaele: The Story Behind the Tragic Victory of 1917* (London: Sidgwick & Jackson, 1987), 131–2.
17. Prior and Wilson, *Command on the Western Front*, 266–7; John Terraine, *The Road to Passchendaele: The Flanders Offensive of 1917, A Study in Inevitability* (London: Leo Cooper, 1977), 23–4. Letter from Robert Nivelle to Douglas Haig, 21 December 1916.
18. Stephen Badsey, 'Cavalry and the Development of Breakthrough Doctrine,' in Griffith, ed., *Fighting Methods*, 158–9; Anthony Clayton, 'Robert Nivelle and the French Spring Offensive of 1917,' in Brian Bond, ed., *Fallen Stars: Eleven Studies of Twentieth Century Military Disasters* (London: Brassey's UK, 1991), 57, 59; Andy Simpson, *The Evolution of Victory: British Battles of the Western Front, 1914–1918* (London: Tom Donovan, 1995), 78–80.
19. Paddy Griffith, *Battle Tactics of the Western Front: The British Army's Art of the Attack, 1916–18* (New Haven, CT: Yale University Press, 1994), 85.
20. Clayton, 'Robert Nivelle,' 59.

21. Burg and Purcell, *Almanac of World War I*, 169–70; de Groot, *Douglas Haig*, 313–6. Burg and Purcell place the end of Arras as the capture of Bullecourt, 17 May. De Groot includes the consolidation of the line until 23 May, and reports a total of 160,000 casualties.
22. *Register*, 293.
23. Ibid., 226.
24. Guin, *British Strategy and Politics*, 230.
25. *Register*, 229.
26. Manning's novel is based on his own Great War experiences. It has been called 'the finest and noblest book of men in war' (Ernest Hemingway) and 'without doubt one of the greatest books about soldiers in the whole of western literature' (Michael Howard), Wilson, *Myriad Faces of War*, 678–9.
27. PRO file WO 32/4993. Original recommendation of Private F. W. Dobson, 28 September 1914, plus chain of command endorsements, 28/29 September 1914.
28. PRO file WO 32/4993. Letter from Douglas Haig, Headquarters, 1st Army Corps, to the Adjutant General [Lt. Gen. C. F. N. Macready], General Headquarters, 30 September 1914.
29. PRO file WO 32/4993. Minute Sheet signed by Major General Frederick Spencer Robb, n.d. The sentence 'The Committee understand that the S. of S. is prepared to accept such recommendations' was typed in the original and then struck through in pencil. A marginal note reads 'S of S has given his intentions to refer this to C in C Sir J. French saying that he concurs with [illegible word] V.C.'
30. PRO file Wo/32/4993. Letter from Field Marshal Sir John French to the Secretary, War Office, 25 November 1914.
31. Haig, *Private Papers*, 79.
32. Charles Edmonds, *A Subaltern's War* (New York: Minton, Balch, 1930), 64–5.
33. Wilson, *Myriad Faces of War*, 473. Major C. A. Bill, 15th Battalion, Royal Warwickshire Regiment, incident during the Third Battle of Ypres.
34. This is not to be confused with Sir John French's assessment that officers should not get the VC for rescuing the wounded. What we are dealing with here are enlisted men awarded for saving the life of an officer.
35. For attitudes toward the High Command, see Wilfred R. Bion, *The Long Weekend, 1897–1919: Part of a Life* (Abingdon: Fleetwood Press, 1982), 131, 172–3; Brown, *Book of the Western Front*, 150–2; Graves, *Farewell to All That*, 110–11; Liddle, *Soldier's War*, 97, 212–14; Morton, *When Your Number's Up*, 113, 178; Harry Siepmann, *Echo of the Guns: Recollections of an Artillery Officer* (London: Robert Hale, 1987), 89–94;.
36. Burg and Purcell, *Almanac of World War I*, 200–3; Niall Ferguson, *The Pity of War* (n.p.: Basic Books, 1999), 285; Anthony Farrar-Hockley, 'Sir Hubert Gough and the German Breakthrough, 1918,' in Brian Bond, ed., *Fallen Stars: Eleven Studies of Twentieth Century Military Disasters* (London: Brassey's UK, 1991), 78–83; John Terraine, *To Win a War: 1918, The Year of Victory* (Garden City, NY: Doubleday, 1981), 43–9; Wilson, *Myriad Faces of War*, 564.
37. Burg and Purcell, *Almanac of World War I*, 204.
38. Wilson, *Myriad Faces of War*, 570.
39. Terraine, *Haig*, 432–3.
40. Aubrey Wade, *The War of the Guns* (London: Batsford, 1936), 57–8.
41. Wilson, *Myriad Faces of War*, 552. Anonymous British Private, relating the events 21 March 1918.
42. H. M. Tomlinson, *All Our Yesterdays* (London: Heinemann, 1930), 481.

# CHAPTER 9

1. PRO file ADM 1/8528/176. Letter from 'O.A.R.M' (Oswyn Murray) to Sir Reginald Brade, 10 June 1918.
2. It is more likely that 'J.P' was Jonathan Peel, who was appointed Undersecretary of State for War under Lord Panmure in 1855 as part of the Palmerston ministry.
3. PRO file ADM 1/8528/176. Memorandum by Assistant Military Secretary Malcolm Graham 'Notes on the V.C. Warrant,' 15 June 1918; Letter from Reginald Brade to Oswyn Murray, 2 July 1918.
4. PRO file ADM 1/8528/176. Untitled internal Admiralty Memorandum outlining the need for warrant revision, 5 July 1918; Letter from Oswyn Murray to Reginald Brade, 8 July 1918; Reply from Reginald Brade to Oswyn Murray, 9 July 1918; Admiralty Board Minute Sheet to officially request the Army approach the King concerning warrant revision, 11 July 1918; Draft of Admiralty letter requesting Army approach the King regarding warrant revision, 20 July 1918; Letter from Bertram Blakiston Cubitt to Admiralty, 30 July 1918. PRO file WO/32/3443. Letter from Malcolm Graham to Lieutenant-Colonel the Right Honorable Sir F. E. G. Ponsonby, 1 August 1918.
5. PRO file WO/32/3443. Letter from Sir Frederick Ponsonby to Malcolm Graham, 3 August 1918.
6. PRO File ZJ1 656. Supplement to the London Gazette, 4 March 1918, 2729.
7. Sanger, *Letters From Two World Wars*, 83. Letter from Miss K. E. Luard, RRC to ? 31 July 1917.
8. Wilson, *Myriad Faces of War*, 711–12.
9. Sanger, *Letters From Two World Wars*, 94. Letter from Marguerite McArthur, with the YMCA in France, to ?, 26 May 1918.
10. Barbara McLaren, *Women in the War* (New York: George H. Doran, 1918), 157. Most of the book is devoted to upper-class women named in the text. Only six pages at the end of the book, in a chapter titled 'Some Army Nurses,' really deal with the common auxiliaries. Not a single one was identified by name.
11. Wilson, *Myriad Faces of War*, 389–93, 508–9.
12. PRO file WO/32/3443. Letters from Francis Davies, War Department, to: Major General Sir Godfrey Payne, Master-General of Personnel, Air Ministry, Hotel Cecil, The Strand; Major General H. G. Ruggles-Brise, Military Secretary, General Headquarters, British Armies in France; Sir George Fiddes, Colonial Office, Downing Street; Rear Admiral A. F. Everett, Naval Secretary, Admiralty, 6 August 1918.
13. PRO file WO/32/3443. Letter from Francis Davies to Frederick Ponsonby, 6 August 1918.
14. Ibid. Letter, Cox to Davies, 7 August 1918; Letter, Air Ministry to Davies, 10 August 1918.
15. PRO file ADM 1/8528/176. Letter from A. F. Everett to Francis Davies, 7 August 1918.
16. PRO file ADM 1/8528/176. Admiralty Memorandum 'Eligibility of Women for the Victoria Cross,' 8 August 1918.
17. PRO file ADM 1/8528/176. Letter from A.F. Everett to Francis Davies, 12 August 1918.
18. The Davies circular is not included in the correspondence held in WO/32/3443. Its content is inferred from the replies to the letter.
19. PRO file WO/32/3443. PRO file ADM 1/8528/176. Circular Letter from Robert U. Morgan, War Office to the Admiralty, the Air Ministry, the Colonial Office, the India

Office, and a 'complimentary copy' to the Home Office, 12 August, 1918. The Home Office was not invited to attend, merely notified that the meeting was to take place.
20. Ibid.
21. Nicolson, *King George the Fifth*, 395n, 469n.
22. 'Minutes of the First Meeting of the "Committee on Co-Ordination etc. of Warrants Relating to the V.C.," 30 August 1918, Whitehall,' 1. The minutes of this meeting will hereafter be cited as 'Committee I' followed by the page number of the original transcript.
23. Committee I, 1.
24. Ibid., 2.
25. Ibid., 3–4.
26. Ibid., 4.
27. Ibid., 5.
28. Macdonald, *They Called it Passchendaele*, 166–7. Undated statement of Sergeant John Carmichael, 9th Battalion, North Staffordshire Regiment.
29. *Register*, 54.
30. Committee I, 6–7.
31. While Graham's assertion was that each and every VC granted during the Great War had two witnesses, the nature of some of them – like that of Todger Jones, operating alone in the German trenches – make it a logical impossibility that the Army always adhered to this standard.
32. For example, see the controversy surrounding Captain William Bishop's solo Victoria Cross in Kennett, *First Air War*, 164.
33. Committee I, 8–9.
34. Ibid., 21.
35. In fact it did not; it was limited to the forces of New Zealand only. The idea that it could possibly cover troops from India was an impossibility as long as the Duke of Cambridge drew breath.
36. Committee I, 21–2.
37. Ibid., 22.
38. *Register*, 296.
39. Committee I, 23–4; Captain Smith was eventually gazetted as a 'Temporary Lieutenant, Royal Naval Reserve' and received a posthumous Victoria Cross on 24 May 1919.
40. See appendix for full text of all warrants; *Register*, 9.
41. Committee I, 41–2.
42. Ibid., 24.
43. Ibid., 28.
44. Clarke, *Gallantry Medals*, 84–5.
45. Committee I, 29–30.
46. Ibid., 30.
47. Ibid., Ponsonby, 31.
48. Ibid., 31.
49. Ibid., Graham, 32. Note that the woman is not mentioned by name.
50. Ibid., Everett, 33.
51. Ibid., Everett, 33.
52. Ibid., 34.
53. Ibid., 36.

54. Ibid., 36–7.
55. Ibid., 39–40.
56. Ibid., 42.
57. 'Minutes of the Conference on the Co-Ordination of Warrants Relating to the Victoria Cross,' The War Office, Whitehall, 12 November 1918, 1. Cited hereafter as 'Committee II.'
58. Ibid., 2.
59. Ibid., 3.
60. Clause V, warrant of 29 January 1856; for full text of all warrants, see appendix.
61. Surgeon-Captain Arthur Martin-Leake won his Cross in 1902 tending the wounded under fire at Vlakfontein, South Africa; his bar came in 1914 for rescuing the wounded under fire in Belgium. Captain [Doctor] Noel Chavasse won his Cross tending the wounded under fire at Guillemont, France in 1916; the bar (posthumous) was earned doing the same thing at Wieltje, Belgium in 1917. *Register*, 189; Ann Clayton, *Chavasse, Double VC* (London: Leo Cooper, 1992), 163–9, 219–21.
62. Frank Dunham, *The Long Carry: The War Diary of Stretcher Bearer Frank Dunham, 1916–1918*, R. H. Haigh and P. W. Turner, eds (London: Pergamon Press, 1970), 5n.
63. It is possible (although outside the scope of this work) that the military's resentment of this aspect of the Victoria Cross warrant along with the new civilian environment for heroism in the face of the Blitz was a factor in the creation of the George Cross in 1940.
64. Committee II, 4–6.
65. Ibid., 6–7.
66. Ibid., 8–12.
67. Ibid., 21–2.
68. PRO file ADM 1/8528/176. Letter from Lord Stamforham to Winston Churchill, 7 March 1919; Letter from J. A. Corcoran to Oswyn Murray, 7 March 1919.
69. David Jablonsky, *Churchill, The Great Game, and Total War* (London: Frank Cass, 1991), 14–5, 32–4, 145.
70. Winston Spencer Churchill, *Thoughts and Adventures* (London: Odhams Press, 1949), 200.
71. For full text of all the warrants, see appendix.

# CHAPTER 10

1. 'Disaster to an Indian Force,' *Times*, 12 June 1897, 9; *Operations in Waziristan, 1919–1920*. 2nd edn (Delhi: Government Central Press, 1923), 109–10.
2. *Register*, 335.
3. World War I: Acting Captain Clement Robertson, Lieutenant Cecil H. Sewell, Acting Captain Richard W. L. Wain and Acting Lieutenant-Colonel Richard A. West. World War II: Major David V. Currie, Acting Captain Michael Allmand, Guardsman Edward C. Charlton, Temporary Lieutenant-Colonel Henry R. B. Foote, Acting Captain Philip J. Gardener and Temporary Lieutenant-Colonel Geoffrey C. T. Keyes. All of these men were either serving with, or members of, armored units; in some cases the individual was on detached duty and not acting alongside armored forces.
4. David Fletcher, *The Great Tank Scandal: British Armour in the Second World War* (London: HMSO, 1989), 57–69; George Forty, *World War Two Tanks* (London: Osprey, 1995), 9, 56–63; A. J. Smithers, *Rude Mechanicals: An Account of Tank Maturity During the Second World War* (London:

Leo Cooper, 1987), 188–9. During the course of the Second World War British industry churned out 29,288 tanks, production that was augmented by American and Dominion manufacturing supplied to British forces.
5. Committee, I, 38.
6. Keegan, *Face of Battle*, 265–70.
7. The figure of 31 percent casualties cited in a previous chapter for First World War casualties was a ratio of combat casualties among combatant troops. These figures are based on total mobilization and include noncombat deaths.
8. These figures are derived from statistics listed in Cook and Stevenson, *Handbook of Modern European History*, 133, 167.
9. *Register*, 107.
10. Ibid., 50.
11. The figures cited in Table 10.1 and in the text for total casualties do not include individuals taken as prisoners of war, unless they were also wounded in the process of winning the VC.
12. Mark K. Wells, *Courage and Air Warfare: The Allied Aircrew Experience in the Second World War* (London: Frank Cass, 1995), 152–4.
13. Johnson, *Breakthrough!*, 147–57, especially 156–7.
14. See Chapter 6 above.
15. Charles Messenger, *'Bomber' Harris and the Strategic Bombing Offensive, 1939–1945* (New York: St. Martin's Press, 1984), 17–26.
16. Sir Arthur Harris, *Bomber Offensive* (London: Greenhill Books, Lionel Leventhal, 1990), 43.
17. Charles Messenger, *'Bomber' Harris and the Strategic Bombing Offensive, 1939–1945* (New York: St Martin's Press, 1984), 17.
18. Ibid., 53; Denis Richards, *The Hardest Victory: RAF Bomber Command in the Second World War* (New York: W. W. Norton, 1995), 69.
19. *Register*, 240.
20. Ibid., 285.
21. Air Ministry, *Bomber Command Continues* (London: HMSO, 1942), 25.
22. Messenger, *'Bomber' Harris*, 70–1.
23. Harris, *Bomber Offensive*, 141.
24. PRO File AIR 16/757. Bomber Command Operational Order No. 143, 18 April 1942.
25. Jack Currie, *The Augsburg Raid: The Story of one of the Most Dramatic and Dangerous Raids Ever Mounted by RAF Bomber Command* (London: Goodall Publications, 1987), 93–4.
26. PRO File AIR 2/5686. Victoria Cross recommendations of Acting Squadron Leader John Deering Nettleton and Squadron Leader John Seymour Sherwood, 19 April 1942. Richards, *The Hardest Victory*, 121–2.
27. Ibid., 93–4.
28. Wells, *Courage and Air Warfare*, 126–7.
29. Due to the small size of the statistical sample, median average (the point at which half of the sample falls before and half after) was deemed more accurate than a raw arithmetical average or modified arithmetical average.
30. *Register*, 112.
31. Ibid., 50.
32. Messenger, *'Bomber' Harris*, 39; Harris, *Bomber Offensive*, 46–7.
33. *Register*, 100, 119.
34. Guy Gibson, *Enemy Coast Ahead* (London: Michael Joseph, 1946), 253–6; Paul Brickhill, *The Dam Busters* (London: Evans Brothers, 1951), 32, 56–7.

35. Harris, Bomber Offensive, 43–4.
36. Register, 325.
37. Richards, The Hardest Victory, 89.
38. Note from Prime Minister to Secretary of State for Air and Chief of the Air Staff, 4 August 1940.
39. Eric J. Grove, ed., The Defeat of the Enemy Attack on Shipping, 1939–1945 (Aldershot: Navy Records Society, 1997), 221, 224.
40. Richards, The Hardest Victory, 80.
41. Winston Spencer Churchill, The Grand Alliance (Boston: Houghton Miflin, 1948), 123–6.
42. Grove, Defeat of the Enemy Attack on Shipping, 38–9. For the war as a whole surface raiders accounted for 188 ships lost out of a total of 4066 lost to all enemy action. U-boats sank 69 percent of the total. George Malcolm Thompson, The Vote of Censure (New York: Stein and Day, 1968), 114. Churchill, The Grand Alliance, 123–6; Richards, The Hardest Victory, 82.
43. Messenger, 'Bomber' Harris, 62.
44. Richard Garrett, Scharnhorst and Gneisenau: The Elusive Sisters (New York: Hippocrene Books, 1978), 77.
45. Richards, The Hardest Victory, 80–1.
46. Peter Kemp, The Escape of the Scharnhorst and Gneisenau (Annapolis, MD: Naval Institute Press, 1975), 12–3.
47. Ibid., 92–4, 101–2.
48. For accounts of the Channel Dash, see Garrett, Scharnhorst and Gneisenau, 92–111; Kemp, Escape of the Scharnhorst and Gneisenau, 41–72; and Peter C. Smith, Hold the Narrow Sea: Naval Warfare in the English Channel, 1939–1945 (Anapolis, MD: Naval Institute Press, 1984), 141–55.
49. John Kilbracken, Bring Back My Stringbag: Swordfish Pilot at War, 1940–1945 (London: Leo Cooper, 1996), 63–5; John Winton, ed., The War at Sea: The British Navy in World War II (New York: William Morrow, 1968), 179.
50. Register, 104.
51. Kilbracken, Bring Back My Stringbag, 64–5.
52. Ministry of Information, Fleet Air Arm (London: HMSO, 1943), 71. In one of the ironies of war, Esmonde had won the DSO for his part in the Bismarck affair. His investment in the Order was held at Buckingham Palace on 11 February, less than 24 hours before his death over the Channel.
53. Winton, The War at Sea, 27–9, 140.
54. Kevin Jefferys, The Churchill Coalition and Wartime Politics, 1940–1945 (Manchester: Manchester University Press, 1991), 86–7.
55. Excerpts from the Diary of Sir Henry Channon, 18 December 1941, 9 January 1942, 20 January 1942, 21 January 1942. Quoted in Kevin Jefferys, ed., War and Reform: British Politics During the Second World War (Manchester: Manchester University Press, 1994), 69–70.
56. Roger Parkinson, Blood, Toil, Tears and Sweat: The War History from Dunkirk to Alamein, Based on the War Cabinet Papers of 1940 to 1942 (New York: David McKay, 1973), 362–3; Winston Spencer Churchill, The Hinge of Fate (Boston: Houghton Miflin, 1948) 60–4, 71.
57. David Jablonsky, Churchill, The Great Game, and Total War (London: Frank Cass, 1991), 107.
58. Churchill, The Hinge of Fate, 81.
59. Parkinson, Blood, Toil, Tears and Sweat, 368.
60. Jefferys, Churchill Coalition, 92.

61. Alexander Cadogan, *The Diaries of Sir Alexander Cadogan*, David Dilks, ed. (New York: Putnam, 1972), 433.
62. Churchill, *Hinge of Fate*, 113–15.
63. Jablonsky, *Churchill, The Great Game, and Total War*, 159.
64. *Register*, 53. Date of Act: 6 April 1941; Date of gazette: 13 March 1942.
65. The ships had sustained damage from high altitude multi-aircraft strikes in July and April, but in these instances no individual person or aircraft could be credited with scoring the hit.
66. Major Kenneth Muir, Lieutenant-Colonel James Power Carne, Lieutenant Philip Kenneth Edward Curtis, and Private William Speakman.
67. *Register*, 232; Argyll and Sutherland Highlander Museum Archive Manuscript 15012 reported his dying words as 'The gooks will never drive the Argylls off this hill!'
68. Argyll and Sutherland Highlander Museum Archive Manuscript 15012.
69. Bob Breen, First to Fight (Nashville: The Battery Press, 1988), 1–11; Terry Burstall, *Vietnam: The Australian Dilemma* (St Lucia: University of Queensland Press, 1993), 217–20; D. M. Horner, *Australian Higher Command in the Vietnam War* (Canberra: Australian National University, 1986), 28–44; Ian McNeill, *The Team: Australian Army Advisers in Vietnam, 1962–1972* (London: Leo Cooper, 1984), 481–4. The four VC winners are Warrant Officer II Kevin A. Wheatley, Major Peter John Badcoe, Warrant Officer II Keith Payne, Warrant Officer II Rayene Stewart Simpson.
70. *Register*, 18.
71. Lance Corporal Rambahadur Limbu, Sarawak, 1965, Lieutenant-Colonel Herbert Jones and Sergeant Ian John McKay, Falklands, 1982.
72. *Register*, 206.
73. Ministry of Defense, 'Latest News: Private Johnson Gideon Beharry-Victoria Cross' http://www.operations.mod.uk/telic/ophons05/beharry.htm Published 18 March 2005. Accessed 25 February 2007.
74. Ministry of Defense, 'Corporal Budd awarded the Victoria Cross' http//www.mod.uk/DefenceInternet/DefenseNews/HistoryandHonour/CorporalBryanBuddAwarded theVictoriaCross.htm published 14 December 2006. Accessed 26 February 2007.
75. PRO File WO/32/7370. Memorandum from Edward Pennington concerning the Heaphy recommendation, 5 October 1866.
76. James Aulich, *Framing the Falklands War: Nationhood, Culture and Identity* (Milton Keynes: Open University Press, 1992), 8, 24.

# Bibliography

## UNITED KINGDOM ARCHIVAL, MANUSCRIPT, AND ORAL SOURCES

Argyll and Sutherland Highlanders Museum, Stirling. Mss 15012. 'For Valour.'
Gordon Highlanders Museum, Aberdeen. File PB1215. Correspondence related to the storming of Dargai Ridge, 20 October 1897.
Interview with Lieutenant Colonel Angus Fairrie, Cameron Barracks, Inverness, 26 July 1995.
Interview with Major (ret) Tony Astle, 22nd (Cheshire) Regiment, Chester, 31 July 1995.
Imperial War Museum. Lummis File.
Imperial War Museum Manuscript Collection. Arthur Surfleet. 'Blue Chevrons: An Infantry Private's Great War Diary.'
Public Record Office File ADM 1/8528/176.
Public Record Office File AIR 16/757. Bomber Command Operational Order No. 143.
Public Record Office File AIR 2/5686. Victoria Cross recommendations of John Deering Nettleton and John Seymour Sherwood.
Public Record Office File WO/32. War Office Documents related to the Victoria Cross
Public Record Office File WO/98. War Office Documents related to the Victoria Cross.
Public Record Office File ZJ1 656. Supplement to the London Gazette, 4 March 1918, 2729.
Royal archives, Windsor Castle: RA VIC /E5/16, 18, 29, 30, 31.
Royal Archives, Windsor Castle: RA VIC/E6/69, 71, 78.
Royal Archives, Windsor Castle: RA VIC/G42/65.
Royal Archives, Windsor Castle: RA VIC/E9/30.

## NEWSPAPER AND JOURNAL SOURCES

'Afghanistan.' *Times* (London). 24 December 1879, 10.
'Afghanistan.' *Times* (London). 25 December 1879, 8.
'Army Regulations.' *Times* (London), 31 July 1858.
'Calcutta,' *Times*, 27 June 1857, 9.
'Disaster to an Indian Force.' *Times* (London). 12 June 1897.
'Distribution of the Victoria Cross.' *Times* (London), 26 June 1857.
'Editorial criticizing the command of Sir Richard England.' *Times* (London). 11 December 1854, 6.
'Leading Story.' *Times* (London), 3 January 1855, 6.
'Leading Story.' *Times* (London), 3 November 1855, 6–7.
'Letter (unsigned) to the Editor of *The Times*.' *Times* (London). 8 January 1855, 5.
'Letter from "FAIR PLAY" To the Editor of *The Times*.' *Times* (London) 8 January 1855, 5.
'Letter from "A Civilian" to the Editor of *The Times*.' *Times* (London). 27 December 1854, 5.

'Letter from "A Civilian" to the Editor of The Times.' Times (London), 11 January 1855, 5.
'Letter from "An Old Soldier" to the Editor of The Times.' Times (London). 20 December 1854, 8.
'Letter from "J. C." to the Editor of The Times.' Times (London). 3 December 1854, 8.
'Letters from the Crimea.' Times (London). 26 December 1854, 9.
'Mons.' Times (London), 22 August 1914, 5.
'Military and Naval Intelligence.' Times (London). 3 November 1855, 10.
'Parliamentary Intelligence: Distribution of the Victoria Cross.' Times (London), 26 June 1857, 7.
'Parliamentary Intelligence, Tuesday 19 December: Order of Merit.' Times (London). 20 December 1854, 3.
'The British Expedition.' Times (London). 18 December 1854, 8.
'The End of A Victoria Cross Man.' United Services Gazette, 9 April 1864.
The Hampshire Chronicle, 5 December 1863 [Private Valentine Bambrick].
'The Indian Mutinies.' Times (London). 6 October 1857, 9.
'The Massacre at Cawnpore.' Times (London). 2 September 1857, 5.
'The Press and the War.' Times (London), 8 January 1855, 10.
'The Victoria Cross.' Times (London), 26 February 1857, 6.
'The Zulu War.' Times (London). 12 February, 1879, 10.

## PRINTED PRIMARY SOURCES

Air Ministry. Bomber Command Continues. London: HMSO, 1942.
Aitken, Max, Lord Beaverbrook. Politicians and the Great War, 1914–1918. London: Butterworth, 1928.
Beaverbrook, Lord, Politicians and the Great War, 1914–1918, 2 vols (London: Butterworth, 1928, 1932; reprint, London: Archon Books, 1968.
Bion, Wilfred R. The Long Weekend, 1897–1919: Part of a Life. Abingdon: Fleetwood Press, 1982.
Bishop, William Avery. Winged Warfare: Hunting Huns in the Air. London: Hodder & Stoughton, 1918.
Bourne, Kenneth, ed. The Letters of the Third Viscount Palmerston to Laurence and Elizabeth Sullivan, 1804–1863. Camden Fourth Series xxiii. London: Royal Historical Society, 1979.
Cadogan, Alexander. The Diaries of Sir Alexander Cadogan. New York: Putnam, 1972.
Callwell, Charles E. Small Wars: Their Principal and Practice. London: HMSO, 1906; reprint, Greenhill Books, 1990.
Carlyle, Thomas. On Heroes, Hero-Worship, and the Heroic in History. Berkeley, CA: University of California Press, 1993.
Churchill, Winston Spencer. The Grand Alliance. Boston: Houghton Mifflin, 1948.
———. The Hinge of Fate. Boston: Houghton Mifflin, 1948.
———. Thoughts and Adventures. London: Odhams Press, 1949.
Corbett-Smith, A. The Retreat From Mons by One Who Shared in it. London: Cassell, 1916.
Craig, Grace Morris. But This is Our War. Toronto: University of Toronto Press, 1981.
Creighton, Mandell. Memoir of Sir George Grey. London: Longmans, Green, 1901.
Crouch, Lionel William. Duty and Service: Letters From the Front. London: Hazell, Watson & Viney, 1917.
Douglas, George. Autobiography and Memoirs of George Douglas, 8th Duke of Argyll. n.p.:n.p., 1906.

Dunham, Frank. *The Long Carry: The War Diary of Stretcher Bearer Frank Dunham, 1916–1918.* R. H. Haigh and P. W. Turner, eds. London: Pergamon Press, 1970.
Edmonds, Charles. *A Subaltern's War.* New York: Minton, Balch, 1930.
Forbes-Mitchell, William. *Reminiscences of the Great Mutiny.* n.p.: n.p., 1893.
Gibbs, Philip. *Realities of War.* London: Heinemann, 1920.
Gibson, Guy. *Enemy Coast Ahead.* London: Michael Joseph, 1946.
Gildas. *The Ruin of Britain and Other Works.* Michael Winterbottom, ed., trans. London: Philmore, 1978.
Gillam, John. *Gallipoli Diary.* Stevenage: The Strong Oak Press, 1989.
Graves, Robert. *Good-bye to All That.* Garden City, NY: Doubleday, 1929.
Haig, Douglas. *The Private Papers of Douglas Haig.* London: Eyre & Spottiswoode, 1952.
Hamilton, Ernest W. *The First Seven Divisions.* New York: E. P. Dutton, 1916.
Hamilton, Ian. *Gallipoli Diary.* London: Edward Arnold, 1920.
———. *Listening For the Drums.* London: Faber & Faber, 1944.
*Hansard's Parliamentary Debates.* New York: Readex Microprint Corp., 1961.
Harris, Sir Arthur. *Bomber Offensive.* London: Greenhill Books, Lionel Leventhal, 1990.
Henty, George Alfred. *Beric the Briton.* New York: Charles Scribner's Sons, 1896.
———. *The Bravest of the Brave, or, With Peterborough in Spain.* New York: Hurst, n.d.
———. *Facing Death, or, The Hero of the Vaughan Pit.* New York: Hurst, n.d.
———. *A Final Reckoning.* New York: Hurst and Company, n.d.
———. *For Name and Fame, or, Through Afghan Passes.* New York: Hurst, n.d.
———. *In Greek Waters: A Story of the Grecian War of Independence.* New York: Charles Scribner's Sons, 1902.
———. *Jack Archer: A Tale of the Crimea.* New York: Hurst, n.d.
———. *One of the 28th: A Tale of Waterloo.* New York: Hurst (1890?).
———. *With Moore at Corunna.* New York: Charles Scribner's Sons, 1897.
———. *Held Fast For England: A Tale of the Siege of Gibraltar.* New York: Charles Scribner's Sons, 1902.
Homer. *The Illiad.* A. T. Murray, trans. Cambridge, MA: Harvard University Press, 1999.
———. *The Odyssey.* A. T. Murray, trans. Cambridge, MA: Harvard University Press, 1995.
Hutchinson, H. D. *The Campaign in Tirah, 1897–1898.* London: Macmillan, 1898.
Kipling, Rudyard. *Kipling: A Selection of His Stories and Poems.* John Beecroft, ed. Garden City, NY: Doubleday, n.d.
———. *Soldiers Three: The Story of the Gadsbys in Black and White.* New York: Doubleday, Page, 1914.
———. *Rudyard Kipling's Verse, Inclusive Edition, 1885–1918.* Garden City, NY: Doubleday, Page, 1920.
———. *Kipling Stories: Twenty-Eight Exciting Tales by the Master Storyteller.* New York: Platt & Munk, 1960.
Macaulay, Thomas Babington, Lord. *Macaulay's Essays on Clive and Hastings.* Charles Robert Gaston, ed. Boston: Ginn, 1910.
———. 'Horatius at the Bridge' in J. E. Pournelle, ed., *There Will Be War, Volume IX: After Armageddon.* New York: Tom Dougherty and Associates, 1990.
Maule, Fox, 2nd Baron Panmure. *The Panmure Papers.* London: Hodder & Stoughton, 1908.
Mills, H. Woosnam. *The Tirah Campaign.* Lahore, India: Civil and Military Gazette Press, 1898.
Milton, John. *The History of Britain, That Part especially now call'd England, From the first Traditional Beginning Continu'd to the Norman Conquest.* London: Ri. Chiswell, 1695.

Ministry of Defense, 'Latest News: Private Johnson Gideon Beharry – Victoria Cross' http://www.operations.mod.uk/telic/ophons05/beharry.htm Published 18 March 2005. Accessed 25 February 2007.
Ministry of Defense, 'Corporal Budd awarded the Victoria Cross' http://www.mod.uk/DefenceInternet/DefenseNews/HistoryandHonour/CorporalBryanBuddAwardedtheVictoriaCross.htm published 14 December 2006. Accessed 26 February 2007.
Ministry of Information. *Fleet Air Arm.* London: HMSO, 1943.
Morely, Thomas. *The Cause of the Charge of the Light Brigade, Oct. 25th 1854 by the 'Man of the Hour'.* Nottingham: Arthur Jackson, 1899.
Newbolt, Henry. *The Island Race.* London: Elkin Mathews, 1902.
——. *Admirals All and Other Verses.* London: Elkin Mathews, 1908.
——. *Poems: Old and New.* London: John Murray, 1912.
*Official History of the Great War.* London: HMSO, 1925.
*The Register of the Victoria Cross.* Nora Buzzell, ed. Cheltenham: This England Books, 1988.
Robertson, William. *From Private to Field Marshal.* Boston, MA: Houghton Mifflin, 1921.
Rogerson, Sidney. *Twelve Days.* London: Arthur Baker, 1933.
Siepmann, Harry. *Echo of the Guns: Recollections of an Artillery Officer.* London: Robert Hale, 1987.
Slessor, Alexander Kerr. *The 2nd Battalion Derbyshire Regiment in Tirah.* London: Swan Sonnenschein, 1900.
Smith-Dorrien, Horace. *Memories of Forty-Eight Years Service.* London: John Murray, 1925.
Sotheby, Lionel. *Lionel Sotheby's Great War: Diaries and Letters From the Western Front.* Donald Richter, ed. Athens, OH: Ohio University Press, 1997.
Tacitus, Julius (Publius) Cornelius. *Life of Gnaeus Julius Agricola* in Herbert W. Bernario, trans. *Tacitus' Agricola, Germany, and Dialogue on Orators.* Norman, OK: University of Oklahoma Press, 1991.
Tennyson, Alfred Lord. *The Best of Tennyson,* Walter Graham, ed. New York: The Ronald Press, 1930.
Tomlinson, H. M. *All Our Yesterdays.* London: Heinemann, 1930.
Victoria, Queen. *Letters of Queen Victoria From the Archives of Brandenburg-Prussia.* Hector Bolithio, ed. New Haven, CT: Yale University Press, 1938.
Wade, Aubrey. *The War of the Guns.* London: Batsford, 1936.
'Wing Adjutant.' *Plane Tales From the Skies.* London: Cassell, 1918.
Wolff, Anne, ed. *Subalterns of the Foot: Three World War I Diaries of Officers of the Cheshire Regiment.* Worcester: Square One Publications, 1992.

# SECONDARY SOURCES

Adkin, Mark. *The Last Eleven?* London: Leo Cooper, 1991.
Anderson, Olive. *A Liberal State at War: English Politics and Economics During the Crimean War.* New York: St. Martin's Press, 1967.
Andrews, Eric Montgomery. *The ANZAC Illusion: Anglo-Australian Relations During World War I.* Cambridge: Cambridge University Press, 1993.
Arnold, Guy. *Held Fast for England: G. A. Henty, Imperialist Boys' Writer.* London: Hamish Hamilton, 1980.
Ascoli, David. *The Mons Star: The British Expeditionary Force, 5th Aug.–22nd Nov. 1914.* London: Harrap, 1981.

Ashley, Leonard M. *George Alfred Henty and the Victorian Mind*. San Francisco: International Scholars Publications, 1999.

Aulich, James. *Framing the Falklands War: Nationhood, Culture and Identity*. Milton Keynes: Open University Press, 1992.

Badsey, Stephen. 'Cavalry and the Development of Breakthrough Doctrine,' in Paddy Griffith, ed. *British Fighting Methods in the Great War*. London: Frank Cass, 1996.

Bailey, Jonathan. 'British Artillery in the Great War,' in Paddy Griffith, ed. *British Fighting Methods in the Great War*. London: Frank Cass, 1996.

Barnett, Correlli. *The Sword Bearers: Supreme Command in the First World War*. Bloomington, IN: Indiana University Press, 1963.

———. *Britain and Her Army, 1509–1970: A Military, Political and Social Survey*. New York: William Morrow, 1977.

Batchelor, Peter and Chris Matson. *VCs of the First World War – The Western Front, 1915*. London: Wrens Park Publishing, 1999.

Beckett, Ian. 'The British Army, 1914–1918: The Illusion of Change,' in John Turner, ed. *Britain and the First World War*. London: Unwin Hyman, 1988.

Bennett, Daphne. *King Without a Crown: Albert, Prince Consort of England, 1819–1861*. New York: J. B. Lippincott, 1977.

Best, Geoffrey Francis Andrew. *Mid-Victorian Britain, 1861–1875*. New York: Shocken Books, 1972.

Bickers, Richard Townshend. *The First Great Air War*. London: Hodder & Stoughton, 1988.

Blatherwick, F. J. *1000 Brave Canadians*. Toronto: Unitrade Press, 1991.

Bolithio, Hector. *Albert: Prince Consort*. London: Max Parrish, 1964.

Bond, Brian. *Victorian Military Campaigns*. New York: Frederick Praeger, 1967.

———. *The First World War in British Military History*. Oxford: The Clarendon Press, 1991.

———. ed. *Fallen Stars: Eleven Studies of Twentieth Century Military Disasters*. London: Brassey's UK, 1991.

Bonner, Robert A. 'Here We Fight, Here We Die!' n.p.: R. A. Bonner, 1998.

Bourne, J. M. *Britain and the Great War, 1914–1918*. London: Hodder & Stoughton, 1989.

Bowen, James. 'Education, Ideology and the Ruling Class: Hellenism and English Public Schools in the Nineteenth Century,' in Clarke, G. W., ed. *Rediscovering Hellenism*. Cambridge: Cambridge University Press, 1989.

Bowyer, Chaz. *For Valour: The Air VCs*. n.p.: Kimber, 1978.

Brantlinger, Patrick. *Rule of Darkness: British Literature and Imperialism*. Ithaca, NY: Cornell University Press, 1988.

Breen, Bob. *First to Fight*. Nashville, TN: The Battery Press, 1988.

Brickhill, Paul. *The Dam Busters*. London: Evans Brothers, 1951.

British Broadcasting Company. *Ideas and Beliefs of the Victorians*. London: Sylvan Press, 1949.

Brown, Malcolm. *The Imperial War Museum Book of the Western Front*. Osceola, WI: Motorbooks International, 1994.

Bruce, Anthony. *The Purchase System in the British Army, 1660–1871*. London: Royal Historical Society, 1980.

Buchan, John. *The King's Grace*. London: Hodder & Stoughton, 1935.

Burg, David F. and L. Edward Purcell. *Almanac of World War I*. Lexington, KY: The University of Kentucky Press, 1998.

Burk, Kathleen, ed. *War and the State: The Transformation of British Government, 1914–1918*. London: George Allen & Unwin, 1982.

Burn, W. L. *The Age of Equipoise*. New York: W. W. Norton, 1969.
Burroughs, Peter. 'An Unreformed Army?,' in David Chandler and Ian Beckett, eds. *The Oxford Illustrated History of the British Army*. Oxford: Oxford University Press, 1994.
Burstall, Terry. *Vietnam: The Australian Dilemma*. St Lucia: University of Queensland Press, 1993.
Carver, Michael, Field Marshal Lord. *The Seven Ages of the British Army*. New York: Beaufort Books, 1984.
Chamberlain, Muriel. *Lord Aberdeen: A Political Biography*. London: Longman Group, 1983.
Chandler, David and Ian Beckett, eds. *The Oxford Illustrated History of the British Army*. Oxford: Oxford University Press, 1994.
Chandler, D. G. 'The Expedition to Abyssinia,' in Brian Bond, ed. *Victorian Military Campaigns*. New York: Frederick Praeger, 1967.
Charlot, Monica. *Victoria, The Young Queen*. Oxford: Basil Blackwell, 1991.
Clarke, G. W. *Rediscovering Hellenism*. Cambridge: Cambridge University Press, 1989.
Clarke, John D. *Gallantry Medals & Awards of the World*. Sparkford, Somerset: Patrick Stephens, 1993.
Clayton, Anthony. 'Robert Nivelle and the Spring French Offensive of 1917,' in Brian Bond, ed. *Fallen Stars: Eleven Studies of Twentieth Century Military Disasters*. London: Brassey's UK, 1991.
Clayton, Ann. *Chavasse, Double VC*. London: Leo Cooper, 1992.
——. *Martin-Leake, Double VC*. London: Leo Cooper, 1997.
Conacher, J. B. *The Aberdeen Coalition: A Study in Mid-Nineteenth-Century Party Politics*. London: Cambridge University Press, 1968.
——. *Britain and the Crimea, 1855–6: Problems of War and Peace*. London: The Macmillan Press, 1987.
Constantine, Stephen. 'Britain and the Empire,' in Stephen Constantine, Maurice W. Kirby, and Mary B. Rose. *The First World War in British History*. London: Edward Arnold, 1995.
Constantine, Stephen, Maurice W. Kirby, and Mary B. Rose. *The First World War in British History*. London: Edward Arnold, 1995.
Cook, Chris and John Stevenson. *The Longman Handbook of Modern European History, 1763–1985*. London: Longman, 1987.
Cowan, James. *The New Zealand Wars: A History of the Maori Campaigns and the Pioneering Period*. Wellington, NZ: n. p.: 1922; reprint, New York: AMS Press, 1969.
Creagh, Sir O'Moore and E. M. Humphries. *The Victoria Cross, 1856 – 1920*. Reprint: London: J. B. Hayward & Son, 1985.
Creswicke, Louis. *South Africa and the Transvaal War*. New York: G. P. Putnam's Sons, 1900.
Crook, M. J. *The Evolution of the Victoria Cross*. Tunbridge Wells: Midas Books, 1975.
Currie, Jack. *The Augsburg Raid: The Story of one of the Most Dramatic and Dangerous Raids Ever Mounted by RAF Bomber Command*. London: Goodall Publications, 1987.
David, Daniel. *The 1914 Campaign: August–October, 1914*. New York: Military Press, 1987.
Davis, Paul K. *Ends and Means: The British Mesopotamian Campaign and Commission*. London: Associated University Presses, 1994.
De Groot, Gerard. *Douglas Haig, 1861–1928*. London: Unwin & Hyman, 1988.
DeWeerd, Harvey A. 'Churchill, Lloyd George, Clemenceau: The Emergence of the Civilians,' in Edward Meade Earle, ed. *Makers of Modern Strategy: Military Thought from Machiavelli to Hitler*. Princeton: Princeton University Press, 1943.
Earle, Edward Meade, ed. *Makers of Modern Strategy: Military Thought from Machiavelli to Hitler*. Princeton: Princeton University Press, 1943.

Edmonds, James Edward, ed. *Military Operations, France and Belgium, 1914*. London: Macmillan, 1922.

Elliot, W. J. *The Victoria Cross in Zululand and South Africa*. London: Dean & Son, 1882.

Eltinge, Le Roy. *Psychology of War*. Fort Leavenworth, KS: Press of the Army Service Schools, 1915.

Erickson, Carolly. *Her Little Majesty: The Life of Queen Victoria*. New York: Simon & Schuster, 1997.

Eyck, Frank. *The Prince Consort: A Political Biography*. London: Chatto & Windus, 1959.

Farrar-Hockley, Anthony. 'Sir Hubert Gough and the German Breakthrough, 1918,' in Brian Bond, ed, *Fallen Stars: Eleven Studies of Twentieth Century Military Disasters*. London: Brassey's UK, 1991.

Farwell, Byron. *Queen Victoria's Little Wars*. New York: Harper & Row, 1972.

———. *The Great Anglo-Boer War*. New York: Harper & Row, 1976.

———. *Eminent Victorian Soldiers: Seekers of Glory*. New York: W. W. Norton, 1982.

———. *Armies of the Raj: From the Mutiny to Independence, 1858–1947*. New York: W. W. Norton, 1989.

Ferguson, Niall. *The Pity of War*. n.p.: Basic Books, 1999.

Fletcher, David. *The Great Tank Scandal: British Armour in the Second World War*. London: HMSO, 1989.

Fraser, Antonia. *The Warrior Queens*. New York: Vintage Books, 1990.

French, David, *The Strategy of the Lloyd George Coalition, 1916–1918*. Oxford: Clarendon Press, 1995.

French, David A. 'A One-Man Show? Civil-Military Relations in Britain During the First World War,' in Paul Smith, ed. *Government and the Armed Forces in Britain*. London: The Hambledon Press, 1996.

Fortescue, John William. *A History of the British Army*. London: Macmillan, 1899–1930.

Forty, George. *World War Two Tanks*. London: Osprey, 1995.

Fulford, Robert. *The Prince Consort*. New York: St Martin's Press, 1966.

Fuller, J. G. *Troop Morale and Popular Culture in the British and Dominion Forces*. Oxford: Clarendon Press, 1990.

Gardyne, A. D. *The Life of a Regiment*. London: Medici Society, 1929.

Garrett, Richard. *Scharnhorst and Gneisenau: The Elusive Sisters*. New York: Hippocrene Books, 1978.

Gibson, Mary. *Warneford, VC*. Chippenham: Picton Publishing, 1984.

Gill, Christopher. *Personality in the Greek Epic, Tragedy, and Philosophy: The Self in Dialogue*. Oxford: Clarendon Press, 1996.

Girouard, Mark. *The Return to Camelot: Chivalry and the English Gentleman*. New Haven, CT: Yale University Press, 1981.

Gliddon, Gerald. *VCs of the First World War – 1914*. London: Alan Sutton, 1994.

———. *VCs of the First World War – The Somme*. London: Alan Sutton, 1994.

———. *VCs of the First World War – Arras and Messines*. London: Alan Sutton, 1998.

Goldberg, Michael K. 'Introduction to Thomas Carlyle,' in Thomas Carlyle. *On Heroes, Hero Worship and the Heroic in History*. Berkeley, CA: University of California Press, 1993.

Gooch, John. 'The Armed Services,' in Stephen Constantine, Maurice W. Kirby, and Mary B. Rose, eds. *The First World War in British History*. London: Edward Arnold, 1995.

Griffith, Paddy. *Battle Tactics on the Western Front: The British Army's Art of the Attack, 1916–1918*. New Haven CT: Yale University Press, 1994.

———. ed. *British Fighting Methods in the Great War*. London: Frank Cass, 1996.

———. 'The Extent of Tactical Reform in the British Army,' in Paddy Griffith, ed. *British Fighting Methods in the Great War*. London: Frank Cass, 1996.

Grove, Eric J., ed. *The Defeat of the Enemy Attack on Shipping, 1939–1945*. Aldershot: Navy Records Society, 1997.

Guinn, Paul. *British Strategy and Politics, 1914 to 1918*. Oxford: The Clarendon Press, 1965.

Haghofer, Natascha U. *The Fall of Arthur's Kingdom: A Study of Tennyson's 'The Holy Grail'*. Salzburg: University of Salzburg Press, 1997.

Haigh, R. H. and P. W. Turner. *World War One and the Serving British Soldier*. Manhattan, KS: Military Affairs/Aerospace Historian, 1979.

Hair, Donald S. *Domestic and Heroic in Tennyson's Poetry*. Toronto: University of Toronto Press, 1981.

Hall, Major Darrell D., 'Field Artillery in the British Army, 1860–1960: Part II 1900–1914,' *Military History Journal*, vol. 2 no. 5 (June 1973).

Hamilton, Ian B. M. *The Happy Warrior: A Life of General Sir Ian Hamilton, GCB, GCMG, DSO*. London: Cassell, 1966.

Harries-Jenkins, Gwyn. *The Army in Victorian Society*. London: Routledge & Keegan Paul, 1977.

Harris, J. P. 'The Rise of Armor' in Paddy Griffith, ed. *British Fighting Methods in the Great War*. London: Frank Cass, 1996.

Harrison, John Fletcher Clews. *The Early Victorians, 1832–1851*. London: Weidenfield & Nicolson, 1971.

Harvey, David. *Monuments to Courage*. n.p.: Kevin & Kay Patience, 1999.

Hattendorf, John B., et. al., eds. *British Naval Documents, 1204–1960*. Aldershot: Scolar Press, 1993.

Hawkins, Angus. *Parliament, Party and the Art of Politics in Britain, 1855 – 59*. Basingstoke: Macmillan Press – now Palgrave Macmillan, 1987.

———. *British Party Politics, 1852–1886*. Basingstoke: Macmillan Press – now Palgrave Macmillan, 1998.

Hayden, A. L. *The Book of the V.C.* London: Pilgrim Press, 1906.

Hill, J. R. and Bryan Ranft. *The Oxford Illustrated History of the Royal Navy*. Oxford: Oxford University Press, 1995.

Hoppen, Theodore K. *The Mid-Victorian Generation, 1846–1886*. Oxford: Clarendon Press, 1998.

Horner, D. M. *Australian Higher Command in the Vietnam War*. Canberra: Australian National University, 1986.

Imperial War Museum. *The Illustrated Handbook of the Victoria Cross and the George Cross*. London: Imperial War Museum, 1970.

Jablonsky, David. *Churchill, The Great Game, and Total War*. London: Frank Cass, 1991.

James, Robert Rhodes. *Prince Albert: A Biography*. New York: Alfred A Knopf, 1984.

James, W. F. *Submariners VC*. London: Peter Davis, 1962.

Jane, Fred T. *The British Battle Fleet: Its Inception and Growth Throughout the Centuries to the Present Day*. n.p.: S.W. Partridge, 1912; reprint, London: Tri-Service Press, 1990.

Jefferys, Kevin. *The Churchill Coalition and Wartime Politics, 1940–1945*. Manchester: Manchester University Press, 1991.

———. *War and Reform: British Politics During the Second World War*. Manchester: Manchester University Press, 1994.

Jenkyns, Richard. *The Victorians and Ancient Greece*. Cambridge, MA: Harvard University Press, 1980.

Johns, W. E. *The Air VCs*. London: Hamilton, 1935.

Johnson, Hubert C. *Breakthrough! Tactics, Technology and the Search for Victory on the Western Front.* Novato, CA: Presidio Press, 1994.

Judd, Denis. *Empire: The British Imperial Experience, From 1765 to the Present.* London: Harper Collins Publishers, 1996.

Keegan, John. *The Face of Battle.* London: Cox & Wyman, 1976.

Keegan, John and Richard Holmes. *Soldiers: A History of Men in Battle.* New York: Viking Penguin, 1986.

Kemp, Peter. *The Escape of the Scharnhorst and Gneisenau.* Annapolis, MD: Naval Institute Press, 1975.

Kennett, Lee. *The First Air War, 1914–1918.* New York: The Free Press, 1991.

Kightley, Charles. *Folk Heroes of Great Britain.* London: Thames & Hudson, 1983.

Kilbracken, John. *Bring Back My Stringbag: Swordfish Pilot at War, 1940–1945.* London: Leo Cooper, 1996.

Laffin, John. *Tommy Atkins, The Story of the English Soldier.* London: Cassell, 1966.

———. *On the Western Front: Soldiers' Stories from France and Flanders, 1914–1918.* Gloucester: Alan Sutton, 1985.

———. *British Butchers and Bunglers of World War One.* London: Alan Sutton, 1988.

———. *Damn The Dardanelles!.* Gloucester: Alan Sutton, 1989.

———. *British VCs of World War 2.* London: Alan Sutton, 1997.

Lambert, Andrew. 'The Shield of Empire,' in J. R. Hill and Bryan Ranft, eds. *The Oxford Illustrated History of the Royal Navy.* Oxford: Oxford University Press, 1995.

Lewis, Bruce. *A Few of the First: The True Stories of the Men Who Flew in and before the First World War.* London: Leo Cooper, 1997.

Liddle, Peter. *The Soldier's War, 1914–1918.* London: Blandford Press, 1988.

———. *The 1916 Battle of the Somme.* London: Leo Cooper, 1992.

Luvaas, Jay. *The Education of an Army: British Military Thought, 1815–1940.* Chicago: University of Chicago Press, 1964.

MacDonagh, Oliver. *Early Victorian Government, 1830–1870.* New York: Holmes & Meier, 1977.

Macdonald, Lyn. *They Called it Passchendaele.* London: Michael Joseph, 1978.

———. *1915: Death of Innocence.* London: Headline Books, 1993.

Machum, G. *Canada's VCs.* Toronto: McClelland and Steward Publishers, 1956.

MacKenzie, John M. ed. *Imperialism and Popular Culture.* Manchester: Manchester University Press, 1986.

Mandler, Peter. *Aristocratic Government in the Age of Reform: Whigs and Liberals 1830–1852.* Oxford: Clarendon Press, 1990.

Martin, Richard P. *The Language of Heroes: Speech and Performance in The Illiad.* Ithaca, NY: Cornell Univesity Press, 1989.

Mason, Peter D. *Nicolson, VC.* Ashford: Geerings, 1991.

McCrery, N. *For Conspicuous Gallantry – A Brief History of the Recipients of the VC from Notts and Derbyshire.* n.p.: n.p., 1990.

McLaren, Barbara. *Women in the War.* New York: George H. Doran, 1918.

McNamee, Maurice B., S. J. *Honor and the Epic Hero: A Study in the Shifting Concept of Magnanimity in Philosophy and Epic Poetry.* New York: Holt, Rinehart & Winston, 1960.

McNeill, Ian. *The Team: Australian Army Advisers in Vietnam, 1962–1972.* London: Leo Cooper, 1984.

Messenger, Charles. *'Bomber' Harris and the Strategic Bombing Offensive, 1939–1945.* New York: St Martin's Press, 1984.

Mitchell, David. *Monstrous Regiment: The Story of the Women of the First World War.* New York: Macmillan, 1965.
Moorehouse, Geoffrey. *Hell's Foundations: A Social History of the Town of Bury in the Aftermath of the Gallipoli Campaign.* New York: Henry Holt, 1992.
Moran, Lord. *The Anatomy of Courage.* London: Constable, 1945. Reprint, Garden City, NY: Avery Publishing Group, 1987.
Morgan, J. A. ' "The Grit of Our Forefathers:" Invented Traditions, Propaganda and Imperialism,' in John M. MacKenzie, ed. *Imperialism and Popular Culture.* Manchester: Manchester University Press, 1986.
Morris, Richard. *Cheshire: The Biography of Leonard Cheshire.* New York: Viking, 2000.
Morrow, John H. *The Great War in the Air: Military Aviation from 1909–1921.* Washington: Smithsonian Institution Press, 1993.
Morton, Desmond. *When Your Number's Up.* Toronto: Random House of Canada, 1993.
Muddock, J. E. *'For Valour' the 'V.C.'* London: Hutchinson, 1895.
Mullen, Richard, and James Munson. *Victoria: Portrait of a Queen.* London: BBC Books, 1987.
Munsell, Darrell F. *The Unfortunate Duke: Henry Pelham, Fifth Duke of Newcastle, 1811–1864.* Columbia, MO: University of Missouri Press, 1985.
Nagy, Gregory. *The Best of the Achaeans.* Baltimore, MD: Johns Hopkins University Press, 1999.
Nicolson, Harold. *King George the Fifth: His Life and Reign.* London: Constable, 1952.
Noon, Geoffrey. 'The Treatment of Casualties in the Great War,' in Paddy Griffith, ed. *British Fighting Methods in the Great War.* London: Frank Cass, 1996.
*Operations in Waziristan, 1919–1920.* Delhi: Government Central Press, 1923.
Palmer, Alan. *The Banner of Battle: The Story of the Crimean War.* London: Weidenfield & Nicolson, 1987.
Parker, Peter. *The Old Lie: The Great War and the Public School Ethos.* London: Constable, 1987.
Parkinson, Roger. *Blood, Toil, Tears, and Sweat: The War History from Dunkirk to Alamein, Based on the War Cabinet Papers of 1940 to 1942.* New York: David McKay, 1973.
Parry, D. H. *Britain's Roll of Glory.* London: Cassell, 1906.
———. *The VC: Its Heroes and Their Glory.* London: Cassell, 1913.
Parry, Jonathan Philip. *The Rise and Fall of Liberal Government in Victorian Britain.* New Haven, CT: Yale University Press, 1993.
Pemberton, William Baring. *Battles of the Boer War.* London: B. T. Batsford, 1964.
Perkins, Roger. *The Kashmir Gate – Lieutenant Home and the Delhi VCs.* Chippenham: Picton Publications, 1983.
Philpott, William James. *Anglo-French Relations and Strategy on the Western Front.* Basingstoke: Macmillan, 1996.
Poovey, Mary. *Making a Social Body: British Cultural Formation, 1830–1864.* Chicago: The University of Chicago Press, 1995.
Pournelle, J. E. ed. *There Will Be War, Volume IX: After Armageddon.* New York: Tom Dougherty and Associates, 1990.
Prest, John. *Lord John Russell.* Columbia, SC: University of South Carolina Press, 1972.
Prior, Robin and Trevor Wilson. *Command on the Western Front: The Military Career of Sir Henry Rawlinson.* Oxford: Blackwell, 1992.
———. *Passchendaele: The Untold Story.* New Haven, CT: Yale University Press, 1996.
Prioreschi, Plinio. *Man and War.* New York: Philosophical Library, 1987.
Puleston, William Dillworth. *The High Command in the World War.* New York: Charles Scribner's Sons, 1934.

Rasor, Eugene L. *Reform in the Royal Navy: A Social History of the Lower Deck, 1850 – 1880.* Hamden, CT: Archon Books, 1976.

Rawling, Bill. *Surviving Trench Warfare: Technology and the Canadian Corps, 1914–1918.* Toronto: University of Toronto Press, 1992.

Reader, W. J. *At Duty's Call: A Study in Obsolete Patriotism.* Manchester: Manchester University Press, 1988.

Regan, Patrick M. *Organizing Societies for War.* Westport, CT: Praeger, 1994.

Rice, Geoffrey W., ed. *The Oxford History of New Zealand.* Oxford: Oxford University Press, 1992.

Richards, Denis. *The Hardest Victory: RAF Bomber Command in the Second World War.* New York: W. W. Norton, 1995.

Ross, Graham. *Scotland's Forgotten Valour.* Isle of Skye: Maclean Press, 1995.

Sanger, Ernest. *Letters From Two World Wars: A Social History of English Attitudes to War, 1914–45.* Stroud: Alan Sutton, 1993.

Selby, John. 'The Third China War, 1860,' in Brian Bond, ed. *Victorian Military Campaigns.* New York: Frederick Praeger, 1967.

Shaw, Marion. 'The Contours of Manliness and the Nature of Woman,' in Herbert F. Tucker, ed. *Critical Essays on Alfred Lord Tennyson.* New York: G. K. Hall, 1993.

Shepperd, Alan. *Sandhurst: The Royal Military Academy, Sandhurst and its Predecessors.* London: Country Life Books, 1980.

Simkins, Peter. *Kitchener's Army: The Raising of the New Armies, 1914–1916.* Manchester: Manchester University Press, 1988.

Simpson, Andy. *The Evolution of Victory: British Battles of the Western Front, 1914–1918.* London: Tom Donovan, 1995.

Skelley, Ramsay. *The Victorian Army at Home: The Recruitment Terms and Conditions of the British Regular, 1859–1899.* London: Croom Helm, 1977.

Slowe, Peter and Richard Woods. *Fields of Death: Battle Scenes of the First World War.* London: Robert Hale, 1986.

Smith, George, ed. *The Dictionary of National Biography.* London: Oxford University Press, 1968.

Smith, Paul, ed. *Government and the Armed Forces in Britain.* London: The Hambledon Press, 1996.

Smith, Peter C. *Hold the Narrow Sea: Naval Warfare in the English Channel, 1939–1945.* Anapolis, MD: Naval Institute Press, 1984.

Smithers, A. J. *Rude Mechanicals: An Account of Tank Maturity During the Second World War.* London: Leo Cooper, 1987.

———. *Cambrai: The First Great Tank Battle, 1917.* London: Leo Cooper, 1992.

Southgate, Donald. *The Passing of the Whigs, 1832–1886.* Basingstoke: Macmillan, 1962.

Spiers, Edward M. *The Army and Society, 1815–1914.* London: Longman, 1980.

'Gallipoli,' in Brian Bond, ed. *The First World War in British Military History.* Oxford: The Clarendon Press, 1991.

St Aubyn, Giles. *The Royal George.* New York: Alfred A. Knopf, 1964.

———. *Queen Victoria: A Portrait.* New York: Atheneum, 1967.

Strachan, Hew. *European Armies and the Conduct of War.* London: George Allen & Unwin, 1983.

———. *Wellington's Legacy: The Reform of the British Army, 1830–54.* Manchester: Manchester University Press, 1984, 101.

———. *From Waterloo to Balaclava: Tactics, Technology, and the British Army, 1815–1854.* Cambridge: Cambridge University Press, 1985.

———. *The Politics of the British Army.* Oxford: Oxford University Press, 1997.

———. *The First World War, Volume I: To Arms.* Oxford: Oxford University Press, 2001.

Stokesbury, James. *Navy and Empire*. New York: William Morrow, 1983.
Streets, Heather Elizabeth Gillis. ' "The Right Stamp of Men:" Military Imperatives and Popular Imperialism in Late Victorian Britain.' PhD diss., Duke University, 1998.
Sweetman, John. *War and Administration: The Significance of the Crimean War for the British Army*. Edinburgh: Scottish Academic Press, 1984.
Taylor, Miles. *The Decline of British Radicalism, 1847–1860*. Oxford: Clarendon Press, 1995.
Terraine, John. *Mons: The Retreat to Victory*. London: B. T. Batsford, 1960.
——. *Douglas Haig, The Educated Soldier*. London: Hutchinson, 1963.
——. *The Road to Passchendaele: The Flanders Offensive of 1917, A Study in Inevitability*. London: Leo Cooper, 1977.
——. *To Win a War: 1918, The Year of Victory*. New York: Doubleday, 1981.
Thompson, George Malcolm. *The Vote of Censure*. New York: Stein & Day, 1968.
Tooley, Sarah A. *The Personal Life of Queen Victoria*. London: Hodder & Stoughton, 1896.
Toomey, T. E. *Heroes of the Victoria Cross*. n.p.: Newnes, 1895.
Travers, Tim. *The Killing Ground: The British Army, the Western Front and the Emergence of Modern Warfare*. London: Allen & Unwin, 1987.
Tucker, Herbert F. *Critical Essays on Alfred Lord Tennyson*. New York: G. K. Hall, 1993.
Turner, Frank M. *The Greek Heritage in Victorian Britain*. New Haven, CT: Yale University Press, 1981.
Turner, J. F. *V.C.'s of the Air*. London: Harrap, 1960.
Turner, John. 'Cabinets, Committees and Secretariats: The Higher Direction of the War,' in Kathleen Burk, ed. *War and the State: The Transformation of British Government, 1914–1918*. London: George Allen & Unwin, 1982.
——. 'British Politics and the Great War,' in John Turner, ed. *Britain and the First World War*. London: Unwin & Hyman, 1988.
——. ed. *Britain and the First World War*. London: Unwin & Hyman, 1988.
——. *British Politics and the Great War: Coalition and Conflict, 1915–1918*. New Haven, CT: Yale University Press, 1992.
Uys, I. S. *For Valour: The History of South Africa's Victoria Cross*. Johannesburg: Uys, 1973.
Vance, Norman. *The Sinews of the Spirit: The Ideal of Christian Manliness in Victorian Literature and Religious Thought*. Cambridge: Cambridge University Press, 1985.
——. *The Victorians and Ancient Rome*. Oxford: Blackwell Publishers, 1997.
Waites, Bernard. *A Class Society at War: England, 1914–1918*. Leamington Spa: Berg, 1987.
Warner, Philip. *Passchendaele: The Story Behind the Tragic Victory of 1917*. London: Sidgwick & Jackson, 1987.
Webster, Graham. *Boudica: The British Revolt Against Rome. AD 60*. Totowa, NJ: Rowman & Littlefield, 1978.
Weintraub, Stanley. *Uncrowned King: The Life of Prince Albert*. New York: The Free Press, 1997.
Wells, Mark K. *Courage and Air Warfare: The Allied Aircrew Experience in the Second World War*. London: Frank Cass, 1995.
Wigmore, L. and B. Harding. *They Dared Mightily*. Canberra: Australian War Memorial, 1963.
Wilkins, P. A. *History of the Victoria Cross*. London: Constable, 1904.
Williams, Richard. *The Contentious Crown: Public Discussion of the British Monarchy in the Reign of Queen Victoria*. Aldershot: Ashgate, 1997.
Williams, W. Alister. *The VCs of Wales and the Welsh Regiments*. Wrexham: Bridge Books, 1984.
Wilson, Trevor. *The Myriad Faces of War*. New York: Basil Blackwell, 1986.
Wilson, David Harris. *A History of England*. New York: Holt, Rinehart & Winston, 1967.

Winter, Denis. *Death's Men: Soldiers of the Great War*. London: Penguin Books, 1978.
——. *The First of the Few: Fighter Pilots of the First World War*. Athens, GA: The University of Georgia Press, 1983.
——. *Haig's Command: A Reassessment*. London: Penguin/Viking Books, 1991.
——. *25 April 1915: The Inevitable Tragedy*. St. Lucia: University of Queensland Press, 1994.
Winter, J. M. 'Britain's Lost Generation of the First World War.' *Population Studies* vol. 31, no. 3 (1977).
Winton, John. ed. *The War at Sea: The British Navy in World War II*. New York: William Morrow, 1968.
——. *The Victoria Cross at Sea*. n.p.: Michael Joseph, 1978.
——. 'Life and Education in a Technically Evolving Navy, 1815–1925,' in J. R. Hill and Bryan Ranft, eds. *The Oxford Illustrated History of the Royal Navy*. Oxford: Oxford University Press, 1995.
Woodham-Smith, Cecil. *Queen Victoria: From Her Birth to the Death of the Prince Consort*. New York: Alfred A. Knopf, 1972.
Woodward, David R. *Lloyd George and the Generals*. East Brunswick, NJ: Associated University Presses, 1983.
Woollcombe, Robert. *The First Tank Battle: Cambrai, 1917*. London: Arthur Barker, 1967.

# Index

Aberdeen, Lord, 31, 33
Aberdeen Ministry, 29, 32, 41
Admiralty Board, 31, 63, 77, 108, 118, 166, 168, 170, 175, 177, 179–80, 186, 196–7
Albert Medal, 72, 176
Albert, Prince Consort, 31, 33
   attitude toward decorations, 37–8
   and creation of VC, 34–8, 40, 41
Andaman Island rescue, 72, 100, 176
Army administration, 29–31, 33
Army demographics, 110, 141–2, 148
Army reform, 26, 29–30, 31–4
   Aberdeen Ministry, 29–32
   Palmerston Ministry, 32–4
Augsburg raid, 192–3, 195

Beatie, Alexander Elder, 171
Bentinck, Rudolf (Walter), Sir, 180
*Bismarck*, 196, 197
Boudicca, 8–9
Brade, Reginald, Sir 136, 165–6
Brereton, H. W., 71
Broadwood, Robert George, 82
Broderick, St John, 91–2
Brooke, Rupert, 116
Buller, Redvers, Sir, 82, 85–6, 88–90, 97, 99, 104, 109, 129, 133

Cadogan, Alexander Sir, 198
Cambridge, George, Duke of, 44, 47, 56–7, 62, 69–70, 76, 78, 79, 80, 97, 106
Campbell, Colin, Sir, 66–7, 102, 203
Canning, Charles, Viscount, 61–2
casualties, 120, 139, 143, 188–9
Channel dash, 197, 205
Churchill, Winston Spencer, 154, 183, 196, 198–9, 205
Clive, Robert, Lord, 16, 22
Coghill, John Joscelyn, Sir, 91–2, 93

Colenso, Battle of, 85–6
Committee on Coordination etc. of Warrants Relating to the Victoria Cross, 171–83
'cost of courage,'
   Victorian, 102–3
   First World War, 139–40, 145–6, 160–1, 162
   Second World War, 187–9
Crouch, Lionell, 116–17
Cubbitt, Bertram Blakiston, 166

Dargai Ridge, 23–5
Daubeney, Henry C. B., 50–3
Davidson, L. E. O., 158–9
Davies, Francis, 136, 138
Derby, Lord, 32, 64
Distinguished Conduct Medal, 35, 81, 89
Distinguished Service Order, 81, 89, 193

Edward VII, King, 92
Ellenborough, Earl (Edward Law), 64–5
Evans, Delacy, Sir, 50
Everett, Allan Frederick, 169–70, 172, 175, 176, 177–9, 186

foreign medals and gallantry awards, 26–7, 38, 40
French, John, Sir, 11, 113, 115, 117–18, 142, 158–9

George Cross, 72, 176
George V, King, 1, 93, 108, 151, 153–4, 159, 166, 170, 171, 183
*Gneisenau*, 196–7, 199
Good Conduct Badge, 26
Gordon Highlanders, 23–4
Gordon, S. D., 171–2, 178–9
Graham, Malcolm, 136, 165–6, 171–2, 173, 174, 176, 178, 179–80

Graves, Robert, 138
Great Mutiny, 60–8
Grenfell, Julian, 116, 117
Grey, Earl, 29–30, 31
Gurney, Ivor, 147

Haig, Douglas, 137, 142, 148–9, 152, 162
  and Lloyd George, 152–4
  and the press, 154
  and the Victoria Cross, 152, 154, 156–60, 165, 168, 177, 179, 189, 190, 201, 204–5
Haldane Reforms, 110–11
Hamilton, Ian, 89–90, 91–2, 104, 134–6, 203
Hampton, Harry, 1
Hardinge, Henry, Viscount, 31, 44
Harris, Arthur, Sir ('Bomber'), 191, 192–3, 195
Havelock, Henry, 4, 66–8, 173, 203
Havelock, Henry Masham, *see under* Victoria Cross winners
Henty, George Alfred, 6, 10–12, 13–14, 15, 16, 17–20, 22–3, 117
Herbert, Sidney, Lord, 33–4, 71, 76
Hereward the Wake, 9–10,
heroism, categories defined, 94–5
heroism, concepts of
  Anglo-Saxon, 6, 9
  Celtic, 8–9
  Greek, 6–7, 19
  Roman, 7–8
  Albert, Prince Consort, 5
  Graham, Malcolm, 165–6, 171–2, 173, 176, 178, 179, 180
  Haig, Douglas, 152, 157–60, 177, 189, 190, 204
  Kitchener, Herbert Horatio, 80–1, 97, 149, 158–9
  Panmure, Lord, 41, 44–7, 54, 58, 63–4, 87, 104
  Ponsonby, Frederick, 174, 177, 180
  Rose, Hugh, Sir, 104
  Victoria, Queen, 5, 15, 39–40, 41, 54, 70–1, 105–6
Hope Grant, James, Sir, 75–6, 106

Howick Commission, 26, 29–30
Hunter-Weston, Aylmer, Sir, 134–6

Indian Imperial Service Troops, 170, 174
Indian Order of Merit, 62

Kipling, Rudyard, 6, 13, 18, 21–2
Kitchener, Herbert Horatio, Lord, 80–1, 89, 115, 141–2, 149, 158–9
Kitchener Armies, 141–5, 148
*Konigsberg*, 197–8
Korn Spruit/Sana's Post, 82–4, 99, 114, 173

Lambert, Henry C. M., 171, 172, 174, 177, 182
Lancashire Fusiliers, 134, 136–7
Legion of Honor, 27, 38, 40
Lloyd George, David, 152–4
Long, Charles, 85
Lucy, John, 116

Macaulay, Thomas Babbington, Lord, 6, 10, 16, 22
Macmillan, Harold, 146
Magadala, seige of, 76, 97
Manning, Frank, *The Middle Parts of Fortune*, 157
Matthias, Henry, 23–4 and n. 234
*Medaille Militaire*, 27, 35
mention in dispatches, 27, 51
Mitchell, Charles, 70
Mons, Battle of, 111–13
Montague-Scott, Herbert A., Lord, 180, 182
More, Robert Henry, 171, 172, 178, 179
Morgan, Robert U., 171, 178, 180, 181
Mundy, Godfrey Charles, 44
Murray, Oswyn Sir, 165–6

Newbolt, Henry, 6, 7, 10, 14–15, 20, 21
Newcastle, Duke of, 29, 31–2, 34–5, 36–7, 39

# INDEX

Order of the Bath, 27, 34, 36, 37–8, 44, 46, 60, 71, 90, 105, 108
Outram, James, Sir, 66

Palmerston, Lord, 31–2, 39, 77
Pamerston Ministry, 32–4, 64, 203
Panmure, Lord (Fox Maule), 31, 32–4, 39–41, 44–7, 54, 58, 63–5, 87, 104
Peel, Frederick, 34
Peel, Jonathan, 64–7, 70–1, 72, 87–8
Pennefather, John L., 50–1
Pennington, Edward, 77–8
Ponsonby, Frederick, Sir, 166, 171, 174–80, 182

questionable VC recommendations, 50–3, 66–8

Raglan, Lord, 28, 35, 50, 54
Rawlinson, Henry, Sir, 145, 149
Robb, Frederick Spencer, 135
Roberts, Frederick Sleigh, Lord, 18, 65, 83, 84–5, 89–92, 97, 99
Roberts, Frederick Sherston, The Honourable, 85–6, 88–9, 109, 180, 203
Robertson, William, Sir, 156
Roebuck, John Arthur, 32
Rourke's Drift, 79–80
Royal Air Force, 124–5, 162, 166, 168, 170–2, 177, 179, 182, 184, 190, 191–6
Royal Flying Corps, 121, 124
Russell, John, Lord, 31–2, 33
Russell, William Howard, 29

Scharnhorst, 196–7, 199
Scobell, Thomas, 35–6
Sherwood, John Seymour, 193
Shoedde, James Holmes, Sir, 52–3
'six VCs before breakfast,' 134–7
Slessor, Arthur Kerr, 11
Smiles, Samuel, 28
Smith-Dorrien, Horace O., 112, 114, 158
Somme, Battle of, 143–8

Sotheby, Lionel, 138–9
Surfleet, Arthur, 146, 147

Taku Forts, 75, 106, 171 and n. 243
Tennyson, Alfred, Lord, 6, 10, 12, 21
*Times* of London, 28, 29, 35, 55, 59, 11–12, 153
  editorials in, 30, 35
  letters to, 29, 35–6, 40
Tirpitz, 190, 196

Victoria, Queen
  attitude toward Army, 15, 39–40
  creation of Victoria Cross, 38–40, 203, 61
  influence on selection process, 41, 46, 54, 106
  political attitudes, 30–1, 32–4, 41, 44
Victoria Cross
  amending warrants, 61, 69–71, 77–8, 175, 176, 184, 209–15, 221–6
  and Bomber Command, 191–3, 195–6, 205
  civilian, 50, 175–7, 180, 186, 211
  creation of, 34–42
  Crimean recommendations, 46–54
  denied/rejected recommendations, 12, 45, 47, 50, 53–7, 61–2, 63–4, 70–1, 72, 75, 76, 79, 81, 102, 104, 135–6, 158–9, 193 and n. 234
  dominion/colonial eligibility, 65, 77–8, 174–5, 182, 184, 199, 212, 214–29
  elective principle, 38, 78, 83–4, 102, 135–6, 165–6, 170, 182
  eligibility, 44, 70–1, 77–8, 87, 106, 170, 174–5, 180, 181–2, 184
  female eligibility, 166–8, 169–70, 171–2, 176–9
  'first-in' Crosses, 74–7, 98, 106
  forfeiture, 23, 106–8, 182, 184, 221, 224
  Indian Establishment, 60–9, 93, 107, 170, 174, 184, 190, 209–10, 213–14, 216–26

# INDEX 279

Merchant Marine, 170, 175, 182, 186, 225, 227
non-combat awards, 69–72, 100, 176
pension, 1, 36, 38, 49–50, 71, 105, 182, 184, 209, 215, 218, 221, 222, 224, 225, 228, 229
persistent claimants, 55–9
posthumous award, 46, 87–8, 90–3, 102, 119, 139, 170, 176, 179–80, 181, 187, 192, 199, 203–4, 205
pre-Crimean claims, 45
provisional bestowal, 60, 65–8, 76, 82–4, 136, 165–6, 170. 173, 182, 203
public perceptions of, 59–60
questionable recommendations, 50–3, 66–8
race, 62–3
ring politics, 104–5
selection process, 41, 44, 46, 49–50, 53, 54, 56, 68–9, 179
temporary rank, 105, 140, 163
test cases, 4, 58–9, 63–5, 69–71, 75, 77–8, 78–9, 82–4, 86, 88, 90–3,
Victoria Cross Winners
Aitken, Robert H. M., Lieutenant, 114
Alexander, Ernest Wright, Major, 113
Allan, William, Corporal, 79
Atkinson, Alfred, Sergeant, 90
Babtie, William, Major, 89
Badcoe, Peter John, Major, 200
Badlu Singh, Ressaidar, 130–1
Bambrick Valentine, Private, 106
Baxter, Frank William, Trooper, 87
Beach, Thomas Private, 52
Beharry, Johnson, Private, 201–2
Beresford, William, Lord, Captain, 123
Bergin, James, Private, 76–7
Bingham, Edward B. S., Commander, 125–6
Bishop, William Avery, Captain, 122, 124
Bradbury, Edward Kinder, Captain, 115

Bromely, Cuthbert, Captain, 134–5, 136
Bromhead, Gonville, Lieutenant, 79–80
Buchanan, Angus, Temporary Captain, 129
Budd, Bryan James, Corporal, 202, 205
Buller, Redvers, brevet Lieutenant Colonel, 129
Burslem, Nathaniel, Lieutenant, 75
Butler, John Paul, Lieutenant, 126–7
Cairns, George Albert, Lieutenant, 188, 194–5
Campbell, Kenneth, Flying Officer, 169, 199
Carmichael, John, Sergeant, 173
Chaplin, John Worthy, Ensign, 75
Chard, John R. M., Lieutenant, 79–80
Coghill, Nevill J. A., Lieutenant, 87
Colliss, James, Gunner, 106
Coltman, William Harold, Lance Corporal, 181
Congreve, Walter Norris, Captain, 86, 88–9
Cookson, Edgar Christopher, Lt Cmdr, 127–8
Corbett, Frederick, Private, 106
Cornwell, Bernard Travers, Boy First Class, 126
Dalton, James Langley, Commissary, 80
Daniel, Edward St. John, Midshipman, 22–3, 107–8
Daniels, Harry, Sergeant Major, 133–4
Dartnell, Wilbur Taylor, Lieutenant, 127
Dease, Maurice, Lieutenant, 112
Dobson, Frederick William, Private, 158–9
Dorrell, George Thomas, Sergeant Major, 115
Edwards, Hughie I., Wing Commander, 195
Elton, Frederick, Cockayne Brevet Major, 52, 99, 117–18

Victoria Cross Winners – continued
  Esmonde, Eugene, Lieutenant Commander, 197, 199
  Fazal Din, Naik, 188, 120
  Findlater, George, Piper, 25
  Foote, John Weir, Honorary Captain, 194
  Gibson, Guy, Wing Commander, 195
  Glasock, Horace Henry, Driver, 83
  Godley, Sidney Frank, Private, 112–13
  Graham, John, R.N., Lieutenant, 130
  Grant, Peter, Private, 102
  Grenfell, Fancis, Captain, 113
  Grimshaw, John Elisha, Lance Corporal, 134–6
  Hall, William, Seaman, 62
  Hampton, Harry, Colour Sergeant, 1
  Hannah, John, Sergeant, 195
  Havelock, Henry Masham, Lieutenant, 66–8
  Haydon, Charles Edward, Sergeant, 83
  Heaphy, Charles, Major (Auckland Militia), 77–8
  Hills, James, Second Lieutenant, 97–8
  Hitch, Fred, Private, 79
  Hodge, Samuel, Private, 62
  Holland, Edward James Gibson, Sergeant, 113
  Hollowell, James, Private, 96
  Hook, Henry, Private, 79
  Hull, Charles, Private, 128–9
  Insall, Gilbert S. M., Second Lieutenant, 123–4
  Johnston, William Henry, Captain, 117–18
  Jones, Herbert 'H,' Lieutenant Colonel, 205
  Jones, Robert, Private, 79
  Jones, Thomas Alfred 'Todger,' Private, 150–1
  Jones, William, Private, 79
  Jotham, Eustace, Captain, 129
  Keneally, William S., Private, 134–6
  Kerr, William Alexander, Lieutenant, 63–5
  Laidlaw, Daniel, Piper, 120
  Lane, Thomas, Private, 75–6, 106
  Leach, Thomas, Lieutenant, 119–20
  Learoyd, Roderick A. B., Flight Lieutenant, 195
  Lennon, Edmund Henry, Lieutenant, 75
  Lloyd, Owen, Surgeon Major, 100
  Lodge, Isaac, Gunner, 83
  Lucas, Charles D., Mate, 100–1
  MacLean, Hector L. S., Lieutenant, 87
  Mahoney, Patrick, Sergeant, 101
  Manger, Michael, Drummer, 76–7
  McDougall, John, Private, 75
  McGaw, Samuel, Lance Sergeant, 127
  McGuire, James, Sergeant, 106–7
  McKay, Ian John, Sergeant, 201
  McKechnie, James, Sergeant, 123
  McNamara, Frank Hubert, Lieutenant, 122–3
  McWheeney, William, Sergeant, 55–6
  Melvill, Teignmouth, Lieutenant, 87, 92
  Melvin, Charles, Private, 130
  Milne, William Johnstone, Private, 155–6
  Moore, Montague S. S., Lieutenant, 156–7
  Morely, Samuel, Private, 68–9
  Muir, Kenneth, Major, 200
  Murphy, Michael, Farrier, 69, 107
  Nelson, David, Sergeant, 115
  Nettleton, John Dering, Squadron Leader, 192–3
  Nicolson, Eric J. B., Flight Lieutenant, 191
  Noble, Cecil Reginald, Corporal, 133–4
  Nurse, Edward George, Corporal, 89
  O'Connor, Luke, Lieutenant, 98
  Odgers, William, Leading Seaman, 74–5
  O'Hea, Timothy, Private, 71–2
  Palmer, Anthony, Private, 95
  Peel, William, Captain, 22–3
  Phillipps Everard Aloysius Lisle, Ensign, 87
  Phipps-Hornsby, Edmund, Major, 83

Pitcher, Ernest Herbert, Petty Officer, 126
Proctor, Andrew F.W. Beauchamp-, Captain, 124–5
Ravenhill, George, Private, 107–8
Reed, Hamilton Lyster, Captain, 88–9
Rennie, James, Commander, 63–5
Reynolds, James Henry, Surgeon, 80
Richards, Alfred Joseph, Sergeant, 134–5
Ritchie, Walter Potter, Drummer, 120–1
Roberts, Frederick Sherston, Lieutenant, 85–6, 89, 109
Roberts, Frederick Sleigh, Lieutenant, 65
Rogers, John Montressor, Lieutenant, 75
Ross, John, Corporal, 99
Russell, Charles, Brevet Major, 96
Ryan, John, Lance Corporal, 101
Ryan, Miles, Drummer, 106–7
Scarf, Arthur S. K., Squadron Leader, 192
Scheiss, Ferdinand Christian, Corporal, 80
Schofield, Harry Norton, Captain, 86–90
Sifton, Ellis Welwood, Lance Sergeant, 155
Sims, John J., Private, 99–100
Smith, Archibald Bissett, Temporary Lieutenant, 175

Spence, Edward, Private, 87
Stanlake, William, Private, 105–6
Stubbs, Frank Edward, Sergeant, 134–5, 136–7
Sutton, William, Bugler, 102
Tollerton, Ross, Private, 118
Trewavas, Joseph, Seaman, 128
Vallentin, John Franks, Captain, 119
Ward, James Allen, Sergeant, 196
West, Ferdinand M. F., Captain, 125
Wheeler, George G. M., Major, 128
Wilkinson, Thomas, Temporary Lieutenant, 186
Williams, John, Private, 79
Willis, Richard Raymond, Captain, 134–6
Wyatt, George Henry, Lance-Corporal, 114
Yate, Charles Alix Lavington, Major, 114–15
Young, Thomas James, Lieutenant, 62

Waddy, Richard, 54
Warre, Henry, 49–50
Wellington, Duke of, 33
Wells, Herbert George, 121–2
Wigham, Robert Dundas, Sir, 136
Wolley-Dod, O. C., 134, 136
Wolseley, Garnett, Sir, 18
women in uniform, 167–9
Wood, Evelyn, Sir, 12, 234
Wynne, Arthur, Sir, 92

Yorke, Charles, Sir, 44, 53, 54